Special Edition

USING
MACROMEDIA
AUTHORWARE 3.5

Special Edition

Using
Macromedia
Authorware 3.5

Written by Robert S. Zielinski

Special Edition Using Macromedia Authorware 3.5

Library of Congress Catalog No.: 96-67559

ISBN: 0-7897-0791-8

99 98 97 96   6 5 4 3 2 1

Interpretation of the printing code: the rightmost double-digit number is the year of the book's printing; the rightmost single-digit number, the number of the book's printing. For example, a printing code of 96-1 shows that the first printing of the book occurred in 1996.

Screen reproductions in this book were created using Collage Plus from Inner Media, Inc., Hollis, NH.

Credits

PRESIDENT
Roland Elgey

PUBLISHER
Joseph B. Wikert

PUBLISHING MANAGER
Jim Minatel

EDITORIAL SERVICES DIRECTOR
Elizabeth Keaffaber

MANAGING EDITOR
Sandy Doell

DIRECTOR OF MARKETING
Lynn E. Zingraf

ACQUISITIONS MANAGER
Cheryl D. Willoughby

PRODUCT DIRECTOR
Lisa A. Bucki

PRODUCTION EDITOR
Caroline D. Roop

EDITORS
Kelli Brooks
Thomas Cirtin
C. Kazim Haidri
Sydney Jones
Patrick Kanouse
Gill Kent

PRODUCT MARKETING MANAGER
Kim Margolius

ASSISTANT PRODUCT MARKETING MANAGER
Christy M. Miller

STRATEGIC MARKETING MANAGER
Barry Pruett

TECHNICAL EDITORS
Jeff Agnew
John Bartlett
Randy Cox
Grace Daminato
Danny Engelman
Paul Hamilton
Ron Kinsey
Jeff Schick
Laurie Southerton

TECHNICAL SUPPORT SPECIALIST
Nadeem Muhammed

ACQUISITIONS COORDINATORS
Jane K. Brownlow
Andrea Duvall

SOFTWARE RELATIONS COORDINATOR
Patricia J. Brooks

BOOK DESIGNER
Kim Scott

COVER DESIGNER
Dan Armstrong

COVER ARTWORK
Christian Moore
The Human Element, Inc.

PRODUCTION TEAM
Erin Danielson
Jenny Earhart
Joan Evan
Bryan Flores
Trey Frank
Kelly Warner

INDEXER
Tim Griffin

Composed in *Century Old Style* and *Franklin Gothic* by Que Corporation.

To Shelly, Lauryn, and Daniel

About the Author

Robert S. Zielinski has been an Authorware user since 1987. In 1988, he joined Authorware, Inc., to participate in the Professional services consulting group. His experience in creating applications, and in teaching Authorware clients, served to assist in the continuing design and development of Authorware.

Mr. Zielinski is cofounder and principal of The Human Element, Inc., an interactive learning and communications company with offices in Cincinnati, Ohio; Minneapolis, Minnesota; San Francisco, California; and Nashville, Tennessee. The Human Element, Inc., is an authorized Macromedia Value Added Reseller, Trainer, Developer, and beta site.

Mr. Zielinski is the author of numerous published articles and has taught at the college and university level. He is a frequent guest speaker at both national and international conferences on such topics as multimedia production methodologies, interactive design, and using Authorware. His educational credentials include a bachelor's degree from Eastern Kentucky University and a master's degree from The Ohio State University. He used the beta version of Course of Action, the original name of Authorware, to complete his thesis research in computer-assisted instruction.

Acknowledgments

This work is a collection of experiences captured through a most wonderful journey. While the technical aspect began in 1987 when I was first introduced to "multimedia," the journey as a whole began much earlier. I am grateful to everyone who has contributed in inspiration, support, and word.

This work would have never been possible without the love, encouragement, and sacrifice of my wife, Shelly, and our two children, Lauryn and Daniel. The hours spent apart can never be recaptured, and the commitment shall never be forgotten. Our Lord Christ has truly blessed me with a wonderful gift.

The compilation of a book of such size and scope is an incredible task, and one which I did not undertake alone. Without the assistance of Scott Risner to lend perspective; Michelle Ritola for editorial assistance; and Shawn Vanbriesen for illustrative support, this work could not have been completed. In addition to these individuals, I owe a special thanks to the following team. They kept The Human Element, Inc. going despite my absence and many interruptions: Tony Adams, Dee Dee Bernhardt, Sheila Childers, Michael Kiffmeyer, Joe Gehling, Karen Furman, Laura Wilmans, Derik Clayton, Bob Kelly, Brandon Blank, Christian Moore, Steve Kitchen, Jonathon Halleen, Jeff Weinberg, Jothan Sargent, Pete Lisowski, Karen Reutzel, Shannon Turner, Joseph Lanham, and Kent Sokoloff.

I must thank Cheryl Willoughby, Lisa Bucki, and Caroline Roop from Que. Without their whip-cracking encouragement and gentle guidance, I could not have endured. Additionally, without the vision of Dr. Michael Allen to create Authorware, and the dedication of Macromedia to make it a leader in authoring tools, there would be no need for this book at all.

Finally, I'd like to thank my friends and family for the hours I spent away, and for your understanding. A special thanks to Todd Ericson, John Beck, Jun Chung, and Rick Anderson for holding me accountable to what really matters.

Contents at a Glance

Table of Contents

IV | Hyperlinking and Branching

V | Creating Media Rich Programs

VII | Exploring Design and Development Methodologies

Foreward

Authorware began in the PLATO R&D labs at Control Data Corporation as a solution to the excessive monetary, time, and talent costs of developing interactive software. We hoped to reduce cost so that average folks could transfer their skills and insights from the software they would create to those people willing to learn.

The goals of cost reduction have been achieved to a very significant level. The widespread adoption of Authorware throughout the industry means that Authorware's object-oriented, icon-based design and development tools are helping both developers and end users.

Authorware is truly different from other development tools. Prior to its development, lengthy in-depth studies were conducted to understand how people did creative work; how software was developed and maintained; what were the roots of project difficulties; and what tasks could and should be given computer assistance. In other words, we studied the current process of interactive software design and development with its successes and pitfalls. We studied creative problem-solving in other fields as well to see if a new process, made viable by supporting software tools, might be effective in decreasing costs and increasing quality.

The outcome has been dramatically positive. Skilled Authorware users can't imagine how others can bear the continuing costs of more traditional development methods and the inflexibility of the resulting products. They can't imagine not being able to click on a screen element to make changes to it or its behavior, even while the software is running. They can't imagine not having a constantly updated flowchart of the logic so that program logic can evolve easily and be modified readily after the development team has gone on to other projects.

But while costs have been reduced, the possibilities and expectations have increased. Today, we must do more than ever before to provide user-friendly navigation, motivating designs, spectacular media, and most important, engaging interactions that result in thought-provoking events. While Authorware is a worthy tool to be used with any development process, to meet today's goals, it's necessary to use a matched set—a development process and tool that take full advantage of each other.

Robert Zielinski takes your hand and guides you through the many-faceted features of Authorware. If you pay close attention, practice, and play, you'll learn Authorware quickly. Keep in mind that you don't have to know all features to be a competent Authorware author—almost no one knows it all. As Authorware has evolved with features applicable to an extraordinary array of interactions, restrictions and limitations have fallen by the wayside. But the resulting power can be overwhelming if you feel that you must master it all—especially at the outset. Fortunately, with only a little knowledge, you can build interactions that will be challenging to program in almost any language. As you refine your work, you'll learn more and more of what Authorware can do.

But don't just learn Authorware's features. Pay close attention to what Robert says about the process of design. Be sure to build prototypes early on. Don't make them perfect (as you'll want to do) before you show them to anyone. Ask for feedback on your prototypes to see if you're on the right track. Some of the feedback will be very helpful, and you'll be glad you didn't put any more work into your first prototype. If you get in the habit of building prototypes, you'll end up developing an application that's successful and user-friendly. And you'll save an amazing amount of time and cost over the more traditional design and development methods.

Michael W. Allen, Ph.D.

Chairman & CEO

Allen Interactions

Introduction

Easy to use! No need to learn a complicated programming language. These are the popular claims for most multimedia development tools today. The question must be asked, however, "Easy for whom?" It is typically after educators, corporate trainers, and independent developers have made the investment in an authoring tool that they discover the hidden truth about the technical proficiency needed to develop even the simplest of applications.

But as you will soon discover, the development of an interactive application with Macromedia's Authorware is incomparable. Authorware's powerful, icon-based development environment allows everyone—instructors, students, artists, subject matter experts, and programmers—to develop sophisticated multimedia pieces.

Creators of interactive learning, electronic performance support, online documentation, kiosk, and entertainment pieces have come to depend on Authorware's reliability and its structures for supporting efficient development. And now, with the release of version 3.5, Authorware is more powerful than ever.

In addition to its traditional strengths in interactivity and user-tracking, this new version of Authorware takes full advantage of the PowerMac, Windows 95, and Windows NT operating systems and performance. Most exciting, however, is Authorware's use of ShockWave—Macromedia's Internet-delivery technology. Interactive pieces that had been traditionally developed for floppy disk or CD-ROM delivery can now be interacted with directly over the Internet.

Special Edition Using Macromedia Authorware 3.5 is designed to gently guide you through the basic steps of creating an interactive piece, as well as to provide direction for utilizing today's multimedia technologies. ■

Who Should Use This Book?

This book is designed for anyone who wants to create truly interactive, multimedia-based pieces.

Novices will find basic steps on how to configure and begin developing with Authorware. Intermediate users will discover tips, tricks, and suggestions for building interactivity that captivates the end user. And advanced users will capture the spirit of authoring and the foresight necessary to provide an effective piece via a variety of delivery media.

How This Book Is Organized

Special Edition Using Macromedia Authorware 3.5 is organized into eight logical parts.

Part I, "Getting Started," provides a quick tour to Authorware. It explains the metaphor that Authorware is based upon, as well as the environment in which authoring takes place.

Part II, "Mastering the Basics," walks you through the basic steps for incorporating text and graphics into your presentation. You will see how graphics are created using the Authorware graphics toolbox and imported from other high-end illustration tools. This part also guides you through animation and transition techniques using Authorware. Finally, this part will provide processes for naming and organizing Authorware code to make development easier and more efficient.

Part III, "Building Interactivity," focuses on defining what interactivity really is and then how to build common methods for interacting with a multimedia piece. For example, it explains how to build push buttons, pull-down menus, and movable objects.

Part IV, "Hyperlinking and Branching," explains how to design interactive documents through the use of hyperlinking. Concepts, such as developing text styles, keywords, and paging, are discussed. Additionally, advanced techniques for implementing searching and content navigation are presented. Finally, methods to create linear, random, and content-driven branching are explained.

Part V, "Creating Media Rich Programs," builds on the knowledge you gained in Parts II, III, and IV by introducing steps for including digital video, audio, and laserdisc video. Additionally, importing external functions to enhance Authorware's utility is covered. Finally, methods for collecting and storing data are explored, as well as methods for using data to control the multimedia piece.

Part VI, "Becoming Efficient in Development," gets you thinking about making development efforts more efficient. By organizing the functionality of the piece into models, and storing media elements in libraries, the benefit of using Authorware rather than similar authoring tools will quickly become apparent.

Part VII, "Exploring Design and Development Methodologies," touches on the non-technical consideration of developing a multimedia-based piece. Issues, such as the level of interactivity, and the development process, must be considered when producing any piece.

Part VIII, "Delivering the Final Program," delves into the final phase of a multimedia project—distribution. Whether you are producing a project that will be distributed via CD-ROM or Shockwave for the Internet, distribution concerns should not be left to the end of the project.

What About the CD-ROM?

Inside the back cover of this book you'll find a CD-ROM containing the Authorware Working Model. This fully featured version of Authorware (limited only in certain features and in the size of the piece that can be created) will allow you to practice the basics of authoring.

Additionally, several clients of The Human Element, Inc.—the interactive learning and communications company that I cofounded in 1992 and of which I am currently a principal—have contributed either a demonstration version, or a fully functioning version, of their multimedia pieces. Each application has been created with Authorware, so you will begin to recognize the types of features inherent to an interactive multimedia piece.

Finally, the CD-ROM contains scripts used to write several External Commands (XCMDs) and Dynamic Link Libraries (DLLs). These scripts were saved as text files so that they can be viewed using any word processing program; however, to use the scripts, you need a C++ compiler.

Conventions Used in This Book

This book applies various stylistic and typographical conventions to make it easier to use.

Keyboard shortcut key combinations are joined by + signs; for example, Ctrl+X means hold down the Ctrl key, press the X key, and then release both. When appropriate, we have also provided shortcuts for both the Macintosh and the Windows platforms together.

Additionally, this book uses several sidebar formats. These items are built to provide hints, serve warnings, and to answer popular questions which come from using Authorware. The formats for these sidebars are explained next.

N O T E Notes provide additional information that may help you avoid problems or offer advice on general information related to the topic at hand. ■

 Tips provide quick and helpful information to assist you along the way.

CAUTION
Cautions warn you of hazardous procedures and situations that can lead to unexpected or unpredictable results, including data loss or system damage.

 TROUBLESHOOTING

Troubleshooting sections anticipate common problems...

...and then provide you with practical suggestions for solving those problems.

Special Edition Using Macromedia Authorware 3.5 uses cross-references like this one to point you to other places in the book with additional information relevant to the topic.

▶ **See** "Taking the Authorware Tour," **p. 9**.

Let's Keep in Touch

There is no doubt that for several reasons not every answer about using Authorware has been provided in this book. First, as multimedia becomes a standard component of training and communication, developers continue to push the envelope on both the capabilities of Authorware and its uses. Additionally, portions of this book were completed before version 3.5 was released.

To address issues that were overlooked, as well as to collect information that might be valuable for the next revision, I invite you to participate in an exciting online dialog in any of the following ways.

Question and Answers
Beginning just after the release of this book, The Human Element, Inc. will be maintaining a Web site—**http://www.theinc.com**—to collect and respond to questions regarding Authorware. As questions are asked, we will post responses.

We recognize that many of the questions will provide an opportunity to demonstrate rather than describe Authorware's ability to address the situation. Therefore, The Human Element, Inc. is committed to using its professional team—located in Cincinnati, Ohio; Minneapolis, Minnesota; Nashville, Tennessee; and San Francisco, California—to build Authorware code which will also be available through the Web site.

Finally, as some questions may concern instructional design or development methodology, we invite you to visit any of our offices to see how our team has developed a process for creating truly interactive multimedia pieces on-time and within budget.

Questions of all types will appear as troubleshooting and tip sidebars in future revisions of this book.

Technical Corner
In addition to the Question & Answer portion of our Web site, we will frequently provide Authorware code or utilities. In many cases, the code examples will be based on the questions provided by you.

General Comments
In addition to technical questions, I would greatly appreciate any comments to improve future revisions. Please feel free to contact me directly, and thanks in advance—your comments will help us immensely.

Robert S. Zielinski
The Human Element, Inc.
8120 Penn Avenue South
Suite 433
Bloomington, Minnesota 55431
USA

612.888.9544 telephone
612.888.9568 fax

ZMyster@aol.com
http://www.theinc.com

Getting Started

Taking the Authorware Tour

In grade school my parents encouraged me to take music lessons and to join the band. Even though they claimed that the experience would be fun, looking back, I think that this was strategically a move to keep me out of trouble. In any case, every morning I stood waiting for the bus with a trombone case that was only slightly taller than I was. In band practice, I learned how to blow that horn, and how to position the slide to precisely hit each note. I knew the scales backwards and forwards, I achieved first seat, and I often played the solo in the annual Christmas program. I could really play that horn!

In high school, I joined a jazz band. This was the opportunity to make music rather than simply play a bunch of notes. Unfortunately, when it came time to ad lib, to play a solo that was not in the score sheet, or to write my own music, I failed miserably. While I was a great technician with the instrument, I really never gained the spirit of music.

Authoring a multimedia piece is like music for many people. They learn what the icons do, and they can recite variables and functions forwards and

Beginning with Authorware

Authorware has several unique characteristics inherent to its design, including its use by non-technical programmers, its position in a product suite, and its support of multiple delivery platforms and the World Wide Web.

Understanding the flowchart metaphor

Developing with Authorware is based on a flowcharting metaphor, the understanding of the Flowline and the use of the Icon palette.

Working in the Presentation Window

Screens are developed in Authorware from the user's perspective using the Graphics toolbox.

Becoming efficient during development

The Authorware tool bar provides shortcuts to functions that are commonly used during development.

Taking advantage of the technology

Authorware allows you to take advantage of the technology to communicate valuable design ideas through prototypes.

backwards, but when it comes to designing outside of those boundaries, they fail to create the masterpiece.

This chapter introduces you to the foundations for creating an Authorware program. It is my hope, however, that you will also receive the spirit of authoring so that you can create beyond the boundaries of the icons. ■

Introducing Authorware

Like many of you, I found myself in a position of needing an interactive learning piece, but not having the programming experience required to build such a piece from scratch. For this reason, I decided to search for an authoring tool.

An authoring tool is a software application designed to create multimedia pieces. To use the tool however, you do not need to master the art of traditional programming. Authoring tools often rely on icons, or objects, that represent such functions as displaying text and graphics; playing a sound; or building an interaction.

There are several authoring tools in the marketplace today, but Authorware is unique for several reasons.

Built for Interactive Learning

Authorware was specifically designed by instructional designers to create interactive learning pieces. Although Authorware can be used to create multimedia pieces that serve a variety of purposes, such as interactive kiosks, online magazines, product catalogues, electronic performance support tools, and simulations, Authorware is most effective when used to create interactive learning, or computer-based training, pieces.

Part

I

Ch

1

Built for Non-Programmers

Authorware was also designed for non-technical users. To accommodate the need for teachers, trainers and subject matter experts to build computer-based pieces, years of research went into the design of an interface and a metaphor for development. The resulting tool requires only a minimal amount of technical skill to create a piece.

Supported by a Multimedia Product Suite

Authorware is a single product in a family of tools used to create multimedia. Macromedia, the creator of Authorware, also produces the leading animation tool (Director), a premier three-dimensional modeling tool (MacroModel), and the sound-editing tool, which is most preferred by multimedia developers (SoundEdit). While most authoring tools are not designed to create 3-D models, realistic animation or audio, Authorware's relationship to its sister products makes full multimedia integration seamless.

Multi-Platform Support

Authorware was created in the Macromedia "Build Once, Play Anywhere" theme. Unlike many other authoring tools that allow you to build on one platform, then simply run on another platform, Authorware allows you to start creation in one environment, then move cross-platform to continue development in another. Authorware is a true multi-platform application.

In the Windows environment, Authorware takes full advantage of Windows 95 as well as Windows NT. Authorware is also Power PC native, so developers who use Power Macintoshes will realize the performance they have come to expect from other native applications.

For delivery on any platform, there are two issues to be considered: multimedia support and performance. Authorware supports video, audio and high-resolution graphics no matter where they were created. For example, if you have created a graphic on the Macintosh that has been imported into Authorware, the graphic will appear just as it did on the Macintosh when the piece is moved to the Windows platform

In terms of performance, Authorware supports most of the lowest performing systems. For example, I have seen quality pieces delivered in environments having a 486/33 mHz processor, 4M RAM, 16 VGA colors, and no audio. Additionally, this piece was distributed by floppy disk.

World Wide Web Authoring

All of the functionalities within Authorware, including animation, interactivity, and data collection, can be experienced over the World Wide Web. Files of any size can be prepared using the Authorware Afterburner, which compresses media up to 50 percent, so that they can be viewed using the Netscape Navigator 2.0 browser.

Understanding the Authorware Flowchart Metaphor

For years computer-based training designers have used paper-based flowcharts to lay out the sequence of events that end users will encounter as they interact with the piece (see Fig. 1.1 for an example). Having a visual guide of the program flow allowed the designer to consider each branch of content, and to design feedback for each interaction, before programming was initiated.

FIG. 1.1
Flowcharts have been used for years in the design of interactive pieces.

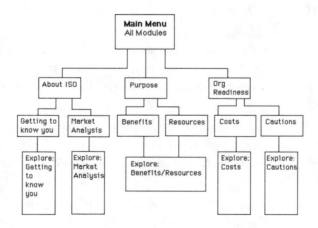

The dependence upon flowcharts by designers, and the benefits that a visual flowchart brings to the interactive design process, was carefully incorporated into the development of Authorware. In fact, the flowchart is the metaphor on which Authorware programming takes place.

Building the Flowline

As you create a multimedia piece using Authorware, you will build a flowchart-like structure that is called the *Flowline*. Like a traditional flowchart, the Flowline contains boxes—the icons—representing certain functions, and a line connecting those functions (see Fig. 1.2). Unlike a traditional flowchart, however, that simply aides in the design process, the Authorware Flowline is actually the programming code.

FIG. 1.2
Authorware uses the flowchart metaphor as its programming language.

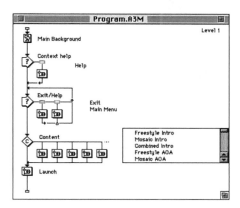

The Authorware Flowline is built by dragging icons from the Icon palette to the Flowline. Like a traditional flowchart, the sequence begins with the icon located at the top of the Flowline and then continues down, executing each icon individually, until it reaches the end of the piece.

For example, you can drag an icon to the Flowline that allows you to display text on the screen, then you can drag another icon that allows you to play a sound. When you run the piece, you will see the graphic on the screen and hear the sound at the same time.

 Becoming familiar with flowcharting and reading an Authorware Flowline, is key to becoming an efficient developer. While you will certainly gain insight by working through the remainder of this book, practice and experience are the best teachers for understanding how Authorware uses the flowchart metaphor.

To help understand this process, I often envision small mites—the Authorware mites—wearing leather jackets and long scarves standing on the platform at the top of the Flowline, as shown in Figure 1.3.

When the piece is run, the Authorware mites leap off of the platform and begin down the Flowline. As the mites encounter an icon, they perform the function of that icon, then they move on.

FIG. 1.3
Envisioning Authorware mites
helps to track the sequence
of events and to solve
problems.

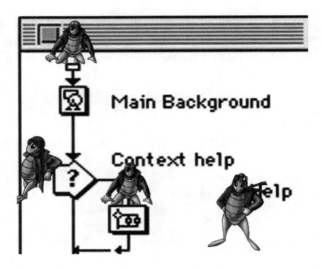

For example, when the mites encounter an Interaction icon, they sit and wait until a response is given by the end user, then they again leap onto the Flowline, executing icons until they reach the end of the Flowline.

Becoming Familiar with the Icon Palette

The Authorware Icon palette (see Fig. 1.4) contains 13 icons that are used to build the Flowline. Each icon represents one or more multimedia functions that the piece performs as it runs. Upon first glance, it may appear that the simplicity of the authoring tool must mean that it is not powerful enough for some applications. As you will soon discover, there are few functions that Authorware cannot perform.

The icons in the Icon palette are placed on the Flowline in the order in which you want them to perform. For example, if you want the user to see a graphic and to hear audio, you first place the icon that contains graphics on the Flowline. You then place the audio icon on the Flowline. If, however, you want the audio to begin before the graphic appears, place the audio icon on the Flowline first, followed by the icon for the graphic.

TROUBLESHOOTING

What if I want several things to happen at once, but the piece pauses before each of the icons on the Flowline is encountered? Many of the icons will either pause the piece until the user interacts or until a certain function is complete. For example, the Authorware mites might pause until a motion is complete or until an entire video sequence has been completed. To prevent this from happening, first identify at which icon the piece is pausing. Next, determine if that icon is set to complete its function before the piece proceeds. Throughout this book, we will explore each icon, and the options that must be considered to prevent automatic pausing.

FIG. 1.4
The Authorware Icon palette contains the icons used for authoring.

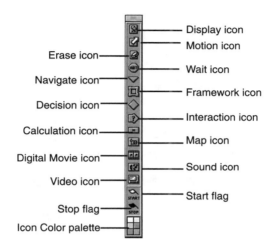

The icons contained in the Authorware Icon palette are described next.

 The Display Icon   The Display icon displays text or graphics used in the piece. You can either import the text and graphics, or create them within Authorware

For example, the interface shown in Figure 1.5 was built in an external graphics package—Adobe Photoshop, I believe—and is being displayed in Authorware using the Display icon.

▶ To learn more about working with text, **see** "Placing Text on the Screen," **p. 68**.
▶ To learn more about creating and importing graphics, **see** "Working with Graphics and Objects," **p. 97**.

 The Motion Icon   The Motion icon moves any displayed object from one screen position to another. Motion is different from animation in that the movement does not change the orientation of the object. For example, a box moving down a conveyor, as seen in Figure 1.6, is motion. The box being filled, closed, then wrapped is animation.

Motion can be used to technically illustrate how something works, or to simply add excitement to the piece.

▶ For information on using the Motion icon, **see** "Making Objects Move," **p. 165**.

FIG. 1.5
The Display icon lets you display text and graphics, such as the interface shown here.

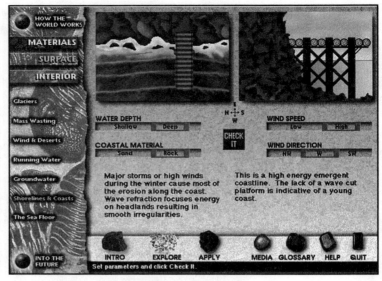

Used by permission from West Publishing.

FIG. 1.6
The Motion icon moves elements within a two-dimensional plane, such as a box along a conveyer.

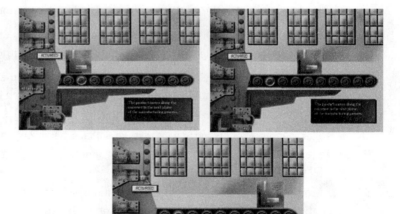

 The Erase Icon The Erase icon erases displayed objects in the Presentation Window. This helpful feature allows the author to treat the Presentation Window like a stage—presenting and removing characters as needed. Once an object is erased from the Presentation Window, it is no longer stored in the computer's memory. It does, of course, remain as a part of the piece.

▶ To learn more about erasing objects from the Presentation Window, **see** "Erasing Media," **p. 353**.

 The Wait Icon　The Wait icon pauses the presentation until the user interacts (by clicking the mouse button or pressing a key, for example) with the piece, or until the specified amount of time expires.

▶ For more information on the Wait icon, **see** "Pausing the Presentation," **p. 155**.

An option for using this icon is to display a little clock counting down the time as seen in Figure 1.7. Using this option, however, might distract the user from other items on the screen and produce unnecessary nervousness.

FIG. 1.7
The Wait icon pauses the presentation.

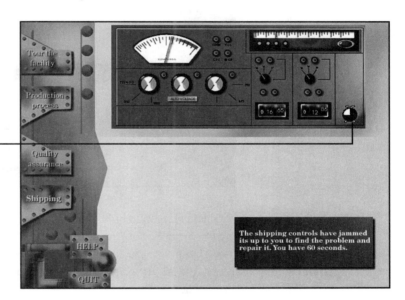

This clock is automatically created by the Wait icon if the Show Time Remaining option is selected.

The shipping controls have jammed its up to you to find the problem and repair it. You have 60 seconds.

N O T E　If you find yourself using the Wait icon quite often, take a second look at the design of your piece. Using the Wait icon typically results in a linear design, and the level of interactivity for the user becomes no more than a monotonous pounding of the keyboard to advance the piece. ▪

 The Navigate Icon　The Navigate icon is used to establish hyperlinks across the piece. While this icon, and hyperlinking in general, can be very helpful, the Navigate icon is a departure from the flowchart metaphor that makes Authorware so easy to use. For more information regarding the Navigate icon, see Chapter 16, "Applying Advanced Interactivity and Searching."

The Framework Icon The Framework icon is used to build a navigation scheme that, by default, produces a book-like metaphor and a control panel graphical interface. The control panel, seen in Figure 1.8, allows the user to page forward and backward, as well as search the contents of the pages.

FIG. 1.8
The Framework icon produces a default navigation control panel that the user can use to move through book-like pages.

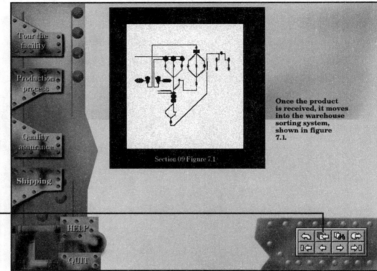

The Framework icon produces a default Navigation control panel.

While the Framework icon allows you to quickly produce a navigation scheme for your multimedia piece, using the metaphor of linear pages results in a piece that is not very engaging for the end user. Users can quickly lose interest in simply paging their way through countless screens. Unless you provide a cue as to how many pages there are in the sequence and where the user is within that sequence, the user can also become frustrated or disoriented.

When using this tool, be sure that each page contains an interaction, such as simulating a control panel, that encourages the users' participation. To learn when to use the Framework icon, see Chapter 15, "Building Interactive Documents."

 The Decision Icon The Decision icon is used to establish branching within the piece. While this tool is most commonly used to build sequential presentations or random-test banks, it can also make your piece responsive to individual users.

The Decision icon is different from the Interaction icon in that the decision as to which branch should be taken is made by the computer. The decision to take a certain path in an interaction loop (discussed next), however, is based on a response made by the user.

For example, each branch associated with a Decision icon may represent an exam question in a training piece. The Decision icon could be set to select the questions randomly until all of the questions have been given. To learn more about the functionality of the Decision icon, see Chapter 17, "Setting Up Branching."

 The Interaction Icon   The Interaction icon, as the name implies, is used to create interactions, or ways in which the end user will communicate with your piece. Navigation schemes, test questions or content exercises are all created with the Interaction icon.

> **N O T E**   For step-by-step guidance on building interactions, see Part III, "Building Interactivity." ■

This icon allows you to create interactions that go beyond the typical push buttons and pull-down menus, and require the end user to arrange objects on the screen or to select specific objects. Figure 1.9 shows an interaction that requires the user to arrange objects on the screen. For the basics of using the Interaction icon, see Chapter 9, "The Fundamentals of Interactions."

FIG. 1.9
The Interaction icon can be used to create complex interactions, such as this one, that require the user to drag boxes.

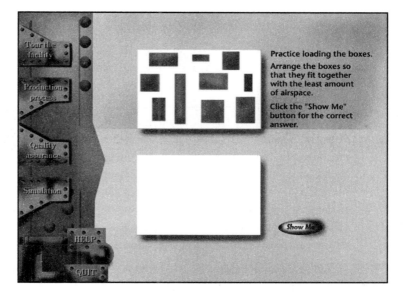

 The Calculation Icon   The Calculation icon is used to manipulate functions, variables, and Authorware scripting codes. While Authorware scripting is very helpful in the collection and recording of user information, it is often overused by authors, especially those coming from a traditional programming background.

Additionally, Macromedia user groups, Internet forums, and many publications focus on the use of functions and variables. I suggest that you not be overly concerned about becoming fluent in the use of functions and variables. You will quickly find that the Authorware icons already do a majority of what you are designing. To learn more about using the Calculation icon, see Chapter 21, "Implementing XCMDs and DLLs."

 The Map Icon   The Map icon is used to group icons that are located on the Flowline. While this icon has no impact on what takes place in the Presentation Window, it is incredibly helpful in the organization of Authorware code and the piece's content.

When working with the Map icon, it might help to think of it as a file cabinet used to hold the content. The value is not the cabinet, but the content. The cabinet is only a way to organize your work. Likewise, the Map icon is only a way to organize your icons.

Figure 1.10 illustrates that if Map icons are clearly named, they help explain the flowchart.

FIG. 1.10
The Map icon can be used to organize code and content.

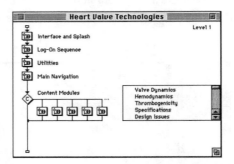

Other authoring tools, though they can be icon- and flowchart-based, typically do not have an equivalent to the Map icon. Instead, the flowchart in these pieces extends indefinitely both horizontally and vertically. Finding specific content information, therefore, requires memorization of the physical diagram, or that you start at the top of the diagram and scroll your way through until you find what you are looking for. To make development efforts more efficient using the Map icon, see Chapter 8, "Organizing Authorware Logic on the Flowline."

 The Digital Movie Icon   The Digital Movie icon is used to display moving pictures or pieces within Authorware. Digital movies include QuickTime, Video for Windows and PICS animation.

Digital movies also include pieces created with Macromedia Director, and include interactivity created using the Macromedia Scripting Language, or Lingo. To learn more about enhancing your piece with digital movies, see Chapter 20, "Working with Digital Movies."

In Figure 1.11, the character walking across the screen was created using Macromedia Director.

FIG. 1.11
The Digital Movie icon can be used to show animation as well as digital video.

 The Sound Icon   The Sound icon is used to play audio that has been created in an external program and saved as an .AIFF, .WAV or .SND file.

> **N O T E**   On the Macintosh, you can record sound right into Authorware through the Macintosh microphone. ▨

Sound is commonly used as an effect when a button is pushed, a menu item is selected, or for narration. One reason that sound has not been used for more than this in the past is because audio requires large amounts of storage space and memory. As technologies change, however, I believe that audio will be used more pervasively for such things as setting tone, like the background music in a movie. To learn how to effectively implement sound into your piece, see Chapter 23, "Importing Audio."

The Video Icon   The Video icon is used to control or to allow the user to control, an external videodisc or laserdisc player. Until digital video, including MPEG, is as real-time as television, videodisc players will continue to be used where picture-perfect quality is required.

For example, multimedia training for a heart surgeon cannot rely on video that does not have perfect quality or display rates. This type of precision video still needs the quality of a laserdisc.

Traditional videodisc technology (see Fig. 1.12) is still very prevalent in the educational setting. Publishers continue to provide video and stills on videodisc, and teachers continue to use materials acquired years ago.

FIG. 1.12
The traditional multimedia system consisted of a laserdisc player and a computer, and often had a touch screen.

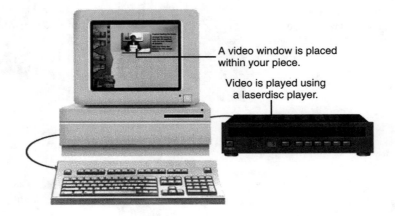

A video window is placed within your piece.

Video is played using a laserdisc player.

Industry trends, however, are to move away from this technology because of the cost of the hardware, and the frustration of coordinating and connecting the computer with a video overlay card to the player. For more information on using laserdisc video, see Chapter 24, "Setting Up Analog Video."

 The Start and Stop Flags The Start and Stop flags are used in the process of development, and have no impact on the functionality of the final piece. The Start flag can be placed on the Flowline, and when the Run From flag is selected from the Try It menu, Authorware will execute the piece beginning at the flag. Likewise, the Stop flag can be used to prevent Authorware from executing icons located after the Stop flag's position.

The Start and Stop flags are beneficial to development when you want to test a specific functionality repeatedly, but you do not want to take the time to run the piece from the beginning each time.

N O T E Start and Stop flags will be ignored when your piece is packaged for final delivery. ■

▶ For guidance on using the Start and Stop Flags, **see** "Introducing The Flags," **p. 490**.

 The Icon Color Palette Use the Icon Color palette to color-code icons on the Flowline. While I have not found this feature valuable, development teammates suggest that color-coding can be used to identify icons that contain certain types of information; to identify who is to work on which parts of the piece; to identify where perpetual interactions are used; to identify unfinished components; or to identify which pieces of logic were developed using a model.

▶ For tips on using the Icon Color palette, **see** "Coloring Icons," **p. 207**.

Editing the Flowline

The greatest benefit of using Authorware is the flowchart metaphor. As you become more familiar with the Flowline, and with each icon's function, you will actually be able to envision how the piece will run by looking at the Flowline.

In addition to the benefit of being able to create a flowchart, however, is the ability to modify it. If you run your piece and determine that the sequence of events is not executing as planned, you can rearrange the icons to change the sequence. Rearranging the icons on the Flowline can be done via cutting, copying, pasting, and deleting, as described next. To conduct any of these operations, the desired icon(s) must first be selected. Select a single icon by clicking it. Select multiple icons by holding down the Shift key while clicking the icons, or by creating a marquee.

▶ For step-by-step guidance on selecting and deselecting icons on the Flowline, **see** "Grouping and Ungrouping," **p. 197**.

Cutting Icons   When an icon has been selected, you can choose the Cut command in the Edit menu to remove the icon from the Flowline. Cutting does not delete the icon, rather it places that icon onto the Clipboard. The icon will remain on the Clipboard until it is overwritten by cutting or copying something else.

N O T E   When an Interaction, Decision or Framework icon has several branches attached, you must select all the icons in the loop, including the Interaction, Decision or Framework icon, to cut the loop. If only some of the branch icons are selected, and the Interaction, Decision or Framework icon has not been selected, only the selected branches will be cut. ■

Copying Icons   When an icon has been selected, you can choose the Copy command in the Edit menu to make a copy of the icon. Copying does not remove the icon from the Flowline, but it places a copy of that icon onto the Clipboard. The icon remains on the Clipboard until it is overwritten by cutting or copying something else.

Pasting Icons   Once an icon, or many icons, has been copied or cut, you can paste that icon onto the Flowline. To paste an icon onto the Flowline, click the Flowline where you want to insert the icon. When the Paste pointer appears (as seen in Fig. 1.13), choose Paste from the Edit menu.

FIG. 1.13
The Paste pointer is used to indicate where a cut or copied icon will be pasted on the Flowline.

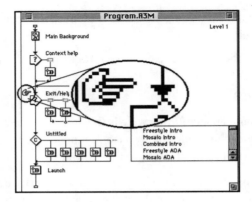

Whichever icon, or group of icons, was previously cut or copied will be pasted onto the Flowline.

N O T E Authorware will not allow you to paste icons when doing so creates an unacceptable structure. For example, you cannot paste a Decision icon as a path to an Interaction icon. ▪

TROUBLESHOOTING

When I try to cut, copy or paste a large number of icons, I get the message that the computer's memory is full and that the operation cannot be completed. How do I get around this? Rather than storing the icons in the computer's memory, create an Authorware model that stores the icons on the hard disk. You can then paste the model in other locations within the current program, or within other programs. See Chapter 26, "Building Models," for information on using models.

Deleting Icons In addition to cutting, copying, and pasting, you can also delete icons from the Flowline. Like cutting, deleting will remove the icon from the Flowline; however, no copy remains in the Clipboard.

To delete a selected icon from the Flowline, simply press the Delete key on the keyboard.

N O T E The Undo command in the Edit menu is used to undo a cut, copy, paste or delete action as long as it was the last action taken. ▪

Shortcuts for Moving Icons If you discover that a single icon needs to be moved, drag the icon to its new location on the Flowline. Dragging an icon is much faster than cutting, inserting the paste pointer, and then pasting.

NOTE Only one icon at a time can be moved by dragging. To learn how to drag multiple icons using a Map icon, see Chapter 8, "Organizing Authorware Logic on the Flowline." ■

When there is more than one icon to be repositioned, you can either cut and then paste them in their new location, or you can group the icons into a Map icon using the Group command in the Edit menu. Once the icons are grouped into a Map icon, drag the Map icon to the new location and choose Ungroup from the Edit menu.

Repositioning icons on the Flowline by dragging, or by using Cut, Copy and Paste, is a great way to experiment with various design ideas.

Previewing Icons Once an icon has been placed on the Flowline, and its contents have been defined, you can view those contents in several ways. First, you can run the piece; however, you will not be able to tell in which icon the displayed objects or media are stored. You can also simply open the icon by double-clicking it; however, if the icon contains a large graphic or digital movie, it can take a while for the Presentation Window to build.

A more efficient way to view the contents of an icon from the Flowline is to use the Preview feature. Previewing places all of the contents of the selected icon in a reduced window (see Fig. 1.14) that is created very quickly rather than building the entire Presentation Window. If the icon being previewed contains a sound, the sound will play, and if the icon being previewed contains a digital movie, the movie will play.

FIG. 1.14
Previewing contents in a reduced window.

To preview the contents of an icon, follow these steps:

1. Select the icon that you want to preview.
2. Choose the Get Info from the Edit menu.
3. Click the Preview button from the Get Info dialog box.

Once the preview window opens, either close it by clicking anywhere on the screen, or close the entire Get Info dialog box by clicking the Close button.

T I P The shortcut keys for previewing the contents of an icon are ⌘+Option (Macintosh) or Ctrl+Alt (Windows).

Defining the Presentation Window

The creation of an Authorware piece occurs from two perspectives. The first perspective is that of the author who places and designs multimedia elements along the Flowline using icons from the Icon palette.

The second perspective is the end user's. When a final piece is distributed, the end user will not see the Flowline, but rather, the graphics, text, sound, animation, and video, which are executed by the Authorware mites as they travel down the Flowline. What the end user will see is defined as the Presentation Window. The Presentation Window can fill the entire monitor or only a portion of it.

FIG. 1.15
The Presentation Window presents your piece from the user's perspective rather than from the computer's.

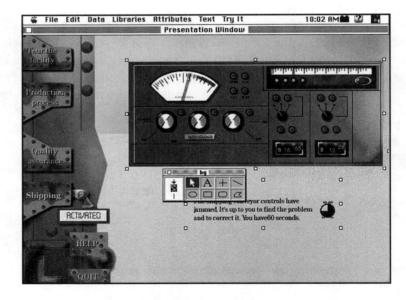

As you are creating a piece, you can continually switch from the author's perspective to that of the end user. In other words, you can toggle between the Flowline (where you place icons) and the Presentation Window (where the content of those icons is executed).

To view your piece running as the end user will see it, choose Run from the Try It menu, or press the ⌘+R (Macintosh) or Ctrl+R (Windows) keys, at any time during authoring.

To return to the Flowline from the Presentation Window, select Jump To Icons from the Try It menu or press the ⌘+J (Macintosh) or Ctrl+J (Windows) keys.

Building the Traditional Presentation Window

Traditional computer-based training development tools, and even many of the popular tools today, require the author to enter information such as the position on the screen where graphics are to be displayed, or a number representing the color for text. Once this data is entered, the author can execute the piece to see the results.

If the elements displayed on the screen do not meet the design specifications, or if the developer finds that a change is necessary, the developer must return to the code and guess what alterations have to be made. The changes are made to the code, the piece is executed, and the cycle begins again until the display finally appears correctly.

Building the Authorware Presentation Window

The designers of Authorware wanted to break the traditional cycle for designing the Presentation Window. To do this, they combined graphical user interfaces and object-oriented development to create an authoring tool that allows you, the author, to design content and create on-screen objects from the perspective of the end user. Rather than editing elements in dialog boxes, then executing the piece to see the resulting changes, Authorware developers can edit screen objects while the piece is actually running. The obvious benefit of this is a reduced development time, and the ability to explore creative ideas born in the development process.

Editing the Presentation Window

To make changes to the position and appearance of objects in the Presentation Window, either open an icon on the Flowline by double-clicking it or double-click an object in the Presentation Window while it is running or paused. In either case, edits to the Presentation Window are made using the Graphics toolbox unless you are editing a bitmap graphic. In that case, you will need to use an external graphics package.

The Authorware Graphics toolbox, shown in Figure 1.16, contains several tools that allow you to edit the Presentation Window. Each of these tools is described next. These tools function much like tools provided in popular graphics or page layout programs. For example, to create graphic objects, simply click the tool in the Graphics toolbox, then drag to create the object. To create text, select the Text tool, then click the Presentation Window at the point where the text is to be placed, then begin typing.

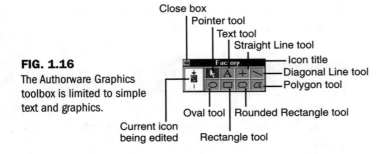

FIG. 1.16
The Authorware Graphics toolbox is limited to simple text and graphics.

Close box
Pointer tool
Text tool
Straight Line tool
Icon title
Diagonal Line tool
Polygon tool
Oval tool
Rounded Rectangle tool
Current icon being edited
Rectangle tool

 The Pointer Tool   This tool is used to select, resize and move objects in the Presentation Window. Like most other object-oriented programs, you select an object by clicking it.

Once an object is selected, handles appear around the object. You can resize an object by dragging a handle, or reposition the object by dragging it to a new location.

> **N O T E**   Resizing bitmap graphics in Authorware will have an unpredictable outcome. Quality is usually reduced as Authorware tries to interpret the bitmap. ∎

 The Text Tool   The text tool is used to place and format text in the Presentation Window. Text can also be imported or pasted from other applications such as Microsoft Word or QuarkXPress, then the layout can be formatted using the Text tool. Characteristics of the text, such as font, size and justification, are edited using the Authorware pull-down menus.

While this tool is good for most applications, Authorware in general does not give the designer very good text control. Kerning, leading and anti-aliasing are not controllable with Authorware. For this reason, I suggest that you format text that is required to have extremely high quality in a product such as Adobe Illustrator or Adobe Photoshop, then import the final text into Authorware as a graphic.

▶ For more information on using the Text tool, **see** "Using the Text Tool," **p. 76**.

 The Straight Line Tool   The Straight Line tool is used to create lines that retain a vertical, horizontal or 45-degree orientation. I often use this tool to create a grid onto which I will align other objects during development. This grid can reside in the same icon as the objects, or in a separate icon. When my piece is finished, I then delete the lines or the additional icon.

▶ For step-by-step guidance on drawing straight lines, **see** "Using the Line Tools," **p. 99**.

 The Diagonal Line Tool   The Diagonal Line tool is used to create a straight line between any two points. If the Shift key is held down while drawing, this tool behaves like the Straight Line tool.

Part

I

Ch

1

▶ For directions on using the Diagonal Line tool, **see** "Using the Line Tools," **p. 99**.

 The Oval Tool   The Oval tool is used to draw ovals or circles. To draw symmetrical circles, hold down the Shift key while drawing. Because the fill and color options within Authorware are fairly basic, I typically create graphic elements in other graphics programs.

▶ To learn more about the Oval tool, **see** "Building Rectangles, Rounded Rectangles, and Circles," **p. 101**.

 The Rectangle Tool   The Rectangle tool is used to draw rectangles or squares. To draw squares, hold down the Shift key while drawing. This tool is also used quite frequently to define areas of the screen in which content will reside.

▶ For a list of steps on using the Rectangle tool, **see** "Building Rectangles, Rounded Rectangles, and Circles," **p. 101**.

 The Rounded Rectangle Tool   The Rounded Rectangle tool is used to draw rectangles with rounded corners. To adjust the degree of roundness on the corners, select the Rounded Rectangle tool and drag the handle on the created object. To reposition or resize the object, select the Pointer tool and drag the object to its new position.

▶ For more information on using the Rounded Rectangle tool, **see** "Building Rectangles, Rounded Rectangles, and Circles," **p. 101**.

 The Polygon Tool   Use the Polygon tool to create closed or open multi-sided objects. For precise editing after the object is drawn, select the Polygon tool and drag the points individually. To reposition or resize the object, select the Pointer tool and drag the object to its new position.

Aside from the tools defined in the preceding sections, the Graphics toolbox also contains the name of, and a picture of, the icon being edited. This is very helpful in reminding you which icon on the Flowline is being edited.

While the tools in the Graphics toolbox are not very sophisticated, they are very helpful for prototyping. Prototyping an idea is key to project communication as you see in the next section.

▶ For details on using the Polygon tool, **see** "Working with the Polygon Tool," **p. 103**.

Editing the Presentation Window While Running Your Piece

Unlike other development tools, Authorware allows you to edit the Presentation Window from the perspective of the end user. This is accomplished in three different ways, described next.

On the Fly   To reposition an element while the piece is running, simply drag the element to its new location. You do not need to stop the piece if you are only making position changes for an object. You will need to stop the piece, however, if you need to make text edits, change the attributes of an object, or to replace a bitmap graphic.

From Pause Mode   The position of an element can be changed when the piece is running by choosing Pause from the Try It menu, or by pressing the ⌘+P (Macintosh) or Ctrl+P (Windows) keys. This changes the piece from Run mode to Pause mode.

Choose Proceed from the Try It menu, or press the ⌘+P (Macintosh) or Ctrl+P (Windows) keys, to return to Run mode.

N O T E   When you drag an object in the Presentation Window to edit either on the fly or in Pause mode, all of the objects in that icon will be moved. ■

From Edit Mode   To resize an object, to edit text, or to import a new graphic, the Presentation Window display must be opened. Double-click the icon containing the object to be edited to open the display and the Authorware Graphics toolbox. When you are finished with the edits, close the Graphics toolbox, choose Proceed from the Try It menu, or press the ⌘+P (Macintosh) or Ctrl+P (Windows) keys, to return to Run mode.

The capability to make edits while running the piece is one of the greatest benefits to using Authorware. This feature alone saves countless development hours.

Using the Authorware Tool Bar

As you are creating your piece, you will be working from either the Flowline perspective, or from the Presentation Window perspective. In either case, the Authorware tool bar (it's just below the menu bar in Fig. 1.17) is used to make accessing some of the more commonly used Authorware commands more efficient.

Accessing the Tool Bar

The Authorware tool bar is constantly available when you are working on the Flowline. You can elect, however, to hide the tool bar by choosing the Hide Tool Bar command from the Attributes menu. To turn the tool bar back on, choose the Show Tool Bar command from the Attributes menu.

 The shortcut keys for turning the tool bar on and off are ⌘+Shift+T (Macintosh) or Ctrl+Shift+T (Windows).

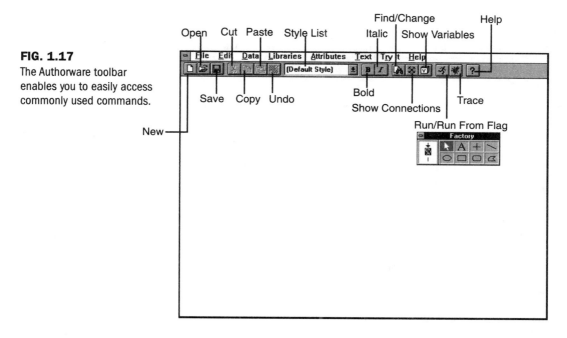

FIG. 1.17
The Authorware toolbar enables you to easily access commonly used commands.

The tool bar is also available from the Presentation Window whenever the piece is paused; either by selecting Pause or by double-clicking an object so that edits can be made.

Working with the Authorware Tool Bar

Each of the buttons on the tool bar corresponds to an option in a pull-down menu. While you may find the tool bar helpful, I have become more familiar with the shortcut keys for each of the commands.

Let's take a closer look at each of the tool bar options in greater detail, beginning with the button on the left and working to the right.

 New The first button in the tool bar is the New button. If you are currently working on a piece, Authorware will prompt you to save any changes before it creates a new, untitled piece.

 TIP The shortcut keys for opening a new piece are ⌘+N (Macintosh) or Ctrl+N (Windows). The New command can also be accessed by choosing the New command from the File menu.

 Open The Open button closes the current piece, and presents the Open File dialog box. Before closing the current piece, Authorware prompts you to save any changes.

TIP The shortcut keys for opening another Authorware piece are ⌘+O (Macintosh) or Ctrl+O (Windows). The Open command can also be accessed from the File menu.

 Save The Save button saves the current piece. If the piece has not been saved previously, Authorware will prompt you to name the piece and to select a location to which it will be saved. If a Library window is currently active, this button accesses the Save Library command rather than the normal save file function.

 TIP The shortcut keys for saving a piece are ⌘+S (Macintosh) or Ctrl+S (Windows). The Save command can also be accessed from the File menu.

 Cut Select the Cut button to cut selected items such as icons from the Flowline or objects from the Presentation Window.

 TIP The shortcut keys for cutting an item are ⌘+X (Macintosh) or Ctrl+X (Windows). The Cut command can also be accessed from the Edit menu.

 Copy Select the Copy button to copy one or more selected items to the Clipboard. Selected items can include icons from the Flowline, or objects from the Presentation Window. Authorware also supports the copying of text files that contain RTF (Rich Text Format) formatting.

 TIP The shortcut keys for copying items to the Clipboard are ⌘+C (Macintosh) or Ctrl+C (Windows). The Copy command can also be accessed from the Edit menu.

 Paste Select the Paste button to paste items into your piece that have been copied or cut to the Clipboard. If the Clipboard contains icons from the Flowline, simply click the Flowline to insert the Paste pointer at the position you want the icons to be pasted.

If the Clipboard contains objects from the Presentation Window, you must first open a Display or Interaction icon, then paste the objects into the Presentation Window. You can position the objects by clicking the point in the Presentation Window where you want the pasted objects centered.

 TIP The shortcut keys for pasting items from the Clipboard are ⌘+V (Macintosh) or Ctrl+V (Windows). The Paste command can also be accessed from the Edit menu.

Undo   Select the Undo button to reverse the last operation you made. For example, if you accidentally delete an icon from the Flowline, selecting the Undo button will replace the icon to the Flowline.

TIP The shortcut keys for undoing the last action are ⌘+Z (Macintosh) or Ctrl+Z (Windows). The Undo command can also be accessed from the Edit menu.

Styles List   You can select a text style to be applied to any selected text. This option is only available when you are working in the Presentation Window. If text is not selected when you select a style from the list, the selected style will become the default.

TIP Text styles can also be applied by choosing the Apply Styles command from the Text menu.

▶ For guidance on creating and applying styles, **see** "Working with Styles," **p. 86**.

Bold   Select the Bold button to make any selected text appear bold. This option is only available when you are working in the Presentation Window. If text is not selected when you select the Bold button, bold will become the default for any new text.

TIP The shortcut keys for applying the bold text style are ⌘+Shift+B (Macintosh) or Ctrl+Shift+B (Windows). Bold can also be applied by choosing the Bold option from the Style portion of the Text menu.

Italic   Select the Italic button to make any selected text appear italic. This option is only available when you are working in the Presentation Window. If text is not selected when you select the Italic button, italic will become the default for any new text.

TIP The shortcut keys for applying the italic text style are ⌘+Shift+I (Macintosh) or Ctrl+Shift+I (Windows). Italic can also be applied by choosing the Italic option from the Style portion of the Text menu.

Find/Change   Select the Find/Change button to display the Find/Change dialog box. This feature allows you to search your piece, including content text and icon titles, for specific words or phrases during authoring.

TIP The shortcut keys for accessing the Find/Change dialog box are ⌘+Shift+F (Macintosh) or Ctrl+Shift+F (Windows). The Find/Change dialog box can also be accessed by choosing the Find/Change command from the Edit menu.

Part
I

Ch
1

Show Connections Select the Show Connections button to access the Show Connections dialog box, which shows the connections between Navigate icons and their destinations.

 The Show Connections dialog box is accessed by choosing the Show Connections command from the Attributes menu.

 Show Variables Select the Show Variables button to access the Show Variables dialog box, which lists all variables: those inherent to Authorware and those that you create.

 The shortcut keys for accessing the Show Variables dialog box are ⌘+Option+V (Macintosh) or Ctrl+Alt+V (Windows). The Show Variables dialog box can also be accessed by choosing the Show Variables command from the Data menu.

 Run Select the Run button to run your piece. If you have inserted the Start flag onto the Flowline, Authorware will run from the position of the flag.

 The shortcut keys for running a piece are ⌘+R (Macintosh) or Ctrl+R (Windows). The Run command can also be accessed by choosing the Run command from the Try It menu.

 The shortcut keys for running a piece from the Start flag are ⌘+F (Macintosh) or Ctrl+F (Windows). The Run From Flag command can also be accessed by choosing the Run From Flag command from the Try It menu.

 Trace Select the Trace button to open the Trace window. This window allows you to view which icons are being executed, enabling you to trace errors.

 The shortcut keys for accessing the Trace window are ⌘+T (Macintosh) or Ctrl+T (Windows). The Trace window can also be displayed by choosing the Trace Window command from the Try It menu.

 Help Select the Help button to access Authorware's online Help.

 The online Help can also be accessed by choosing the Help command from the Apple menu (Macintosh) or the Help command from the File menu (Windows).

Prototyping and the Development Process

As stated earlier, the benefit of using Authorware is the ability to rapidly experience your design ideas. Unfortunately, most people fall into one of two traps when developing multimedia pieces with Authorware.

The first trap is to approach development using the same techniques used for other media. The traditional approaches, even for multimedia, suggest that you conduct a thorough analysis, create a detailed design document or a set of storyboards, then head into development. The problem with this approach, however, is that it does not take advantage of the ability to rapidly prototype your ideas, experience the interactivity, or determine the technical feasibility of your design. Therefore, ideas and designs are often changed during the development phase to accommodate newly acquired ideas or information. With the traditional approach, that means starting from the beginning.

A more conventional development methodology can be used with Authorware. This methodology still requires that you conduct an analysis, but rather than creating a detailed design document or written storyboards, you then use Authorware to quickly prototype your ideas. The prototype not only tests the technical feasibility of your design, but it allows you to communicate your design ideas to colleagues, end users, or members of the development team in the same media that the final piece will be presented. The end result is a more creative piece that requires fewer changes during the development phase and satisfies the pieces objectives more completely.

The second trap, however, is to spend too much time on developing a prototype. Because development can be captivating, authors have a tendency to follow a design idea through to the smallest detail. Rather than drawing a simple square and labeling it "Car," the author makes sure that the angle of the windshield is correct, that the automobile has dual side-view mirrors, and the wheels have spoked covers. At this point, it is no longer a prototype! And if the design evolves so that the prototype no longer meets the objectives, many hours will have to be thrown away.

The art of prototyping is to create as little as possible in order to communicate your idea. Once you receive feedback, incorporate changes as you see necessary into the next iteration, again keeping from over-developing by creating just enough to communicate your ideas for the piece or a portion thereof. Soon enough you will reach a point where you can move forward with conducting fully rendered graphics, and you can incorporate all aspects of multimedia. By this point, however, you can also rest on the fact that major revisions are unlikely. ●

Setting Up an
Authorware Piece

Before you jump into authoring a multimedia piece,
there are a few decisions that must be made, such as
the piece's screen resolution, or which color palette
should be used. Unfortunately, I had to learn this the
hard way! I was working on a driver's training program that was to be run in a standard 640×480 VGA
resolution. To do the authoring, I used a Macintosh
with a single 13" monitor set to the appropriate resolution.

After a few weeks of development, my team gave a
formal presentation to the client. We had a great presentation room with an overhead projection system
hooked to a very powerful computer with two 13"
monitors; one driven by the standard video card and
the other supported by a plug-in card.

The section of the piece that we planned to present
dealt with motorcycle safety. The opening screen had a
motorcycle starting from one side of the screen, traveling across the screen, and then exiting the opposite
side. When the clients came in and took their seats, the
lights lowered, the projector came on, and we began
the show. To my amazement, however, the motorcycle
came squealing in from the side of the screen, buzzed

Launching Authorware

The first step to working with any
application is to launch the program.

Opening and naming files

Establishing a convention for naming files saves time in locating
specific files and tracking development progress.

Saving and backing up files

Each time you are about to begin, or
have just completed, a major piece
of development, save or back up the
piece.

**Understanding the Authorware
file setup features**

Before you begin authoring, consider the size of the Presentation
Window, background color, return
transition, and font mapping.

Working with fonts

Font mapping allows you to determine which fonts will be substituted
during development when your
piece is passed between the
Macintosh and Windows platforms.

**Choosing a resolution and
screen size**

Authorware allows you to develop a
multimedia piece that will take
advantage of any screen resolution.

across the main screen, then parked in the center of the second screen and remained there for the rest of the presentation. How embarrassing! You see, I did not set up the Authorware piece properly before development, and even though I did all my development on a single monitor, the piece was actually set to run on all monitors attached. For this presentation, there were two monitors.

This chapter addresses the benefits of thinking through setup before authoring begins. This preparation takes far less time than having to reengineer the piece if you determine that you must change a setting somewhere down the road. ■

Opening and Naming a Piece

From the time you turn on the computer to begin prototyping your piece, you must start thinking about the end users and how they will be using your piece. You have to consider the machines they will be working on, the physical and digital environments in which they will use your piece, and the emotions, such as fear and anxiety, they may be experiencing with regard to the information you're presenting.

As a part of this analysis, you will be required to make some decisions that you will have to live with for the remainder of the development effort, and that will determine the technical requirements on the part of the end user's computer system.

To step through these decisions, let's start at the beginning by launching a new Authorware piece and taking a look at the file setup process.

Launching Authorware for Macintosh or Windows

To launch Authorware, follow the same process as you would any other executable application, depending on the operating system (Macintosh or Windows).

On the Macintosh, follow these steps to launch Authorware.

1. Locate and open the Authorware folder that is installed on your hard drive.

2. Double-click the Authorware 3.5 desktop icon, as seen in Figure 2.1.

FIG. 2.1
Launch the Authorware for Macintosh application by double-clicking the application icon.

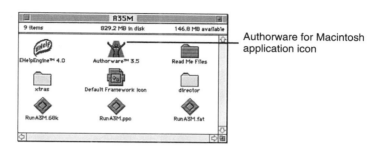

Authorware for Macintosh application icon

In Windows 95, there are several methods that can be used to launch the application. First, you can click the Start button to launch Authorware just as you would any other Windows 95 application, as seen in Figure 2.2. The steps for launching Authorware are as follows:

1. Click the Start button.

2. Select the Programs option from the menu.

3. Select the Macromedia option.

4. Select the Authorware 3.5 option to launch Authorware.

FIG. 2.2
Launch the Authorware for Windows program using the Windows 95 Start button.

Authorware for Windows application icon

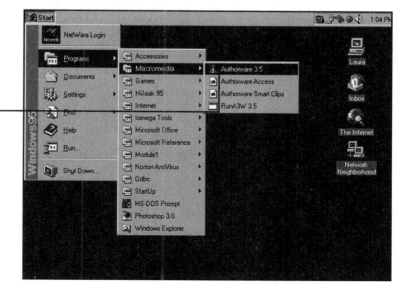

You can also use the Windows 95 Explorer, as seen in Figure 2.3, to launch Authorware by following these steps:

1. Click the Start button.
2. Select the Windows Explorer option from the menu.
3. Locate the A35W directory that contains the Authorware application.
4. Double-click the A35W application file to launch Authorware.

FIG. 2.3

Launch the Authorware for Windows application using the Windows 95 Explorer feature.

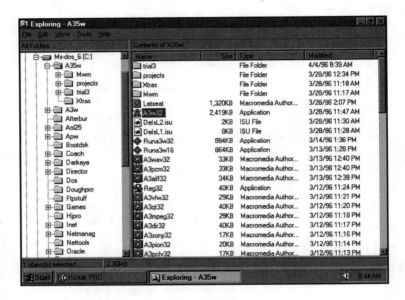

You can also use the Windows 95 desktop, as seen in Figure 2.4, to launch Authorware by following these steps:

1. With no other window open, double-click the "My Computer" icon. This icon may have another name if you have changed it.
2. Double-click the icon representing the drive to which you installed Authorware.
3. Locate the A35W directory that contains the Authorware application.
4. Double-click the A35W application file to launch Authorware.

FIG. 2.4
Launch the Authorware for Windows application using the Windows 95 Desktop feature.

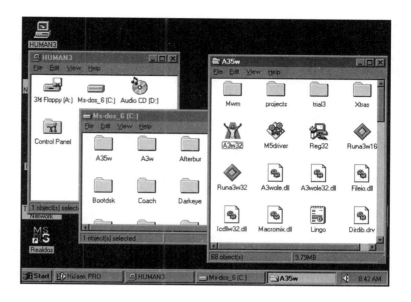

In Windows 3.*x*, there are also several options for launching Authorware depending on how you installed the application. When installing Authorware, you will be prompted to create a program group, as seen in Figure 2.5. If you did this, follow these steps:

1. Open the Authorware program group using Program Manager.
2. Double-click the Authorware 3.5 application icon.

FIG. 2.5
Launch the Authorware for Windows program using Program Manager just as you would any other Windows 3.*x* application.

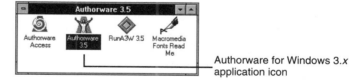

Authorware for Windows 3.*x* application icon

You may also use File Manager to launch Authorware, as seen in Figure 2.6, using the following steps:

1. Locate and open File Manager.
2. Locate and open the A35W directory.
3. Double-click the A35W.exe file.

FIG. 2.6

Launch the Authorware for Windows application using File Manager just as you would any other Windows 3.x application.

Authorware for Windows 3.x application icon

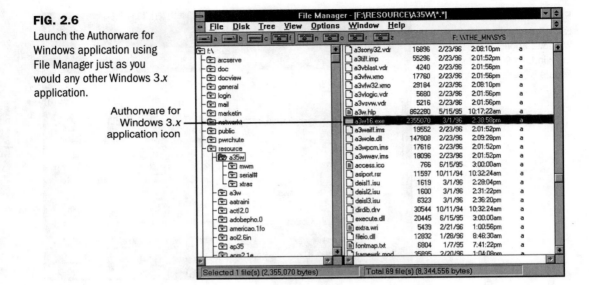

Opening an Existing Piece

To open an existing piece on the Macintosh, either double-click the piece's icon, or drag the piece's icon and drop it onto the Authorware application icon.

In the Windows 95 environment, select the Explorer or My Computer feature to locate and select the piece.

In Windows 3.x, an existing piece can be opened in several ways. If you have created a program item icon for the piece, simply double-click that icon. You can also locate and select the piece using File Manager. In either case, the piece must be associated with the Authorware application using standard Windows procedures.

On any platform, you can also first open the Authorware application, then select to open a piece. To open a piece once the Authorware application has been launched, follow these steps:

1. Select the Open command from the File menu.

2. Use the Open File dialog box to locate the piece you wish to open.

3. Click the piece's name, then click the Open button.

Saving and Backing Up

If any law applies to computers, it must certainly be Murphy's Law. No matter how solid you believe that your system is, "If anything can go wrong, it will!" For this reason, I strongly suggest that as soon as you open a piece, save your work and make backups. (Save frequently throughout the development process as well.)

When you first open a new piece, the title is shown across the top of the Flowline window (see Fig. 2.7).

FIG. 2.7

A new piece is untitled by default.

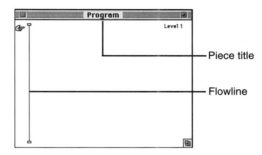

Piece title

Flowline

To save your piece for the first time, follow these steps:

1. Choose Save from the File menu.

 T I P The shortcut key sequence for saving is ⌘+S (Macintosh) and Ctrl+S (Windows).

2. When the Save File dialog box appears, use the pop-up menu to select where you want your piece to be saved.

3. Enter the name of your piece. Be sure to follow Macintosh or Windows conventions, depending on the system on which you are working.

   While the .A3W extension is automatically added to Windows files, adding .A3M to your Macintosh files will better accommodate cross-platform development.

4. Once your file name and extension have been entered, click the Save button. When the Save File dialog box closes, the name you gave your piece will appear across the top of the Flowline window.

After you have initially named and saved the piece, continue to save your work periodically. This is tremendously important if you have just spent a great deal of time developing something that you do not want to re-create if there is a computer error.

To save your work throughout development, simply reselect Save from the File menu or use the shortcut keys. Because you have already determined the name and location for your piece, Authorware does not present the Save File dialog box again. Rather, it just overwrites the previous version using the same name, with the new version containing your most recent changes.

The shortcut key sequences for saving are ⌘+S (Macintosh) and Ctrl+S (Windows).

Using Save As to Create Backup Files   You may also find it helpful to use the Authorware Save As command throughout development as opposed to the Save command. Save As creates a new piece on the hard drive just as if you were starting from the beginning, but it includes all your work to that point. Instead of saving your changes over the existing piece, Save As creates a new piece with a new name, leaving the older, previously saved piece on disk. This enables you to create successive versions of the piece on disk, so you can go back to an earlier version if you need to.

To use the Save As command, follow these steps:

1. Choose Save As from the File menu.

2. When the Save File dialog box appears, use the pop-up menu to select the directory where you want your piece to be saved.

3. Notice that the dialog box already contains the name you gave the piece initially. Modify this name, or overwrite it completely, with a new name. Whether you modify it or overwrite it, however, all work completed since the last Save or Save As will be used to create the new piece. Be sure to follow Macintosh and Windows naming conventions, depending on the system on which you are working.

4. Once your file name and extension have been entered, click the Save button. When you close the Save File dialog box, the new name will appear across the top of the Flowline window.

When naming such files, members of my team include a reference to the date, and to the version, such as ORA0329a.A3W. This helps us to archive versions of the piece if we need to come back to previous programming for any reason, or if the client would like to review the progression of development.

 I use an eight-character naming convention. The first three digits refer to the client, the next two to the month, the next two to the day, and the final character to the version saved for that day. A standard naming system helps you organize your projects.

Use Save As for the reasons described in the next sections to protect you from losing days' or weeks' worth of development work.

Before Major Rework   During Authorware development, it is not uncommon to rip apart something that you developed earlier because you believe there is a more efficient way to build it, or simply because someone has requested a change.

Before beginning the overhaul, however, I recommend that you use Save As just in case the modification leads you to a dead end and you need to return to a working version.

For Archival Purposes The development team in my company has found it very helpful to use Save As several times a day in order to track development progress. Additionally, the security of a backup is critical. I learned this the hard way.

A few years ago we were working on a fairly large piece with an already tight deadline. We were to deliver the final product, a kiosk, for an international trade show that began the Saturday after Thanksgiving. The Wednesday before Thanksgiving, just as we were putting the finishing touches on the piece, we suffered a system error. All attempts to rescue the piece were hopeless.

Without panic, we turned to our archive of backups. One by one we found that each Save As, each backup, carried the error. We finally found a two-week old version that worked. The next day we had turkey sandwiches from a local sub shop as we rebuilt the lost work. All in all, the two-week old version, which was created using Save As, rescued us from having to rebuild months' worth of development.

Part
I

Ch
2

Closing a Piece

When working in Authorware, there are several ways in which a currently open piece can be closed. You can choose the Close command from the File menu, click the Close box located in the upper left-hand corner of the Flowline window (Macintosh), or use the window's Control box located in the upper left-hand corner of the Flowline window (Windows 3.x and Windows 95).

Selecting to open another piece, including a new piece, also causes the currently open piece to close.

In either of these cases, if you have made any changes to the piece, you will be prompted to save those changes before the piece closes.

Specifying the Authorware File Setup

What to name the piece and where to save it are only the beginnings of the decisions you need to make before development begins. For example, the final multimedia application's title, the location of external content files, the design of the Pause button, and the contents and configuration of the Presentation Window must be well thought out.

In general, these decisions will determine what the user will see when the piece is launched, what the multimedia piece will look like on-screen, and what will happen when the user quits the piece. The options to specify all of these settings are located in the File Setup dialog box.

Becoming Familiar with the File Setup Dialog Box

After you have opened a new piece, named it, and then saved it, you need to "set up" your piece. The File Setup dialog box allows you to establish what the user will see when the piece is launched, what the window will look like on-screen, and what will happen when the user quits the piece. Unfortunately, setting up a piece is a step that is usually not taken by many developers until late in the development process, when some changes may require major rework.

To access the File Setup dialog box, as seen in Figure 2.8, choose Setup from the File menu.

FIG. 2.8
Before authoring, consider all the options in the File Setup dialog box.

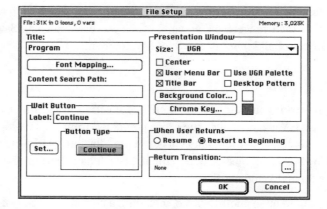

Let's look at each of the options in the File Setup dialog box, and consider when each is useful.

Title   The title of the piece may not necessarily be the name used by the development team, but rather, is the name that you want the end user to see. The title appears in the following places: in the About box for the packaged piece; across the top of the Presentation Window of the final application if the title bar is activated; in the dialog box that is displayed when pressing Alt+Tab to toggle between Windows applications; and on the piece's icon if the piece is minimized in a Windows environment. This can be the same name you use in marketing material, or on an introduction or splash screen within the piece itself.

The default title for your application is the name you gave the Authorware piece the first time you saved it. You can overwrite this title; however, the Authorware piece name will not be affected when you change the title. The section "Saving and Backing Up" earlier in this chapter shows you how to save files with the Save and Save As command.

Font Mapping   The Font Mapping button opens the Font Mapping dialog box. This feature is used to identify which fonts your piece is using, which substitute fonts can be used instead, and for cross-platform development, which fonts must be used during conversion.

We will discuss the Font Mapping dialog box in greater detail later in this chapter, in the section "Using the Font Mapping Dialog Box."

Palette   The Palette feature (available in Authorware for Windows only) is incredibly helpful if you plan to use a color palette other than the standard Windows palette. When you click the Palette button, the Palette dialog box, as seen in Figure 2.9, appears and contains the following options:

Option	Description
Preserve System Colors	Ensures that the standard Windows colors that are used for menu bars, icons, and borders remain constant even though the balance of the palette consists of your custom colors.
Use Default	Restores the standard Windows palette.
Load	Allows you to select a custom palette.
Optimize	Provides a series of options that allows you to optimize the palette for the entire piece; all icons, including those stored in libraries; and all icons in the piece for which links to libraries exist.

Part

I

Ch

2

FIG. 2.9
Authorware for Windows
provides several options for
loading custom palettes.

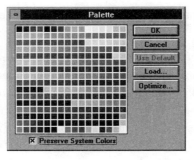

The Optimize feature is helpful if you are planning to use a custom palette, but have not adjusted the colors in each of the graphics to take advantage of that palette. For example, if you create a graphic using a standard palette and then import it into an Authorware piece that uses a custom palette, Authorware will adjust the colors in the image using those available in the custom palette. This adjustment is for display purposes only, and the colors in the actual graphic are not changed. As you can imagine, this exercise takes some processing effort and may impact performance.

If you select to Optimize the piece, however, Authorware will modify each of the graphics in the piece, or any associated library files, so that the colors match those available in the custom palette. When the piece is run after optimization, Authorware no longer needs to do the adjustment to the graphics, so display time increases.

CAUTION

Using a custom palette will negatively impact performance if you load the palette after graphics have already been created or imported into your piece. To enhance performance, either load the palette before you start creating graphics, or use the Optimize option.

TROUBLESHOOTING

How do I use a custom palette in Authorware for the Macintosh? Loading a custom palette into Authorware for the Macintosh can be a complex effort. You can use either an XCMD to call an external palette or a ResEdit to change the Authorware CLUT resource. The identification number for the 8-bit palette is 212.

Content Search Path   The Content Search Path field is where you enter the name of the location where you plan to store external elements used in your piece, such as digital movies or content libraries. As you consider the name and location of these elements, be sure to address the conventions used in both the Windows and the Macintosh environments for directory names should you be developing a multi-platform solution. Additionally, be sure that the location is standard across all systems and is not unique to your development station.

When Authorware encounters an icon that is linked to external content, it will check the directory specified in the search path first. If no directory is specified, or if the linked content cannot be found in that location, Authorware will then check a directory, known as the record location, which is automatically created by Authorware in the system directory and labeled A3MData (Macintosh) or A3W_Data (Windows). If Authorware cannot locate the linked information in the record location, it finally looks in the same folder or directory in which your piece is stored.

To enter a Content Search Path, use a colon (Macintosh) or backslash (Windows) after each volume, directory or folder name. Use semicolons to separate multiple search paths.

Wait Button   When using a Wait icon, or an automatic pause associated with the Interaction or Decision icon, Authorware will automatically create a labeled button, called the Pause button. This button appears in the Presentation Window, and therefore, will be seen and used by the end user.

▶ For step-by-step guidance on using the Wait icon, **see** "Using the Wait Icon," **p. 157**.

TROUBLESHOOTING

How can I develop an application that uses more than one Pause button graphic? Unfortunately, Authorware only allows one default Pause button. You can create a custom push-button interaction, however, that can be used in place of the Wait icon or automatic pause. (See button responses in Chapter 10, "Creating Buttons.")

The Pause button associated with the Interaction icon and the Wait icon will only be displayed if the Show Button option (in the Wait Options dialog box) has been selected. The Pause button associated with the Decision icon, however, is displayed when the automatic pause option is selected. In the File Setup dialog box, change these settings to control the appearance of the labeled button:

- Label—Enter the label you want to appear on the Pause button throughout the piece should you elect to show the button. The button automatically is sized to accommodate your label.

  Be careful when creating this label. Many times a label may make sense to you, but it can be confusing to the end user. The default for the button is "Continue," for which you can easily substitute "Next" or "Go On."

- Button Type—This window displays the currently selected graphic that will be used for the pause button, as well as the label you have created.

■ Set—Click this button, or click the Button Type window, to open the Button Library. The Button Library allows you to select a different button style, to edit the currently selected button style using the Button Editor, or to import buttons created in a graphic program.

 TIP Extensive use of the Wait icon is a sign of very low level interactivity within your piece. If you find yourself relying on the Wait icon, I suggest that you revisit your design and build in other, non-linear ways for the user to move through the piece.

▶ To change the button graphic, **see** "Using the Button Editor," **p. 245**.

▶ For information on applying Wait options to a decision loop, **see** "Taking Advantage of Automatic Pausing," **p. 349**.

Presentation Window Size   The Presentation Window is the window in which your finished piece will run, independent of the size of monitor. The key to the size of the Presentation Window is resolution; that is, the number of pixels high and wide your piece requires and not the physical dimensions of the monitor. The most common resolution is 640 pixels wide by 480 pixels high.

NOTE   In most cases, monitors running 640×480 pixels are displaying 72 dots per inch, and those running 1024×768 pixels are displaying 96 dots per inch. ■

It was my lack of attention to the Presentation Window Size option that caused the embarrassing situation with the motorcycle presentation that I discussed earlier.

Authorware provides a pop-up list, shown in Figure 2.10, containing predefined settings.

FIG. 2.10
Authorware provides a list of predefined Presentation Window settings.

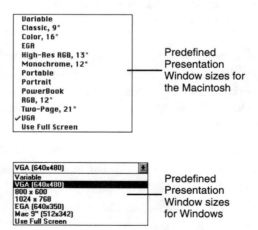

Predefined Presentation Window sizes for the Macintosh

Predefined Presentation Window sizes for Windows

There are three main categories in which these settings fall, including:

- Variable—Use this option to set the Presentation Window size to any set of pixel dimensions (see Fig. 2.11). This is very helpful if you are attempting to simulate exactly a piece of machinery, or an odd-shaped monitor. It also allows you to create pieces that can be run side-by-side, or for one window to overlap another window without totally covering it.

FIG. 2.11
Variable window sizes can be used to simulate other computer screens.

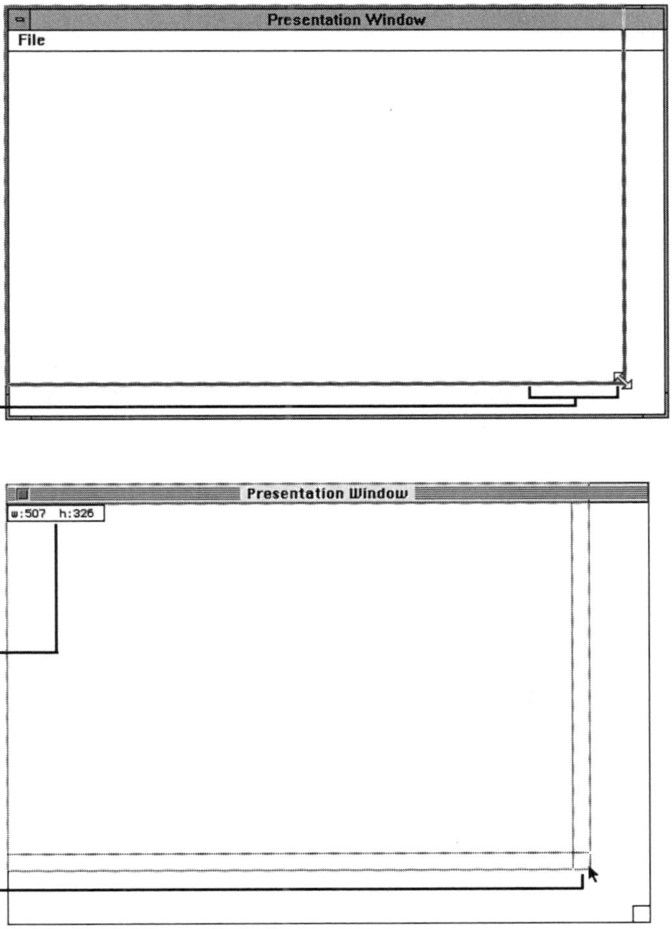
Presentation Window
File
The Windows Presentation Window can be resized using any corner or side.
Presentation Window
w:507 h:326
Width and height coordinates are displayed during resizing.
The Macintosh Presentation Window can be sized from the corner.

To set a variable window size, select the Variable option, then close the File Setup dialog box.

Next, choose Run from the Try It menu, then pause the piece by selecting the Pause command from the Try It menu.

The shortcut key sequences for Run are ⌘+R (Macintosh) and Ctrl+R (Windows). The shortcut key sequences for Pause are Command+P (Macintosh) and Ctrl+P (Windows).

On the Macintosh, drag the size box located in the lower-right corner of the Presentation Window. As soon as you click the size box, height and width dimensions are shown in the upper left-hand corner of the Presentation Window. Continue to resize the Presentation Window until these dimensions meet your specifications.

In Windows, drag any side or corner to resize the Presentation Window. Authorware for Windows does not give pixel dimensions like the Macintosh does.

Choose Proceed from the Try It menu to continue. The Presentation Window retains the set size until you change it.

 The shortcut key sequence for Proceed is ⌘+P (Macintosh) and Ctrl+P (Windows).

N O T E In Windows, as the mouse pointer crosses over an edge of the Presentation Window, it turns into a double arrow, signaling that the Presentation Window can be resized. ■

■ Fixed Settings—Authorware provides several pre-set definitions (refer to Figure 2.10) that range from the Macintosh 9" monitor up to a two-page 21" monitor. The numbers in Windows (such as 640×480) along with the description, refer to the width and height of the window in pixels.

■ Use Full Screen—Select this option to fill the entire monitor.

CAUTION

Be careful when selecting the Full Screen option, however, because this is how I got into trouble with the motorcycle example. If your final application will run on a monitor that is the same size as the one used for development, then everything seems to run all right. But if the monitor used for the presentation is larger, or if there are two monitors, your presentation may overhang into a visible area, just as mine did. If the presentation monitor is smaller than the one used for development, however, some of your presentation will be cut off.

 For cross-platform development, I suggest selecting either High Res 13" or VGA. Either of these settings works well on each platform and supports the greatest number of systems.

I will further discuss selecting a Presentation Window size later in this chapter in the section "Selecting a Presentation Window Size."

Presentation Window Location and Appearance   Along with considerations as to the size of the Presentation Window, you must also consider where the Presentation Window will be located on-screen, which window features will be displayed, and what palette will be used.

To do this, use the following File Setup dialog box options:

- Center—Select this option if you want the Presentation Window to be centered on-screen, no matter what size or resolution monitor the user has.

- Overlay Menu —This Authorware for Windows option causes the menu bar to overlay the Presentation Window, as opposed to the Presentation Window beginning just below the menu bar. Therefore, when this option is selected, the objects located within the top twenty pixels of the Presentation Window will be hidden from view.

N O T E   Selecting the Overlay Menu option results in approximately 20 less pixels vertically for your piece. Be sure that you do not change the setting once you begin development.

- User Menu Bar (Macintosh) or Menu Bar (Windows)—Authorware by default creates a user menu bar with a pull-down menu header titled "File." Within the File menu is a command called "Quit."

  If you do not want to show the user menu bar, deselect this option; however, you must remember to provide an alternative means for your user to exit the piece.

  I have often found that leaving the menu bar turned on distracts from a highly graphical user interface. Additionally, pull-down menus are for the computer aficionado and may hide content from the end user. In any case, decide the effectiveness of pull-down menus based on your target audience.

TROUBLESHOOTING

I don't want the menu bar to be seen by the end user, but I often need to access it for authoring when I am running the piece. How do I do this? The menu bar can be turned on and off during authoring and during runtime, by pressing the ⌘+Shift+? (Macintosh) or Ctrl+Spacebar (Windows) keys.

- Title Bar—Authorware also automatically creates a title bar if the Presentation Window is smaller than the screen. This is actually very helpful because it allows the user to move the Presentation Window by dragging the title bar.

  If the Presentation Window is as large as, or larger than, the screen, however, you can deselect this option to hide the title bar.

■ Use VGA Palette—This Macintosh option allows you to set the Windows VGA palette as the default palette while working on the Macintosh. This is very helpful if you are planning to convert your piece to the Windows platform after development.

As a word of warning, however, the Windows VGA palette, and even the Windows 256-color palette, is difficult to work with. The colors in the Windows palette are very vibrant, causing photos to appear unrealistic looking (see Fig. 2.12). For this reason, there is a tendency to use the Macintosh 256 palette, even for cross-platform applications.

FIG. 2.12
There are color differences in the Macintosh 256, Windows 256, and Windows VGA palettes.

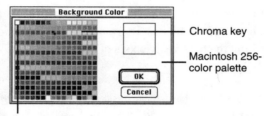

Chroma key

Macintosh 256-color palette

Currently selected color

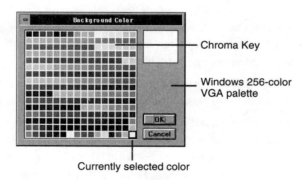

Chroma Key

Windows 256-color VGA palette

Currently selected color

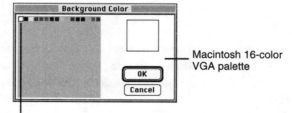

Macintosh 16-color VGA palette

Currently selected color

■ Path Type—The Path Type setting is designed to make the 32-bit version of Authorware for Windows more flexible in terms of handling Windows 95 or Windows NT environments. This option allows you to determine which convention will be used by system variables and functions that return a network path name. If your piece will only be run on networks using the Universal Naming Convention (such as Windows NT), then select the UNC option. If, however, your piece will be run on a variety of networks, then select the DOS (Drive Based) option.

On the Macintosh, the system variables and functions that will be affected by Path Type always return Macintosh-formatted path names, therefore, this File Setup dialog box option is not needed.

- Naming—Like Path Type, you can also determine the convention to be used for file names that are returned by system variables and functions. The DOS option allows a maximum of eight characters, where the long format will allow up to 255 characters. If you are not sure on which system the piece will run—the safest selection is the DOS option.

- Task Bar—The Windows 95 task bar contains buttons that make it easy to switch from one running application to another. If you design your piece to occupy the entire Presentation Window, and the user has the task bar turned on, then part of your piece will be covered by the task bar. Because the task bar can be positioned along any edge of the Presentation Window, however, accounting for this scenario is difficult.

To overcome this conflict, Authorware's default is to hide the task bar if it will overlap the Presentation Window. Select this option if you want to override this default, potentially allowing the task bar to cover a portion of the Presentation Window.

- Match Window Color—Because Windows 95 allows users to set their own window color for executable files, you can allow that setting to be used for your piece. Selecting this option overrides your selection for a background color. The risk, of course, is that the user may have selected a background that aesthetically conflicts with your piece.

- Standard Appearance at Runtime—Just as the users can establish a custom window color for their Windows 95 system, they can also select an appearance for buttons. Selecting this option allows the users' selection to override the Authorware default for all system buttons and objects.

- Windows 3.1 Metrics—The Windows 95 menu bar, title bar and window borders differ from earlier versions of Windows. Therefore, if you are designing a piece that is to run in both environments, you will either overlay one pixel at the top of the Presentation Window, or you will be a pixel short at the bottom of the Presentation Window.

While the solution to select the Windows 3.1 Metrics will allow these items to appear the same on both platforms, there are a few drawbacks. For example, if you select this option, every window of every application will be changed to use Windows 3.1 Metrics. Additionally, future versions of Authorware may not contain this option, as Windows 95 Metrics become the standard.

■ Use Desktop Pattern—This Macintosh option creates a Presentation Window that contains the same background pattern currently being used by the end user's Macintosh desktop.

To date, the only use I have found for this option is for playing practical jokes on my coworkers. I create a small piece that looks like their desktop, but when they try to click on an icon, the icon animates away.

■ Background Color—This button presents a palette from which you can select a background color to be used throughout your entire piece. The default color is white, and the currently selected background color is shown in the chip to the right of the button.

This option is very helpful if your background color is solid, or if it contains a lot of one color. You can set the background color instead of displaying a graphic containing the needed color; this means your piece will use less RAM and disk space, and will display faster.

■ Chroma Key—Use this option if you are using a video overlay card and the card supports chroma keys. Just like setting the Background Color, you click a color in the palette, and the currently selected color is displayed in the chip next to the button.

When analog video is played in a computer screen, it will map to a specific color only. This color is known as the *chroma key*.

Because the use of video overlay is quickly giving way to digital video, I will only spend a little time discussing its use.

▶ For detailed guidance on using analog video and a chroma key, **see** "Don't Forget the Chroma Key," **p. 477.**

N O T E   To identify which color is being used as the chroma key, look for a color in the palette that has two small inverse colored boxes in it (Macintosh) or a "C" overlaying the color in the palette (Windows). ■

When User Returns   Another decision you must make when using the Authorware File Setup dialog box is to define what happens when the user quits and later returns to the piece.

There are two options for directing the user when returning to the piece, including:

■ Restart At Beginning—This default option restarts your piece from the beginning each time it is launched. Restarting from the beginning resets all the variables used to control the piece.

This option is most commonly used when multiple users will share the same executable piece. If you still desire the capability to save information created by one user, and you do not want the current user to pick up where the previous user left off, you can store each user's information in an external file. At the beginning of the piece, you can build a log-on function, which then reads the external file and sets the variables and controls.

- Resume—This option forces the current user to start at the point where the previous user exited, regardless if that user was the last person to use the piece. Resume also saves all variables and current settings.

Both the Restart At Beginning and the Resume options can be overridden using the Restart and QuitRestart functions, which are explained in the Authorware Functions dialog box.

▶ For information on accessing the Functions dialog box, **see** "How Authorware Functions Are Organized," **p. 373**.

▶ For a sample log-on sequence, **see** "Building a Log-on Sequence," **p. 427**.

Return Transition   This option allows you to select a transition to be used when the user returns to the piece. For example, you can select a transition that causes the entire Presentation Window to slide up from the bottom of the monitor each time the piece is launched by the end user.

▶ For step-by-step instructions on selecting a transition, **see** "Working with Xtras Transitions," **p. 149**.

TROUBLESHOOTING

I selected a return transition, but when I distributed the application, it did not work. What happened? As discussed in Chapter 5, "Working with Display Effects and Transitions," transitions are read from external Authorware plug-ins that are stored in the Xtras folder or directory. When distributing the final application, you must also deliver and install the Xtras plug-ins, otherwise, the transitions will be ignored.

If you carefully consider each of the options in the File Setup dialog box, you will avoid spending hours reengineering your piece.

Using the Font Mapping Dialog Box

As I will discuss later in this book, working with fonts is a real trick, and developing cross-platform applications makes font issues an even greater nightmare. Many developers have taken a certain but long road around font issues by converting all text to a graphic before moving to a second platform. While this does certainly solve the font-conversion problem, it also creates an application that may be quite large, have text that requires great effort to change, and results in content that cannot be searched using Authorware's search features.

▶ For an introduction to placing text in the Presentation Window, **see** "Placing Text On-Screen," **p. 68**.

The selection of fonts is a concern both during development and delivery. If you are developing for the Macintosh platform only, however, this concern is reduced. The Macintosh treats fonts as a resource to the application (unless they are Type 1 Postscript fonts) and when you package an Authorware piece on the Macintosh for distribution, you can include the fonts so that end users are not required to have the fonts installed on their system. If the font is a TrueType font, Authorware provides the option to convert it to a bitmap during packaging, which creates the executable piece.

> **CAUTION**
>
> Converting text to bitmaps eliminates the capability to include the content when searching for particular words.

Development and delivery in a Windows environment is not so simple, however. Windows treats fonts as a resource to the system, so if the end user does not have the same fonts you used during development, your piece will not look in delivery as it looked when you created it.

Developing for a cross-platform solution, of course, adds even more confusion because the fonts between the platforms can be named differently, and because their physical characteristics are treated differently on each platform. For this reason, Authorware provides font mapping, which is controlled using the Font Mapping dialog box. Using Font Mapping, unlike the other options in the File Setup dialog box, typically occurs after development has begun, or at least a prototype has been developed. If you are planning to develop a multi-platform solution, you may want to include font samples as a component of your first prototype.

▶ For hints to using fonts when developing for multi-platform delivery, **see** "Dealing with Fonts," **p. 575**.

> **CAUTION**
>
> Be careful when using font mapping. Just because a font has the same name in Windows as it does on the Macintosh, does not mean it is the same font. Be sure to test the results of font mapping selections before continuing with large amounts of development.

To access the Font Mapping dialog box, shown in Figure 2.13, click the Font Mapping button located in the File Setup dialog box. Font mapping is most commonly used during cross-platform development. It can also be used, however, to ensure that your piece retains a specified look even if it is running on a single platform.

FIG. 2.13
The Font Mapping dialog box.

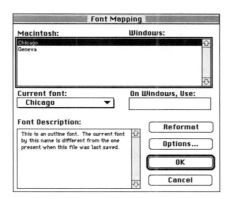

Part
I
Ch
2

The left column in the Font Mapping dialog box shows all fonts used in the piece you have built. If you are working on a Macintosh, the right column is blank. You can select alternative fonts to be placed in the right column if the font you have selected is not installed on the user's system, and you do not intend to include fonts when you package the application for delivery. While the Macintosh is pretty good about selecting alternative fonts automatically, this feature will override the automatic selection.

If you move the Macintosh piece to Windows, you can select an alternative Windows font to replace the Macintosh font. The list of alternative Windows fonts then occupies the right column.

CAUTION
Selecting alternative fonts can dramatically impact screen design and layout. The result can be text that possibly overlaps other elements on-screen or extends beyond the bounds of the Presentation Window.

The additional options and buttons in the Font Mapping dialog box are described in the following sections.

Current Font   The Current Font list shows all of the fonts currently installed on the system. Select a new font from the list to be used in place of the selected font in the left column.

You will notice that font sizes are automatically selected because each platform uses unique sizing conventions.

On Windows, Use   Enter the name of a Windows font in the On Windows, Use text box. Authorware then substitutes the selected Macintosh font with the identified Windows font during conversion to the Windows platform.

On Macintosh, Use   Enter the name of a Macintosh font in the On Macintosh, Use field. Authorware then substitutes the selected Windows font with the identified Macintosh font during conversion to the Macintosh platform.

Font Description   If there are special considerations for the font you have selected, Authorware will provide details in this message window. Use this information to determine how to best proceed.

Reformat   The Reformat option reformats any text that Authorware mapped to a different font.

Options   The Options button displays the Font Problem Options dialog box, which gives you control over the types of errors that make the Font Problem dialog box appear.

Steps for Mapping a Font   To use font mapping, follow these steps:

1. Select a font that is currently used in the piece by clicking it. A list of currently used fonts appears in the scrolling list located on the left-hand side of the Font Mapping dialog box.

2. Enter the name of the font you want to be used when the piece moves cross-platform. If you are working on a Macintosh, the entry field will be labeled "On Windows, Use" and in Windows, it will be labeled "On Macintosh, Use."

3. Click the Reformat button, or select another font to map, to save your entry.

4. Click the OK button when you have established all of the font maps.

Selecting a Presentation Window Size

Determining a Presentation Window size is just as critical as font selection in terms of the successful delivery of your piece. While the hazards are not quite as prevalent as font issues, they may prove to be more detrimental to the functionality of your piece. Selecting a font that your end user's system does not support usually results in a piece that does not look good, and in the worst case, is difficult to read. Selecting the wrong Presentation Window size, however, can result in a piece where the entire main menu is out of view and unselectable, or critical graphics are cropped by the edge of the monitor.

CAUTION

Do not change the size of the Presentation Window during development. If you select a larger-sized Presentation Window after development begins, the monitor will not be filled with the content. If you select a smaller size, some elements, or menus, will be cropped from view.

Most computers today support, or even come set to, 640×480 pixel resolution. There have been a few instances recently, however, where this standard was deviated from. For example, Apple built a series of computers that has a 512×304 resolution (the Plus and SE series), as well as a series of systems that has a 512×365 resolution (the LC series). Today, many Windows-based systems, while they support 640×480, ship with a resolution of 1024×768 or 800×600.

While you can develop for any resolution, you must consider which resolution your end user's system is most likely to have. The following sections explain what happens if the end user runs your piece in a resolution other than what you develop in.

The Piece Is Executed Using a Smaller Resolution   When the user's system has a lower resolution than the size of Presentation Window you set, the Presentation Window will be larger than the monitor, resulting in a portion of the piece being unusable and unviewable (see Fig. 2.14). Avoid this combination at all costs.

FIG. 2.14
Never deliver in a resolution smaller than what you developed in.

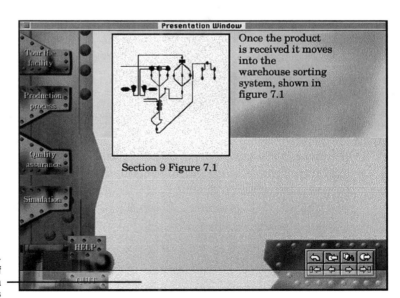

This portion of the Presentation Window will be cut off if the piece is running in a smaller resolution than it was developed in.

CAUTION

Selecting 640×480 resolution on a large monitor causes the image to distort slightly because the pixels become enlarged. Running at a higher resolution, however, enhances the quality of the image because the pixels are smaller and less noticeable individually.

The Piece Is Executed Using the Same Resolution   When the end user's system displays in the same resolution you developed in, the piece will fit the monitor just as it did during development (see Fig. 2.15). The graphics will appear exactly the same, as will the text. Keep in mind the size of the monitor does not matter; only resolution matters.

FIG. 2.15
The best solution is to deliver the application in the same resolution it was developed in.

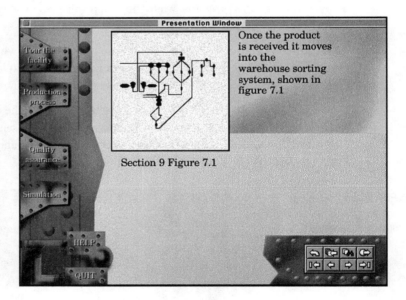

The Piece Is Executed Using a Higher Resolution   When the end user's system displays in a higher resolution than you used during development, the piece will occupy only a portion of the screen, with other files or pieces visible in the background (see Fig. 2.16). The higher resolution makes text appear smaller and more difficult to read due to the greater number of pixels per inch.

FIG. 2.16
While this configuration is tolerable, it is not the optimum.

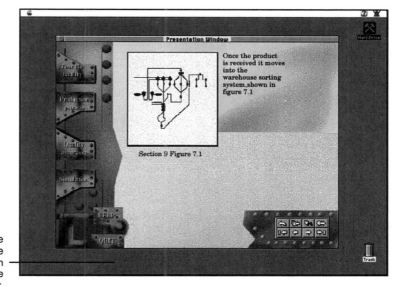

Other windows behind the Presentation Window are visible when the Presentation Window does not fill the entire monitor.

Mastering the Basics

Presenting Text

One of the earliest uses of the personal computer by business and home enthusiasts was for word processing. Newsletters, proposals, reports, résumés, and homework assignments quickly took on a new appearance as the traditional typewriter blocks of text gave way to hanging indents, stylized characters, and word wrapping. The availability of a wide range of fonts, varying in size and style, allowed even the novice designer to add pizzazz to a document.

This so-called pizzazz quickly found its way into the computer-based presentation as well. Adorned with color and displayed with a variety of Hollywood-like special effects, text has remained the main tool for on-screen communication in many multimedia training, educational, and reference applications.

Authorware makes it easy to display text, and supports a variety of fonts, sizes, and styles. This chapter

Recognizing the design considerations for using text

When designing with text, consider such issues as column width, point size, font type, and text color.

Introducing the Display icon

The Display icon is primarily used to hold text and graphics.

Building and working with text in Authorware

The Authorware Text tool is used to create text just as it is created in most word processing or page layout programs.

Implementing tabs, margins and scrolling text

The Authorware margin line is used to set character tabs, decimal tabs and hanging indents.

Defining and applying styles to make development more efficient

Styles contain characteristics as font, size and alignment, as well as information regarding hyperlinking.

Hyperlinking

Hyperlinks contain the characteristics of the text that contain a link, and the creation of the link itself.

introduces you to working with text, as well as to a few design techniques to consider when building pieces that incorporate on-screen text. ■

Placing Text On-Screen

Despite countless studies, as well as human intuition, that proclaim people do not like to read text from the computer screen, we continue to see programs that assume a book metaphor. The designer takes pages of content, which have been created for one medium (a book), and with the assistance of a scanner for digitizing text and graphics, converts the content so that it can be presented on-screen.

Often, this content ends up in "pages" separated by forward and backward buttons. The content in this form, therefore, behaves much like it did in its original medium. To accommodate large amounts of text, each page may contain a scrolling window in which the content is presented. Designers of such applications get away with calling this type of piece "interactive multimedia" because they often include a graphic or two among the text. They may also include an interface that allows the user to "interact" with the content.

While I do not believe that such applications are either "interactive" or "multimedia," I do believe that these types of applications have their place in the digital world for such reference applications as encyclopedias, technical documentation, and phone books. I also believe that text is a necessary medium in the multimedia experience. The issue, however, is how much and how it is used.

Before discussing how to incorporate text into an Authorware application, let's quickly look at a few obvious dos and don'ts when using text.

Design Considerations for On-Screen Text

The proliferation of the print industry has resulted in several publications, reference materials, and books that address issues surrounding print layout. If you plan to produce truly effective text-based applications, I suggest that you refer to these materials for further guidelines on displaying text. But for now, I'll present some overarching guidelines to help you get started.

While you can never say never when talking about the design of a multimedia piece, the following issues can at least be given a "most of the time" label in regard to the presentation of text.

Column Width   The designers of print-based materials have understood for years that the human eye cannot easily track or follow a wide column of text. For this reason, newspapers are written in narrow columns, and text books are often divided into blocks or columns.

The same rules that have been used in the print world can also be applied in the digital world. If large amounts of text are required, design the screen in blocks or columns. Figure 3.1 compares two screen designs, both of which handle the same, large amount of text. While the first design maintains all of the text in one column stretching across the monitor, the other employs narrower columns. Narrower columns are more readable because the content is easier for the eye to follow.

Point Size   Just like the layout of a page has a tremendous impact on its legibility, the point size of the text also plays a major role in a piece's legibility. Unfortunately, like layout, point size is often sacrificed for the need to get more content on-screen.

TIP   Choose one font, point size, style, and justification for all content text throughout the piece. Never succumb to the temptation of decreasing the point size or changing any other characteristic just to fit a large amount of content on a single screen. Additionally, the consistency will actually increase usability.

With most fonts, the smaller the point size, the more that jagged edges appear, making the text difficult to read. While this may be tolerable for such uses as labels or instructions, major bodies of text must be clearly readable, even if it means adding screens to accommodate large amounts of text. Figure 3.2 demonstrates how text becomes unreadable as it gets smaller and how adding screens can benefit your piece in the long run.

FIG. 3.1
Try to avoid stretching text all the way across the monitor. Break the text into columns for better legibility.

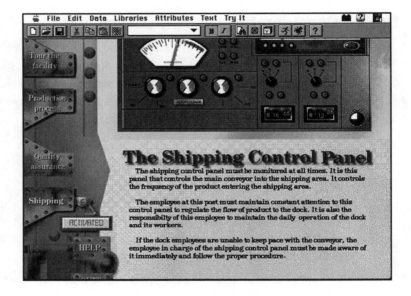

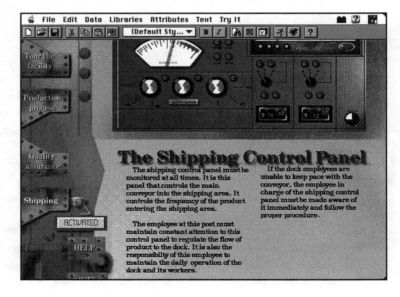

FIG. 3.2
Adding screens instead of decreasing the font size makes a piece more usable.

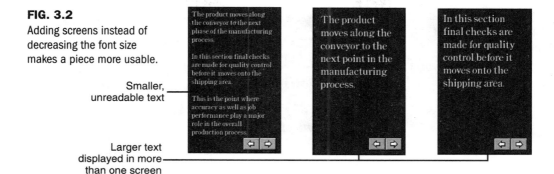

Smaller, unreadable text

Larger text displayed in more than one screen

To help you select which font to use as you get started developing multimedia pieces, I suggest that you create a paragraph of text on-screen. You can then print that screen, change the point size, and print the screen again. Continue this process for each point size and for every font. When you are done, you will have a notebook showing what fonts look like in each of the sizes on-screen.

N O T E Do not use the notebook of fonts to make your final selection without seeing your choice on-screen. The effects of light coming from behind the text (back-light) as you read it versus the light source being in front of the text (front-light), and the fact that fonts raster (show the stair-step or jagged edges) when displayed on the screen, may cause you to alter your selection. ■

Serif Versus Sans Serif   The rule in the print world has been that serif fonts are easier to read. Serif fonts are the ones that have little "feet" on each letter and have a tendency to be more stylistic. Examples of serif fonts include Times Roman, Palatino, and New York. Alternatively, in the digital world, sans serif fonts are easier to read for large blocks of text. Examples of sans serif fonts include Arial, Helvetica, and Futura.

The primary reason why sans serif fonts are easier to read on-screen than serif fonts is screen resolution. Most computer screens have a display resolution of 72 pixels per inch, as opposed to as many as 200 lines per inch on printed paper. Therefore, the screen cannot draw enough pixels to build the perfectly smooth curves used in serif fonts. The result is jagged lines that require the eye to study the text to interpret it rather than simply to glance over the text while reading.

Figure 3.3 compares several serif fonts with sans serif fonts. While the diagram shows examples of various fonts, I suggest that you experiment with sans serif and serif fonts to truly feel the impact of using one over the other on-screen.

FIG. 3.3
Carefully consider the use of
serif and sans serif fonts.

These are serif fonts

Allegro
Bookman Light
Century Old Style
Clarion
New Century Schoolbook
New York
Palatino
Times
Zapf Chancery
ALEXANDER

These are sans serif fonts

Univers
Avant Garde
BroadbandICG Regular
Chicago
Monaco
PACIFICA CONDENSED
Piano
Arial
Helvetica
Futura

The jagged edges of serif fonts on-screen can be removed using an anti-aliasing feature found in most graphic programs. I will discuss anti-aliasing later in this section.

Text Color   Why is it that just because we have the ability to use 256 colors on the screen, we do? We don't (at least I hope) use that many colors when we paint the outside of our home, even though that many colors of paint (and more) are available.

While novice designers believe that using several text colors enhances the "fun" of the piece, I believe that it makes the screen look like a bad day at the circus. Please understand, I am not referring to coloring text that serves a function, such as hypertext markings or highlights. Rather, I am referring to inconsistency: to the use of color for the sake of color.

So if you need to avoid using every color on the palette, how do you determine which colors to use? Well, there is not necessarily one right answer. In fact, there is an entire science called *Color Theory*, which studies the psychological impact that certain colors have. This science explains why fire engines and stop signs are red and why the inside of the doctor's office is blue.

What we do know is because the computer display is back-lit, unlike a book or a poster, which is front-lit, light text on a dark background is the easiest to read in an environment where the light level is low (compare the images in Fig. 3.4; however, you are looking at a front-lit example).

T I P The key to legibility is contrast, and creating light text on a dark background achieves contrast.

FIG. 3.4
Light text on a dark background (right) is easier to read in a low-light environment.

To determine which text color combinations work best, I suggest that you evaluate each design on a case-by-case basis for each piece that you develop. Be sure to test several combinations with your end users (if you can) before moving into full-scale production. Let the users determine which combinations are easiest to read.

Remember, it is your end user that will have to look at the piece for hours on end, and if the content text is difficult to read, they will avoid it at all costs. Building familiarity and comfort with what to expect from screen to screen, however, will keep your user attentive.

Anti-Aliasing   Selecting a font in terms of serif versus sans serif, as well as point size, is not as critical if you plan to anti-alias the text. Anti-aliasing is a function of many graphic programs that mathematically uses colors from the background to blend out the jagged edges. While jagged edges are more common on serif fonts, they can also appear on sans serif fonts.

Unfortunately, Authorware does not have the ability to anti-alias text either at the point of creation or at the point of packaging for delivery. Therefore, to take advantage of this technology, you must apply the following process to use anti-aliased text in your Authorware piece:

1. Create a mock-up of the screen layout (preferably in Authorware) so that you know how much text will be used. To determine the size of the text necessary to make all of the content fit on-screen, define the physical dimensions of the text area for the screen. If this area changes throughout the piece, you will need to do a layout for each variation.

2. For a particular screen, open a word processing program such as Microsoft Word, and enter the text. The font size, style, and so on are not important because you will

create the layout in a graphics program. Use the spell check capability to ensure that no errors exist.

3. Copy the graphic background for the screen out of Authorware and paste it into a graphics program such as Adobe Photoshop or Macromedia xRes. The selected program must support anti-aliasing.

 TIP Adobe Photoshop allows you to separate graphics into layers. Placing the background into layer one and then pasting text into subsequent layers will save time, as well as allow you to make changes with minimal effort.

4. Copy the text out of the word processing program and paste it into the graphic program. At this point, you will select the font, size, and style according to the specification defined when the layout was created.

5. Select to anti-alias the text onto the background graphic. The specifics for using the anti-aliasing function are dependent on the selected graphics program.

   Once you make this change, the text is no longer treated as text, but it becomes a part of the graphic.

6. Copy the portion of the graphic that now includes the text and the background, and return to Authorware. The graphic should then be pasted in place of text in the Presentation Window.

 TIP Capturing just the portion of the background that contains the text, rather than copying the entire background, will make your piece's finished file size smaller, as well as increase performance. Before capturing, be sure that all text is properly positioned. If the text is repositioned later, another screen capture will have to be made.

As you can see, this is a time-consuming and tedious process. And if the text changes for any reason, then you must begin all over again. The end result, as shown in Figure 3.5, however, is text that is easy to read and fits graphically into your piece.

The success of a piece is based in part on the design considerations for on-screen text. Choosing the right font and its point size, selecting readable colors, setting a reasonable column width, and determining whether or not to use anti-aliasing all contribute to a piece's success or failure.

A more fundamental concern, however, comes into play when designing a piece. That is, just how much text will be used, and will it be the foundation media in your piece or simply a supporting one? I challenge you to consider breaking the traditional book metaphor by attempting to create a new metaphor that takes greater advantage of today's interactive media and technology.

FIG. 3.5
Anti-aliasing removes the jagged edges by altering the background colors.

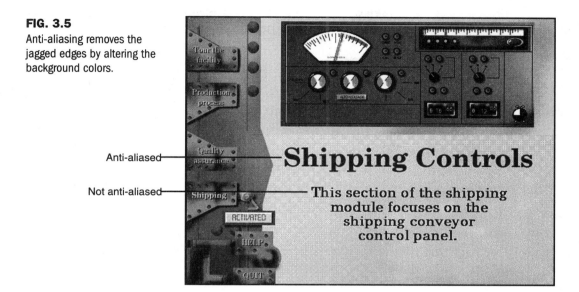

Anti-aliased

Not anti-aliased

Working with the Display Icon and Presentation Window

Now that we have looked at the design considerations for building on-screen text, let's take a look at how text is created using Authorware. To do this, however, the Display icon must be introduced.

The *Display icon*, shown in the Flowline window in Figure 3.6, is the vessel that holds text and graphics that are to be displayed in the Presentation Window and viewed by the end user. Although the Interaction icon shown in Figure 3.7 can also be used to display text and graphics, for the remainder of this discussion, we will focus on the Display icon.

To create text or graphics, you must open the Display icon. To open a Display icon, follow these steps:

1. Drag a Display icon to the Flowline.
2. Open the Display icon by double-clicking it.
3. When the Display icon opens, the Presentation Window will appear. As you create objects that will be displayed in the Presentation Window, you will be defining precisely what the end user will be seeing when the Authorware mites execute that icon.

FIG. 3.6
The Display icon is the primary vessel used to hold text and graphics. Double-click the Display icon in the Flowline to display the Presentation Window.

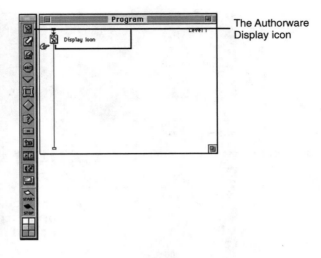

The Authorware Display icon

FIG. 3.7
The Interaction icon, like the Display icon, can also contain text and graphics.

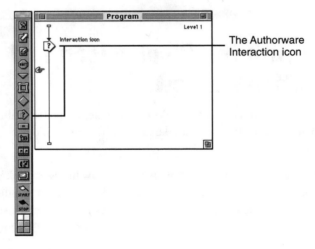

The Authorware Interaction icon

For the remainder of this book, I will assume that you are familiar with accessing the Presentation Window through a Display icon using the previously defined steps. You may find it helpful to practice these steps so that they become second nature.

Using the Text Tool

 In Chapter 1, "Taking the Authorware Tour," I introduced the Presentation Window and the Authorware Graphics toolbox. One of the tools in the Graphics toolbox is the Text tool. The Authorware Text tool works like text tools found in most word processing or text-layout programs.

▶ To refer to the definition of the Presentation Window, **see** "Defining the Presentation Window," **p. 26**.

▶ To refer to the introduction of the Text tool, **see** "The Text Tool," **p. 26**.

To create text in the Presentation Window using the Text tool, follow these steps:

1. Access the Presentation Window through a Display icon. The Graphics toolbox appears in the window.

2. Click the Text tool so that it becomes highlighted in the Graphics toolbox as shown in Figure 3.8. As you move the mouse pointer away from the Graphics toolbox, you will notice that it changes from an arrow to an I-beam pointer.

FIG. 3.8
When using the Text tool, Authorware creates a margin line for entering text in the Presentation Window.

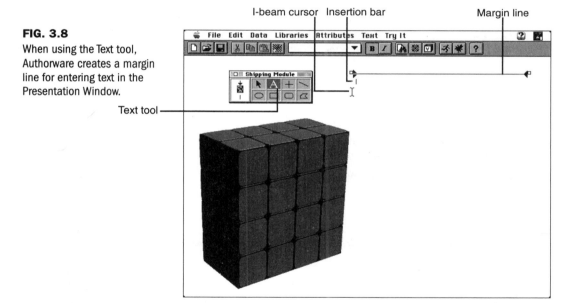

3. Click the location in the Presentation Window where you want to insert text. Once you click, a margin line appears with a blinking insertion bar that awaits text entry. The margin line defines where the left and right margin for the text block will occur within the Presentation Window and is used to establish tabs and hanging indents.

N O T E The default setting for alignment (left, center, or right) will determine where the blinking insertion bar appears. The left edge of the margin line, however, appears where you click the I-beam cursor in the Presentation Window. (See "Alignment" later in this chapter.) ▩

Part
II
Ch
3

4. Type the desired text. You can use the Return key on the Macintosh or the Enter key on the Windows keyboard to add extra carriage returns (lines). In the section titled "Changing Text Characteristics," we will explore changing the font, size, style, and other display characteristics of the text.

TROUBLESHOOTING

How do I produce a drop-shadow for text? Authorware does not have an offset or shadow feature like many graphics packages do. Therefore, to create a drop-shadow, you must create the text block then select it using the Pointer tool and copy it to the Clipboard. Color the remaining text block a color appropriate for the shadow and then paste the copy of the text block so that it overlays the original text block. Select a color for the overlying text block; then using the arrow keys, position the overlying text block so that it is slightly offset from the underlying text block. Using two text blocks, you can create the illusion of a shadow.

Selecting, Positioning, and Resizing a Text Block

Once you have completed entering text, select the Pointer tool to more precisely position the block of text in the Presentation Window. When you do this, you will notice that handles appear around the text block, as shown in Figure 3.9. Authorware will now treat the text block as an object. You can either drag the text to position it, use the arrow keys to position it, or drag one of the handles to adjust the column's width.

FIG. 3.9
Handles appear on the text block, allowing you to resize or reposition the text block.

Pointer tool —

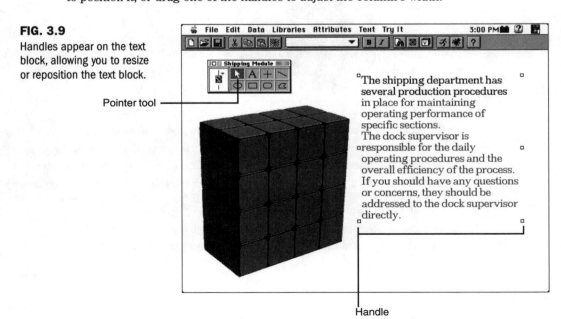

Handle

▶ To refer to the introduction of the Pointer tool, **see** "The Pointer Tool," **p. 28**.

To make revisions to the text within a text block, once again select the Text tool, move the mouse pointer away from the toolbox, and then click the I-beam cursor on the text block to which you want to make changes. Authorware changes the text block from an object to text.

> **N O T E** Keep in mind that you are working from the user's perspective when in the Presentation Window. What you see on the screen is exactly what the user will be seeing, so be sure that edits are exactly how you want them to appear in the final piece. ■

Changing Text Characteristics

Now that you know how to put text in the Presentation Window, let's look at how to change the characteristics of the text. Text characteristics, such as font, size, style, and justification, can be changed for either a single word or up to an entire block of text. In fact, a single block of text can contain as many characteristics as you can imagine. I do suggest, however, that you restrain yourself from using them all in one text block.

To change the characteristics of text, follow these steps:

1. Select the text you want to change. If you want to change an entire text block, use the Pointer tool to select the block. When the block is selected, handles will appear around it.

   If you want to change the attributes for a single word, or group of words, you must use the Text tool. Using the I-beam cursor, click within the text block so that the margin line appears. Double-click the single word, or drag the I-beam over the group of words to highlight them.

2. Select a font characteristic from the Text menu. As soon as you make your selection, the text will change to reflect the new font characteristic.

> **N O T E** Authorware only allows you to set one font characteristic at a time unless you are defining a style. (Styles are covered later in this chapter.) Simply changing a few characteristics can become a time-consuming process. Let's hope that Macromedia moves toward a font characteristics menu similar to that used in Photoshop or when defining an Authorware text style for setting all text characteristics. ■

Next, you'll learn about each of the different font characteristics you can manipulate. Each of the characteristics described in the following sections appear in Authorware's Text menu.

Part
II

Ch
3

Font   Use the Font selection to change from one typeface to another. Any font that is installed on your system can be used within Authorware. Keep in mind, however, if you are working in a Windows environment, or if you are using Type 1 Postscript fonts on the Macintosh, your end users will also be required to have the font installed on their system.

To help insure that a font similar to the one you are designing with is used in the final presentation, you might consider using the Authorware Font Mapping utility.

▶ To learn how to use Font Mapping, **see** "Using The Font Mapping Dialog Box," **p. 57**.

Size   Use the Size option to change selected text from one point size to another. Authorware supports any font size that is supported by the typeface itself.

If you choose the Size option in the Text menu, you will be presented with a list of supported font sizes for the current font in a hierarchical menu, as well as the following:

- Other—If you select Other, a dialog box appears that allows you to enter a point size. The dialog box also offers a preview of the current font in the selected size. This is helpful in selecting a point size if you are not familiar with how each font will appear in the various sizes.

CAUTION

If a font size other than one currently installed on the system is selected, Authorware will do its best to create the font. Unfortunately, selecting a bitmap font using Other will more than likely have a poor result.

- Size Up—Selecting this option will raise the point size of the currently selected characters to the next highest point size.
- Size Down—Selecting this option will lower the point size of the currently selected characters to the next lowest point size.

Style   Authorware supports all of the popular font styles available in most graphics and word processing packages, including bold, italic, underline, outline, and so on. Select a font style from the list of styles to be applied to the selected text.

Be careful when selecting font styles. Not only do some fonts not look good when a font style is applied, but selecting several font styles to be used either on a single screen or throughout the piece adds visual clutter (sometimes called the "ransom note effect") and inconsistency in design.

Additionally, using font styles in a Windows environment does have a few drawbacks. For example, if you select to apply bold to text, not only are the characters set to bold but so are the spaces between the characters. This can add to the difficulty in reading the text, as well as expand the spatial requirements for the text block.

Alignment   The Alignment option on the Text menu allows you to format the text block to be either left-aligned, centered, justified, or right-aligned. Once again, I recommend that you find one alignment for the main body of content and stick to it, not only within one screen but throughout your piece.

> **CAUTION**
> Centering is great for labels, but centering, or even right-aligning entire blocks of content can make it more difficult for the eye to find the next line, making it more difficult to read.

Scrolling Text   Choosing this option turns your block of text into a scrolling window. When you make a block of text scrolling, there are several issues that must be addressed. First, because the scrolling window looks and feels like a normal scrolling window, it may not fit into your interface graphically.

Second, novice users may not have the experience to use scrolling windows, and the last thing you want to do is alienate your users by creating an environment that is difficult to use.

Finally, you must take a hard look at your piece and determine if that much text is absolutely necessary. If it is, challenge yourself with the question, "Would this content work better in a book?" Remember, people do not like to read on the computer, and if you need a scrolling window, then the end user will obviously be required to do a lot of reading.

 Scrolling windows are good for the presentation of lists or for reference-based information, but try to avoid them for main bodies of content.

Other Text Attributes   In addition to the characteristics just described, you are able to change the color and mode for text. You will learn how to change these attributes when working with graphics in the next chapter.

▶ To learn how to change text color, **see** "Using the Color Palette," **p. 119**.

▶ To learn how to change text mode, **see** "Understanding Modes," **p. 114**.

Setting Text Defaults

Each of the text characteristics, such as the font and size, has a default setting. Therefore, every time you open a Display icon or Interaction icon to create a block of text, it will have characteristics according to the default. In the course of development, however, you may find it desirable to change the defaults.

There are two ways to change a default setting: manually or automatically.

Manually Changing Text Defaults   To manually change a default for font, size, style, or alignment, follow these steps:

1. Open a Display or Interaction icon.

2. Be sure no text is selected. If text is selected, you will be adjusting the characteristic for that text only, rather than setting the default.

3. Choose the characteristic you want to change the default for from the Text menu. For example, you can select the Alignment characteristic.

4. Select the new default setting for that characteristic from the options presented, such as Center.

From this point forward, all newly created text will be centered.

Automatically Changing the Text Defaults   Authorware will also automatically adjust the defaults as you are building your piece. It does this anytime you select more than one text block and then apply a new characteristic. For example, if you select two text blocks in the Presentation Window and then select bold, the default for any new text that you create will be bold.

Later in this chapter in the section, "Working with Styles," we will look at defining and applying styles, which enable you to change or set a group of characteristics for text.

Setting Tabs and Margins

Placing text on-screen is a relatively easy process. The issue, of course, is treating text like a design element so that it compliments the design of your piece. So far, we have looked at selecting fonts, styles, and other related text characteristics, as well as techniques for making text more visually pleasing or legible through processes such as anti-aliasing.

Another method for controlling the layout of text is through the manipulation of tabs, margins, and indents. Let's look at how each of these can be used to enhance the presentation of text in your piece.

Margins   When you select the Text tool and then click to place text in the Presentation Window, the margin line, as seen in Figure 3.10, appears. The left margin for the text is based on where you click in the Presentation Window, and the right margin then extends as far as it can within the Presentation Window.

FIG. 3.10

The margin line is used to set tabs, indents, and margins.

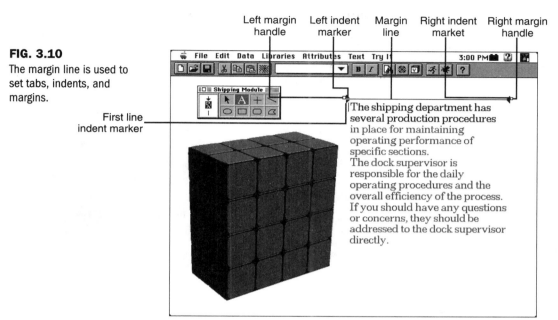

Left margin handle • Left indent marker • Margin line • Right indent market • Right margin handle

First line indent marker

The shipping department has several production procedures in place for maintaining operating performance of specific sections. The dock supervisor is responsible for the daily operating procedures and the overall efficiency of the process. If you should have any questions or concerns, they should be addressed to the dock supervisor directly.

To adjust either the left or the right margin, you can either drag the appropriate handle on the margin line, or you can drag a handle on the text block using the Pointer tool. In either case, Authorware will automatically word wrap the contents of the text block when the margins are adjusted; however, word wrapping does not automatically create hyphenation.

Indents Authorware allows you to place indents in several ways, including:

- First Line—The first line of each paragraph in your text block can be indented by dragging the bottom half of the left triangle (the first line indent marker shown in Fig. 3.10) to the point of the indent, as seen in Figure 3.11.

  The first-line indent applies to the entire text block, not just the paragraph containing the insertion bar at that time.

- Right Edge—To indent just the right edge of the text, drag the top half of the triangle marker located at the right side of the margin line to the left. You will notice that the entire triangle actually moves when you do this.

  Additionally, the margin indent only applies to the paragraph containing the insertion bar or highlighted text and not the entire text block. This feature, as seen in Figure 3.12, is helpful for wrapping text around a graphic. Without this feature, you would need to create two separate text blocks, each with a different right margin.

FIG. 3.11
First-line indents are created by dragging the bottom of the left-margin line marker.

First-line indent marker

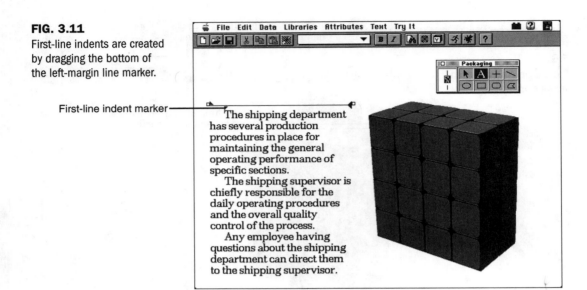

Right-indent marker

FIG. 3.12
Right-margin indents are created by dragging the top of the right-margin line marker to the left.

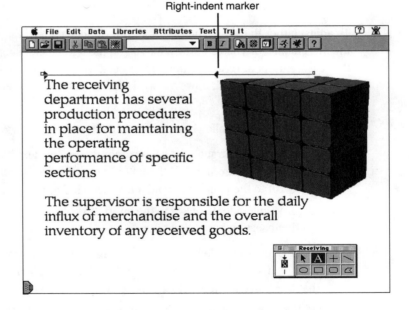

■ Left Edge—Like a right indent, the left side of a text block can also be indented. To indent just the left edge of the text, drag the top half of the triangle marker located at the left side of the margin line to the right. When you do this, you will notice that the upper and lower triangles actually move.

Additionally, the margin indent only applies to the paragraph containing the insertion bar and not the entire text block. This feature, as seen in Figure 3.13, is helpful for wrapping text around a graphic. Without this feature, you would need to create two separate text blocks, each with a different left margin.

FIG. 3.13
Left-margin indents are created by dragging the top of the left-margin line marker to the right.

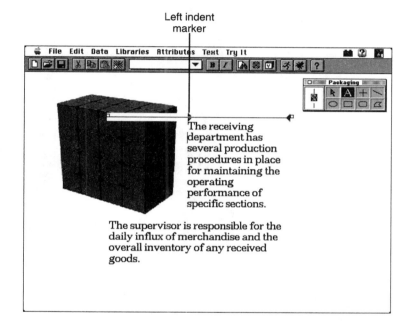

Left indent marker

Tabs Authorware allows you to create as many tab stops along the margin line as you need. To create a tab stop, simply click the margin line. To position the tab stop, drag it along the margin line to a new location. To remove a tab stop, drag it off of either end of the margin line and release the mouse button.

Within Authorware, there are two types of tab stops including:

- Character tabs—This normal type of tab is represented using a solid triangle pointing down toward the margin line and results in text that is left justified.

- Decimal Tabs—This special type of tab is represented using an arrow pointing toward the margin line. These tabs are very useful when aligning numbers.

TIP   Decimal tabs can also be used for right-aligning text as well as numbers.

To change from one type of tab stop to another, simply click the marker to toggle it. Additionally, tab settings must be applied to each paragraph separately, unless several paragraphs are selected when the tab stop is first placed.

Refer to Figure 3.14 to become more familiar with the different types of tab markers available in Authorware.

FIG. 3.14
Authorware supports both character and decimal tabs.

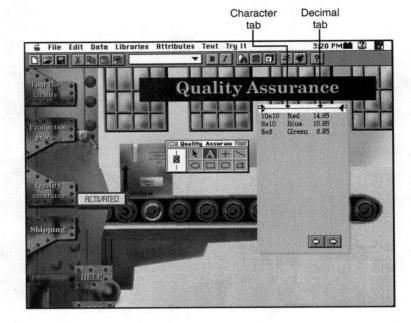

Character tab   Decimal tab

Working with Styles

So far in this chapter, we have focused on considerations for using text, as well as how to make text look better as a screen element. The remainder of this chapter will focus on potential development efficiencies when using text, as well as how to create hypertext links.

Now that we have taken a look at the various characteristics that can be applied to text on-screen, let's look at how styles can be defined and applied to text in order to make the development process, in particular the creation of text, more efficient.

Styles typically contain a predefined set of characteristics, such as a particular font, size, and alignment. Styles, however, can also contain information regarding hyperlinks. We will look at the use of styles for hyperlinking later in this chapter in the section, "Building Hyperlinks," but for now let's focus on the display characteristics of styles.

Style Settings

Earlier we looked at how to set various display characteristics for text on-screen. As you can imagine, however, if you had to manually set these characteristics for each block of text, the development process could drag on indefinitely. In an attempt to make the development process more efficient, Authorware provides the ability to define a style that can be applied to other text blocks throughout development.

To begin defining a style, simply select Define Style from the Text menu. After this selection has been made, the Define Styles dialog box, as seen in Figure 3.15, will appear.

The Define Styles dialog box contains the features described next.

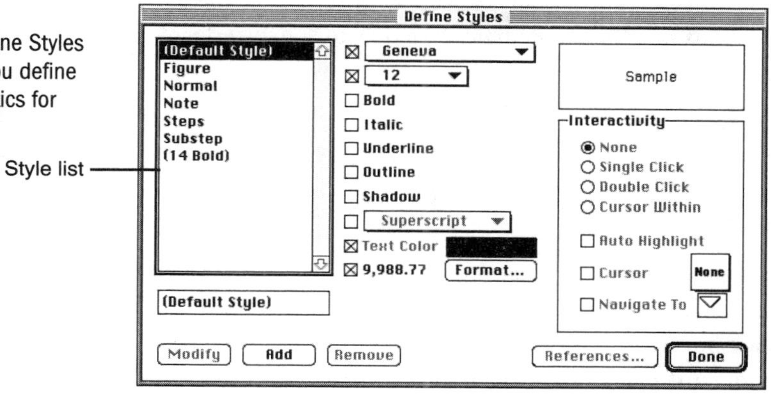

FIG. 3.15
The Authorware Define Styles dialog box allows you define specific characteristics for each style.

Style list —

Style List   Along the left side of the Define Style dialog box is the Style list, which contains the names of all the styles that have been defined, as well as a list of unnamed styles. Unnamed styles, such as the one named "14 Bold" are created automatically by Authorware whenever you manually set font, size, style, or color characteristics.

To see the characteristics of a style in the list, simply click the name of the style to select it. Once the style is selected, the formatting characteristics that apply to that style will be shown in the center of the Define Style dialog box.

In the text box located under the Style list, you can enter a name for a newly created style or rename the currently selected style.

Formatting Style Characteristics   The center of the Define Styles dialog box contains check boxes that allow you to set the display characteristics for the selected style. The attributes/characteristics that we have not previously looked at include

■ Color—To set a color for the text, double-click the color chip and select a color from the palette that appears. We will look at setting colors manually in the next chapter.

■ Number Format—Numbers that are contained in a block of text can also contain a format regarding the number of decimals that appear in front of and past the decimal point or the type of separator that is used. To set the Number Format for the style, select the check box and then click the Format button to edit in the Number Format dialog box.

▶ To learn more about setting the color of an object, **see** "Using the Color Palette," **p. 119**.

Sample Area   The sample area, located in the upper-right corner of the Define Styles dialog box, illustrates what the style text will look like with the selected display characteristics. Having this viewing area eliminates the need to bounce between this dialog box and the Presentation Window to see the effect your selections have on the displayed text.

Interactivity Attributes   The Interactivity characteristics define what characteristics the defined style has in terms of hyperlinking or navigation. We will look at these characteristics in greater detail in the "Defining the Hyperlink Text Style" section later in this chapter.

References Button   If you want to see where a style is used within the piece, select the style and then click the References button. When this button is selected, the references dialog box, shown in Figure 3.16, appears revealing a list of all the Flowline icons that contain text using the selected style.

You can click one of the references and then click the Show Icon button, and Authorware will position the Flowline window to that icon so that you can change the style applied to the text.

FIG. 3.16
The Authorware references dialog box allows you to view where a selected style is used throughout your piece.

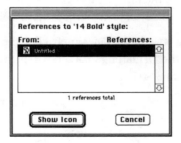

Defining a Style

You've now taken a look at the different characteristics you can set when creating your own styles. To define a style within Authorware, follow these steps:

1. Select Define Styles from the Text menu.

2. When the Define Styles dialog box appears, click the Add button.

3. Enter a name for the new style.

4. Use the check boxes and pop-up menus in the Define Styles dialog box to set the characteristics for the style.

5. Watch the sample area in the upper-right corner of the dialog box to be sure the text is appearing as you intended. Continue to make adjustments to the characteristics.

6. Click the Modify button, or another named style, when finished to save your changes.

Defining styles does reduce development time if you have several different styles being used throughout the piece. If you are only using one format for text layout, however, defining a style and then applying that style to each screen isn't as beneficial as setting defaults (as discussed earlier in this chapter) for each of the characteristics or copying a text template into each display.

Modifying and Deleting Styles

In addition to using the Define Styles dialog box to create styles, you can use it to make changes to existing styles or to delete styles altogether. You perform these actions with the following buttons in the Define Styles dialog box:

- Modify—To modify an existing style and, therefore, change the original characteristics of that style, select the style from the list, set the new characteristics, and then click Modify.

- Add—To create a new style and add its name to the list, click Add, enter the name of the new style, define the characteristics, and then click Modify.

- Remove—To remove a defined style from the list, select the style, and then click Remove. A style cannot be removed if it is currently being used within the piece.

Applying Styles

Now that you have walked through creating a style, let's look at two different ways to apply a style to a block of text. In either case, however, you must have the Presentation Window for the appropriate Display icon open and the text block selected.

To apply a style using the Apply Style option in the Text menu, follow these steps:

1. Once your text block, or a portion of the text block, is selected, select the Apply Style option in the Text menu. The Text Styles dialog box, shown in Figure 3.17, will appear listing the defined styles for your piece.

Part
II

Ch
3

2. Select a style from the list to be applied. As soon as you select the new style, it is applied to the text.

3. Close the Text Styles dialog box and continue modifying the Presentation Window. You can also elect to leave the Text Styles dialog box open as a floating window so that it can be easily accessed in other Presentation Windows.

FIG. 3.17
The Text Styles dialog box lists all defined styles for your piece.

Authorware also provides a means to change styles using the tool bar that appears below the menu bar. To apply a style using the tool bar option, follow these steps:

1. Once your text block is selected, select the styles drop-down list in the tool bar, shown in Figure 3.18. The drop-down list provides a listing of the defined styles for your piece.

FIG. 3.18
The tool bar can also be used to change text from one style to another.

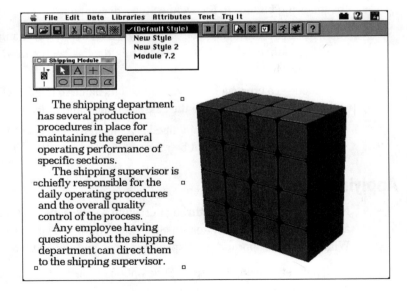

2. Select a style from the list to be applied. As soon as you select the new style, it is applied to the text.

▶ For more information on the tool bar, **see** "Using The Authorware Tool Bar," **p. 30**.

Authorware allows you to apply more than one style to a selected text block. When you do this, the characteristics of the style that is selected first remain until they are overwritten by a second style. For example, you can define a style titled "Main" having the characteristics of red, bold, and 12 point, and then define a second style titled "Header" to be blue, italic, and 18 point.

If you apply the style "Main" to a block of text and then you apply the style "Header" to that same block, the result will be blue, bold, italic, and 18 point. The text is blue and 18 point because these characteristics, contained in the style which was applied second, overwrote the red and 12 point characteristics of the first style. It will be both bold and italic, however, because these characteristics do not overwrite one another. If you apply "Header" first, however, then you apply "Main," the result will be red, bold, italic, and 12 point.

While predicting the outcome of applying multiple styles does take some experience, the ability to apply several styles once again adds to the efficiency of development. For example, you can set certain styles to contain display characteristics and other styles to contain hyperlink qualities. Combining these styles will result in a palette of options that can otherwise take quite some time to manually set.

Building Hyperlinks

The final feature associated with using text in an interactive piece is hyperlinking. Hypertext and the entire notion of hyperlinking blossomed in popularity in the early 1980s. While many applications (such as the World Wide Web, online encyclopedias, some online Help systems, and so on) that use this technology are very successful, there are a few issues to be aware of if you plan to incorporate hyperlinking into your piece.

The first applications for hyperlinking were massive technical manuals that had associated material located in several noncontiguous portions of the document. Through the use of hyperlinking, however, the linear nature of the documentation was quickly replaced with a system that allowed the user to access information quickly and in a seemingly contiguous order.

Unfortunately, many multimedia developers attempted to use this tool for applications beyond reference-based materials. For example, many traditional book publishers started converting their collections of printed material to CD-ROM-based, hyperlinked programs. Trainers and educators anxious to adopt technology also made a place for hyperlinking by dumping information onto a CD-ROM, linking associated topics, and labeling it as training.

In my opinion, which is now being backed by a few studies, hyperlinking may not aid as much as one thought in the learning process as it does in the research process, and in fact, it may hinder learning. While you would want a technician researching possible failure points in a piece of equipment to be able to bounce from topic to topic, this type of functionality may not always be desirable. Think about the problems that brain surgeons would have if they learned to operate in a non-linear, non-guided method.

There is a benefit to having an educator—the expert in the learning experience—who looks in the student's eyes and has the ability to determine how well the student understands the material. This person, or system, guides the student, constantly reacting to what the student believes to be correct, until the student has learned what is correct.

Replacing this guidance with an all-knowing and infinite body of information is like placing a teacher who can only answer questions asked by the student in the classroom. The answers will only be provided, however, if the student is smart enough to ask the question in the first place. If there is no prompting or guidance by the teacher but the student is left to their own exploration, can we guarantee the student will learn? Removing the guidance of the teacher, in its most basic format, is hyperlinking.

As you move forward with designing interactive pieces, you must carefully study the purpose of your piece. If you are building a reference or performance-support piece, then hyperlinking is more than likely appropriate. If you are building a training or educational piece, however, you must consider the costs of unguided instruction. Perhaps eliminating hyperlinking for the sake of greater retention would be beneficial.

Defining the Hyperlink Text Style

In Authorware, hyperlinking combines the definition of a style with the creation of interactivity using the Navigation icon. In this section, we will focus on the creation of a style which contains interactivity or hyperlinking. In Chapter 16, "Applying Advanced Interactivity and Searching," we will focus on the Navigation icon and how to establish the point to which Authorware will jump when the hyperlink is activated.

▶ To learn how to establish the linking portion of a hyperlink, **see** "Introducing the Navigate Icon," **p. 307**.

Previously in this chapter, we looked at defining a style and the Define Styles dialog box. In the Define Styles dialog box, we only discussed the display characteristics of the text and ignored the Interactivity options. Let's now return to the Define Styles dialog box, as shown in Figure 3.19, to explore these options.

The Define Styles dialog box contains the features described next for establishing interactivity.

FIG. 3.19
The Authorware Define Styles dialog box also allows you to define interactivity characteristics for each style.

Determine what type of interactivity will trigger the hyperlink.

Change the mouse pointer as it passes over text that can be clicked.

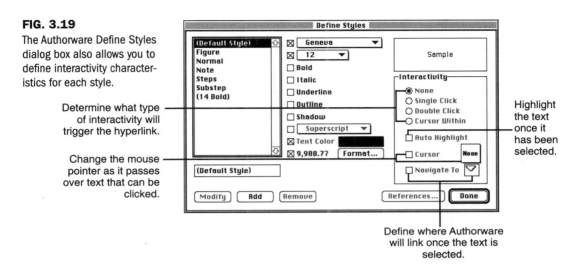

Highlight the text once it has been selected.

Define where Authorware will link once the text is selected.

Part
II

Ch
3

Actions   Use the upper portion of the Interactivity area within dialog box to select the action you want to trigger the hyperlink. Options include a single-click, double-click, or simply placing the cursor (mouse pointer) over the text containing the defined style. If None is selected, the other interactivity options, such as Automatic Highlight, Cursor, and Navigate To, will not be available.

Auto Highlight   Select this option to display an inverse image over the hot text area after the reader has selected it using the specified action. Displaying this inverse image lets the user know that the action was accepted and that the computer is processing their request.

All too often authors forget that the end user may be working on a slower system. When this is the case, the user may make a selection, and if nothing happens, grow impatient and make the selection again thinking that the computer did not register the first selection. In reality, however, the computer did register the first selection, but the Authorware mites did not have time to process it. The worst part is that it now has also registered the second interaction, and the user is caught in a frustrating loop waiting for the computer to respond.

Cursor   Select this option if you would like the cursor (mouse pointer) to change shape when it passes over text containing the hyperlink style. Click the pop-up palette of available cursors to select a cursor to be displayed.

▶ To learn how to change the cursor type, **see** "Selecting a Custom Cursor," **p. 256**.

When something can be interacted with, changing the cursor is a wonderful way to visually cue the end user. This type of visual cue begins to eliminate the need for elaborate instructions on how to use the piece and allows for exploration by the end user. The best example of this type of cueing exists in many of the Broderbund programs for children. While there are no directions as to what the child should select, the cursor shape changes or the item animates as the cursor passes over a region that can be selected.

TIP Making objects look like they can be clicked is another great way to cue the end user. With text, I suggest that you change the color of the text that can be clicked.

The palette of cursors can be edited using the Cursor Editor, as we will discuss in Chapter 11.

Navigate To   Select the Navigate To option if you plan to incorporate hyperlinking as a part of the style. Keep in mind that if hyperlinking is a part of the style, then every body of text that contains the style will be subject to the same hyperlink conditions.

Once this option is defined, click the navigate symbol (the down-pointing arrow beside it) to define the navigation criteria. Defining navigation is discussed further in Chapter 16.

▶ For step-by-step instruction of defining linking, **see** "Navigating Through Frameworks," **p. 306**.

Including Navigation in the Style

As we have just seen, you can identify—as a part of a style—the point to where Authorware will jump if a hyperlink is executed. When you do this, however, every block of text that contains the style will also contain the same navigation criteria.

In some cases, this may be very desirable. For example, you may be building a very technical piece in which you want the user to be able to access a calculator by simply clicking a formula. In this case, the style will always link directly to a single location that displays the calculator.

In another example, you may be creating a product catalog, and whenever the user clicks the name of the product, you want to display a list of related products the user can link to. In this case, the navigate criteria may be based on a keyword search, which results in a displayed list. If, however, you want each link to be uniquely defined, then you do not want to include the navigate criteria as a part of the style.

Building Navigation Separate from the Style

If you want a style to have the same display characteristics yet you do not want the navigate criteria to be the same for each use of the style, then don't select the Navigate To option when defining the style. Rather, each time you apply the style, Authorware will prompt you to define the link for the unique text block that you're applying the style to.

For example, you may want a certain block of text in your piece to be linked to a unique definition. While you want the hot text (hyperlink) to be the same font, size, style and color, and the cursor to change as it crosses over the text, the point where the link is to navigate to will be different for each definition.

In this case, you will define each of the display characteristics, but you will not define the navigation criteria as a part of the style. When you apply the style, however, Authorware will ask you to define the navigation. It is at this point that you draw a unique link for each of the terms in your piece to its definition.

▶ For step-by-step instruction for defining linking, **see** "Navigating Through Frameworks," **p. 306**.

When a link is identified separate from a style, Authorware adds a small symbol to the upper-right corner of the Display icon that contains the linked text (in the Flowline window), as shown in Figure 3.20. This symbol helps you to identify which icons contain links to other icons.

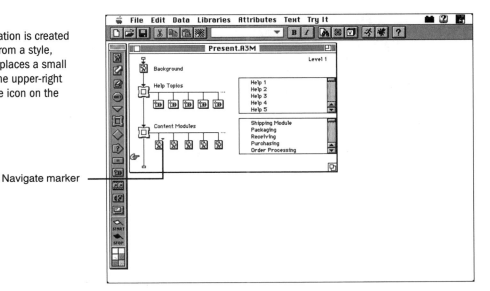

FIG. 3.20
When navigation is created separately from a style, Authorware places a small triangle in the upper-right corner of the icon on the Flowline.

Navigate marker

Introducing the Find/Change Feature

When authoring, you may find it necessary to search for words or phrases which have been used throughout your piece. Similar to most word processing programs, Authorware provides a fairly extensive Find/Change function.

Authorware's Find/Change feature allows you to search the contents of the Presentation Window, unless the text is stored as a graphic. Additionally, icon titles, keywords, and Calculation icons may all be searched.

Using the Find/Change Feature

To use the Find/Change feature, follow these steps:

1. Select the Find/Change option from the Edit pull-down menu from either the Flowline window or the Presentation Window. When this selection is made, the Find/Change dialog box will appear.

 The shortcut key sequence for opening the Find/Change dialog box is ⌘+Shift+F (Macintosh) and Ctrl+Shift+F (Windows).

2. Enter the word or phrase for which you want to search in the Find field.
3. Enter the word or phrase to which you want to change any matches in the Change To field.
4. Adjust the search criteria to more accurately modify your piece.
5. Select the Find button.
6. When a match is made, you may elect to Change, which changes that single instance, or Change All, which will modify all future instances without asking you first.

CHAPTER 4

Working with Graphics and Objects

I am a firm believer that while developers can be trained, artists must be born. Despite three years of design school, countless hours of perspective drawing, and the chapters of reading about color composition, balance, and unity, the only thing that I can draw is a cartoon dog and stylistic people holding balloons.

Maybe the reason I work so well in Authorware is that the program does not expect me to be an artist. The graphic tools that Authorware provides are very rudimentary, and because of their ease of use, even I can't get in trouble trying to draw something with them.

Our development team has set a rule in place. Although the rule may have been established to keep me away from creating graphics, I think that it might apply in your development team as well. "Let the artists work in their high-end graphics programs to create high-end graphics, and let the developer assemble these graphics in Authorware."

Sure, I sometimes get to draw a highlight or maybe even a menu in Authorware, but for the most part, the Authorware tools are best used for prototyping and not

Building objects in the Presentation Window

Learning the most efficient way to develop graphics is key to maximizing a piece's performance. Issues, such as using bitmap verses vector-based images and color depth, are addressed.

Learning to use the tools

Authorware provides six tools for creating graphics: the Straight Line tool, the Diagonal Line tool, the Oval tool, the Rectangle tool, the Rounded Rectangle tool, and the Polygon tool.

Importing text and graphics

Text and graphics can be imported from external programs using Cut, Copy, Paste, and the Authorware Import feature.

Using the drawing attributes

Objects created in Authorware, or imported as vector-based graphics, can be adjusted using the Line Width, Fill Pattern, Color, and Mode attributes.

Setting attribute defaults

Setting defaults for commonly used attribute options makes development much more efficient.

for creating final graphics. This chapter focuses on how to use each of the graphic tools as well as how to import and work with high-end graphics. Additionally, we explore working within the Presentation Window. ■

Drawing Objects

The Authorware Graphics toolbox is very simple and straightforward. The tools can be used for creating objects, but not bitmaps. They are for drawing, but not for painting. And if you want photo-realistic pictures with elegant effects and stylized text, then the Authorware Graphics toolbox is not for you.

NOTE Bitmaps are created with a paint program and can be edited pixel by pixel. Object-oriented graphics, or vector-based graphics, are created using the Authorware Graphics toolbox or a drawing package and can only be edited by manipulating handles around the objects making up the graphic. ■

The tools in the Authorware Graphics toolbox are, however, great for building simple graphics, such as buttons and text boxes, and are better yet for prototyping. All too often, multimedia authors spend great amounts of time trying to create fully rendered images to be placed in the first draft of the interactive application, rather than making a small investment in prototyping graphics and interactivity.

The result of this can be catastrophic. If the idea for the interaction is modified or an enhancement is suggested, then either the artwork has to be thrown away—along with the investment required to build the graphic—or else the ego kicks in and, because of the high degree of ownership that comes from spending hours working on something, the better idea is forgone.

In Chapter 1, "Taking the Authorware Tour," I introduced the Authorware Graphics toolbox and each of the tools used for enhancing the Presentation Window. Throughout this chapter, we will look in detail at how to use each of the tools in the toolbox as well as how each graphic tool can be used for prototyping or making the development process more efficient.

 TIP Authorware performs best in the Windows environment when graphics are bitmaps, which requires that they be created in external programs; Authorware performs best on the Macintosh when graphics are object-oriented. You may want all graphics to be bitmaps, however, for better portability between platforms.

As you may recall, the Authorware Graphics toolbox is used to create or import text and graphics into the Presentation Window. To access the Graphics toolbox, follow these steps:

1. Drag either an Interaction or a Display icon to the Flowline.
2. Double-click the icon to open it. If you are using an Interaction icon, a dialog box will appear when you attempt to open the icon. You must click the OK, Edit Display button in order to access the Presentation Window.
3. When the icon opens, the Graphics toolbox appears. You can make edits to the Presentation Window using the provided tools. When finished, simply click the close box located in the upper left-hand corner of the toolbox.

Using the Line Tools

The line tools, as their names imply, are used for creating lines. Lines can vary in length, line width, fill pattern, and color. As you saw in Chapter 1, there are two types of line tools within the Authorware Graphics toolbox, as follows:

- Straight Line tool—This tool is used to create lines that retain a vertical, horizontal, or 45-degree orientation.
- Diagonal Line tool—This tool is used to create a straight line between any two points. If the Shift key is held down while drawing, this tool behaves like the Straight Line tool.

    ▶ For an introduction to the Straight Line tool, **see** "The Straight Line Tool," **p. 28**.
    ▶ For an introduction to the Diagonal Line tool, **see** "The Diagonal Line Tool," **p. 28**.

Part
II

Ch
4

Whenever possible, I suggest avoiding diagonal lines unless you are prototyping. Just as we saw when working with text, the screen resolution sometimes has difficulty displaying all the pixels required to make a smooth line and, therefore, creates a line with jagged points.

N O T E I find that the Diagonal Line tool is great for designing a path along which an object will be animated. If several objects are to follow the same path, I will create a guide using the line tools. ▪

In many cases, a diagonal line can be replaced with a combination of horizontal and vertical lines. If this is not possible, you may want to consider the anti-aliasing techniques discussed in Chapter 3, "Presenting Text."

▶ For step-by-step details on anti-aliasing, **see** "Anti-Aliasing," **p. 73**.

To use either of the line tools, follow these steps:

1. Open the Presentation Window of a Display icon or an Interaction Icon by double-clicking the icon on the Flowline.

2. Click either of the line tools to highlight it in the Graphics toolbox, as shown in Figure 4.1. As you move the pointer away from the Graphics toolbox, you will notice that it changes from an arrow pointer to a crosshair pointer.

FIG. 4.1
Click and drag to create a line using either of the line tools.

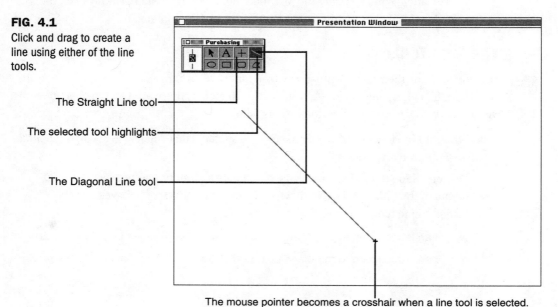

The Straight Line tool——

The selected tool highlights——

The Diagonal Line tool——

The mouse pointer becomes a crosshair when a line tool is selected.

3. Click in the Presentation Window at the location where you want to start drawing the line; then begin to drag. As you drag, the line will be drawn.

4. When you are finished with the line, release the mouse button. Handles immediately appear on the line object that was just drawn. As you move the crosshair close to the object, it reverts to an arrow pointer. You can use the pointer to position the object by dragging, or you can resize the object by dragging one of the handles.

I most commonly use the line tool to create guidelines for positioning objects. If I have several items that must be aligned, I will draw a line, position the objects along the line, then delete the line. I also commonly build templates or grids for text, as shown in Figure 4.2, then delete the grids before final packaging.

Lines created with the line tools can be used to align text and graphics

FIG. 4.2

The line tools can be used to create a set of layout templates for your application.

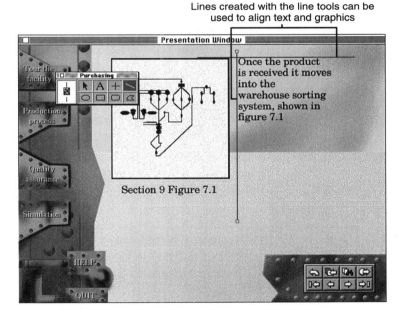

Part

II

Ch

4

Building Rectangles, Rounded Rectangles, and Circles

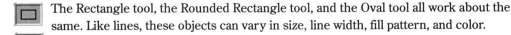

The Rectangle tool, the Rounded Rectangle tool, and the Oval tool all work about the same. Like lines, these objects can vary in size, line width, fill pattern, and color.

To use an object tool, follow these steps:

1. Open the Presentation Window of a Display icon or an Interaction icon by double-clicking the icon on the Flowline.

2. Click the desired tool to highlight it in the Graphics toolbox. As you move the pointer away from the Graphics toolbox, you will notice that the pointer changes from an arrow to a crosshair.

3. Hold the mouse button down, then begin to drag in the Presentation Window at the location where you want to place the object. As you drag, the object will be drawn. To constrain the shape to a square or a circle, hold the Shift key down while dragging.

4. When you are finished with the object, release the mouse button.

   If you have created an oval or a rectangle, handles immediately appear on the object that was just drawn. As you move the crosshair close to the object, it reverts to an arrow pointer.

N O T E The most common mistake when trying to position an object is attempting to grab the center of the object. Unfortunately, this is much like trying to move a Hula-Hoop by grabbing the hollow center. You must grab the object on the rim in order to move it, unless it is filled with a pattern. ▪

You can use the mouse pointer to position the object by dragging it, or you can resize the object by dragging one of the handles. Hold the Shift key down while resizing the object, and it will be resized proportionately.

When a rounded rectangle is drawn, a single handle appears. This handle is used to control the roundness of the corners. To adjust the roundness, drag the handle. As you drag the handle closer to the center of the object, the corners become more rounded.

T I P To edit the roundness of a rounded rectangle, be sure that the Rounded Rectangle tool and the object are both selected. Selecting the Pointer tool and the object will not allow you to edit roundness—only the object's size and position.

Select the Pointer tool and handles will appear on the rounded rectangle. Use these handles to resize the object just as you did the oval or rectangle.

5. To reposition an object, select the Pointer tool and drag the object to its new position.

I find that the object tools are very helpful for two things: prototyping and spatial alignment. As I am working through a concept, I will use the rectangle to identify regions on the screen, as seen in Figure 4.3, that are reserved for certain functions. For example, I will draw a rectangle where the menu will be placed, and inside of that several smaller rectangles representing the icons or buttons. I can also define a region for text or for instructional prompts.

FIG. 4.3
The object tools are used to create regions defining general screen layout or to space elements on the screen.

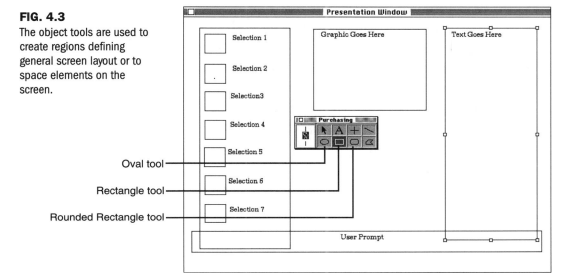

Oval tool
Rectangle tool
Rounded Rectangle tool

As I get closer to rendering the interface, I can use the Rectangle tool to create a grid so that I know that each icon is exactly the same size and the same distance apart.

▶ For an introduction to the Oval tool, **see** "The Oval Tool," **p. 29**.
▶ For an introduction to the Rectangle tool, **see** "The Rectangle Tool," **p. 29**.
▶ For an introduction to the Rounded Rectangle tool, **see** "The Rounded Rectangle Tool," **p. 29**.

Working with the Polygon Tool

 The Polygon tool is used to create open or closed, multi-sided objects. Like the other object tools, polygons can vary in size, line width, fill pattern, and color.

To use the Polygon tool, follow these steps:

1. Open the Presentation Window of a Display icon or an Interaction icon by double-clicking the icon on the Flowline.

2. Click the Polygon tool to highlight it in the Graphics toolbox. As you move the mouse pointer away from the Graphics toolbox, you will notice that the mouse pointer changes from an arrow to a crosshair.

3. Click the mouse button to set the starting point for the polygon.

4. Move the crosshair to a new location, and click again to set the next point. Notice as

you move the mouse, a line is drawn from the first point to the position of the crosshair pointer. Once you click, this line becomes set as a side of the polygon.

If you hold the Shift key down while dragging, the line will become constrained to horizontal, vertical, and 45-degree orientations, just like the line tools. (See "Using the Line Tools," earlier in this chapter.)

5. Continue setting points until you have built the desired shape.

6. When you are ready to finish the object, either double-click to set the last point and create an open polygon, or single-click the same point as you started with to create a closed polygon.

7. Handles appear when you are finished drawing the object. As you move the crosshair close to the object, it reverts to an arrow pointer. You can use the pointer to edit the shape of the polygon.

 To edit the polygon after it has been created, be sure that the Polygon tool and the object are both selected. Selecting the Pointer tool and the object will not allow you to edit the points, but only the size and position of the object.

If you select the Pointer tool, handles appear around the polygon. You can use these handles to resize the object just as you did ovals and rectangles. Hold down the Shift key while dragging, and the object will resize proportionately.

▶ To refer to the introduction of the Polygon tool, **see** "The Polygon Tool," **p. 29**.

Selecting, Deselecting, and Deleting Objects in the Presentation Window

Once you have created an object in the Presentation Window, you will need to select it so that it can be deleted or moved, or so that an attribute can be applied to it. Let's take a quick look at selecting, deselecting, and deleting objects.

Selecting an Object   Objects can be selected in several ways when you're working in a Display or Interaction icon, as follows:

■ Selecting a Single Object—To select a single object, use the Pointer tool and click the object. When an object has been selected, handles appear around it.

■ Selecting Multiple Objects—To select multiple objects, start by selecting the Pointer tool. Then, either hold down the Shift key and click objects one by one, or use the Pointer tool to draw a selection marquee around the objects, as shown in Figure 4.4. If the marquee does not fully encompass an object, it isn't selected.

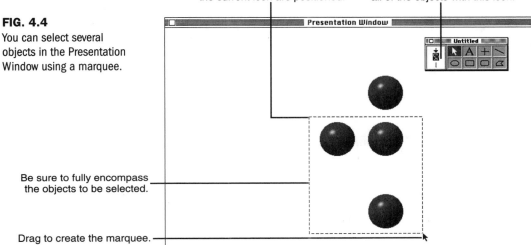

Click where no objects for the current icon are positioned.

Double-click this icon to select all of the objects with this icon.

FIG. 4.4
You can select several objects in the Presentation Window using a marquee.

Be sure to fully encompass the objects to be selected.

Drag to create the marquee.

■ Selecting all the objects—To select all of the objects in the current icon, either choose Select All from the Edit menu, or double-click the Display or Interaction icon symbol at the left side of the Graphics toolbox (see Fig. 4.4).

 TIP The shortcut keys for Select All are ⌘+A (Macintosh) and Ctrl+A (Windows).

N O T E When an Interaction icon or a Display icon is opened in the Windows environment, all objects are automatically selected. On the Macintosh, however, no objects are automatically selected. ■

Deselecting Objects To deselect an object, or several objects, press the space bar, either select a different object, or click where there are no objects for that icon in the Presentation Window.

To deselect a single object from a group of selected objects, hold down the Shift key and click the object you want to deselect.

Deleting Objects Removing objects from the Presentation Window can be done using any of the following methods:

- Using the Delete key—Once an object, or several objects, have been selected, pressing the Delete key will permanently remove them from the icon.

- Cutting—Once an object, or several objects have been selected, choosing Cut from the Edit menu permanently removes the object from the Presentation Window. However, the objects will remain on the system's Clipboard until another cut or copy function is performed.

TIP | The shortcut keys for cutting are ⌘+X (Macintosh) or Ctrl+X (Windows).

- Clearing—Once an object, or several objects, have been selected, choosing Clear from the Edit menu permanently removes the object from the icon.

Moving Objects

Once an object has been created using any of the tools in the Graphics toolbox, or has been imported into the Presentation Window, it can be moved or positioned using either the Pointer tool, or the arrow keys on the keyboard.

To move an object using the Pointer tool, follow these steps:

1. Select the Pointer tool from the Graphics toolbox.
2. Drag the object to its new location. Be sure to grab the object. Clicking inside an object that does not have a fill pattern, for example, will not allow you to drag the object.

To move an object using the arrow keys, follow these steps:

1. Select the Pointer tool from the Graphics toolbox.
2. Select the object by clicking it. To select multiple objects, hold down the Shift key while clicking.
3. Press any of the arrow keys to move the selected object(s) one pixel in any direction.

So far, we have looked at creating graphics using the Authorware Graphics toolbox. Because this toolbox is very limited in its use, let's look at how graphics can be imported from other applications that provide more sophisticated illustration tools.

TROUBLESHOOTING

I didn't have the icon open, and the toolbox was not present, but I was able to move objects in the Presentation Window. Did I do anything wrong? No, changing the position of an object while in Run mode is called editing on the fly. As long as the object is not associated with a target area response, you can change its position without taking the time to open the icon. If you accidentally move something, simply choose Undo from the Edit menu.

Importing Graphics

Authorware is more a tool for the assembly of media than it is a tool for the creation of media. While Authorware does have the functionality to create text, graphics, and even sound (recording sound is a Macintosh feature only), its real strength is in the capability to generate interactivity.

As an assembler, therefore, Authorware relies on the strengths of other applications for the creation of the various media. Once graphics have been created using an external application, they can be imported into Authorware and combined with interactivity and other media. An imported graphic becomes a part of the Authorware piece and is no longer dependent on the program in which it was created. If you are importing the graphic into an Authorware for Windows piece as an object linking and embedding (OLE) object, however, an association with the program that created the graphic will remain for ease of editing purposes.

When selecting which external graphics program to use, try to select one that produces images that do not require great amounts of RAM or hard disk space. The larger the graphic that is imported into Authorware, the greater the negative impact on performance.

TROUBLESHOOTING

The graphics in my piece seem to be quite large, which is causing the whole piece to run slowly. What can I do? First, be sure that your graphic is not taking advantage of more colors than you are capable of displaying. For example, if you have 256 colors, there is no need to have a final graphic containing thousands of colors. The same is true for resolution. Since you will be presenting the graphic on the screen, which has 72 or 96 dots per inch, there is no need to have a graphic with 150 or 300 dots per inch.

Part
II

Ch
4

Using the Import Function

Graphics can be imported into Authorware with either of two methods. The first method uses the Authorware Import feature, which enables you to import graphics, as well as text, directly into an Interaction or a Display icon. Central to the Import feature is the Import dialog box, as seen in Figure 4.5.

FIG. 4.5
Authorware enables you to import text and graphics using the Import dialog box.

Preview the image in a reduced size.

Use the pop-up menu and scrolling window to locate the file to import.

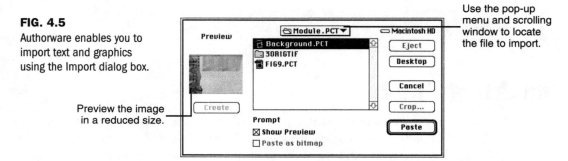

The Import dialog box contains the following options:

- Opening the File—Use the directory pop-up list, scrolling window, Eject button, and Desktop button to locate the graphic to be imported. This feature works just like the dialog boxes for saving or opening an Authorware piece.

- Preview—Once you have located the graphic to be imported, you can click the Create button to get a preview of the graphic before importing it.

- Crop—When a graphic is imported into Authorware, the entire graphic, or all the graphics in the file, will be imported. If you only want a portion of the graphic to be imported, however, you can use the Crop option. When you click the Crop button, a new window displaying a reduced image of the graphic appears. This window enables you to use a marquee to define the portion of the graphic you want to import.

- Paste—Once you have selected the graphic to be imported, or have selected the portion of the graphic to be imported, click the Paste button to add the image to the icon which is currently open.

To use the Import feature, follow these steps:

1. Open a Display or Interaction icon by double-clicking it on the Flowline.

2. Choose Import from the File menu.

3. When the Import dialog box appears, use it to select or edit the desired graphic. You use the Import dialog box just as you would use the dialog box to open or save a piece. Click the Paste button to paste the graphic into the Presentation Window.

4. Use the Pointer tool to position the graphic. After clicking the tool, click the graphic to select it. Drag the graphic into place. If the graphic comprises objects, you can re-size the individual objects, or the entire graphic, by dragging the handles.

CAUTION

Resizing a bitmap graphic that has been imported into Authorware will produce unpredictable results if done by dragging the handles. Since Authorware is not a true graphics program, and does not support scaling, you should perform all resizing in an external graphics program.

Copy and Paste

Because my development team has a tendency to work in several packages at one time and because we continually like to try an idea, adjust things, then try again, we have found it more efficient to just copy graphics from one package and paste them into the other than using the Import function to import graphics into Authorware.

For example, we may be working on a graphic interface. To use the Import function, we would have to do all the work in the graphic package, save the graphic file, then open Authorware and step through the procedure to import a graphic. Once the graphic is imported, we would position it. If, however, we determine that an edit must take place, then we would again access the graphic file, make the edits, save the file, and repeat the process for importing graphics. This cycle would continue until the graphic fits perfectly into the piece.

Using copy and paste, however, this cycle is shortened tremendously. Rather than open-ing and closing the applications and the files, we simply toggle from one application to the other to make the adjustments. For example, we open the graphics program, create the graphic, then select the graphic and copy it to the Clipboard. Next, we open the Authorware piece, open the Display icon that is to contain the graphic, and choose Paste from the Edit menu. If changes to the graphic are required, we simply switch back to the graphics program, make the edits, select the graphic, copy it to the Clipboard, and return to the Authorware piece where the graphic can again be pasted into the open icon.

NOTE You can also take advantage of object linking and embedding (OLE) to shorten this process even more. If the object was created with an application which supports OLE, you only need to double-click the object within Authorware and the program that created that object will become active. This allows you to edit the object within the Authorware window. ■

Moving Objects from One Icon to Another

The standard copy and paste features, located in the Edit menu, can be used for more than importing graphics and text into Authorware. They can also be used to move text and graphics from one Flowline icon to another.

When objects are moved from one icon to another, Authorware begins to make some assumptions in an attempt to make development more efficient. For example, if you select then cut an object from one icon, then open the Presentation Window for another icon and immediately select to paste, the object will be pasted in the same screen location it held in the Presentation Window from which it was cut. If you click anywhere in the Presentation Window before you select to paste, however, the graphic will be pasted where you clicked.

To cut an object from one icon and paste it into another icon, follow these steps:

1. Open the Display icon that contains the object to be moved to another icon.
2. Select the object by clicking it. If multiple objects are to be selected, hold down the Shift key while clicking.
3. Choose Cut from the Edit menu.

 The shortcut keys for cutting are ⌘+X (Macintosh) or Ctrl+X (Windows).

4. Close the Display icon by clicking the close box on the toolbox, or choose Jump To Icons from the Try It menu to return to the Flowline window.

 The shortcut keys for jumping to the Flowline window from the Presentation Window are ⌘+J (Macintosh) or Ctrl+J (Windows).

5. Locate on the Flowline the icon in which you will paste the object(s). Double-click the icon to open it.
6. Choose Paste from the Edit menu to place the objects in the Presentation Window. Use the Cursor tool and arrow keys to position the objects.

 The shortcut keys for pasting are ⌘+V (Macintosh) or Ctrl+V (Windows).

7. Once the object(s) are positioned, close the icon by clicking the close box on the toolbox, or choose Jump to Icons from the Try It menu to return to the Flowline window.

 The shortcut keys for jumping to the Flowline window from the Presentation Window are ⌘+J (Macintosh) or Ctrl+J (Windows).

Keeping Graphics Small

Whether you are using the Import feature or you are using copy and paste, a goal should be to keep graphics as small as possible in terms of file size. Small file sizes are easier to work with in that they may be copied to removable media, and they better accommodate backing up multiple versions throughout the day. Additionally, smaller graphics will ensure the best performance possible.

The careful implementation of graphics can make or break your application. Before moving into mass production, I suggest that you experiment with the techniques covered in this section to determine which produces the most efficient graphic in terms of file size, quality, and performance.

When creating graphics for multimedia, you may want to consider the tips and tricks described next.

Building for 8-Bit   In the creation of a graphic, one of the first issues to be resolved is color depth (see the following table for a description of terms), or the number of colors that will be used in the final image. While this is not an issue for designers who are creating for print, it is critical to the success of a multimedia piece. When designing for print, file size, or the size of the image, it is rarely an issue since the file will never be widely distributed in its digital form. In multimedia, if the graphic requires a great amount of memory, it will take a long time to be displayed, causing the end user to lose interest in the piece. Therefore, no matter what color depth you are using, you should always try to produce graphics with the smallest possible file size.

Part
II

Ch
4

Term	Description
1 Bit	Lowest graphic form where the pixels that comprise the image are either on or off. The image can contain only one color, which is applied in Authorware.
4 Bit	The image can contain up to 16 colors. Earlier Windows systems had a standard of 16 colors.
8 Bit	The standard for almost all Macintosh computers, and now the standard for Windows systems. Allows up to 256 colors.
16 Bit	Many computers today offer both 8 bit and 16 bit (thousands of colors).
24 Bit	The format typically used in the print industry where photo quality (millions of colors) is the primary concern, and file size is not an issue.

While you may have a special situation, and control over the final delivery platform, most systems use an 8-bit (256 color) palette. Therefore, to reach the greatest number of people with the best possible quality of images, graphics should be designed to take advantage of the 8-bit environment.

Our team has found it beneficial to create images using 24 bit (known in most graphics tools as RGB mode), but when they are in final form, index them to an 8-bit (256 colors) palette. When graphics are indexed, the graphics program studies the image in an attempt to match the unavailable colors as closely as possible with colors from the 8-bit palette, thus reducing or even eliminating distortion to the image.

TROUBLESHOOTING

Even though I am indexing the graphics, I am still getting some banding of pixels. How can I improve the quality of the 8-bit image even further? Try creating a custom palette. Use a program such as DeBabelizer, which studies your graphic files and creates a custom palette most suitable to those images and then index the graphics to that palette rather than the system palette. When the custom palette is loaded into Authorware, your graphic should look just like it did within the graphics program.

Working in Small Regions   If only a small portion of a larger graphic changes, do not cover over or replace the entire original graphic with a copy containing the change. Instead, just cover the part of the graphic that actually changes. Unlike a graphics program that modifies the base graphic when you paste changes onto it, Authorware actually maintains both the original image and the changes as separate objects. Therefore, the file size would double if you pasted a replacement graphic on top of the original because two objects would exist.

Working with smaller pieces will save file size and increase performance.

Working with the Final Dots per Inch   Most graphic programs enable you to create bitmaps with a resolution of 150 to 300 dots per inch (dpi). While this resolution is necessary for print, the computer monitor typically only displays 72 (Macintosh standard) or 96 (Windows standard) dpi. To reduce your file size without reducing any visual quality, create all graphics in the same resolution in which your final piece will be delivered.

Using Attributes

Whether you create an object within Authorware or import it from another application, Authorware provides the capability to adjust the display characteristics of the graphic.

Some attributes only apply to objects drawn with the Graphics toolbox, and others apply to objects and imported bitmaps.

Each display attribute is set using a unique palette, which is accessible through the pull-down menus at the top of the Authorware screen. To make the development process more efficient, once a palette is opened, it remains open until you elect to close it. Additionally, more than one palette can be opened at one time.

To apply an attribute, open the icon that contains the object to format, select the Pointer tool and click to select the object so that the handles appear, then select the attribute to be changed from the Attributes menu. Finally, select the desired display characteristic from the palette that appears.

Let's spend a little time looking into each of the display attributes, and when each one can be used.

Setting Line Widths

The Line command on the Attributes menu is used to adjust the line width of vector-based graphics, including both those created in Authorware as well as those created in external graphic programs. The Line command is also used to set the line width for the border of objects created using the Oval, Rounded Rectangle, Polygon, or Rectangle tools.

If you have created a graphic in a paint application or if you have made a screen capture of the graphic and have pasted or imported the graphic into Authorware, then this attribute will have no effect when it is applied. If you created the graphic in a draw program or within Authorware, however, then the modification of the Line attribute will have an effect on the graphic.

To open the Line Width palette, shown in Figure 4.6, choose Line from the Attributes menu.

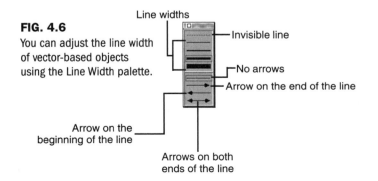

FIG. 4.6
You can adjust the line width of vector-based objects using the Line Width palette.

Line widths

Invisible line

No arrows

Arrow on the end of the line

Arrow on the beginning of the line

Arrows on both ends of the line

Keep in mind that the Line Width palette only works with objects and not with bitmaps. If you need to adjust the line width in a bitmap, you will need to copy the graphic to an external graphic package to make the change.

 TIP The shortcut for opening the Line Width palette is to double-click either of the line tools.

The top half of the palette is used to establish the line width, and the bottom half is used to place arrowheads on the line. Once the Line Width palette opens, there are a few key areas of which you should be aware. I'll describe each of these next.

Invisible Line The first option, Invisible line, located at the very top of the palette, is used to set lines to be invisible. This is helpful if you do not want the borders of circles or squares to be seen.

Line Widths The remainder of the options in the top half of the palette are used to establish the line width. Simply click to select a line width, and the graphic will change to reflect your selection.

Arrows The lower half of the palette is used to determine if the line is to contain arrowheads, and if so, which direction they will point. If you need high quality arrows, I suggest either creating them in an external graphics package or trying your luck at creating them using the Polygon tool.

Understanding Modes

The Mode option is used to adjust the transparency and opacity of an object as it lays on top of another object. Whether the objects are created in Authorware or you have imported them from an external program, the Mode option can be applied.

To open the Modes palette, shown in Figure 4.7, choose Modes from the Attributes menu.

FIG. 4.7
You can adjust the opacity of an object using the Modes palette.

Once the Modes palette opens, there are five options to choose from. These are described next.

Opaque   If an object is set to Opaque, all background pixels within the object take on the background pattern color, and the underlying object is blocked from view. For example, in Figure 4.8, the letter *A* laying on top of the graphic is set to Opaque and the background pattern color is white; therefore, the background to the letter is blocking a portion of the graphic from view.

FIG. 4.8
An object set to Opaque
hides an underlying object
from view.

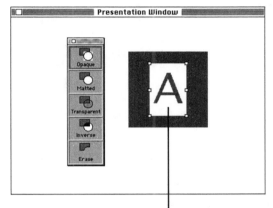

Opaque mode causes all background pixels to block objects behind them.

The Opaque setting is really only useful if you are working on a solid colored background. If you are working on a textured or patterned background, the backdrop to the objects will be filled with the background colors while areas outside of the object will contain the texture.

Matted   If the *A* is set to Matted, as shown in Figure 4.9, all background pixels outside of the colored boundary (the outermost set of non-white pixels) will be invisible; however, the enclosed background pixels, such as those inside the *A,* will remain Opaque.

FIG. 4.9
An object set to Matted only
hides an underlying object
from view for areas inside
the boundary of the graphic.

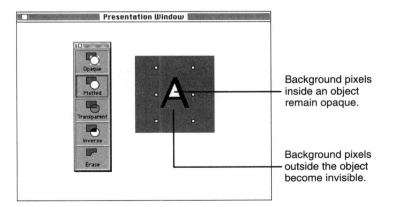

Background pixels
inside an object
remain opaque.

Background pixels
outside the object
become invisible.

Part

II

Ch

4

Transparent Setting the object to Transparent would make all background pixels—even those that are a part of the graphic—invisible (see Fig. 4.10). This is the most common setting for graphics that are being layered together.

FIG. 4.10
An object set to Transparent makes all background pixels invisible.

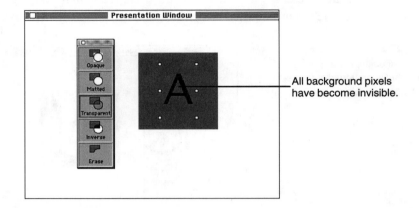

All background pixels have become invisible.

CAUTION

If your graphic contains any white pixels that you want to remain white, setting the Mode to Transparent will make them invisible, or see-through. I suggest using the lightest gray instead of white for these pixels.

Inverse Setting an object to Inverse not only makes all background pixels invisible, but it changes the colors in the graphic to the mathematical inverse of the combination of the top graphic laying on the bottom graphic.

Determining the resulting color could be a party game perhaps. While black is white and white is black, anything beyond that is a mystery. Look what happens to our graphic in Figure 4.11 when it is set to Inverse.

Erase The only thing stranger than Inverse mode is Erase mode. When an object is placed on top of another object and the overlaying object is set to Erase, the overlying object will assume the color that you have established as the background color for your piece in the File Setup dialog box.

In Figure 4.12, therefore, the letter *A,* assumes the piece background color when set to Erase mode.

FIG. 4.11

An object set to Inverse makes all background pixels invisible as well as changes the color of the overlying graphic.

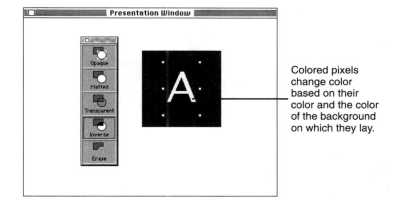

Colored pixels change color based on their color and the color of the background on which they lay.

FIG. 4.12

An object set to Erase assumes the piece background color unless it is a colored bitmap.

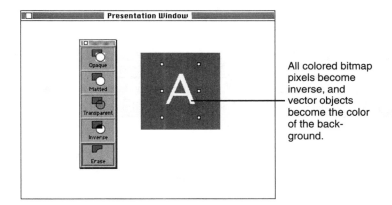

All colored bitmap pixels become inverse, and vector objects become the color of the background.

However, if an overlaying object is a colored bitmap and is set to Erase, it produces the same unpredictable results as setting it to Inverse mode. (See the previous section, "Inverse.")

▶ To set the background color for an Authorware piece, **see** "Presentation Window Location and Appearance," **p. 53**.

Mode Tips Using the Mode settings can be a guess in many cases. There are a few instances, however, in which modes are extremely beneficial. For example, if you have a colored or textured background upon which you plan to place text, you will want to set the text to Transparent so that you can see the background. Otherwise, a colored rectangle will appear behind the text block.

Part

II

Ch

4

In another case, you may have created an illustration that contains a fair amount of white in the graphic. If you plan to place this graphic on top of a colored background or on top of another graphic, you will want to set the Mode to Matted. Matted will remove the solid white rectangle behind the object; however, it will not set the white pixels in the graphic to be invisible.

 The shortcut for opening the Modes palette is to double-click the Pointer tool.

Working with Fills

The Fill option is used to adjust the pattern within an object created using the Oval, Rectangle, Rounded Rectangle, or Polygon tool. Fills can also be applied to objects that were created with drawing tools external to Authorware; however, the Fill option has no effect on bitmaps.

To open the Fills palette, as shown in Figure 4.13, choose Fills from the Attributes menu.

 The shortcut for opening the Fills palette is to double-click the Rectangle, Rounded Rectangle, or Polygon tool.

FIG. 4.13
You can adjust the fill pattern of an object using the Fills palette.

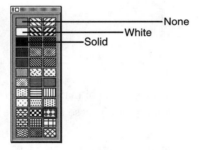

None
White
Solid

Fills comprise two components: the foreground color and the background color. While in the palette the foreground is shown in black and the background is shown in white, the colors can be adjusted using the Authorware Color palette, which is covered in the section, "Using the Color Palette," later in this chapter.

There are a few options that you may want to give particular attention to in the Fills palette.

None (No Fill)   The selection in the upper left-hand corner of the Fills palette is used to assign no fill to the object. This is most commonly used if you simply want to draw a border around another object on the screen.

Solid White   The selection located directly under the No Fill option will fill the object with all white pixels. If the object has an Opaque or Matted Mode, the pixels will be visible. (See the sections, "Opaque" and "Matted," earlier in this chapter.) However, if the object is Transparent, these pixels will be invisible.

Patterns   The remainder of the options fill the object with the selected pattern (with "solid" being one of the patterns).

The strange thing about fill patterns is that the fill pattern is not actually painted into the object, but rather occupies a place on the screen. It may be helpful to picture your object as a window moving over a stationery background that contains your fill pattern. Therefore, if you change the position of the object, either by positioning the object or using the Motion icon, the fill pattern will also change to show the portion of the stationery background now visible through your object.

▶ For information on using the Motion icon, **see** "All About Moving Objects," **p. 166.**

 You may want to create fill patterns as a part of a bitmap if you are going to animate the object using the Motion icon. That way, when the object animates, the pattern will not change as the object moves across the screen.

Fill patterns can be used to create designs in static objects such as a shadow on a text box. In conjunction with fill patterns, however, you will more than likely want to apply colors.

Using the Color Palette

The Color palette is used to adjust the color of an object's border, the display text, or the foreground and background of a fill pattern. Like fill patterns, colors can only be applied to objects, whether created in Authorware or in an external drawing program. Using the Color option has no effect on bitmaps.

To open the Color palette, shown in Figure 4.14, choose Color from the Attributes menu.

 The shortcut for opening the Color palette is to double-click the Oval tool. I believe this is counter-intuitive because double-clicking any other tool opens the Fills palette. The shortcut keys for opening the Color palette are ⌘+K (Macintosh) and Ctrl+K (Windows).

Once the Color palette opens, there are three main options to choose from. These are described next, as well as one other setting that's displayed in the palette.

Border Color and Text Color   Use this option to set the color of highlighted text or to set the color of the border for a highlighted object.

Part
II

Ch
4

FIG. 4.14
You can adjust the color of an object's border, text, or the foreground and background of a fill pattern using the Color palette.

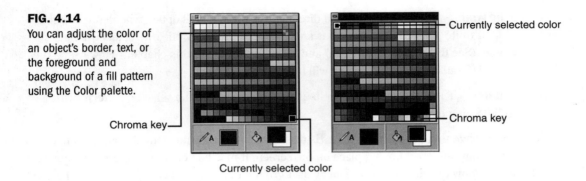

Currently selected color

Chroma key

Chroma key

Currently selected color

To set the color using this feature, first click the color chip located in the lower left-hand corner of the Color palette, then select the color you desire from the palette by clicking it.

Foreground Color   Use this option to set the foreground color of a highlighted object's fill pattern.

To set the color using this feature, first click the overlying color chip located in the lower right-hand corner of the Color palette, then select the color you desire from the palette by clicking it.

Background Color   Use this option to set the background color of a highlighted object's fill pattern.

To set the color using this feature, first click the underlying color chip located in the lower right-hand corner of the Color palette, then select the color you desire from the palette by clicking it.

N O T E   The currently selected color in the palette will have a white border highlight. Additionally, the color chip for the feature icon itself will change to the currently selected color.

Chroma Key   In addition to the options for setting border, text, foreground, and background colors, the Color palette identifies which color is currently being used for the video chroma key.

As we discussed in Chapter 2, when analog video is played in a multimedia piece using a laserdisc player, the video will appear within the Presentation Window only where a defined color—the chroma key—is placed. If you do not want video to play in a certain area, or within a certain graphic, the chroma key color should be avoided.

To identify which color is being used as the chroma key on the Macintosh, look for a color in the palette that has two small inverse colored boxes in it. In Windows, the color that is being used for the chroma key will have a *C* in the small box used to select the color.

▶ For an introduction to the chroma key, **see** "Presentation Window Location and Appearance," **p. 53**.

▶ To learn more about using analog video, **see** "Introducing the Video Icon," **p. 475**.

Setting Defaults

Each of the display attributes has a default setting just as the characteristics of text do. Therefore, every time you create an object, it will have attributes according to the default. In the course of development, however, you may find it necessary to change the defaults, just as we did when working with text.

▶ For step-by-step guidance on setting defaults for text, **see** "Setting Text Defaults," **p. 81.**

For example, you may have come to a point in your piece where you will be creating several charts, each with a light blue background. If the default is currently set to red, you will need to edit the color each time you draw an object. To shorten the process, you could change the default so that each time you draw an object it is automatically created with the correct light blue color.

There are two ways to change the default setting: manually or automatically.

Manually Changing Graphic Attribute Defaults   To manually change a default for line width, fill pattern, mode, or any of the color settings, follow these steps:

1. Open the Presentation Window for a Display or Interaction icon by double-clicking the icon on the Flowline.
2. Be sure that no objects are selected. If an object is selected, you will be adjusting the attribute for that object rather than setting the default.
3. Select the attribute for which you want to change the default, and open its palette.
4. Select the new default setting from the palette.
5. Close the palette.

Automatically Changing Graphic Attribute Defaults   Authorware will also automatically adjust the defaults as you are building your piece. It does this anytime you select more than one object, then apply an attribute.

For example, if you select two objects in the Presentation window, open the Fills palette, and apply the cross hatch pattern, the default for any new objects that you create will be cross hatch.

Working in the Presentation Window

Whether you are working with text or with graphics, there are a few functions that can help you in the organization of graphics and other objects in the Presentation Window. To use each of these functions, you must have the Display or Interaction icon open.

Using Send to Back and Bring to Front

As graphics and text objects are created or imported, they are placed in layers within the Presentation Window. This type of layer is different than the layering between icons, which you'll learn more about in Chapter 5, "Working with Display Effects and Transitions."

Layers within an icon's Presentation Window are similar to the layers of paper that accumulate on your desk. The most recently created item is on top, while the older items work their way to the bottom. Additionally, the top layers begin to cover lower layers, and it becomes difficult to access lower layers without first moving or shuffling the upper layers.

To shuffle objects within a Display icon or Interaction icon, you must use the following commands found in the Attributes menu.

▶ To gain an understanding for the concept of layers, **see** "Knowing the Various Types of Layers," **p. 145.**

Bring To Front   The Bring To Front command will take all the selected items and move them to the top of the stack of objects in the Presentation Window (see Fig. 4.15). If more than one item is selected, the relative positions of those items will not change as they move to the top.

 T I P   The shortcut keys for Bring to Front are ⌘+ + (plus sign) (Macintosh) and Ctrl+ + (plus sign) (Windows).

FIG. 4.15
The Bring To Front command moves all selected objects to the top of the stack.

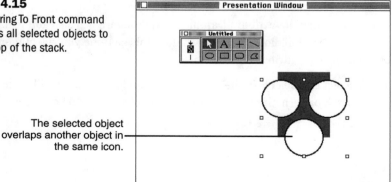

The selected object overlaps another object in the same icon.

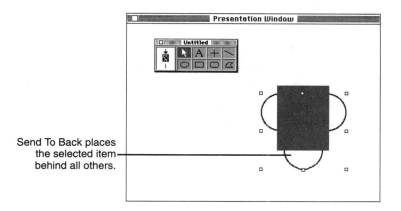

Send To Back places
the selected item
behind all others.

Send To Back   Likewise, this command will take all the selected items and move them to the bottom of the stack of objects in the Presentation Window (see Fig. 4.16). If more than one item is selected, the relative positions of those items will not change as they move.

 T I P   The shortcut keys for Send To Back are ⌘+ - (minus sign) (Macintosh) and Ctrl+ - (minus sign) (Windows).

Part
II

Ch
4

FIG. 4.16
The Send To Back command
moves all selected objects to
the bottom of the stack.

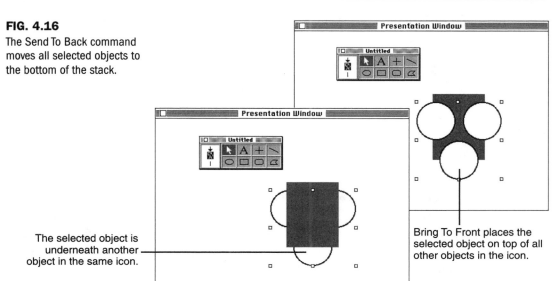

The selected object is
underneath another
object in the same icon.

Bring To Front places the
selected object on top of all
other objects in the icon.

Positioning in a Grid

In the section, "Using the Line Tools," earlier in this chapter, I discussed using the Line Tool to create a layout for aligning objects in the Presentation Window. Authorware also provides a grid that you can use during development.

To access the grid, simply select the Show Grid option from the Attributes pull-down menu. This option acts as a toggle, so to hide the grid, you must select this same option again.

Once Show Grid is selected, a grid with 32-pixel spacing is placed on the screen (see Fig. 4.17). This grid will not be seen by the end user when your piece is packaged for distribution.

FIG. 4.17
Authorware's grid is based on a fixed, 32-pixel spacing.

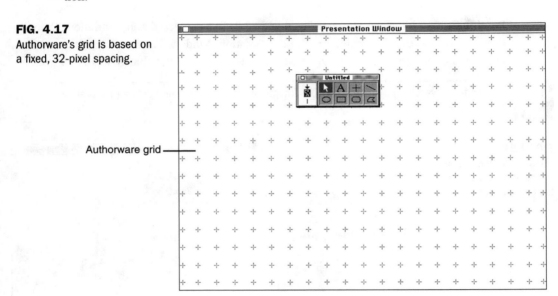

Authorware grid ——

The grid may be useful in helping beginners align objects. It would be of even more value if Authorware allowed you to adjust the grid spacing or set rule lines like most page layout programs; however, this isn't the case. As you develop more and more applications, you may find few instances where your designs fit Authorware's 32 pixel grid. In such cases, try creating your own design grid with the Straight Line tool, as I described earlier in the chapter.

Aligning Objects

Consistent with the notion of using style guides and grids is that of aligning objects. The Authorware Align Objects command in the Attributes menu enables you to align imported or created objects, as well as push buttons created by the Interaction icon, in relation to one another. It also allows you to equally space objects apart from one another.

To use the align feature, follow these steps:

1. Open the Presentation Window of a Display or Interaction icon.

2. Select two or more objects using the Pointer tool.

3. Open the Align Objects palette using the Align Objects option in the Attributes menu. The Align Objects palette appears (see Fig. 4.18).

 TIP The shortcut keys for opening the Align Objects palette are ⌘+H (Macintosh) or Ctrl+H (Windows).

4. Select the desired alignment option.

5. Close the Align Objects palette.

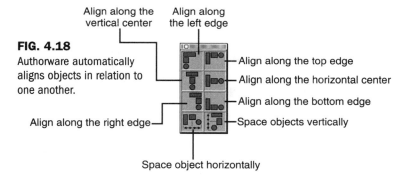

FIG. 4.18
Authorware automatically aligns objects in relation to one another.

Align along the vertical center

Align along the left edge

Align along the top edge

Align along the horizontal center

Align along the bottom edge

Space objects vertically

Align along the right edge

Space object horizontally

The Align Objects palette (in Figure 4.18) functions just like any other attributes palette. Once the palette is opened, it can remain open as a floating window. You cannot, however, set a default alignment.

Authorware supports the alignment tools described next.

 Left Vertically   Use the Left Vertically option to align all of the selected objects vertically according to the left-most edge of the object positioned closest to the left-hand side of the screen.

 Top Edge   Use the Top Edge option to align all of the selected objects horizontally according to the top-most edge of the object positioned closest to the top of the screen.

 Centered Vertically   Use the Centered Vertically option to align all of the selected objects vertically along a common center. Authorware will determine the vertical center of all the selected objects, then align the center of each object individually with that point.

Centered Horizontally   Use the Centered Horizontally option to align all of the selected objects horizontally along a common center. Authorware will determine the horizontal center of all the selected objects, then align the center of each object individually with that point.

Right Vertically   Use the Right Vertically option to align all of the selected objects vertically according to the right-most edge of the object positioned closest to the right-hand side of the screen.

Bottom Edge   Use the Bottom Edge option to align all of the selected objects horizontally according to the bottom-most edge of the object positioned closest to the bottom of the screen.

Space Vertically   Use the Space Vertically option to space all of the selected objects vertically. Authorware will determine the upper-most and lower-most points of the selected objects, then align the center of the other selected object equally between those points.

Space Horizontally   Use the Space Horizontally option to space all of the selected objects horizontally. Authorware will determine the left-most and right-most points of the selected objects, then align the center of the other selected object equally between those points.

Using the Alignment Options to Place Buttons   The alignment options are great for quickly placing buttons on the screen. For example, if you have five buttons along the bottom of the screen that you want equally spaced and aligned, follow these steps:

1. Place the left-most button in the lower left-hand corner, as shown in Figure 4.19. Be sure that it is positioned according to the left and bottom edges of your piece.

2. With the left-most button already selected, select the right-most button, as shown in Figure 4.20, by holding down the Shift key while clicking the right-most button. Be sure that the right-most button is not closer to the bottom of your piece than the left-most button.

FIG. 4.19
Place the left button first.

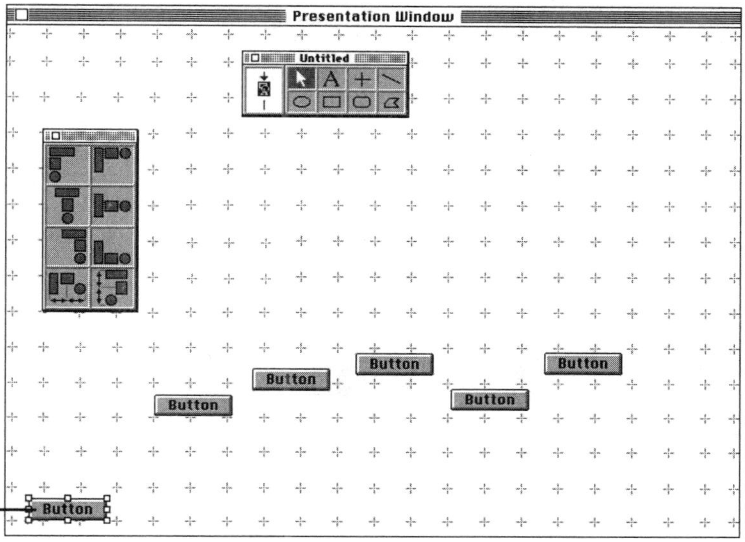

Place the first object off of which all other objects will be positioned.

FIG. 4.20
Select the right-most button to align the two buttons.

Once the objects are selected, choose the align bottom edge option.

Select the second object that is to be positioned.

Be sure that the first object remains selected.

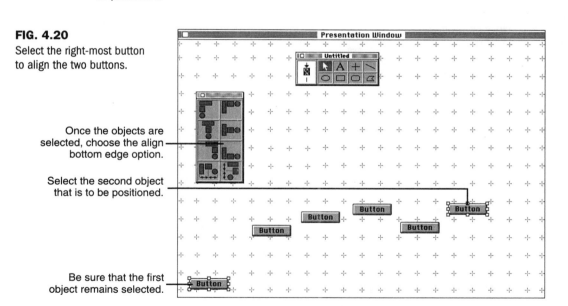

3. Select the Bottom Edge option from the Align Objects palette to align the two buttons along the bottom edge.

4. Without changing the vertical position, drag to place the right-most button the desired distance away from the right edge of your piece.

5. Select all of the buttons that are to be placed, as shown in Figure 4.21. Make sure than none of them are further to the left, right, or bottom than the one that you have already placed.

FIG. 4.21
With the left-most and right-most buttons in place, select the remaining buttons.

Select the Bottom Edge option.

Select the Space Horizontally option.

Select the remaining objects.

Authorware aligns this object with the one on the far left.

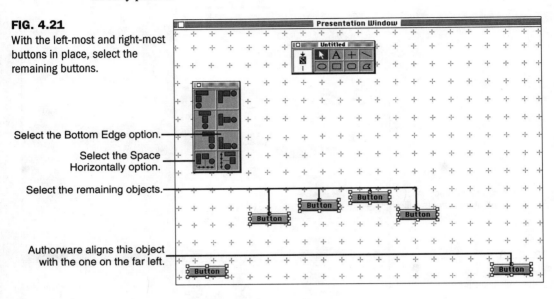

6. Select the Bottom Edge option to align all of the buttons along the bottom.

7. Select the Space Horizontally option to automatically space the buttons along the bottom of the screen, as shown in Figure 4.22.

FIG. 4.22
The alignment tools are used to perfectly align and space the buttons along the bottom of the screen.

The Space Horizontally option.

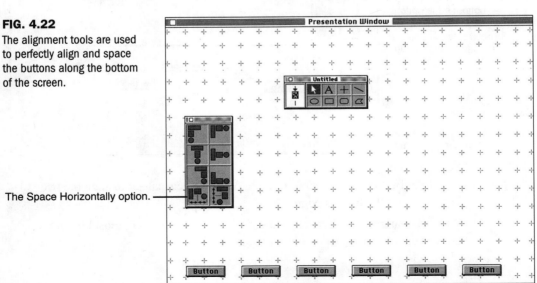

Working with Display Effects and Transitions

"I want every screen to come up using a different transition!" It was this directive from the client that made me realize that, once again, Hollywood won out over the value of content. Moreover, it confirmed that this person had no sense of design.

For years, the film and video industry has been applying effects to the transition from one scene to another. As soon as computer-based presentation builders hit the market, they too provided the opportunity for bullet points to slide onto the screen and for text to tumble out of nowhere.

Display transitions can be used quite effectively. For example, the television comedy, *Home Improvement,* uses effects for scene changes. The transitions not only provide a bit of humor, they prepare the viewer for a new scene. Unfortunately, transitions in many computer-based presentations don't seem to have such a sense of purpose.

Transitions in computer-based presentations are often implemented to provide a sense of *fun*. I believe that

Using the display effects and transitions

Display effects are used to determine how a Display, Interaction, or Digital Movie icon will be positioned on the screen, what automatic erase features it will have, and how embedded content will be treated. Transitions define what special effect will be applied when the icon is executed.

Calculating the initial display position

The initial display position of an icon can be defined within an area or along a path. Additionally, the objects within a display can be constrained to this same area or path.

Understanding layers

Objects are placed in layers as they are displayed in the Presentation Window. You can adjust the value of an icon's layer using values, variables, or expressions.

Working with the Authorware Xtras and transitions

Authorware uses Xtras plug-ins to create special effects that are used when an object is displayed in the Presentation Window, as well as when it is erased using the Erase icon. Additionally, a transition can be applied to the piece to be seen when the piece is executed, or during automatic erasing.

many pieces use this sense of fun to overcompensate for the lack of interactivity or content in the first place

In this chapter, we explore applying display effects and transitions within Authorware. Authorware display effects include not only transition effects, but controls to position the display and to give the display special qualities when the piece is running. ■

Setting Display Effects

In Chapter 4, "Working with Graphics and Objects," we looked at building or importing objects and text into the Presentation Window. We also considered how to apply several characteristics, such as a fill pattern, color, or mode, to the objects. Each of these characteristics were used to enhance the piece.

In addition to the display characteristics, Authorware enables you to control how those objects are positioned, whether the display is movable by the end user, and several other considerations that are given to the contents of the icon when the piece is running. In this chapter, we explore how to use each of the options as well as explore practical applications for each.

▶ To review placing text in the Presentation Window, **see** "Placing Text On-Screen," **p. 68**.

▶ For more information on creating graphics in the Presentation Window, **see** "Drawing Objects," **p. 98**.

▶ To learn how to apply display characteristics to objects within the Presentation Window, **see** "Using Attributes," **p. 112**.

Understanding Display Effects and Transitions

When the piece encounters a Display icon or an Interaction icon, the contents of that icon are drawn in the Presentation Window. Using the Effects attribute, you can control how all of that icon's contents are presented.

▶ To refer to the introduction of the Display icon, **see** "The Display Icon," **p. 15**.

▶ To refer to the introduction of the Interaction icon, **see** "The Interaction Icon," **p. 19**.

To use the Effects attribute, you must access the Effects dialog box, shown in Figure 5.1, from either the Flowline or from the Presentation Window. When the Effects dialog box is opened, the name that appears across the top of the dialog box is based on what you named the icon along the Flowline. Descriptively naming the icon helps remind you of the purpose of the icon while editing the dialog box.

FIG. 5.1
Use the Effects dialog box to control the positioning of the displayed objects.

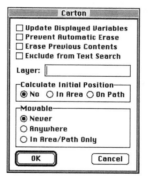

To access the Effects dialog box from the Flowline, select the icon you want to apply the effect to, then select the Effects command from the Attributes menu. To access the dialog box from the Presentation Window, simply choose Effects from the Attributes menu.

The shortcut key for accessing the Effects dialog box is ⌘+E (Macintosh) or Ctrl+E (Windows). When the Effects dialog box opens, the Presentation Window also opens. To prevent the Presentation Window from opening, press the Option key (Macintosh) or Alt key (Windows) while using the shortcut keys.

Part
II

Ch
5

Once the Effects dialog box is opened, you will notice that it contains a varied collection of check boxes, text boxes, and radio buttons. Let's take a quick look at each of these, then an in-depth look at those that are more complex.

Selecting the Update Displayed Variables Option

If the Display icon contains information that is calculated by the computer (embedded) rather than placed in the Presentation Window using the Text tool, you can select the Update Displayed Variables check box to enable the information to be updated without requiring Authorware to execute the icon again.

▶ To review placing text in the Presentation Window, **see** "Placing Text On-Screen," **p. 68**.

▶ For step-by-step guidance on using variables and functions, **see** "Working with Variables and Functions," **p. 366**.

▶ To learn how to place data that is contained in a variable on the Presentation Window, **see** "Embedding Data in the Presentation Window," **p. 434**.

This feature is very helpful if you plan to display information that will update continually throughout the piece, such as the user's score in a game. One of my favorite uses is in the construction of a prompt bar used to guide the user. The prompt is changed from screen to screen by adjusting a variable, but there is only one Display icon to present the text information.

CAUTION

Updating displayed variables will slow your piece down so use this feature sparingly.

Prevent Automatic Erase

Authorware has the capability to automatically erase the content of icons from the Presentation Window. Although this functionality is very helpful, there are times when you may not want the contents of the icon to be automatically erased. In such instances, check the Prevent Automatic Erase option. An Erase icon will consequently be required to make the objects go away.

▶ For an overview of automatic erasing, **see** "Exploring Alternatives to the Erase Icon," **p. 361**.

CAUTION

Selecting Prevent Automatic Erase can create confusion for new Authorware developers because this option has no impact on the Flowline icon where it has been applied (that is, there's no way to easily tell that the icon must be manually erased with an Erase icon). I suggest applying a color to the icon so that everyone can see that there is something special about the icon that carries the Prevent Automatic Erase effect.

Erase Previous Contents

Selecting the Erase Previous Contents check box for an icon will cause everything in the Presentation Window to be erased at the same time that it executes the selected icon. Although this feature enables you to build a piece with fewer icons (no need for Erase icons), it does force you to build a piece using the book or slideshow metaphors: one screen presented at a time.

CAUTION

Selecting this option can again create confusion should you later decide that you don't want everything to disappear. Again, I suggest applying a color to the icon so that everyone can see that there is something special about the icon. In this case, the icon carries the Erase Previous Content effect.

The Erase Previous Contents option will not erase an icon that has the Prevent Automatic Erase option selected.

Exclude from Text Search

In Chapter 16, "Applying Advanced Interactivity and Searching," you learn about searching the text in a piece for keywords or for phrases in the content itself. Selecting the Exclude from Text Search check box, however, excludes the contents of the selected icon from such search activities.

Once again, if you select this option, I suggest color-coding the icon to show that something is special about it.

▶ For guidance on searching the content text of a piece, **see** "Creating a Search Destination Link," **p. 321**.

Part

II

Ch

5

Using the Layer Option

As Authorware travels along the Flowline encountering icons, objects naturally begin to accumulate on top of one another within the Presentation Window. As this happens, the objects within the most recently encountered icon assume a position on top of previously displayed objects much like papers accumulate on a desktop.

In conjunction with this natural layering action, Authorware uses display layers in which the content of an icon is displayed. By default, an icon assumes layer zero. If, however, an icon is assigned a layer with a higher value, such as five, the objects within the icon with the layer of five will always reside on top of icons with layers that have a lower value, even if the icon with a lower layer value is executed after the icon with the layer of five.

Later in this chapter, in the section "Understanding Layers," I discuss using layers with reference to the Layer setting in the Effects dialog box. To set the layer of an icon, you must enter a value into the Layer text box.

> **CAUTION**
>
> Be sure that your strategy for using layers has been well thought out. I have often seen people use layers as a remedy for solving display problems. Once you start down this path, there is no returning to constructing a solid Flowline structure.

Calculate Initial Position

In the center of the Effects dialog box is a region titled Calculate Initial Position. The default selection for the Calculate Initial Position setting in the Effects dialog box is No. If this option is selected, Authorware will not position the objects in the Presentation Window in any way other than how you positioned the objects when you created them.

Selecting the In Area option under Calculate Initial Position expands the Effects dialog box, enabling you to define an area in which the contents of the icon are positioned. Additionally, you can set parameters used to determine where in that area the contents will be positioned.

Likewise, if you select On Path, the Effects dialog box expands to provide controls that enable you to define a path along which the contents of the icon are positioned. You can set parameters to position the contents on that path. (See "Creating a Path for Positioning Objects," later in this chapter for more information on the In Area and On Path options.)

Movable

Finally, the bottom portion of the Effects dialog box enables you to determine whether the objects in the icon are movable by the end user.

By default, objects in the Presentation Window are not movable by the end user when your piece is packaged for distribution. The default option, Never, automatically changes to Anywhere, however, if you identify the contents of the selected icon as the objects to be moved in association with a Target Area interaction type. For example, if you define a Target Area interaction in which the end user is to drag labels to a diagram, the icons containing the labels will automatically change to the Anywhere movable option.

▶ For step-by-step guidance on creating an interaction with a Target Area response, **see** "Creating Target Areas," **p. 284**.

Authorware also provides a variable (Movable) that can be used to override the default setting when your piece is run. You can change the value of this variable using a Calculation icon, or you can use the value of the variable in dialog boxes that accept variables. For example, if you want to set a particular icon so that it cannot be moved, use the following expression: `Movable@"IconTitle":=FALSE`.

As the name implies, the Anywhere option enables the user to move the contents of this display anywhere, including outside of the Presentation Window.

N O T E When authoring, every object in the Presentation Window is movable. This makes it difficult to determine if the object will also be movable by the end user. ■

CAUTION

Give careful consideration to the impact of this selection before it is applied. If users drag valuable components out of the Presentation Window with no way of returning them, they will not be able to use the piece as you have designed it.

The In Area/Path Only option enables the end user to move the objects anywhere in the Presentation Window as long as it is along the defined positioning path or within the defined positioning area. Even though the user can drag the mouse outside of the area, the objects themselves are constrained to the defined area. In most cases, this is a preferred method to the Anywhere selection just described.

 T I P Constraining the movement of all movable objects to a path or to an area is the safest way to ensure that valuable components of the content will not be lost outside of the Presentation Window. Additionally, it is a great way to quietly guide the use of the piece.

Creating an Area for Positioning Objects

The Effects dialog box can do more than control special characteristics of an icon during execution of the piece. The Effects dialog box can also be used to determine where and how the objects in the icon are initially positioned in the Presentation Window, as well as where the user will be able to drag movable objects.

The first option to look at is In Area under Calculate Initial Position, which is used to determine where and how the objects in the display are placed. When this selection is made, the Effects dialog box expands to the In Area dialog box, as shown in Figure 5.2.

FIG. 5.2
The In Area dialog box enables you to define an area within the Presentation Window and the parameters to control where in that area the contents of this icon will be displayed.

Enter a value to position the objects horizontally.

Enter a value to position the objects vertically.

Select Base to adjust either base position.

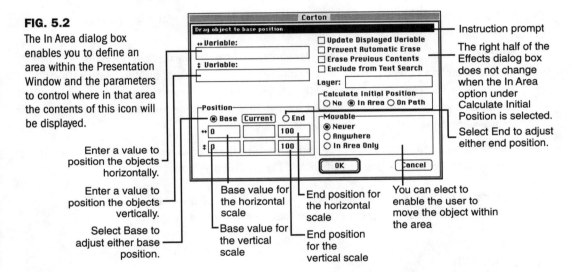

Instruction prompt

The right half of the Effects dialog box does not change when the In Area option under Calculate Initial Position is selected.

Select End to adjust either end position.

Base value for the horizontal scale

Base value for the vertical scale

End position for the horizontal scale

End position for the vertical scale

You can elect to enable the user to move the object within the area

The In Area option is particularly helpful if you have created an object that the user is to move within the Presentation Window, and you want to control the area in which it is moved. In this case, after choosing In Area, define an area by dragging and using the Position section of the In Area dialog box, then select In Area Only from the Movable portion of the In Area dialog box. The In Area Only option constrains the movable object within the area you have defined.

An example for the use of the In Area option is the creation of a game, such as chess or checkers. In this case, you set the area around the gameboard so that the pieces can only be moved within the board.

To define an area in which the contents of the icon will be positioned or in which the user can move the objects, perform the following steps:

1. Select an icon on the Flowline that contains the object to be moved by the end user, or open the icon and create the object.

2. Once the icon is either selected or opened, choose the Effects command from the Attributes menu.

TIP The shortcut keys for accessing the Effects dialog box are ⌘+E (Macintosh) or Ctrl+E (Windows). When the Effects dialog box opens, the Presentation Window also opens. To prevent the Presentation Window from opening, press the Option key (Macintosh) or Alt key (Windows) while using the shortcut keys.

3. Select the In Area option from the Calculate Initial Position section of the Effects dialog box. When you do this, the In Area dialog box appears.

TIP When the In Area dialog box is open, directions for using it appear just under the title bar of the dialog box.

4. Drag the object in the Presentation Window to the base position of the area you plan to create. The base position is typically the upper left-hand corner of the bounding area.

5. Select the End option radio button located in the Position section of the dialog box.

6. Drag the objects to the end position of the area you plan to create. The end position is typically the corner opposite the base position.

When you release the mouse, an outline of the area appears, as shown in Figure 5.3. The area is defined by the center of the objects you dragged, so if you have more than one object in the icon, Authorware calculates the center of all the objects to define the area.

Let's look next at how Authorware calculates the display position of the game piece by placing a scale to the area. If you assign a scale, each time you move the game piece, the variable tracking the current position of the game piece changes to reflect the object's current position according to the scale.

Setting the Horizontal Scale

The horizontal scale is a measurement in incremental units from one side of the area to the other horizontally. The scale can be any size you want. For example, if you have a map with a scale in miles in the Presentation Window, the horizontal scale for the area can go from 0 to 100. In this example, the map is divided into increments from 0 to 100.

To establish a horizontal scale, you must set both a Base and an End value in the Position area of the In Area dialog box, described as follows:

Part

II

Ch

5

■ Horizontal Base Value—This value, placed in the entry text box in the upper left-hand corner of the Position area in the In Area dialog box, establishes the beginning value for the scale.

■ Horizontal End Value—This value, placed in the entry text box in the upper right-hand corner of the Position area in the In Area dialog box, establishes the ending value for the scale.

FIG. 5.3
The defined area is shown on the screen after both the Base and the End positions have been determined.

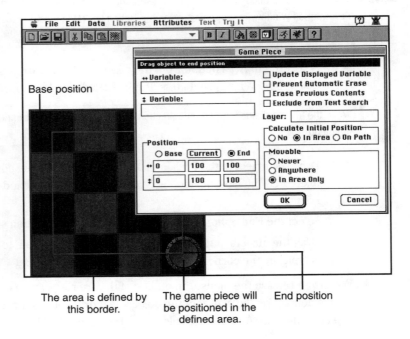

The area is defined by this border.

The game piece will be positioned in the defined area.

End position

Setting the Vertical Scale

The vertical scale is a measurement in incremental units from one side of the area to the other vertically. As the horizontal scale, this scale can also be any size you want. For example, if you have a picture of the earth's atmosphere in the Presentation Window, the vertical scale can again go from 0 to 100 miles.

To establish a vertical scale, you must set both a Base and an End value, described as follows:

■ Vertical Base Value—This value, placed in the entry text box in the lower left-hand corner of the Position area in the In Area dialog box, establishes the beginning value for the scale.

■ Vertical End Value—This value, placed in the entry text box in the lower right-hand corner of the Position area in the In Area dialog box, establishes the ending value for the scale.

T I P To test the accuracy of the scale that you defined for the area, enter a value for the horizontal and the vertical axes in the center text box located just under the Current button, then click the Current button. Authorware positions the contents of the display within the area based on the values you entered. You can then adjust the area by clicking either the Base or End radio button and dragging the object to its new location.

It is possible to set your scale to read backwards. For example, you could create some sort of tracking device that, like the ball drop in Times Square on New Year's Eve, is used to count down the time required to complete the piece. If the time remaining, however, was in direct proportion to the user's score so that as they came closer to a mastery level, the amount of time could be reduced and the scale could read backwards.

While in some cases this may be desirable, in most cases it is an error in defining the area.

Creating a Path for Positioning Objects

A second option to determine where and how the objects in a display are placed is On Path. When this selection is made, the Effects dialog box expands to the On Path dialog box, as shown in Figure 5.4.

Part
II

Ch
5

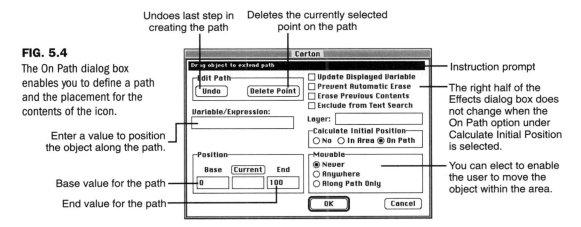

Undoes last step in creating the path

Deletes the currently selected point on the path

FIG. 5.4
The On Path dialog box enables you to define a path and the placement for the contents of the icon.

Enter a value to position the object along the path.

Base value for the path

End value for the path

Instruction prompt

The right half of the Effects dialog box does not change when the On Path option under Calculate Initial Position is selected.

You can elect to enable the user to move the object within the area.

The On Path option is helpful if you have created an object that the user is to move in the Presentation Window, but you want to control its path. In this case, define the path and select Along Path Only from the Movable portion of the On Path dialog box. The user is now able to move the object only on the path you have defined.

One popular application for the On Path effect is to control the path of a slider bar, as shown in Figure 5.5. In this case, you can set the effect for the sliding part of the widget and define the path so that the bar cannot slide past the ends of the slider.

FIG. 5.5
The On Path effect enables you to restrict the movement of a display along a path.

The user only moves this object along the defined path.

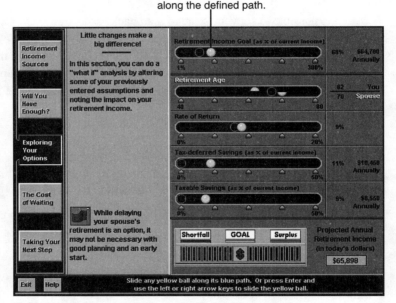

Used with permission from Lutheran Brotherhood Insurance Co.

To define the path on which the contents will be positioned or along which the user can move the object, perform the following steps:

1. Select an icon on the Flowline that contains the object to be moved by the end user, or open the icon and create the object.

2. Once the icon is either selected or opened, choose the Effects command from the Attributes menu.

T I P The shortcut keys for accessing the Effects dialog box are ⌘+E (Macintosh) or Ctrl+E (Windows). When the Effects dialog box opens, the Presentation Window also opens. To prevent the Presentation Window from opening, press the Option key (Macintosh) or Alt key (Windows) while using the shortcut keys.

3. Select the On Path option from the Calculate Initial Position section of the Effects dialog box. When you do this, the On Path dialog box appears.

TIP When the On Path dialog box is open, directions for using it appear just under the title bar of the dialog box.

4. When the On Path dialog box opens, you will see a small triangle placed in the center of the objects for that icon. This point represents the Base point for your path. You can drag the triangle to set a new Base point if needed.

5. Drag the objects to another position in the Presentation Window. When you release the mouse, another point is created. Unlike creating or positioning objects, holding down the Shift key while dragging will not constrain the object vertically or horizontally.

You can continue creating points until the desired path is complete. Figure 5.6 shows a path that has been created by dragging the objects.

FIG. 5.6
Drag the display to create a path. Release the mouse button each time you want to set a point.

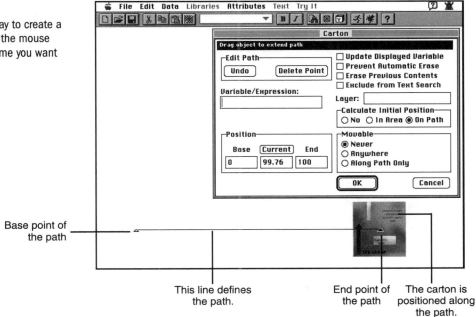

Base point of the path

This line defines the path.

End point of the path

The carton is positioned along the path.

Part II

Ch 5

> **CAUTION**
>
> I have seen many people try to drag the display all over the screen thinking that Authorware would trace its position to create the path. You must release the mouse button to create a point on the path, then drag the display to create the next point.

Editing the Path

As you create the path, there are several methods you can use to edit the path. Each of these is described next.

Adding a Point   You can add a point to the path at any time: Simply click the path line and another triangle appears. In some cases, it may be easiest to define the first and last points by dragging the display, then create the remainder of the points using this method.

Moving a Point   Once a point has been created, it can be moved anywhere in the Presentation Window. To move a point, simply drag the triangle to its new location.

For example, if you are attempting to trace a detailed map, you will have difficulty accurately guessing each of the points by dragging an object. In this case, it is easier to create the first and last points, then add additional points one by one. As the points are created, they can be positioned much more precisely than by dragging an object.

Specifying Curve or Angle Points   When a point is first created, it is represented by a triangle. Triangle-shaped points identify angles along the path. If you double-click a triangle, however, it becomes a circle. Circle-shaped points represent curves in the path. You can toggle between angled and curved points by double-clicking the symbol.

Deleting a Point   Any point along the path can be deleted. Click to select (highlight) the point to be deleted, then click the Delete Point button from the Edit Path portion of the On Path dialog box.

> **N O T E**   The normal procedure for deleting (pressing the Delete key) does not function when this dialog box is open. ■

Undoing a Path Change   If you make an error while using any of the previously described path editing techniques, click the Undo button from the Edit Path portion of the On Path dialog box.

N O T E The normal procedure for selecting Undo by pressing the ⌘+Z key (Macintosh) or Ctrl+Z key (Windows) does not function when the On Path dialog box is open. ■

Specifying the Path Scale

The next step in enabling Authorware to position an object along a path is to define the parameters described next.

Authorware uses these values when determining where an object is along the path or where it should be placed along the path. For example, you may identify the Base value for the slider as 100 and the End value as 200. If you move the slider along the path to the half-way point, Authorware will understand the value for the position is 150.

Base Value   The Base value, which you enter in the text box on the lower left-hand side of the Position area of the On Path dialog box, establishes the beginning value for the scale along the path.

End Value   The End value, which you enter in the text box to the right of the Base value in the On Path dialog box, establishes the end value for the scale along the path.

T I P   To test the accuracy of the scale that you defined for the path, enter a value in the center text box located under the Current button, then click the Current button. Authorware positions the contents along the path based on the values that you entered. You can then adjust the path by editing any of the points.

Part
II

Ch
5

Calculating the Display Position

The last two sections of this chapter cover building an area or a path in which an object can be moved, and how Authorware knows where the object is within that area or path. This section describes how to provide information to Authorware so that it can position the objects within the area or path that you defined. In Chapter 22, "Working with Data," I go into greater depth to illustrate how the position of an object can be adjusted by Authorware.

As you recall, when I defined the area or path, I established a horizontal and vertical scale for the area and a linear scale using base and end values for the path. The purpose of these values was to tell Authorware the position of the object within the area or along the path in terms of my scale.

In many cases, however, we don't want the user to move the object and Authorware to recognize the value; we want Authorware to move the object based on a value it interprets from the user's interaction with the piece. For example, you may have a pointer that is used to highlight the best application for a product, and as the user clicks on the various products, you want the pointer to reposition itself accordingly.

The value that you use to drive the repositioning of the pointer is going to be based on each individual product (in this example). Therefore, you must create a holder for a value rather than simply enter a number into the Effects dialog box. This holder is referred to as a *variable*.

▶ To learn more about using variables in a text box, **see** "Exploring Variables," **p. 373**.

As you can see in Figure 5.7, the path along which the pointer moves stretches from the top price to the bottom price. Because there are four prices, the Base value for the path is 1 and the End value is 4 (that is, the scale starts at 1 and ends at 4).

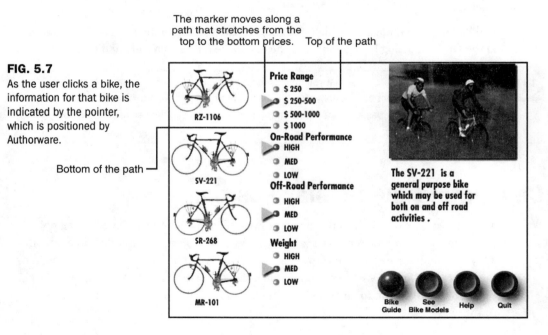

FIG. 5.7
As the user clicks a bike, the information for that bike is indicated by the pointer, which is positioned by Authorware.

In this case, I have also created a variable called BikeUse, and rather than entering a number into the Variable/Expression text box located in the upper left-hand portion of the Along Path dialog box, I entered the variable BikeUse. I have now told Authorware that I want it to use the value of BikeUse to position the pointer along the path.

N O T E If I had been defining the display position within an area, I would have to define a value for both the horizontal and the vertical axis. ■

Even if Authorware receives a value that is outside of the range that I established for my path or area, it will not go beyond the defined region. For example, if the value for the variable, BikeUse, was set to 6, Authorware would move the pointer to the highest possible value, which would be 5. The same holds true for numbers below the defined range as well.

As we have seen, the Effects dialog box can be used to position objects vertically and horizontally on the screen. These objects can be positioned in an area or along a path, and if the user is able to move the object, it can be constrained to the defined region.

In the next section, you see how the Effects dialog box can be used to position objects along the z-axis, or depthwise, using layers.

Understanding Layers

Just as Authorware can determine the horizontal and vertical position of a displayed object using the Effects dialog box, it can also determine the way in which objects layer together in the Presentation Window.

Knowing the Various Types of Layers

In Chapter 4, "Working with Graphics and Objects," I used the metaphor of papers collecting on a desktop to describe how objects were layered within the Display and Interaction icons. Objects naturally assume the highest layer—that which is closest and most visible to the end user—when they are created or imported. Using Bring to Front and Send to Back, you are able to adjust their layered position within an icon as necessary to create the desired design in the Presentation Window.

▶ For more information on layering objects within an icon, **see** "Using Send to Back and Bring to Front," **p. 122**.

As the piece travels along the Flowline, it encounters Display and Interaction icons containing objects to be drawn in the Presentation Window. Like layering within an icon, the objects in the most recently encountered icons naturally assume the highest layer, therefore overlaying objects previously drawn to the screen when earlier icons were encountered.

Part
II

Ch

5

The difference in these two occurrences of layers is that the layering within an icon is established by you, the author, and it cannot be adjusted during the piece's execution. If you have created two objects in a Display icon—one on top of the other—they will appear that way every time the icon is executed. The natural layering between icons, however, may be disrupted, either according to your design or according to variables set as the piece is running.

Shuffling the Layers

When you create a Display or Interaction icon, the default layer for that icon is 0. This means that the objects in the icon will be displayed on top of any other icons having the default setting and that are already displayed. When future icons are executed, they will be placed on top of that icon if they too have the default setting of 0.

If you create an object that you always want to appear on top of whatever else is placed on the screen after it, you can adjust the layer for that icon. For example, you may have created a very complex interaction that encompasses the entire screen, leaving no room for instructions, as shown in Figure 5.8.

FIG. 5.8
Because information in the Presentation Window updates, you need to adjust the layer for the instructions screen.

The user can move the equation box anywhere in the Presentation Window.

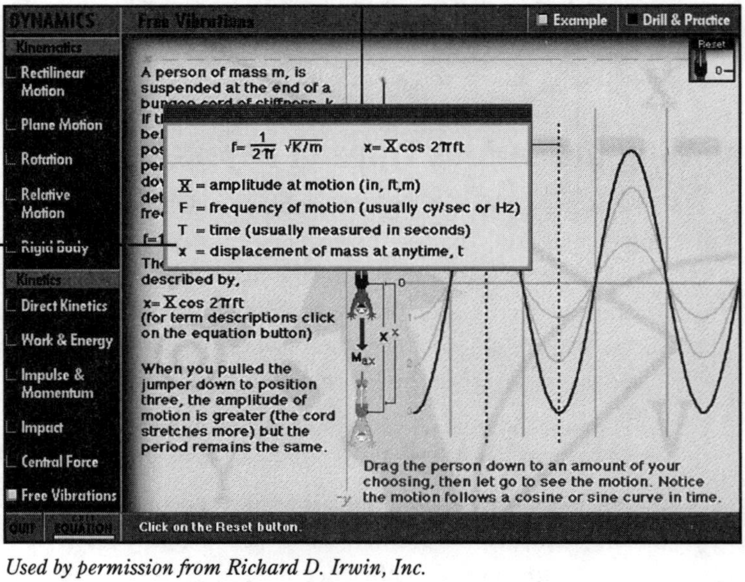

Used by permission from Richard D. Irwin, Inc.

Because you don't want to block any of the information, the instructions need to be in a movable window. As the user interacts, new information is displayed on the screen; therefore, the movable window needs to be set to a layer higher than the default so that it continues to float above the interaction.

To set the layer of an icon, perform the following steps:

1. Select an icon on the Flowline that contains the object to be moved by the end user, or open the icon and create the object.

2. Once the icon is either selected or opened, choose the Effects command from the Attributes menu.

TIP The shortcut keys for accessing the Effects dialog box are ⌘+E (Macintosh) or Ctrl+E (Windows). When the Effects dialog box opens, the Presentation Window also opens. To prevent the Presentation Window from opening, press the Option key (Macintosh) or Alt key (Windows) while using the shortcut keys.

3. Enter a value into the Layer text box. If all of the other icons that will be displayed at the same time as the one you are applying the effect to are using the default setting, then you can enter any value greater than 0. Otherwise, you must enter any value greater than the highest layer currently used by the icons that will be displayed at the same time as the one to which you are setting the layer.

N O T E You can also use negative numbers when setting a layer value. ■

4. Click OK and continue authoring.

CAUTION
Performance may be negatively affected if too many objects have layer values other than the default of 0.

Part

II

Ch

5

Although layers are most commonly associated with Display and Interaction icons, layers can also be set to animation and the Digital Movie icon.

▶ To learn about assigning a layer to an animation, **see** "Animating in Layers," **p. 178**.

Whenever an object is being moved by a Motion icon, it will assume the highest layer unless you have specifically assigned it—and the objects that it will encounter—to a layer different than the default of zero.

Movies also always play on top of other objects and by default assume a layer value of 1. To have objects displayed on top of a digital movie, the digital movie must be an internal movie and not a reference to an external movie file (for example, QuickTime or Director), and the layer value for the object must be set higher than 1.

A Word of Warning

Although layers certainly have their place in development, more often than not they are overused. I have noticed that once layers are established for a few icons, they become the quick and easy solution if things are not displaying, erasing, or animating properly.

Before employing the use of layers, I challenge you to look hard at your design and at the structure of the Authorware icons to find a better solution. Usually, there is a solution that does not require the patch that layers can provide.

Setting Transitions

Although display effects are used to control the positioning of objects as they are first displayed in the Presentation Window, transitions are used to determine what visual effect is used when the objects are displayed. For example, you might want an object to slowly fade in or slide across the screen.

Authorware 3.5 contains over 50 unique transitions that can be used to move from one screen to another. Furthermore, these transitions have been created as plug-ins, or Xtras. As Macromedia, you or third-party suppliers create additional transitions, the functionality within Authorware is extended by using Xtras, instead of by updating the Authorware application.

> **CAUTION**
>
> Although using Xtras is greatly beneficial during authoring, it creates one more concern when the piece is complete and ready for distribution. You must remember which Xtras were used, and you must be sure to distribute them for your end user. If the Xtras folder is misplaced, no transitions will be applied.

Installing Xtras

Although Xtras are incredibly beneficial for enabling quick extendibility of the Authorware application, they do cause an added degree of instability to the piece. For example, if you do not place the Xtras into the proper location on your computer; if the Xtras become misplaced or damaged; or if you do not properly distribute and install the Xtras for your end user, the transitions will not occur. Each platform supported by Authorware has unique requirements of the positioning of the Xtras.

Location requirements for Xtras are described next.

Xtras Under Windows 95 and Windows NT   In the Windows 95 and Windows NT environment, the Xtras directory must be placed in one of the following locations:

- A35W\Xtras\
- Program Files\Common Files\Macromedia\Xtras\
- Directory containing the program\Xtras\

Xtras Under Windows 3.1x   In the Windows 3.1x environment, the Xtras directory must be placed in either of the following locations:

- A35W\Xtras\
- Windows\Macromed\Xtras\
- Directory containing the program\Xtras\

Xtras on a Macintosh   In the Macintosh environment, the Xtras folder must be placed in either of the following locations:

- Authorware 3.5 Folder:Xtras:
- System Folder:Macromedia:Xtras:
- Folder containing the program:Xtras:

Working with Xtras Transitions

Like effects, transitions can be applied to a specific Display or Interaction icon from either the Flowline or the Presentation Window. In either case, transitions are set using the Transition dialog box (see Fig. 5.9).

To access the Transitions dialog box from the Flowline, select an icon then choose the Transition command from the Attributes menu. To access the Transition dialog box from the Presentation Window, simply choose the Transition command from the Attributes menu. The transition will be applied to the icon in which you are currently working or which has been selected.

Part
II

Ch
5

 TIP The shortcut keys for accessing the Transition dialog box are ⌘+Shift+E (Macintosh) or Ctrl+Shift+E (Windows). When the Transition dialog box opens, the Presentation Window also opens. To prevent the Presentation Window from opening, press the Option key (Macintosh) or Alt key (Windows) right after using the shortcut keys.

N O T E   The Transition command in the Attributes menu is available only when a Display, Erase, Interaction, or Framework icon is selected or opened. ■

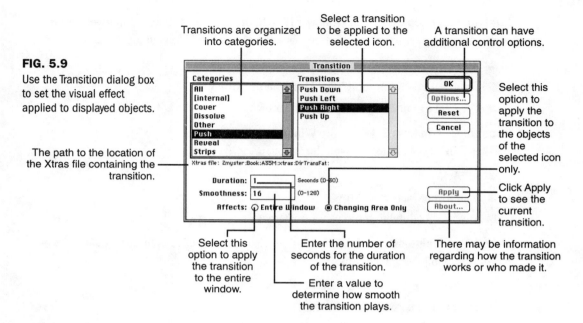

FIG. 5.9
Use the Transition dialog box to set the visual effect applied to displayed objects.

Transitions are organized into categories.

Select a transition to be applied to the selected icon.

A transition can have additional control options.

Select this option to apply the transition to the objects of the selected icon only.

The path to the location of the Xtras file containing the transition.

Click Apply to see the current transition.

Select this option to apply the transition to the entire window.

Enter the number of seconds for the duration of the transition.

There may be information regarding how the transition works or who made it.

Enter a value to determine how smooth the transition plays.

Let's take a quick look at each of the options in the Transition dialog box.

Categories   The list of Transitions has been broken into categories for easier reference. When a category name is selected in the Categories list, all of the transitions in that category appear in the Transitions list. If you do not know in which category a transition is located, select All to view all transitions in a single list.

> **N O T E**   Transitions can be created using the Xtras Developers Kit (XDK). Transitions, stored as Xtras, are typically written using the C++ programming format. ■

Transitions   Select a transition from the Transitions list to apply that transition to the selected icon.

> **N O T E**   Transition Categories and Names are established when the transition is created. ■

Transition Location   Transitions, by default, are stored in the Xtras directory. The path to the Xtras file containing the currently selected transition is shown just under the Categories window.

Duration   No matter which transition has been selected, you can establish the time required to complete the transition by entering a value, variable, or expression in the

Duration text box. The value must not be greater than 30 seconds; however, it can incorporate fractions such as 2.5.

N O T E Some transitions have a fixed Duration value that cannot be changed. ■

Smoothness Smoothness defines the rate at which the objects within the selected icon are displayed. The lower the value, variable, or expression in this text box, the finer or smoother the transition. Transitions are seen as smoother because smaller portions of the screen change in each unit of time.

For example, if you have selected an object to fade in and you set the Smoothness value to 1, the object displays a few pixels at a time based on the Duration setting. If, however, in the same Duration you set the Smoothness value to 128—the maximum—the objects appear in larger groups of pixels.

N O T E Some transitions have a fixed Smoothness value that cannot be changed. ■

Determining the Affects Setting A transition can either be applied to the entire Presentation Window or simply to the area of the Presentation Window in which new objects are being placed, depending on the choice you make in the Affects area of the Transition dialog box.

Considering Other Transition Effects Within the Transition dialog box, there are four command buttons that can be used to further fine-tune the transition, as follows:

- Options—If there are additional settings associated with the selected transition, this button will be active. Additional settings vary, based on the transition. For example, there may be additional timing settings, or possible opportunities to change color settings.
- Reset—This button restores the selected transition's original defaults for both duration and smoothness. This option is helpful if you have been experimenting with these settings, yet want to return to their initial values.
- Apply—Clicking this button enables you to preview the selected transition.

TIP A transition can be immediately completed by pressing the Escape key either during authoring or by your end user during the running of the final piece.

- About—If there is additional information associated with the selected transition, this button will be active. For example, the producer of the transition may have included contact information such as the address and phone number.

Part
II

Ch
5

N O T E   If two adjacent Flowline icons have the same transition setting, the contents of those
icons are displayed at the same time. To display each icon independently, separate
the icons with a Wait icon that uses the Time Limit option and a value of 0.1 seconds. ■

Other Places Transitions Are Used

Transitions are most commonly associated with the Display and Interaction icons. Transitions, however, can also be set in other locations.

Erase Icon   Just as transitions can be set for objects being displayed in the Presentation Window, they can also be set for objects being erased from the Presentation Window. (See Chapter 18, "Erasing Media," for more information.) To access the Transition dialog box from the Erase Options dialog box, click the Transition button shown in Figure 5.10.

FIG. 5.10
You can use the Transition
dialog box to set the visual
effect applied to erased
objects.

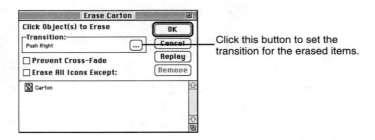

Click this button to set the
transition for the erased items.

 T I P   You can also select the Erase icon on the Flowline, then choose the Transition command from the
Attributes menu to set the transition for an Erase icon.

Interaction Icon   A transition can be applied to the automatic erase associated with the Interaction icon. To access the Transition dialog box from the Interaction dialog box, click the Transition button shown in Figure 5.11.

FIG. 5.11
Use the Transition dialog box
to automatically erase an
Interaction icon.

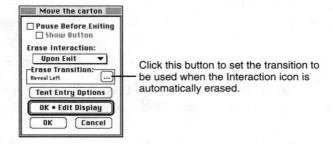

Click this button to set the transition to
be used when the Interaction icon is
automatically erased.

▶ To learn more about applying a transition to an Interaction icon, **see** "Erase Transition," **p. 233**.

▶ For guidance on erasing the contents of an Interaction icon, **see** "Automatically Erasing the Contents of an Interaction Icon," **p. 361**.

> **CAUTION**
>
> You must click the Transition button from the Interaction dialog box to set the transition to be used when the contents of the Interaction icon are automatically erased. If you select the Interaction icon on the Flowline and then choose the Transition command from the Attributes menu, you will set the transition used when the contents of the Interaction icon are displayed, not erased.

Return If you have selected the Resume option in the When User Returns portion of the File Setup dialog box, you can also define a transition to be used when the piece is executed. To access the Transition dialog box from the File Setup dialog box, click the Transition button shown in Figure 5.12.

FIG. 5.12
The selected transition is used each time the piece is executed.

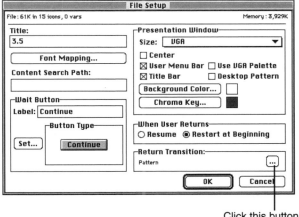

Click this button to set the transition to be used when the user returns to the program.

▶ For more information on applying a return transition, **see** "Return Transition," **p. 57**.

CHAPTER 6

Pausing the Presentation

Timing. Not only is it the most important element in comedy, it also plays a major role in interactive multimedia. In fact, the biggest proponents of interactive learning have always agreed that a strong benefit of this media is the ability for the end user to control the pace of the presentation.

If you think about the context out of which that benefit arose, you will see that controlling the pace is only the first step in the movement from a linear monologue to a truly interactive dialog. Prior to interactive multimedia, all forms of presented instruction—the classroom lecture and video, for example—hindered the user from learning if his or her rate of absorption varied from the rate in which the information was presented. With the capability to control the pace, those rates can be matched more closely, and therefore increase learning.

The problem today is that many multimedia authors have not moved away from the traditional art of placing control points within a linear monologue. And while

Pausing the flow of a multimedia piece

The Authorware Wait icon is used to pause the flow of a multimedia piece until the user clicks a button, presses a key, or until a specific amount of time elapses.

The pausing of a multimedia piece can occur automatically

Both the Decision icon and the Interaction icon have features that cause the piece to automatically pause.

Why would I use the Wait icon?

The Wait icon is used to create pauses. Pauses are used in the linear presentation of information that is either controlled by the end user, or sequenced within a specific amount of time.

Creating a custom pause button

The default button can be substituted with a custom, graphically designed object.

they may be able to achieve increased learning, they have yet to recognize the greater benefits of creating a dialog between the user and the piece.

This chapter presents several methods for controlling the pace of a piece created using Authorware. At the same time, I will continue to urge you to quickly move past linear presentations and on to the creation of "interactive" multimedia. ■

Building Pauses

Controlling the pace of a multimedia piece can be done in either of two ways. You can create interactivity or simply pause the presentation until the user clicks a button, presses a key (keep in mind, that the drone-clicking of a button is not interactivity because the user's mind may never become engaged), or until a given period of time elapses.

▶ For guidance on building interactions, **see** "Introducing Interactions," **p. 212**.

▶ For assistance in determining which form of interactivity is appropriate for the content, **see** "Defining Interactivity," **p. 536**.

N O T E Interactive multimedia, by definition, suggests that the user will be interactive or—at the root of the word—be active. If the piece needs to be paused, therefore meaning it is self-running, the user is typically in a passive state. Try creating a design that keeps the user involved. ■

Using the Wait Icon

There are several ways to build pauses into an Authorware piece without using interactivity. The most common is to place a Wait icon, as seen in Figure 6.1, onto the Flowline where the pause is to occur.

▶ To refer to the introduction of the Wait icon, **see** "The Wait Icon," **p. 17**.

The Authorware Wait icon

FIG. 6.1

The Wait icon is used to pause the flow of the multimedia piece.

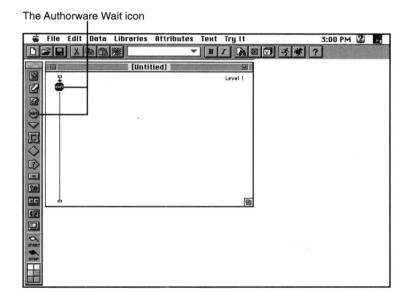

When a Wait icon is encountered along the Flowline, the piece pauses until certain parameters that you established are met. Parameters for a particular Wait icon are established within the Wait Options dialog box, as seen in Figure 6.2. Each Wait icon placed on the Flowline can be set with different parameters; however, each one will use the same on-screen button if the Show Button option is used. I will discuss the Show Button option later in this section.

To open the Wait Options dialog box, double-click the Wait icon on the Flowline.

When the running piece encounters a Wait icon, the piece does not stop so that the Wait options can be defined, as with other undefined icons or options. The default settings for the Wait icon are enough to pause the flow of the piece. When the end user clicks the Wait button, or presses a key that is also a default option, the piece continues.

Although the Wait icon is commonly used without altering the default settings, you can control any of the options in the Wait Options dialog box. If the Wait icon options are not

Part

II

Ch

6

altered, a Pause button is placed in the Presentation Window. To proceed with the piece, the end user must click the Pause button, or press any key on the keyboard.

FIG. 6.2
Wait options are set within the Wait Options dialog box.

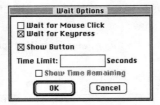

Wait for Mouse Click   The Wait for Mouse Click option concludes the pause, causing the piece to continue when the user clicks the mouse button. If the Pause button is present, the user does not have to click it but can click anywhere in the Presentation Window.

I like to use this option when presenting a brief amount of information, like in a dialog box. Rather than selecting to show the button, or requiring that the user select the button, the user can click anywhere in the Presentation Window to have the information go away and the piece continue.

 If the Pause button is not present, provide a prompt that informs the end users that they are required to click anywhere in the Presentation Window in order to continue with the piece.

Wait for Keypress   The default option Wait for Keypress causes the Wait icon to act somewhat like it does when the Wait for Mouse Click option is selected; however, in this case, pressing any key will cause the piece to continue.

N O T E   When the Wait for Keypress option is selected, the Wait icon does not respond to the Command (⌘), Option, Shift, Cap Locks, or Control keys on the Macintosh, or the Ctrl or Alt keys in Windows. ■

 If the Pause button is not present, provide a prompt to inform the end users that they must press a key on the keyboard to continue with the piece.

Show Button   Another default option, Show Button, causes the Pause button to be placed in the Presentation Window when the piece pauses. The pause button graphic is dependent on what you have established in the File Setup dialog box.

▶ To refer to the introduction of the File Setup dialog box, **see** "Wait Button," **p. 49**.
▶ For information on using the Button Editor to change the Pause button, **see** "Using The Button Editor," **p. 245**.

If neither the Wait for Mouse Click nor Wait for Keypress option is selected, and there is no time limit, the user must click directly on the Pause button for the piece to continue beyond the wait.

When authoring, the button can be repositioned or resized when the flow of the piece is paused. Once the flow of the piece is paused, click the button so that handles appear, and then either drag the object to reposition it or drag a handle to resize the button.

 To pause a running piece, choose Pause from the Try It pull-down menu, or press the ⌘+P (Macintosh) or Ctrl+P (Windows) keys.

If you reposition or re-size a Pause button, any new Pause buttons that are created thereafter will be automatically placed in the same position and sized accordingly. We will look at customizing the Pause button in the next section.

 If you double-click the Pause button that appears in the Presentation Window, the Wait Options dialog box will appear.

Time Limit   The Time Limit option causes the piece to automatically continue after the designated amount of time specified in seconds has expired. If the user clicks the mouse button or presses a key before the amount of time expires, and the Time Limit option is selected, the piece will continue.

> **CAUTION**
>
> I have seen many pieces that use timed waits to separate screens of textual content. This is not a good idea for several reasons. First, if you happen to read faster than your slowest-reading end user and you set the time to match your pace, the piece will continue before the user has read all the content. Second, if the person sneezes, answers the phone, or says hello to a passer-by, the piece could change screens without the end user being aware. Remember, one benefit to interactive multimedia is that the user is in control of the pace.

I have found it very helpful to enter the Authorware variable `IconTitle` into the Time Limit field and then title the icon with a number representing the number of seconds I want the piece to pause. This has allowed me to quickly change the pause time without opening the Wait Options dialog box. Additionally, I am more able to determine how my piece will run when this information exists on the Flowline level by seeing the number of seconds the piece will pause.

Part
II

Ch
6

IconTitle is an Authorware general variable. We will discuss using variables in greater detail in Chapter 19, "Using Functions and Variables."

▶ For further guidance on using functions and variables, **see** "Working with Variables and Functions," **p. 366**.

If the Time Limit option is selected, the Show Time Remaining option becomes available. Checking the Show Time Remaining option produces a small clock on the screen, as seen in Figure 6.3.

FIG. 6.3
The clock counts down the time remaining until the piece continues.

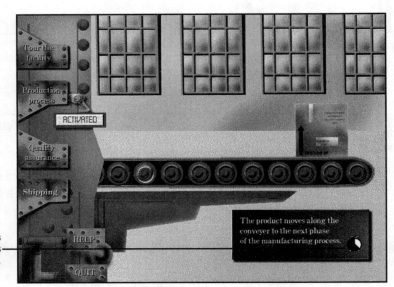

If Show Time Remaining is selected, the clock counts down the remaining time.

TIP If you double-click the clock that appears in the Presentation Window, the Wait Options dialog box will appear.

Other Methods for Pausing

Pauses are also associated with the Interaction icon or the Decision icon. Each of these icons gives you the option to pause the piece before further branching occurs.

▶ For instruction on setting automatic pausing using the Interaction icon, **see** "Pause Before Exiting," **p. 231**.

▶ For guidance on establishing automatic pausing using the Decision icon, **see** "Taking Advantage of Automatic Pausing," **p. 349**.

Common Uses for the Wait Icon

The Wait icon is designed to allow you, the author, to pause the final piece for a specific period of time or until the user clicks the mouse or presses a key. While I do not use the Wait icon for this purpose very often, I have found the Wait icon to be tremendously helpful in other aspects of the development process.

Let's look at two methods for employing the Wait icon.

Linear Presentations

The Wait icon is used to momentarily pause the piece, and after the pause is terminated, the piece continues. The result of this sequence is a linear presentation, whether it is two screens or two hundred screens in length.

Linear presentations are created using the Wait icon in either of the two ways described next.

User-Controlled Pace   By separating screens of content with the Wait icon, the user can control the pace at which those screens are displayed. When the flow of the piece is paused, the user can either press the button if it has been displayed, or press a key, to proceed. Both of these controls are based on the settings established in the Wait Options dialog box.

 T I P   This same linear sequence can be produced using the Decision icon.

Self-Running Pieces   Self-running pieces, unlike user-controlled pieces, separate screens of content with a pause that only lasts a determined amount of time. Without being prompted by the user, the piece automatically moves from one screen of information to the next.

While there are a few places where automatically advancing the piece is appropriate, in most cases, this is a bad habit to adopt. A good use for automatic advancing is in the presentation of a title screen for your piece. This screen appears for a few seconds, then goes away. If the user does not get a chance to study the contents, no harm is done.

Additionally, if you are simulating a piece of equipment or an animated process, you might need to pause the flow of the piece for a few seconds throughout the sequence.

Part
II

Ch
6

> **CAUTION**
>
> Timed pauses behave differently as you move the multimedia piece from machine to machine. Processor speed and RAM each affect the performance and the time it takes to re-draw the screen after a pause.

With these examples in mind, avoid automatically advancing the piece when text or new information, which may require study by your end user, is presented.

Debugging

The best use that I have found for the Wait icon is as a tool for development rather than as a feature for my final piece. For example, if I created a piece with several branches, one of which will be selected via some complex formula, I will place Wait icons in each of the branches.

When the piece begins running down the Flowline, it executes the formula, selects one of the many branches, and then hits the Wait icon and halts. At that point, I can go to the Flowline and see which branch has been chosen. If the correct branch was chosen, I will proceed with the piece by clicking the button. If the wrong branch was chosen, I will adjust the formula, then try running again.

When the piece is running correctly, I simply delete the Wait icons and then move on to the next area to be developed. Using the Wait icon in this manner makes it a tool to assist in development, more than a feature for the end user.

Allowing the user to control the pace of the presentation by using the Wait icon will return some benefits; however, I urge you to seek out a design with greater interactivity. Use the Wait icon to control the pace of animation, or to quickly present information on the screen, but avoid long linear presentations of information.

Changing the Wait Button

When the running piece encounters a Wait icon, a labeled Pause button is displayed in the Presentation Window by default. You can change the characteristics of this button using the File Setup dialog box, which was covered in detail in Chapter 2, "Setting Up an Authorware Piece," and is shown in Figure 6.4.

▶ To refer to the introduction of the File Setup dialog box, **see** "Wait Button," **p. 49**.

▶ For information on using the Button Editor to change the Pause button, **see** "Using the Button Editor," **p. 245**.

FIG. 6.4

The default Pause button can be changed in the File Setup dialog box.

Because Authorware globally sets the Label and Button Type for the Wait icon, you must select an appropriate combination for your entire piece. For this reason, I use an Interaction loop rather than the Wait icon for pauses that require the user's response before continuing. By using an interaction loop, I can incorporate a variety of custom graphics that the end user can interact with to proceed the piece.

Part

II

Ch

6

Naming the Wait Icon

Unlike other icons within Authorware, when a Wait icon is placed on the Flowline, it does not have the default name "Untitled." Naming the Wait icon is commonly avoided because Wait icons are fairly simple, and they do not hold content that is displayed.

▶ For details on selecting the name for an icon, **see** "Naming and Identifying Icons," **p. 200**.

 TIP I suggest naming the Wait icon if you have changed any of the default settings so that you can see that it is not a normal Wait icon on the Flowline.

CHAPTER 7

Making Objects Move

Since the birth of the computer, we have all been fasci-
nated by the capability to make objects move across
the screen. In fact, one of the very first computer
games, Pong, was nothing more than a dot, which
represented a ball, and two lines, which represented
paddles, moving in tandem. The thrill of the ball bounc-
ing and the user's capability to control the movement of
the paddle, however, were enough to captivate early
computer gamers.

This fascination with on-screen movement continues
today, even though our imagination and our expectations for computer animation have grown. Interactive
entertainment titles, reference pieces, and instructional
pieces alike all seem to incorporate moving objects.

All about moving objects

Within Authorware there are two
basic forms of movement: path
animation and realistic animation.

Understanding the To Fixed Point motion

The To Fixed Point motion moves
an object from the point in which it
is displayed to a specific destination.
This is the most simple, and the
default, motion type.

Using the To End motion

The To End motion allows objects to
be moved along a path that contains
angled corners and curves.

Creating movement using the Calculated Point On Line motion

The Calculated Point On Line motion moves objects along a designated line based on a value, variable,
or expression.

Using the To Calculated Point motion

The To Calculated Point motion
allows objects to be moved along an
irregurlarly shaped path based on a
value, variable, or expression.

Understanding the To Calculated Point On Grid motion

Sophisticated positioning of an
object can occur using the To Calculated Point On Grid motion.

Authorware provides five types of movement. This chapter introduces you to these movement types, as well as to the specialized functions. ■

All About Moving Objects

Within Authorware, there are two basic kinds of movement: path animation and realistic animation. Although this chapter will focus on path animation, it is helpful to have an understanding of the difference between the two types. In Chapter 20, "Working with Digital Movies," we will take a closer look at realistic animation when we discuss the Digital Movie icon.

▶ For a closer look at realistic animation, **see** "Introducing the Digital Movie Icon," **p. 395**.

Path animation, created using the Motion icon, enables an object, such as the graphic of a ball, a video, or some text, to traverse the Presentation Window within a given amount of time. During movement, the object will not change orientation, shape, or size. For example, the carton moving along the conveyor in Figure 7.1 demonstrates path animation, but the rotating of the conveyor wheels evinces realistic animation.

Realistic animation does enable a ball to spin, video to scroll, and text to morph. The physical location of the animation, however, might not change position within the Presentation Window, as in the example in Figure 7.2.

FIG. 7.1
Path animation does not
change the orientation of
an object, but merely the
object's position within the
Presentation Window.

This object will simply move
across the Presentation
Window without changing
orientation.

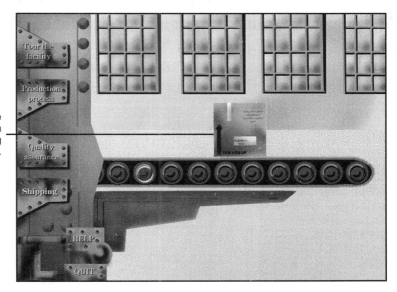

FIG. 7.2
Realistic animation enables
the attributes and the
orientation of an object to
change.

With realistic animation, the helicopter blades can turn.

N O T E You can use path animation to change the position of a realistic animation in the
Presentation Window. For example, the realistic animation of the helicopter in
Figure 7.2 can be moved across the screen using path animation. ▇

Part

II

Ch

7

When to Use Path Animation

To better define path animation, let's look at a few places where it is commonly used. In each of the examples described next, you will note that the object that is being moved does not physically change, but merely its position in the Presentation Window changes.

Moving a Static Object   The most obvious form of path animation is the movement of a static object within the Presentation Window. In the example in Figure 7.3, the car is the object being moved along the roadway by the Motion icon.

FIG. 7.3
The most obvious form of path animation is a static object moving across the screen, such as a car traveling along a roadway.

The static graphic of a car is animated across the Presentation Window.

Using the Motion Icon to Build Highlights   Motion does not have to be as obvious as an object moving across the Presentation Window. In some cases, you can use the Motion icon to create the illusion of one object erasing, then reappearing in another location.

In Figure 7.4, the pointer graphic that is used as a highlight to indicate which option was selected was positioned using the Motion icon. When the pointer moves to the new location, it moves in zero seconds, giving the illusion that it was erased and then redisplayed.

 TIP   Using the Motion icon to position highlights—rather than creating multiple graphics—can dramatically reduce file size. Additionally, because only one graphic is required for the entire menu of options, rather than one graphic for each of the possible selections, the effort required to make edits to the graphic is minimal.

FIG. 7.4
Motion can be used to position menu or selection highlights rather than erasing and redisplaying the graphical object.

Motion is used to position this menu selection highlight.

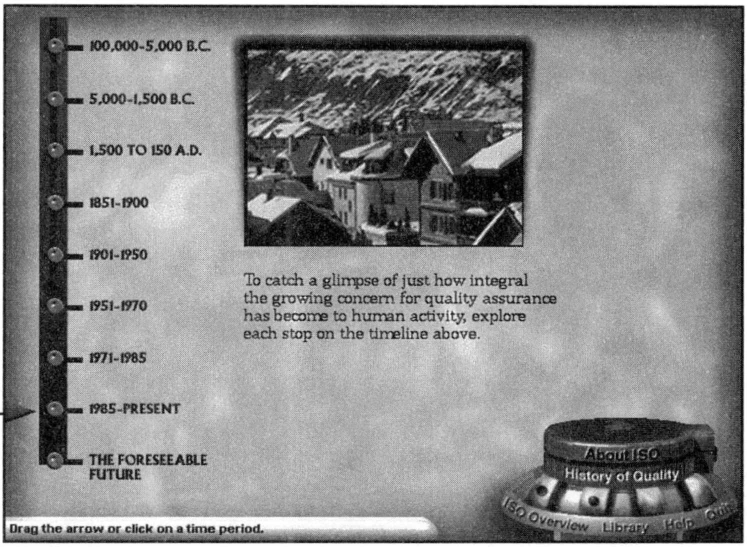

Used with permission by QTech, Inc.

Moving a Digital Movie with the Motion Icon   While the Motion icon cannot be used to create realistic animation, it can be used to move a realistic animation created elsewhere across the Presentation Window.

For example, if you want a helicopter, complete with rotating blades, to buzz across the screen, you will first need to create the helicopter with rotating blades using an external animation application such as Macromedia Director. Once the helicopter movie is created, you must import it into Authorware using the Digital Movie icon.

Finally, you can move the helicopter animation across the Presentation Window, as illustrated in Figure 7.5, using the Motion icon.

Thinking about motion as the repositioning of an object or media within the Presentation Window, based on a specified period of time, will help you recognize other opportunities for using the Motion icon.

▶ For step-by-step guidance on importing a digital movie into Authorware, **see** "Introducing the Digital Movie Icon," **p. 395**.

FIG. 7.5
The Motion icon can be
used to move a realistic
animation.

Motion Types Within Authorware

Authorware supports five types of motion, as seen in the Motion Type dialog box shown
in Figure 7.6. Let's take a closer look at the five motion types that you can create using the
Motion icon, and a few pointers regarding each.

FIG. 7.6
You can select one of five motion types for a Motion icon.

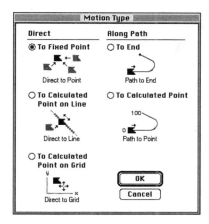

To Fixed Point (Direct to Point)   The To Fixed Point, or Direct to Point, motion type moves an object from the point it is displayed in a straight line to a specified ending position. No angles or curves can exist in the course that the movement takes.

 T I P   You can give the illusion that an object starts from outside of the Presentation Window by setting the initial display position out of view. Likewise, you can make an object "run off" of, or exit, the Presentation Window by adjusting the end point of the motion. If you use this trick, however, be sure that the object is erased once it is out of view.

In the conveyor belt example (refer to Fig. 7.1), the carton moved from the point it was displayed to a fixed ending point using the To Fixed Point motion type.

N O T E   The To Fixed Point motion type is the default for the Motion icon. ■

To End (Path to End)   The To End, or Path to End, motion type moves an object from the point it is displayed in the Presentation Window along a specified path to an ending point. Unlike the To Fixed Point motion type, the path for the To End motion type can contain angles and curves.

N O T E   I could have used this motion type to create a path along the conveyor in Figure 7.1, but because the carton was going to move in a straight line to a fixed destination, it was easier to use the default To Fixed Point motion type. ■

For example, if I have a schematic drawing of the manufacturing facility, I can move a ball around that diagram to illustrate product flow.

When implementing a To End motion, be sure the design of your object logically coincides with its intended motion. In the schematic drawing example just mentioned, the ball can be moved in any direction. If I selected an arrow, however, it might be pointing in the wrong direction in some cases.

To Calculated Point (Path to Point)   The To Calculated Point motion type moves an object from the point it is displayed, along a path for which you determine a beginning point and ending point value, to a relative stopping point along that path.

To better understand this motion type, think of the path as a tape measure for which you set the scale. You can then move the object along the path to a specific point according to the scale. For example, you might need to precisely position a gauge on a piece of equipment during a simulation.

N O T E   Unless you are precisely determining the object's position, you can use the To End motion type to create the same movement as the To Calculated Point motion. Both motion types allow you to create a path, but only the To Calculated Point allows you to precisely position the object along the path.

To Calculated Point On Line (Direct to Line)   The To Calculated Point On Line, or Direct to Line, motion type moves an object from the point it is displayed in the Presentation Window, along a line for which you determine a beginning point and ending point value, to a relative stopping point along that line.

This motion type is much like the To Calculated Point option, except the object can only move along a linear path. No curves or angles can be incorporated in the motion path. For example, we could use this motion type to position the gauge in our simulation if the path is a straight line.

To Calculated Point On Grid (Direct to Grid)   The To Calculated Point On Grid, or Direct to Grid, motion type moves an object from the point it is displayed to a relative stopping point within a grid for which you determine a vertical and a horizontal scale.

For example, you might have a control panel with a series of switches, as shown in Figure 7.7. The object that you will be positioning is a graphic of the switch in the On position, which would mask over the switch in the Off position. Using the To Calculated Point On Grid motion type, you could position the *On* switch.

Later in this chapter, I will give step-by-step instructions for creating each of the five motion types, as well as provide further guidance as to when one motion type would be used rather than another.

FIG. 7.7
The To Calculated Point On Grid motion type is used to position objects within an established grid in the Presentation Window.

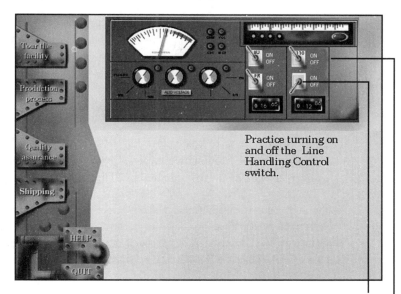

The Off switch can be positioned using a To Calculated Point On Grid motion.

The four switches are aligned in a grid.—

Setting Up the Motion

The Authorware Motion icon, shown in Figure 7.8, is the tool used to develop path animation. As we have seen, movement can occur along a path, within the parameters of the Presentation Window, or simply to a final destination, which might be outside of the Presentation Window.

FIG. 7.8
The Motion icon is used to create path animation.

The Motion icon —

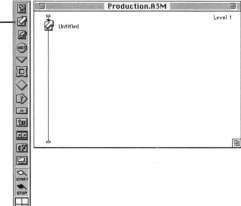

Similar to the Erase icon, the Motion icon is applied to the object(s) within an icon that has been previously displayed in the Presentation Window (see Fig. 7.9). The previously displayed object(s), however, does not need to be within the icon immediately preceding the Motion icon. For an understanding of how the Erase icon and the Motion icon are similar, see Chapter 18, "Erasing Media."

To apply the Motion icon to an object, follow these steps:

1. Create an object to be displayed in the Presentation Window. Objects that can be moved by the Motion icon include those created in a Display icon or Interaction icon, as well as those contained in a Digital Movie icon.

N O T E If you are displaying more than one object in an icon, and you intend for only one of the objects to be moved, it is necessary to place the object that will move into a separate icon. All of the contents of a single Display icon are moved with a single Motion icon, just like all of the objects of a single icon are erased by the Erase icon.

Additionally, the course of the motion is based on the center point for all objects in an icon. Therefore, if you have several objects, or an irregularly shaped object, the course or path of the Motion may be different than anticipated. ■

FIG. 7.9

Objects that will be moved by the Motion icon need to be displayed separately from objects that either will not be moved or will be moved by a different Motion icon.

The background will not move.

The carton will move.

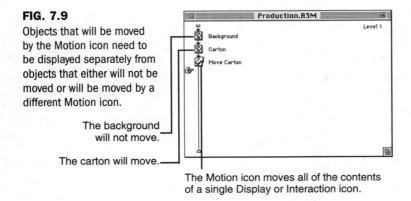

The Motion icon moves all of the contents of a single Display or Interaction icon.

2. Place a Motion icon on the Flowline. The Motion icon will be encountered after the object that is being moved has been displayed. Name the Motion icon so that it helps describe what motion it will be used to create.

3. Open the Motion dialog box by double-clicking the Motion icon. The title across the top of the Motion dialog box is based on the title that you gave to that Motion icon, as we will discuss in the next section "Understanding the Motion Dialog Box."

At this point you can either proceed with the default To Fixed Point motion type, or you can click the Change Type button to select a different motion type. I will discuss changing motion types in greater detail in the section "Changing Motion Types."

4. Once the motion type has been established, you must define the motion by dragging the objects to be moved and entering values into the requested fields. I will cover the details for the various motion types later in this chapter.

5. Click the Replay button to check the accuracy of the motion.

6. Click the OK button to close the Motion dialog box and to save your settings.

For the remainder of this chapter, I will refer to these steps as *setting up* a motion. To learn more about creating objects and moving objects into separate icons, see Chapter 4, "Working with Graphics and Objects."

Understanding the Motion Dialog Box

As mentioned in Step 3 of the preceding section, once a Motion icon is opened, the Motion icon dialog box is presented. Each motion type has a unique dialog box, depending on the type of motion that has been selected. The type of motion for which the dialog box is used, however, is displayed in the upper right-hand corner of each dialog box (see Fig. 7.10).

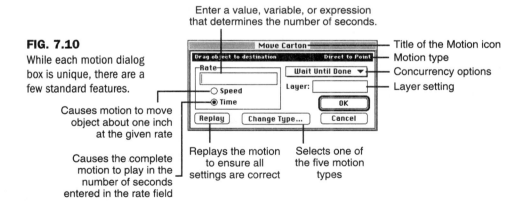

Enter a value, variable, or expression that determines the number of seconds.

FIG. 7.10
While each motion dialog box is unique, there are a few standard features.

Causes motion to move object about one inch at the given rate

Causes the complete motion to play in the number of seconds entered in the rate field

Replays the motion to ensure all settings are correct

Selects one of the five motion types

— Title of the Motion icon
— Motion type
— Concurrency options
— Layer setting

In Step 1 of the preceding section, you were instructed to title the Motion icon on the Flowline according to the motion for which it will be used to create. The title that you give the Motion icon will be displayed across the top of the dialog box (refer to Fig. 7.10). Since each icon can be titled differently, it is more than likely that each dialog box will have a unique heading. In all cases, I will refer to this dialog box as the Motion dialog box.

Part
II

Ch
7

Changing Motion Types

When a Motion icon is first introduced to the Flowline, its default motion type is To Fixed Point. You may elect to use the To Fixed Point motion or change to another motion type. To change from one motion type to another, follow these steps:

1. Open the Motion icon by double-clicking it. When you do this, you will be able to see the object you intend to move as well as the current motion dialog box.

> **N O T E** Keep in mind that the default motion type is the To Fixed Point. If you are opening the Motion icon for the first time, you will see the To Fixed Point Motion dialog box. ■

2. Click the Change Type button to change from the current motion type to the new motion type (refer to Fig. 7.10).

3. Select the desired motion type option from the Motion Type dialog box, seen in Figure 7.11.

FIG. 7.11
You can select one of five motion types for each Motion icon.

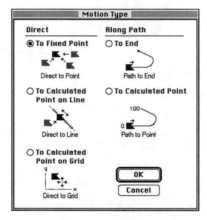

4. Click OK to save your selection. You notice that the Motion dialog box changes to reflect your current selection.

From this point, I will assume that you know how to perform these steps, which I will refer to as *changing* the motion type.

Understanding the Rate Settings

The rate settings are used to determine the speed—in seconds—at which the defined motion will occur. You establish a rate by entering a value, variable, or expression into the Motion dialog box Rate field (refer to Fig. 7.10). This rate is initially determined based on the amount of time it took you to establish the ending point for the motion, or it is a minimum value based on the selected motion type.

To change the rate, simply overwrite this value with a new rate.

N O T E Placing a zero in the rate field, or leaving it blank, causes the object to jump into position rather than animating across the Presentation Window.

Within the Motion dialog box there are two additional settings for Rate, described next.

Time Selecting the Time option causes the motion to play back at the precise number of seconds entered in the Rate field. The movement of the object plays back at this exact rate, regardless of the distance to be traveled.

CAUTION

When an animation is set to play at a high rate, yet it is played on a machine with a slow processor, such as a 386/33mHz, fewer displays per second can be generated. This results in a jumpy animation.

The Time option is used when the animation must take place within a given amount of time, regardless of the distance traveled. For example, you may have an animation that shows that if a planet with a smaller orbit completed its journey in the same amount of time as a planet with a larger orbit, the planet with the smaller orbit would have to cover the distance at a much slower pace. In this example, the Rate setting would be the same for both animations, but the planet with the larger orbit would travel faster because it has a greater distance to travel in the same amount of time as the planet with the smaller orbit.

Speed Selecting the Speed option button, on the other hand, causes the object to move about one inch (72 pixels, for example) at the rate (time) you specify. Therefore, the distance to be traveled greatly affects the amount of time it will take to complete the movement.

N O T E The default rate setting is Time.

For example, if you set up an animation to move an object from one side of the Presentation Window to the other (640 pixels) and you have selected a rate of two seconds, the object will travel across the screen in two seconds if the Time option is selected. If the Speed option is selected, however, it will take roughly 18 seconds (640 pixels divided by 72 pixels per inch multiplied by two seconds per inch equals 18 seconds) for the entire motion to play.

Using the planet example from above, if the Rate settings were the same, and the Speed option were selected, the planets would travel the same distance in an equal amount of time. The planet with the smaller orbit, however, would make more trips around the center point than the planet with the larger orbit since the overall distance is shorter.

Setting the Concurrency Options

Within the Motion dialog box there are several options for Concurrency. Concurrency settings are used to determine what Authorware will do while the motion is taking place. The Concurrency settings are described next.

Wait Until Done   This option causes the motion to play completely before the next Authorware icon on the Flowline is executed.

For example, if you want a motion to play completely before a question is asked about the motion, select Wait Until Done.

> **N O T E**   The default for this option is Wait Until Done. ▪

Concurrent   Unlike Wait Until Done, Concurrent suggests that as soon as the current motion begins, the next Authorware icon on the Flowline is executed.

For example, if you design audio to accompany the motion, setting the motion to Concurrent will start the motion playing and then Authorware will move on to start the audio.

Perpetual   A Motion icon with a Perpetual concurrency setting will play whenever the object to be animated is displayed and a given expression is true. We will explore controlling a Motion icon with data in Chapter 22, "Working with Data."

▶ For information on controlling a motion with a value, variable, or expression, **see** "Using Data to Control Perpetual Motion Icons," **p. 441**.

> **N O T E**   The Perpetual option is only available for To End, To Calculated Point On Line, To Calculated Point, and To Calculated Point On Grid motion types. The Perpetual option is not available for To Fixed Point motions. ▪

Animating in Layers

In many instances, you will want one object to pass in front of or behind another when in motion. For example, you might want the carton moving along the conveyor to pass behind an equipment operator (see Fig. 7.12). To accomplish this, you must animate the objects in layers.

The carton is moving behind the operator.

FIG. 7.12
Animating in layers enables one object to pass behind another.

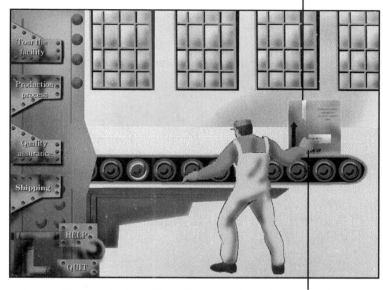

The operator is positioned in a higher layer than the moving carton.

Using animation layers is no different than using the layer option within the Effects dialog box. When an object passes in front of another (that is, it appears to be closer to you visually), it is animating at a higher layer. Therefore, the equipment operator will be on a higher layer than the carton so that the carton passes behind it visually.

Animating objects in layers can be accomplished in two ways. First, if several Motion icons are executed at once by setting them to play concurrently (using the Concurrent option), the last one to start playing will animate at the highest layer (that is, the "top" layer that appears closest to the viewer). In the example of the carton and the operator, you can start the animation of the carton moving across the screen, then begin the animation of the operator. Because the animation of the operator was the last to be executed, the operator assumes the highest layer and will pass in front of the carton visually.

The second way to animate an object on a layer is to actually assign a layer to the animation. Layers can be assigned a position by entering a value or variable into the Layer field. By assigning a layer to a Motion icon, the object will pass in front of any objects that are animating at a layer with a lower value assigned, or that have been assigned a lower display layer. Likewise, the object will pass behind any objects that are animating at a higher layer.

Part
II

Ch
7

▶ To gain a better understanding of using layers, **see** "Understanding Layers," **p. 145**

▶ To learn more about assigning layers, **see** "Shuffling the Layers," **p. 146**.

 T I P You may also set the layer of a Display icon to a higher value than that of the animation, which will cause the animation (the carton) to move behind the objects within the Display icon (the operator.)

N O T E If you do not assign a layer to a Motion icon, the default is zero. Zero is typically the lowest layer, although layers may be set to a negative number. Even though the layer of the motion is zero, however, when an object is in motion, it assumes a higher layer than other objects that have the same layer setting and are not in motion. ▪

Now that we have explored attributes the five motion types have in common, let's look at each of the motion types in greater detail to understand their differences, as well as to see how each motion type is applied.

Moving Objects Using the To Fixed Point Motion Type

The To Fixed Point motion is the default for the Motion icon. This motion type moves an object from the point it is displayed in the Presentation Window to a destination you establish.

To Fixed Point motions are the simplest in functionality and the easiest to set up. You can use To Fixed Point motions whenever you have an object that will move from the point it was displayed to a final destination along a straight path.

N O T E To Fixed Point motions can only be used if you do not intend to control the motion with a variable or expression. If you must control the movement using a variable or expression, consider using the To Calculated Point or To Calculated Point On Line motion types. ▪

Creating a To Fixed Point Motion

Once you have set up a motion, as discussed in the section "Setting Up the Motion," earlier in the chapter, establishing a To Fixed Point motion is relatively simple. To create a To Fixed Point motion, follow these steps:

1. Open the Motion icon by double-clicking it. When you do this, you will be able to see the object you intend to move as well as the To Fixed Point Motion dialog box shown in Figure 7.13.

Prompt

FIG. 7.13
The To Fixed Point Motion dialog box is the default for a Motion icon.

The object will move at the rate entered in this field.

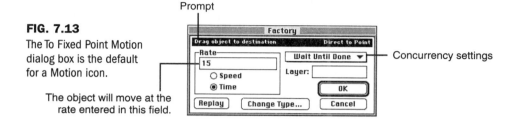

Concurrency settings

2. Drag the object you intend to move from the point it was displayed to the point where you want it to remain once the motion is complete.

3. The amount of time that it took you to drag the object will appear in the Rate portion of the dialog box. You can overwrite this entry with the amount of time you want it to take for the object to move to the destination point. (See "Understanding the Rate Settings," earlier in this chapter.)

4. Click the Replay button to see the motion replay. To make adjustments to the final destination, simply drag the object being moved to the new position. To adjust the rate, simply overwrite the displayed time with a new entry.

5. Click the OK button to save the settings.

Moving Objects Using the To End Motion Type

The To End motion type moves an object from the beginning point of an established path to a fixed end point. Unlike the To Fixed Point motion type, however, you can edit the path so that it is not a direct line to the destination.

N O T E The beginning point of the path may be positioned differently than the point at which the object was initially displayed in the Presentation Window. If this is the case, the object will jump to the beginning point of the path from its initial display position when the motion begins. This functionality may be either a problem, or a benefit, depending on your design. ▪

Part
II

Ch
7

Creating a To End Motion

Defining a To End motion is a little more involved than defining a To Fixed Point motion. With this motion type, you must define a path by creating critical points within the Presentation Window through which the object will move.

Once you have set up the motion, as discussed in the section "Setting Up the Motion," earlier in this chapter, follow these steps to create a To End motion:

1. Open the Motion icon by double-clicking it. When you do this, you see the object you intend to move as well as the default To Fixed Point Motion dialog box.

2. Change the motion type to a To End motion type, as discussed previously in this chapter in the section "Changing Motion Types." Notice that the Motion icon dialog box has changed to the To End Motion dialog box as seen in Figure 7.14.

FIG. 7.14

The To End Motion dialog box is different than the To Fixed Point Motion dialog box in that it allows you to create a path along which the motion will occur.

3. Unlike the To Fixed Point motion, you do not drag the object to create a path. Instead, you first click the object you want to move.

 TIP   The prompt along the top of the dialog box instructs you for each step in creating a To End motion.

Once you have clicked the object, a small triangle appears in its center. This is the beginning point for the motion path.

4. Now that you have established the beginning point of the path, drag the object you intend to move to the next point on the path. Release the mouse when the object is at the point you want to create. When the mouse is released, another triangle point marker will appear.

TROUBLESHOOTING

Every time I try to move my object, I grab the point marker. How can I create a path if I can't drag the object? Dragging the object can be difficult to do if the object you are moving is small. If this is the case, create a larger object in the Display icon, set the path, delete the extra object, then go back and fine-tune the path using the triangle markers. Because a Motion icon moves all objects within a single Display icon, the smaller object will automatically adjust to the path.

5. Continue dragging the object to extend the path by creating additional points. Each time a point is created a small triangle marker will appear. Points can also be created by clicking on the path where a point is to be placed. (See "Adding a Point to a Path," later in this chapter.)

N O T E Authorware does not trace your movement to create the path like a pencil tool would in a drawing piece. Therefore, do not try to create a curved or complex path simply by dragging. You must release the mouse button to create critical points for the path. ■

Once a point has been created, it can be moved to a new position (see "Moving a Point on a Path," later in this chapter), or simply deleted (see "Deleting a Point on a Path," later in this chapter).

6. The default rate for the object to travel from the beginning point to the ending point in a To End motion is one second. You can overwrite this entry with the amount of time you want it to take for the object to move along the path.

7. Click the Replay button to see the motion replay. To make adjustments to the final destination, simply drag the object being moved or the triangle-shaped markers to a more precise location. To adjust the rate, simply overwrite the displayed time with a new entry.

8. Click the OK button to save the settings.

Editing Points of a Path

As you create a path along which an object will move, there are several ways to edit the points along that path, including adding, deleting, transforming, or moving. These different ways to edit a point are described next.

Adding a Point to a Path   To add a point to a path, simply click the path. When the point is set, a new marker will appear (see Fig. 7.15).

FIG. 7.15
You can edit the path
created by a To End motion.

Deletes currently selected marker

Undoes last action ⎯⎯

Circular critical point marker ⎯⎯

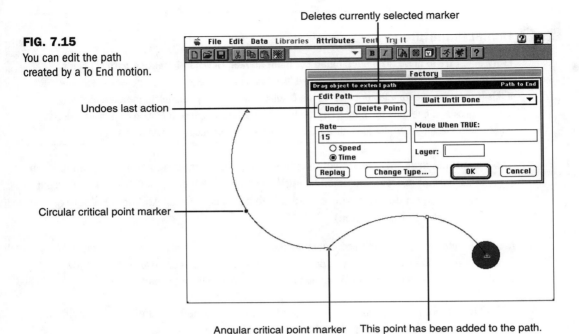

Angular critical point marker   This point has been added to the path.

Deleting a Point on a Path   To delete a point, select the point you want to delete, and click the Delete Point button in the To End Motion dialog box. To undo a deletion, click the Undo button in the To End Motion dialog box.

 While editing a path, the Delete key on the keyboard, and the Cut and Undo commands for both the Edit menu and the keyboard, are inactive.

Transforming a Point on a Path   By default, points along a path are angular. Angular points create corners along the path. By double-clicking the point marker—the small triangle—the angular point will turn into a curved point marker. Curved points smooth out the corner resulting in a curved path. Double-clicking the curved point marker reverts it to an angular point. To see a path that contains both angular points and curved, or circular points, refer to Figure 7.15.

 If while editing a path, you accidentally click an object located in an icon other than the one you intend to animate, Authorware will assume you now want to animate the newly identified object. To revert to the intended icon, simply click an object located in that icon, then continue editing the path.

N O T E Circular points are not edited using Bezier tools, as they are in most graphics applications. Unfortunately, therefore, the precise editing of a curved path can take some guesswork to create. ▦

Moving a Point on a Path   Any point marker can be moved by dragging it to a new location. The new location does not have to be located along the path. If the marker is moved off the path, the path will adjust to incorporate the new marker location.

TROUBLESHOOTING

I have to develop several To End motions that will all follow the same path. How do I make sure each path is the same? I often use the Line tool, or capture the screen of the first path I establish, to create a template. I place the template in a Display icon immediately preceding the Motion icon. When editing the Motion icon, I then develop the path according to the template. When I finish editing the motion, I delete the Display icon containing the template.

Moving Objects Using the To Calculated Point On Line

The To Calculated Point On Line motion type is used to create a perfectly straight line between two points along which an object will move. It differs from the To End motion type in that you can only create a beginning and an ending point. (See "Moving Objects Using the To End Motion Type," previously in this chapter), and from the To Fixed Point motion type in that a variable or expression may be used to control the placement of the object along the defined path. (See "Moving Objects Using the To Fixed Point Motion Type," previously in this chapter.)

Creating a To Calculated Point On Line Motion

Once you have set up the motion, as discussed earlier in this chapter in the section "Setting Up the Motion," follow these steps to create a To Calculated Point On Line motion:

1. Open the Motion icon by double-clicking it. When you do this, you will be able to see the object you intend to move as well as the default To Fixed Point Motion dialog box.

2. Change the motion type to a To Calculated Point On Line motion type, as discussed previously in the section "Changing Motion Types." Notice that the Motion icon

Part

II

Ch

7

dialog box has changed to the To Calculated Point On Line Motion dialog box, as shown in Figure 7.16.

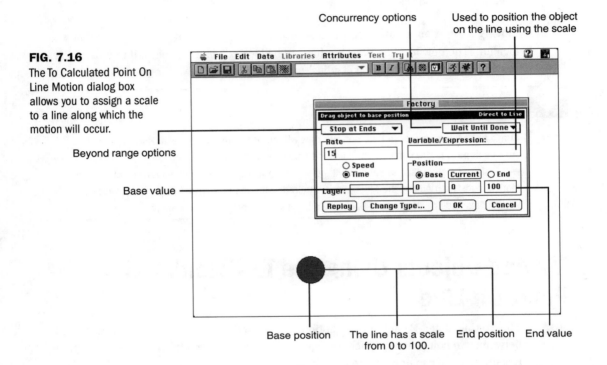

FIG. 7.16

The To Calculated Point On Line Motion dialog box allows you to assign a scale to a line along which the motion will occur.

Concurrency options

Used to position the object on the line using the scale

Beyond range options

Base value

Base position

The line has a scale from 0 to 100.

End position   End value

3. The next step is to identify the base position of the line along which the object will move. To do this, drag the object to that point. If the object is already at the base position of the line, simply click the object so that Authorware can identify it.

   Once you have clicked the object, notice that a small dot shows up in its center. This is the base position for the animation path.

4. Now that you have established the base position of the line, the prompt at the top of the dialog box instructs you to drag the object you intend to move to the end position of the line. Do so. (Be careful to grab the object. Getting too close to the center point does not enable you to move the object.)

   The default value for the base position of a line is zero, and the default value for the end position is 100. You can overwrite these entries with other values or control them with variables.

   The default Rate for a To Calculated Point On Line motion is one second. You can overwrite this entry with the amount of time you want it to take for the object to move along the path.

5. Click Replay to see the motion. To make adjustments to the final destination, simply drag the object being moved more precisely. To adjust the Rate, simply overwrite the displayed time with a new entry.

6. Click the OK button to save the settings.

▶ To learn more about controlling movement with variables, **see** "Controlling Motion Icons with Data," **p. 437**.

Using the Beyond Range Options

The To Calculated Point On Line motion is typically controlled using variables and expressions. Although we will look at this in more detail in Chapter 22, "Working with Data," it is important to understand the Beyond Range options now.

The Beyond Range options are used to control what happens when the value controlling the motion is lower than the value for the base position or greater than the value for the end position. The Beyond Range options include the ones described next.

Stop at Ends   The Stop at Ends option prevents the object from being moved outside of the line that you have defined. For example, if the value, variable or expression controlling the animation is greater than the end value of the line, the object will only move as far as the end position of the line.

Loop   The Loop option treats the linear path as if its end position and base position were connected. For example, if the base value of the path is zero and the end position is 100 and the value controlling the motion is 150, then the object would move to the position on the line equal to 50: 150–100=50.

This option may be helpful when you are creating simulations or mechanical displays. For example, I once had a calculation in which the result was conveyed to the user in two ways: a display presenting a number from one to ten, which represented the hundreds portion of the value, and a gauge, which represented the remainder of the value. The gauge moved along a scale that ranged from 1 to 99, and was positioned based on the value of the calculation. Using the Loop option, the gauge was properly positioned no matter if it was "267" or "867."

Go Past Ends   The Go Past Ends option establishes a line that is infinite in length and assumes that the base and end positions and values are simply reference points along the line.

Part

II

Ch

7

For example, if the base value is 0 and the end value is 100 and the value controlling the animation is 1,000, then the object will be positioned off of the established path and roughly ten times the distance of the line from the end position.

I once used this option to position an object that was used to indicate the cumulative score for a person as he progressed through a set of challenging questions. The scale ranged from 0 to 100, and ran across the bottom of the screen. Rather than developing the path to run from 0 to 100, I only developed the portion which ran from 0 to 20. Using the Go Past Ends option, however, the remainder of the scale was interpreted by Authorware.

Editing the Motion Path

The To Calculated Point On Line motion path can be edited once it is created by either adjusting the base position or by adjusting the end position.

To adjust the base position, first select the Base radio button in the Position area of the dialog box. When this selection is made, the object being moved will move to the base position of the path. Simply drag the object to a new location to establish a new base position for the line.

The end position can be edited in a similar manner by first selecting the End radio button, then dragging the object to a new ending location.

To check the accuracy of the scale, which is determined by the base and end values of the line, enter a value in the box directly under the Current button, then click the Current button. The object will move to the point on the path where the value is equal to the value that you have entered.

Moving Objects Using the To Calculated Point Motion Type

The To Calculated Point motion type moves an object from the base position of an established path to an established end position. Like the To Calculated Point On Line motion type, however, the movement along the path is based on establishing a scaled beginning and ending value for the path.

Creating a To Calculated Point Motion

Once you have set up the motion, as discussed earlier in this chapter in the section "Setting Up the Motion," follow these steps to create a To Calculated Point Motion:

1. Open the Motion icon by double-clicking it. When you do this you should be able to see the object you intend to move as well as the default To Fixed Point Motion dialog box.

2. Select the Change Type button to change from the default To Fixed Point motion type to a To Calculated Point (Path to Point) motion type. Notice that the Motion icon dialog box has changed to the To Calculated Point Motion dialog box, as shown in Figure 7.17.

FIG. 7.17
The To Calculated Point Motion dialog box allows you to assign a scale to a path along which the motion will occur.

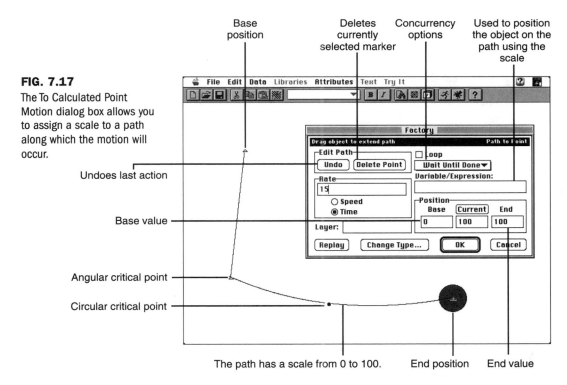

Base position

Deletes currently selected marker

Concurrency options

Used to position the object on the path using the scale

Undoes last action

Base value

Angular critical point

Circular critical point

The path has a scale from 0 to 100.   End position   End value

3. The prompt along the top of the dialog box instructs you to click the object you want to move. The base position of the path is based on the initial display position and once you start moving the object you will be creating critical points for the path.

Once you have clicked the object, notice that a small triangle shows up in the center of the object. This is the base position for the animation path.

4. Now that you have established the base position of the path, the prompt at the top of the dialog box instructs you to drag the object you intend to move to create the next point on the path. Do so. (Be careful not to drag the beginning point of the path—the triangle—but to drag the actual object.)

5. Continue dragging and dropping the object to extend the path by creating additional points.

6. The default Rate for a To Calculated Point motion is one second. You can overwrite this entry with the amount of time you want it to take for the object to move along the path.

7. Click the OK button to save the settings.

N O T E Because this motion type is controlled by a variable or expression, the motion will not play when the Replay button is clicked. ■

Editing Points of a To Calculated Point Path

Points for a To Calculated Point motion path can be added, deleted, or moved using the same techniques as you used for editing the End of Path motion. (See "Editing Points of a Path," earlier in this chapter.)

To check the accuracy of the scale, which is determined by the base and end values of the line, enter a value in the box directly under the Current button, then click the Current button. The object will move to the point on the path where the value is equal to the value that you have entered.

Using the Loop Option

The Loop option is used to control what happens if the value controlling the motion is lower than the value for the base position or greater than the value for the end position, just as the Beyond Range Options do for a To Calculated Point On Line motion.

Selecting the Loop option treats the path as if its end position and base position were connected. For example, if the base value of the path is 0 and the end point is 100 and the value controlling the motion is 150, then the object would move to the position on the path equal to 50: 150–100=50.

Moving Objects Using the To Calculated Point On Grid Motion

The To Calculated Point On Grid motion type is used to create a scaled grid within which an object will move. This motion type is similar to the To Calculated Point On Line motion except that it contains both a vertical and a horizontal axis.

Creating a To Calculated Point On Grid Motion

Once you have set up the motion, as discussed earlier in this chapter in the section "Setting Up the Motion," follow these steps to create a To Calculated Point On Grid motion:

1. Open the Motion icon by double-clicking it. When you do this, you should be able to see the object you intend to move as well as the default To Fixed Point Motion dialog box.

2. Click the Change Type button to change from the default To Fixed Point motion type to a To Calculated Point On Grid motion type. Notice that the Motion dialog box has changed to the To Calculated Point On Grid Motion dialog box, as shown in Figure 7.18.

FIG. 7.18
The To Calculated Point On Grid Motion dialog box allows you to assign a vertical and horizontal scale within which the motion will occur.

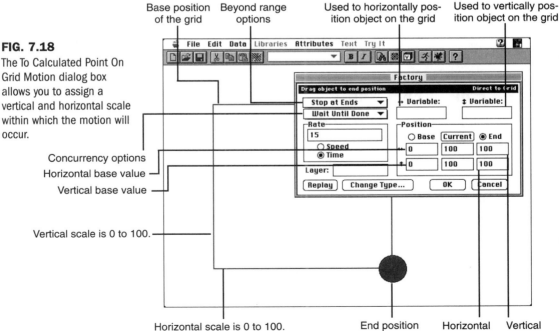

Base position of the grid · Beyond range options · Used to horizontally position object on the grid · Used to vertically position object on the grid

Concurrency options
Horizontal base value
Vertical base value

Vertical scale is 0 to 100.

Horizontal scale is 0 to 100. · End position of the grid · Horizontal end value · Vertical end value

Part
II

Ch
7

3. The next step is to identify the base position of the grid in which the object will move. To do this, drag the object to a corner of the area in which you intend the object to move. Notice that the Base radio button option is already selected.

4. Now that you have established the base position of the grid, click the End radio button in the Position area of the dialog box.

5. Drag the object to the corner of the motion area, which is diagonally opposite the base position. Upon releasing the mouse, you will notice a rectangle that defines the boundary of the grid that is formed.

6. To establish a scale value for the grid, enter a base and an end value for both the horizontal and the vertical axes in the Position area of the dialog box. The default value for the base positions is 0, and the default value for the end positions is 100.

7. The default rate for a To Calculated Point On Grid motion is one second. You can overwrite this entry with the amount of time you want it to take for the object to move within the grid.

8. Click the OK button to save the settings.

Using the Beyond Range Options

The Beyond Range Options function is just like those found in the To Calculated Point On Line motion type (see "Moving Objects Using the To Calculated Point On Line," earlier in this chapter). With these options, you can control what happens when the value controlling the motion is lower than the value for the base position or greater than the value for the end position of an axis.

Editing the Motion Grid

The To Calculated Point On Grid motion area can be edited once it is created by either adjusting the base position or adjusting the end position.

To adjust the base position, first select the Base radio button in the Position area of the dialog box. When this selection is made, the object being moved will move to the base position of the grid. Simply drag the object to a new location to establish a new base position for the grid. The end position can be edited in a similar manner by first selecting the End radio button then dragging the object to a new ending location.

To check the accuracy of the scale, which is determined by the base and end values of the grid, enter a value in the box directly under the Current button, then click the Current button. The object will move to the point within the grid where the value is equal to the value that you have entered. ●

CHAPTER 8

Organizing Authorware Logic on the Flowline

The most overwhelming aspect of creating a multimedia application is the need to keep track of the countless illustrations, sound, video clips, and blocks of text that make up even the simplest of pieces. While most developers pay close attention to these elements on the hard drive, or maybe even across a network, attention is rarely given to the need to organize such elements within the piece itself.

A traditional way to address this need for organization is to adopt a development methodology that dictates strict conventions for storing and identifying the individual media or structural components. Such methodologies typically require extensive documentation to define and continually track the whereabouts of the elements.

An alternative to incorporating a time-consuming documentation procedure is to rely on a few unique characteristics of Authorware. Authorware allows you to organize and document media elements, as well as Flowline structures, while authoring. This inherent characteristic of Authorware provides a mechanism to quickly locate specific elements, as well as interpret the

Using the Map icon

The Map icon is used to organize icons along the Flowline, which makes development more efficient.

Naming and identifying icons

Descriptively naming icons on the Flowline allows you to quickly locate specific content, and allows other members of the development team to quickly understand your Flowline.

When icon names are important

Icon names affect functionality for button responses, pull-down menu responses, text-entry responses, conditional responses, and icons referenced by a function.

Including comments

Comments are created in association with icon names without impacting functionality.

Taking advantage of icon names

There are several opportunities to use icons, such as when working with the Display icon, Motion icon, Wait icon, and Decision icon.

Coloring icons

A final feature Authorware provides for distinguishing icons on the Flowline is the ability to color-code icons.

functionality of the piece as a whole by viewing no more than the Flowline structure. Like a signpost providing guidance, the Authorware Flowline may be used to provide direction to the various media elements, as well as the content segments.

This chapter introduces you to organizing and naming icons within Authorware, and suggests helpful tips for taking advantage of the Flowline. ■

Grouping Icons

The most practical benefit of Authorware is the capability to create a flowchart of icons on the Flowline, through which you can visually track how the piece will run. At first glance, however, you quickly discover that the Flowline window is only large enough to hold a few icons. The larger the monitor you are working on, the larger you can make the window, and therefore, the greater the number of icons that can be placed on the Flowline. Nonetheless, because the Flowline window does not scroll vertically or horizontally, you will find that you quickly run out of room to place additional icons.

▶ To refer to the introduction of the flowchart metaphor, **see** "Building the Flowline," **p. 12**.

▶ For basic information regarding the Map icon, **see** "The Map Icon," **p. 20**.

N O T E   If you continue to add icons to the Flowline, they will extend out the bottom of the Flowline window. You will not be able to see the icons or to select them, yet they will be encountered when the piece runs. ■

Rather than providing an environment in which you can endlessly scroll vertically and horizontally, Authorware provides a mechanism that allows you to organize the icons into self-contained groups. The icon that Authorware uses to group other icons together is called the Map icon, which is discussed next.

Introducing the Map Icon

 The Authorware Map icon, shown in Figure 8.1, is the mechanism used to organize the Authorware Flowline structure (also known as *logic*) into related groups. Unlike most of the other icons, the Map icon serves no functional purpose: It does not display objects, it does not alter performance, and the user does not know when the piece encounters the Map icon.

The Authorware Map icon

FIG. 8.1
The Map icon is used to organize Authorware code (the Flowline icons) into logical groupings.

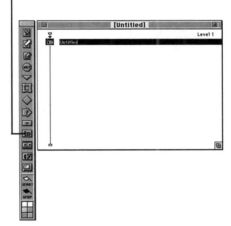

The sole purpose of the Map icon is to assist you in organizing the Flowline icons. To set up the Map icon, follow these steps:

1. Drag a Map icon to the Flowline.
2. Double-click the Map icon to open it. Each Map icon contains an extension of the Flowline that is used to hold more icons.
3. Drag other icons onto the new Flowline level that was created when the Map icon was opened.
4. Close the Map icon by clicking the close box in the upper left-hand corner of the window (Macintosh) or by double-clicking the Control menu box (Windows). Closing the Map icon returns you to the next higher level of the Flowline.

The Map icon is most commonly used to group icons or create multiple levels, as shown in Figure 8.2, so that there is a greater amount of space on the Flowline. There is a more strategic use of the Map icon, however. Just as you consciously organize and label directories on your hard drive, Authorware logic can be organized for ease of use and maintenance.

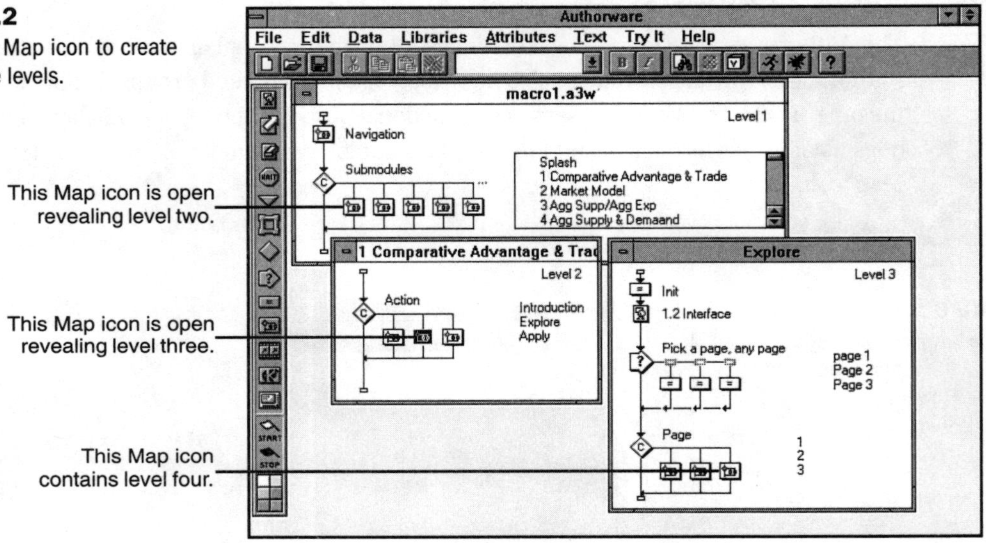

FIG. 8.2
Use the Map icon to create multiple levels.

This Map icon is open revealing level two.

This Map icon is open revealing level three.

This Map icon contains level four.

For example, you can place all of the icons relating to a logon and splash screen presentation sequence in a Map icon titled Intro. (You'll learn how to name Flowline icons later in this chapter.) Following Intro might be a Map icon titled Menus, which contains a series of perpetually available menus enabling the user to freely move from module to module. Finally, you can create a map titled Content that contains all the application content as well as the module highlights. This icon structure is shown in Figure 8.3.

FIG. 8.3
Map icons can be used to group particular parts of the application, such as intro or content information.

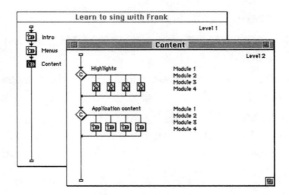

When the Authorware mites encounter a Map icon, they enter the Map and execute all of the icons within it. Upon reaching the bottom of the Flowline within the Map icon, the Authorware mites leave the map and continue down the Flowline at the next highest Flowline level. For example, if the application finished executing the contents of a Map icon in the third level of your application, it would go to the next Flowline icon in the second level of the application—it would not go all the way back to the initial level of the Flowline. If the map is attached to a Decision or Interaction icon, all of the icons within the Map are executed prior to branching.

 T I P A Map icon can be used to create an empty branch for exiting an interaction. When the piece encounters the Map icon, it enters into the new Flowline level. Since the Map icon has no contents, however, the piece quickly exits the Map icon and proceeds down the Flowline. See Chapter 9 through Chapter 14 for more information about creating interactions.

Grouping and Ungrouping

There are two ways to work with the Map icon. You can either begin development by dragging a Map icon to the Flowline, opening it, and then developing within the new level as described in the previous section, or you can group icons together into a Map icon after you've added those icons to the Flowline.

To group icons that have already been brought onto the Flowline, follow these steps:

1. Select all the icons you want to group together. To select multiple icons, hold down the Shift key and individually select the icons by clicking them.

   You can also draw a marquee around the icons that you want to select by clicking next to an icon then dragging, as seen in Figure 8.4. A flowing dashed line will appear as you drag. Each of the icons that the marquee either encounters or surrounds will become highlighted when the mouse button is released.

2. Once the icons that you want to group together are highlighted, choose the Group command from the Edit menu. When the Group command is selected, the highlighted icons will be replaced by a Map icon, as seen in Figure 8.5. The icons that were originally on the Flowline have now been moved to the Flowline level within the Map icon.

 T I P The shortcut keys for selecting Group are ⌘+G (Macintosh) and Ctrl+G (Windows).

FIG. 8.4

To select multiple icons, draw a marquee around them.

The mouse button was clicked here to begin drawing a marquee around the icons.

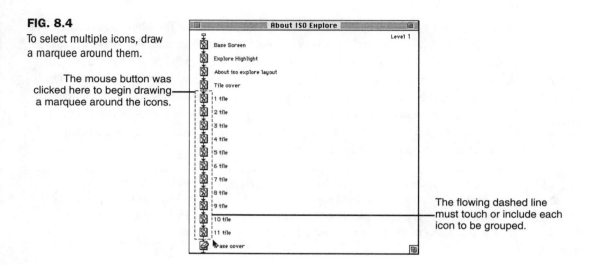

The flowing dashed line must touch or include each icon to be grouped.

FIG. 8.5

Grouping icons together creates a Map icon containing the highlighted icons.

The Map contains the icons that were grouped.

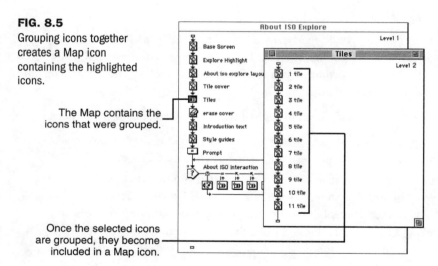

Once the selected icons are grouped, they become included in a Map icon.

When icons are grouped resulting in the creation of a Map icon, the Map icon is labeled "Untitled" just as if it were a new icon brought to the Flowline. In the next section, we will look at the importance of naming an icon, and the steps for changing the name of an icon on the Flowline.

N O T E   If only a single icon is highlighted when the Group command is chosen from the Edit menu, the name of the Map icon is the same as the name of the single icon. ■

Icons that have been grouped can also be ungrouped. When a Map icon is ungrouped, all the icons contained in that Map icon are displayed on the Flowline level on which the Map icon existed. That is, they replace the Map icon on its level.

To ungroup a Map icon, follow these steps:

1. Click the Map icon or draw a marquee around the Map icon to select it.

2. Once the Map icon that you want to ungroup is highlighted, choose the Ungroup command from the Edit menu. All of the icons that were contained on the Flowline within the Map icon are moved to the higher level Flowline to replace the Map icon, as seen in Figure 8.6.

T I P The shortcut keys for selecting Ungroup are ⌘+U (Macintosh) and Ctrl+U (Windows).

FIG. 8.6

Ungrouping a Map icon causes all the icons to replace the Map icon, which resides on the higher Flowline level.

When a Map icon is ungrouped, all of the icons in that Map replace the position of the Map icon.

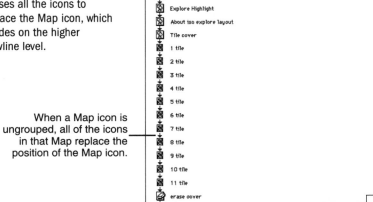

TROUBLESHOOTING

When I ungrouped a series of icons, the Flowline at the higher level became so crowded that the icons ran off the bottom of the window and I could no longer see all of the icons on that level. How do I access the icons that are out of view? The best way to get to the icons that are out of view is to begin grouping icons back into maps.

Naming and Identifying Icons

Consistent with the notion of grouping icons into Maps is the notion of naming icons descriptively. For most of the icons, naming is not critical to the performance or operation of the application. I do believe, however, that it has a tremendous effect on the efficiency of the development team. If conventions for naming are adhered to throughout development, multiple authors will be able to participate on the project with minimal confusion.

Providing a descriptive name for each icon on the Flowline allows members of the development team to locate specific media elements, or to identify the location where a specific value is established, without having to open each icon to view its contents. For example, you can have several Display icons whose contents are animated using Motion icons. By labeling the Display icons according to their contents, and labeling the Motion icons according to which Display icon they are associated with, will eliminate guesswork should editing be required.

Within a short period of time using Authorware, you learn how to read the icons and interpret what will happen functionally. Your clue to the specific details of the piece lies in your ability to descriptively name the icons.

While looking at the Flowline in Figure 8.7, see if you can interpret the functionality described next.

FIG. 8.7
Icons that are descriptively named tell the story as to what will happen functionally.

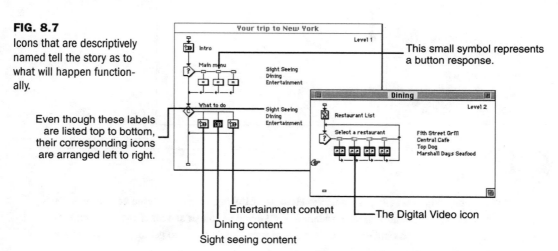

Even though these labels are listed top to bottom, their corresponding icons are arranged left to right.

This small symbol represents a button response.

The Digital Video icon

Entertainment content
Dining content
Sight seeing content

After an introduction sequence, the user will be able to select one of three buttons that are perpetually available on the screen. The buttons are labeled Sight Seeing, Dining, and Entertainment.

▶ For guidance on building button responses, **see** "Creating Buttons," **p. 235**.

If the Dining button is clicked by the user, a list of restaurants will appear. The user could click an item on the list to view a video clip.

When the user is done watching the video about a particular restaurant, he could elect to view the information about another selection or choose to enter the Sight Seeing or Entertainment modules.

As you can see, understanding the functionality of the icons and naming them descriptively aids in the understanding of how the piece will flow.

Naming Icons for the First Time

When an icon is first brought to the Flowline, it is given the default label of "Untitled." Unfortunately, I have seen thousands of icons that were left this way. By leaving icons labeled "Untitled," you will quickly become confused as you edit the Flowline.

To give an icon a name once it is brought to the Flowline, you can simply begin typing as long as you have not clicked on any other icon on the Flowline or within the Icon Palette. An icon title can be infinitely long, however, depending on the size of the Flowline window, you may not be able to see the entire name. I suggest limiting your titles to a few words, yet long enough to be meaningful.

Changing Icon Names

If you want to edit the name of an icon, you can simply select the icon then begin typing to overwrite the current label. You can also select the icon whose label you want to edit, then move the mouse pointer toward the name. As the mouse pointer approaches the name, the pointer changes into an I-beam, which can be used as in a word processing piece.

If you have several icons on the Flowline for which you want to create a label, you can select the first icon, type the new label, then press the Return (Macintosh) or Enter (Windows) key. When this key is pressed, the label for the current icon will change and the next icon on the Flowline will become selected. You can now enter a name for that icon, then repeat the process until the entire list of icons has been named.

When Names Are Important

In most cases, what you name an icon will have no effect on the functionality of the piece. In the following cases, however, naming the icon is critical to the performance of the Authorware piece.

Part
II

Ch
8

Button Responses   When creating an interaction that uses button responses, the title of the icon that is used to create the push button will become the label on the button when it is displayed in the Presentation Window. Therefore, changing the name of the icon in turn changes the label of the button.

For example, the push buttons created by the piece shown in Figure 8.7 contain the labels "Sight Seeing," "Dining," and "Entertainment." To change the "Dining" label to "Restaurants," you simply change the name of the icon.

▶ For step-by-step guidance on creating button interactions, **see** "Creating Buttons," **p. 235**.

Pull-down Menu Responses   The title of the Interaction icon that is used to create a pull-down menu is also critical in that it becomes the label for the menu. For example, if we created a pull-down menu that contained the "Sight Seeing," "Dining," and "Entertainment" options, we may want to title the interaction icon "Activities." By doing this, the label "Activities" will appear in the menu bar.

Additionally, the title of the icons representing each branch of the interaction will become the label within the menu. Using the previous example, title the icons "Sight Seeing," "Dining," and "Entertainment" in order for these options to appear when the "Activities" pull-down menu is activated.

▶ For step-by-step guidance on building pull-down menus, **see** "Creating Pull-down Menus," **p. 266**.

Text-Entry Responses   The title of the icon that will be encountered if the user types a specific response is also critical. For example, if I built an interaction using a text-entry response (one that requires the end user to type a response), the title of the branch icon is actually the anticipated response that the user is to enter. Therefore, if I title the icon "Dining," the entry will not be accepted unless the user types "Dining" exactly. For instructions for creating text-entry responses, refer to Chapter 13, "Setting Up Text-Entry Boxes."

TROUBLESHOOTING

When I type something into the text-entry field, the previous response blinks, but the entry doesn't seem to match the anticipated response. What could be wrong? Keep in mind that the name of the icon has to be exactly what you are expecting the end user to enter. Be sure to check spelling and capitalization. Additionally, be sure there are not any extra spaces in the icon name because you cannot see it on the Flowline. Authorware uses the icon name to judge the response.

Conditional Responses   Much like a text-entry response, the title of a conditional response path icon is the condition that must be matched in order for the path to be matched. For example, you can build a log-on sequence in which the end user will enter some information, and after a bit of evaluation, you set a variable (let's call it "Access") to either "Yes" or "No," depending on the end user's ability to access the training.

If the variable was set to "Yes" and the title of the icon is "Access=YES," then the path would be matched. If the title of the icon was "Access=No," however, this path would not be taken.

▶ For more information on conditional responses, **see** "Using Conditional Response Types," **p. 448**.

TROUBLESHOOTING

Why can't I get the conditional response path to match? While there may be a number of reasons, a good place to start is to look at the name of the icon. Many times I find that people leave the name blank; therefore, no condition exists to match.

Icons Referenced by a Function   In many instances, one icon may reference another. For example, you can determine where on a path an object has been moved by referencing the icon that contains the object that has been moved. To do this, Authorware refers to the icon that is being referenced by name. If more than one icon has the same name, however, Authorware is not able to distinguish which icon is to be referenced. Therefore, the title of an icon that is being referenced must be unique.

Including Comments in an Icon Name

Although naming icons descriptively leads to efficient development, what do you do when you can't be descriptive because the name of the icon affects its functionality—for example, if you have an icon that is used to create a push button.

To get around this dilemma, Authorware provides a mechanism by which you can leave comments on an icon title. You will later see that this convention can also be used within the Calculation icon.

▶ **See** "Introducing the Calculation Icon," **p. 369**

To add a comment to the name of an icon for which the functionality of the icon is affected by its name, simply place two hyphens (--) within the icon's name preceding the comment, as shown in Figure 8.8.

FIG. 8.8
Comments will be ignored in cases where the icon's name affects functionality.

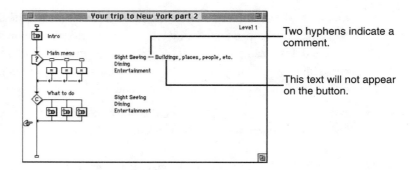

Two hyphens indicate a comment.

This text will not appear on the button.

Be sure that the two hyphens and the comment follow the name of the icon; otherwise, the name will be included in the comment, and Authorware will not perform as you expect.

Taking Advantage of Icon Titles

Previously, we looked at when it was critical to title an icon in order for its functionality to be carried out. The benefit of this is that you can tell from the Flowline exactly what Authorware is expecting or what it will do. You do not need to access information that is hidden away in a dialog box.

This same efficiency can be realized by incorporating the following tricks as you develop using icons whose functionality is not affected by their names.

The Display Icon When rapidly prototyping, you may want to build a logic shell complete enough to execute so you can check the flow of the piece, but void of the elements that are time-consuming to create such as graphics, video, and sound.

When you label Display icons in situations like this (and in general), be very specific as to the purpose of their contents. Then double-click to open the icon and insert the text "{IconTitle}" anywhere within the Presentation Window as seen in Chapter 3, "Presenting Text." IconTitle is an Authorware variable that contains the name of the most currently executed icon. When this variable is placed in the Presentation Window, Authorware will display the name of the icon in the Presentation Window during running. Now, from both Run and Flowline perspectives, you have a good description of what the piece will do without having invested much time in the development of time-consuming media, or by spending time entering information into each Display icon (see Fig. 8.9).

▶ For assistance with placing variables in the Presentation Window, **see** "Embedding Data in the Presentation Window," **p. 434**.

The Motion Icon The timing of an animated sequence is often a very precise science. It is not uncommon to have to make several guesses as to the appropriate amount of time needed to play the motion to make it look as you want it to for the end user. You commonly will need to make this determination by running the piece repeatedly to see the sequence played out. Opening the Motion icon dialog box by double-clicking to tweak the rate of play each time you run, however, can become very tedious and time-consuming.

FIG. 8.9
Use the variable `IconTitle` to display the icon's name in the Presentation Window during Run mode.

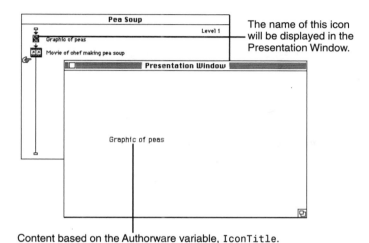

Content based on the Authorware variable, `IconTitle`.

▶ For more hints on using data to control the Motion icon, **see** "Controlling Motion Icons with Data," **p. 437**.

To make this process more efficient, open the Motion dialog box by double-clicking, then place the Authorware variable, `IconTitle`, in the Rate field (see Fig. 8.10). Click OK to close the dialog box. Change the title of the Motion icon so the title is the number of seconds the motion should play, followed by a comment describing the motion itself. (See "Including Comments in an Icon Name," earlier in this chapter.)

Changing the rate now only requires that you change the icon name to a number representing a different number of seconds.

The Wait Icon Like the timing of the Motion icon, setting the correct timing of the Wait icon is usually an exercise of trial and error. Opening the Wait icon dialog box to tweak the time limit each time you run can become very tedious and time-consuming.

▶ For more information on using the time limit for a Wait icon, **see** "Time Limit," **p. 159**.

To make this process more efficient, open the Wait icon dialog box by double-clicking, then place the Authorware variable, `IconTitle`, in the Time Limit field of the Wait Options dialog box (see Fig. 8.11). Change the name of the Wait icon so that the name is the number of seconds Authorware should pause, followed by a comment describing the pause itself. Changing the time limit now only requires that you change the icon name again.

FIG. 8.10
Use the variable `IconTitle` to control the rate of play for a Motion icon.

Changing the title of the Motion icon will change the rate.

The title of the icon will determine the motion's rate.

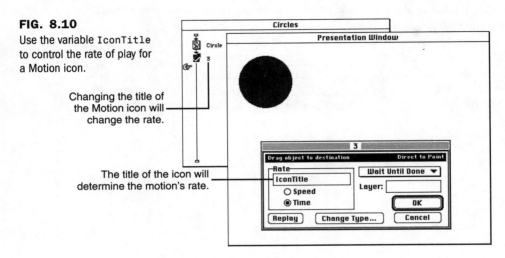

FIG. 8.11
Use the variable, `IconTitle`, to control the time limit for a Wait icon.

Change the name of this icon to change the pause time.

The pause time is based on the name of the Wait icon.

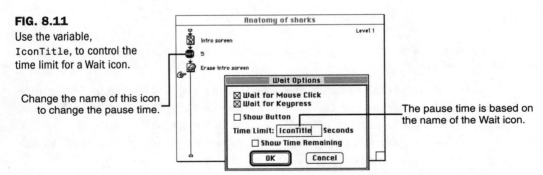

The Decision Icon   Decision icons are used to establish branching, or paths, which Authorware follows. Most of the controls to determine how the Decision icon is to function are based on radio button selections in the Decision Icon Options dialog box, which is accessed by double-clicking the Decision icon. I often use this functionality to establish various testing scenarios, each branch representing a unique scenario.

▶ For guidance on using variables in conjunction with the Decision icon, **see** "Building Calcu-lated Path Decision Branches," **p. 444**.

To control which scenario is played, place the Authorware variable, IconTitle, in the To Calculated Path field (see Fig. 8.12); then change the title of the Decision icon to the number representing which path you want to take, followed by a comment regarding the branching in general. Paths are numbered from left to right, so if you want the path next to the Decision icon to be taken, you enter a "1."

FIG. 8.12
Use the variable, IconTitle, to control which path of the Decision will be taken.

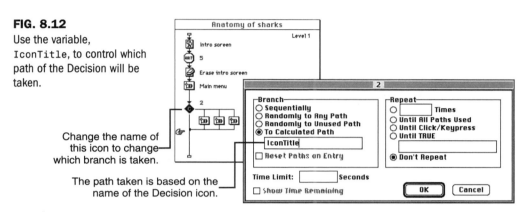

Change the name of this icon to change which branch is taken.

The path taken is based on the name of the Decision icon.

To change which path will be taken, simply change the number in the icon name. If you want no path taken, replace the number with a zero.

These scenarios are but a few of the many ways that you can use the title of an icon to control the functionality of that icon or of the piece as a whole. As you are developing your application, keep an eye out for similar efficiencies.

Coloring Icons

To support maintaining your application from the Flowline level, Authorware provides the capability to color-code icons. At this time, Authorware enables you to select one of the six colors located in the palette at the bottom of the Icon Palette.

▶ For an overview of the Icon Color palette, **see** "The Icon Color palette," **p. 22**.

To color-code an icon, follow these steps:

1. Select the icon you want to color-code by clicking it in the Flowline. To select more than one icon, hold down the Shift key and click each icon or click beside an icon and drag to draw a marquee around the desired icons.

2. Select a color from the Icon Color palette located at the bottom of the Icon Palette.

Color can best be used to identify icons that have special characteristics that are otherwise difficult to detect. For example, you may have established that certain Display icons will be set so that they cannot be automatically erased (see Fig. 8.13). Identifying these icons with a particular color will make them easier to locate later in the development phase.

FIG. 8.13
Use the Icon Color palette to visually associate icons.

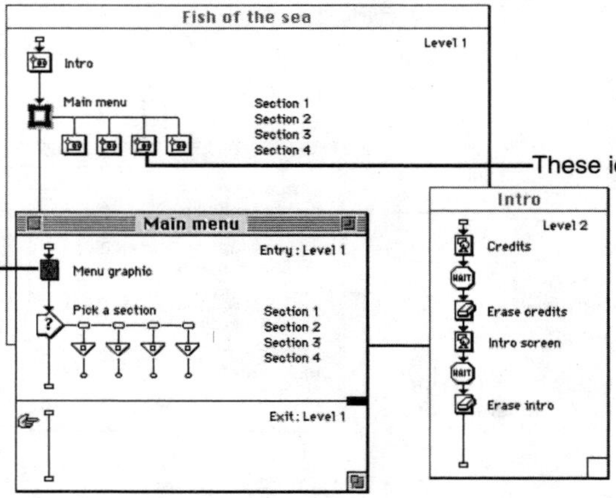

This icon is set to prevent automatic erase.

These icons contain video.

▶ For more information on preventing automatic erasure, **see** "Prevent Automatic Erase," **p. 132**.

▶ For information on placing variables in the Presentation Window, **see** "Embedding Data in the Presentation Window," **p. 434**.

Another occasion when color-coding is appropriate is for icons that contain variables in the Presentation Window. Coding these icons will enable you to see that they are special when viewing the Flowline. ●

Building Interactivity

The Fundamentals of Interactions

Multimedia is typically defined as the incorporation of text, sound, video, graphics, and animation. The problem with this definition, however, is that it ignores the most crucial and ultimately beneficial element of a multimedia experience: *interactivity*.

Interactivity in its simplest form is the action of the user controlling the pace and sequence of events in a multimedia piece through a variety of interface mechanisms. These mechanisms include push buttons, pull-down menus, clickable areas, keypress, text entry, and movable objects.

The definition of interactivity can be expanded beyond this technical definition, however. The traditional definition of interactivity is *to act on one another.* By definition, therefore, interactivity is more than simply enabling the user to control the pace and the sequence of events. True interactivity enables the computer and its user to enter into a dialog, each reacting to the other until understanding is reached.

Getting started with interactions

At the heart of every interaction is the Interaction icon.

Recognizing the interaction loop

The interaction loop is comprised of four parts: the Interaction icon, the response, the response type symbol, and the response branching.

Working with the response types

There are ten response types within Authorware: push button, hot spot, hot object, target area, text-entry, keypress, pull-down menu, time limit, tries limit, and conditional.

Using the response options

Several options are common across all response types: automatic erasing, automatic judgment, branching, and perpetual.

Authorware provides ten total interaction types—seven types of interactions by which the user can communicate with the computer, and three ways in which the computer can monitor the interactive dialog. This chapter introduces you to these interaction types as well as suggests practical applications for each. ■

Introducing Interactions

Interactivity can be used as either a mechanism to control the pace and sequence of a multimedia piece, or as a means to create a dialog—an experience which has greater meaning than the simple delivery of information—between the computer and the user. In either case, incorporating interactivity into your piece will create a rich experience for the end user.

Introducing the Interaction Icon

The Interaction icon, shown in Figure 9.1, is central to creating interactivity within Authorware. While the Interaction icon by itself does not provide the interactivity, it is the icon used as the foundation for creating an interaction.

FIG. 9.1

The Interaction icon is used to create interactivity.

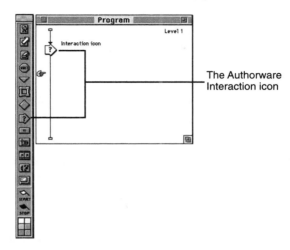

The Authorware Interaction icon

▶ To refer to the introduction of the Interaction icon, **see** "The Interaction Icon," **p. 19**.

An Interaction icon is the combination of the Display icon, which enables you to present text and graphics to the end user; the Decision icon, which provides unique branches along which the piece can flow; the Wait icon, which pauses the piece; and the Erase icon, which removes displayed objects from the Presentation Window.

▶ For more information on how the Display icon is used to present text, **see** "Placing Text on the Screen," **p. 68**.

▶ For more information on using graphics, **see** "Drawing Objects," **p. 98**.

▶ To understand how objects are erased from the Presentation Window, **see** "Erasing Objects," **p. 354**.

N O T E In the past, I have seen Authorware developers place Interaction icons on the Flowline without creating any interactivity or branching. They used the single icon to replace the Display icon, Wait icon, and Erase icon used in a linear presentation. That linear structure—should you want to create such—can more easily be created using the Framework icon or the Decision icon. ▪

Upon encountering an Interaction icon on the Flowline, the piece pauses until the end user performs an anticipated interaction, such as clicking a button or moving an object. When the interaction is complete, the piece continues down the Flowline, following a unique path, known as the response path, according to the specific interaction.

Defining the Interaction Loop

The interaction is more than the Interaction icon; it is also the complete experience the user is engaged in while encountering that portion of the piece. The interaction, or interaction loop, is comprised of the Interaction icon, the response type, the response, and the response branching (see Fig. 9.2). These elements—and how they interact with each other—are described next.

The Response Type   The response type is the way in which the end user will interact with the piece. For example, the user clicks a button or enters text. Within Authorware there are ten response types, as described in the section "Interacting with Authorware," later in this chapter. The anticipated response types are identified by the response type symbol, shown in Figure 9.2.

I will provide step-by-step guidance on building an interaction and selecting a response type in the section, "Building an Interaction Loop."

The Response   Once the end user interacts with the piece, it proceeds down the Flowline. The path taken along the Flowline is referred to as the response path, and the icons that are encountered along the response path are called the response. The response and response path are shown in Figure 9.2. The response can be as simple as a single display or as complex as an entire module of a training piece.

 T I P   To have more than one item within a response, use the Map icon with an additional Flowline structure inside as the response.

The Response Branching   The final component of the interaction loop is the response branch. The response branch, illustrated using the branch path symbol, shown in Figure 9.2, is the portion of the Flowline located just under a response path, which illustrates in what direction on the Flowline the piece will go once the response is complete.

FIG. 9.2
The interaction loop is made up of the Interaction icon, the response type, the response path, and response branching.

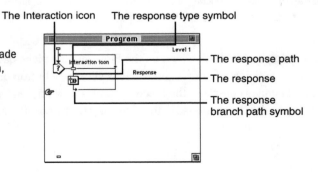

Building an Interaction Loop

Now that we have explored the individual pieces of the interaction loop, let's look at how to set up the interaction. Although there is a unique method for creating an interaction using each of the response types, we can begin by looking at the steps that are common to building all interactions. We explore the procedures for creating a few interaction types in more detail over the next five chapters.

To set up the interaction loop, follow these steps:

1. Drag an Interaction icon to the Flowline.
2. Drag another icon to the Flowline and place it to the right of the Interaction icon, as shown in Figure 9.3. The icon you place to the right of the Interaction icon is called the response. Responses can be created using the Display, Motion, Erase, Wait, Navigate, Calculation, Map, Digital Movie, Sound, or Video icons.

FIG. 9.3

Place an icon to the right of the Interaction icon to build a response path.

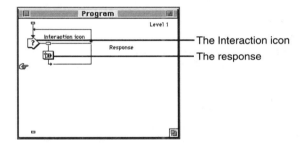

3. Upon releasing the first response icon beside an Interaction icon, the Response Type dialog box, shown in Figure 9.4, will appear. Select the type of interaction you want the end user to perform (such as clicking a button) in order for the piece to perform the response (such as executing a Display icon). Response types will be covered in greater detail in the section "Interacting with Authorware," later in this chapter.

FIG. 9.4

Authorware supports a variety of ways to interact with the piece.

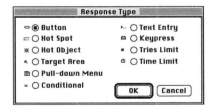

4. Drag additional response icons to the Flowline. Continue to place the icons to the right of the Interaction icon, as shown in Figure 9.5.

FIG. 9.5
Interactions can contain
more than one response
path.

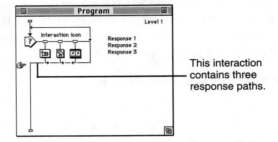

This interaction
contains three
response paths.

Once you have created the first response path to the right of the Interaction icon, you can continue placing icons on the interaction loop. You can place additional branches to either the left or to the right of the first response. Additionally, you can move the icons to adjust their position.

 If you place a response to the right of an existing response, the response type will be assumed, but if you place a response in the first position next to the Interaction icon, the Response Type dialog box appears.

 You can create an infinite number of responses in an interaction loop. The most I have ever created for one interaction loop was 258.

As soon as you create the sixth response, Authorware builds a scrolling window (see Fig. 9.6), which presents only five branches at a time. To view icons located closer to the Interaction icon, scroll up. To see icons further from the Interaction icon, scroll down. When you select an icon, its title will highlight in the scrolling list, and vice versa.

FIG. 9.6
When more than five responses
are used, Authorware organizes
them in a scrolling window.

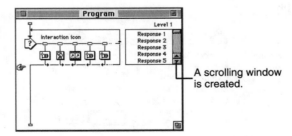

A scrolling window
is created.

Interacting with Authorware

In this chapter, we begin to explore the types of interactivity supported by Authorware. In the next five chapters, I explain the most common interaction types in greater detail, including step-by-step guidance on how to create such interactions.

Recognizing the Interaction Types

There are several ways in which the user can interact with an Authorware program. Although a few of these mechanisms create standard computer-interface controls, most of them enable you to create a more custom interface.

The options for interactivity and control are briefly described next.

Button   Selecting the Button option automatically creates a computer standard button in the Presentation Window with which the end user can interact. You can set the size and location of the button or replace the default button with a custom-designed button that was created using the Button Editor.

When the user clicks the button, the piece continues past the Interaction icon and down the Flowline. The specific Flowline taken is based on the response of the end user.

 TIP   Standard buttons are great for building pieces such as performance-support tools. For education or entertainment pieces, however, you may want to stay away from such conventional controls by creating your own look and feel.

▶ For more information on using the Button Editor, **see** "Using the Button Editor," **p. 245**.

Hot Spot   *Hot spots* create an invisible area in the Presentation Window in which the user must single-click, double-click, or simply position the mouse pointer over. When the user interacts with the invisible area, the piece continues past the Interaction icon and down the Flowline. The specific Flowline taken is based on the response of the end user.

▶ For step-by-step directions to creating a hot spot interaction, **see** "Building a Hot Spot Response Type," **p. 252**.

CAUTION

Common graphical user interface practices suggest that when an area is selected by the user, there should be immediate visual feedback. To do this in Authorware, you must either automatically inverse the colors graphically or manually display a custom highlight after the selection was registered.

As we saw in Chapter 4, "Working with Graphics and Objects" inversing the colors may not be graphically appropriate, and the speed of the system will determine the effectiveness of a custom highlight. You should test a few scenarios before implementing either option throughout the program.

Hot Object   A *hot object* is a graphical object that acts as a button. When the user clicks the object, the piece continues past the Interaction icon and down the Flowline. If the user selects a hollow spot (void of pixels) in the object, the piece will not continue.

For example, if the hot object was a doughnut and the end user clicked the hole, the piece would not continue down the Flowline. If the end user selected the cake portion of the doughnut, however, the piece would continue.

N O T E   All of the objects found in a Display or Interaction icon specified as a hot object are considered part of the hot object. If you only want a single object to be selectable by the user, place it in a separate Display or Interaction icon. ▦

Target Area   *Target areas* enable you to identify an object that must be moved to a specific area, or to define an area in which any object can be moved. When the user moves the object to the designated target area, the Authorware piece continues along the Flowline. If the user moves the object outside of the target area, the piece will not continue.

T I P   Remember to limit the movement of the object by the end user to an area or path so that the object may not be moved outside of the Presentation Window.

Pull-down Menu   This option automatically creates a heading that contains a pull-down menu in the menu bar of your piece. When the user selects an item in the menu, the Authorware piece continues down the Flowline.

TIP Pull-down menus are the least intuitive mechanisms for the novice computer user to compre-
hend. If you are building a piece that is to be used by a general audience, I suggest avoiding pull-
down menus.

▶ To learn how to show or hide the menu bar, **see** "Presentation Window Location and
Appearance," **p. 53**.

 Text Entry Use the Text Entry option to create a field in which the user can enter both
characters and numbers. When the user ends the input by pressing an action key, such as
Tab or Enter, the Authorware piece continues down the Flowline.

TIP Text-entry options are best used when you are gathering data from the user or when the typing
supports the content. For example, if you are creating a training piece to teach heavy machine
operators cleaning procedures, it would not add value to the content to require the end user to
enter responses via the keyboard since typing is not a normal part of the job function. If you are
teaching database-management procedures, however, using some text-entry responses may be
appropriate.

N O T E Authorware supports the use of wild cards. When a wild card is used instead of a
specifically identified entry, any entry is accepted. Within Authorware, the asterisk (*)
is used as a substitute for an open number of characters, and the question mark (?) is used as a
substitute for a single character. A place that I commonly use wild cards is in the creation of a
log-on sequence. Since I want to accept any possible name, I use the asterisk as the anticipated
text entry.

Keypress This option enables you to identify a specific key or key sequence that can be
selected by the user. When the user presses the selected key or key sequence, the
Authorware piece continues down the Flowline.

In addition to the interaction types that we have seen so far, there are also interaction
types that do not require the direct action of the user, but rely on other interaction circumstances. These interaction types are described next.

Conditional *Conditional* interactions cause the Authorware piece to follow the Flowline
when the specified condition is true. For example, you may elect to present a specific
graphic only after the user has achieved a score greater than 70 percent.

▶ For guidance on creating conditional interactions, **see** "Using Conditional Response
Types," **p. 448**.

> **N O T E**   As your pieces become more sophisticated, you will find yourself using the conditional response option more and more. This option enables you to create an intelligent piece that branches based on its understanding of the end user. ■

Tries Limit   *Tries Limit* responses cause the Authorware piece to automatically follow the Flowline when the user has interacted with the current interaction a specified number of times. For example, you can give a hint to the solution of a problem if the user has already attempted to answer two or more times.

Time Limit   *Time Limit* responses cause the Authorware piece to automatically follow the Flowline when the user has failed to interact within a specified amount of time. For example, you can give the user thirty seconds to solve the problem before providing a hint.

CAUTION

Be careful to use the time limit response type in areas where the content would be supported by the race against time. Users may already be hesitant about using the piece, and unnecessarily increasing anxiety would not be helpful.

One place that I have seen the time limit response used well was in emergency response training. Medical personnel were given a brief period of time to make a diagnosis, and as they contemplated their response, the clock counted down the time remaining.

TROUBLESHOOTING

How do I get a touch screen or keypad to work within Authorware? System peripherals, such as a touch screen, voice command system, or key pad, typically have interface software that allows the computer to interpret its response as either a mouse or keyboard activity. For example, a touch screen activity is converted into a mouse activity, so you can use either hot spots, hot objects, or push button response.

Introducing the Response Type Dialog Box

The ten interaction response types that were introduced in the last section are listed in the Response Type dialog box, shown previously in Figure 9.4. This dialog box is automatically presented when an interaction is created. (See the section, "Building an Interaction Loop" earlier in this chapter.)

To change from one response type to another, the Response Type dialog box must be accessed again. To access the Response Type dialog box once the interaction has been built, you must first open the Response Options dialog box, then select the Change Type button. (See the section, "Changing the Response Types," for more information on the Response Options dialog box.) When the Change Type button is clicked, the Response Type dialog box opens and you can select a new response type.

Changing the Response Types

The first time that you place a response path on an Interaction icon, you are given the opportunity to select a response type from the Response Type dialog box. Subsequent response paths, however, will default to the response type of the last placed path.

N O T E Anytime that you drag an icon to the first position to the right of an Interaction icon, the Response Type dialog box opens. ■

To change the response type of a path, follow these steps:

1. Double-click the response type symbol for the path you want to change. When the response type symbol is double-clicked, the Response Options dialog box is presented. This dialog box is unique for each response type, and will be explored in detail in Chapters 10 through 14.

2. When the Response Options dialog box opens, click the Change Type button to open the Response Type dialog box.

 To prevent the Response Options dialog box from opening and to avoid the additional step of clicking Change Type, hold down the ⌘ key (Macintosh) or Ctrl key (Windows) while double-clicking the response type symbol.

3. Select the desired response type from the Response Type dialog box.

4. Click the OK button to save your selection in the Response Type dialog box.

5. Click OK or press Return (Macintosh) or Enter (Windows) to save the settings in the Response Options dialog box.

From this point forward in the book, I will refer to this process as *changing the response type*.

Shortcuts for Accessing the Response Type Dialog Box

To quickly open the Response Type dialog box, hold down the ⌘ key (Macintosh) or the Ctrl key (Windows) and double-click the response type symbol for the branch path you want to change (see Fig. 9.7). You will notice that the response options dialog box did not open, but only the Response Type dialog box appeared. You can then change the response type (see "Recognizing the Interaction Types," earlier in this chapter).

FIG. 9.7
Hold down the ⌘ key
(Macintosh) or the Ctrl key
(Windows), and double-click
the response type symbol to
change the response type.

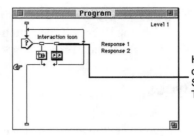

Hold down the shortcut keys and
double-click the Response Type
Symbol to access the Response
Type Options.

Understanding the Response Options

Each response of an interaction has several options that must be considered. While many of those options are unique to the type of interaction, there are a few that are common to all interactions, including branch type, automatic judgment, automatic erasure, and perpetual.

To change any of the options associated with a response, you must access the Response Options dialog box. The Response Options dialog box is unique for each response type, and therefore, will be introduced when I explain building an interaction that takes advantage of the specific response type. (See Chapter 10 through Chapter 14). The portion of each dialog box that is common across all response types, however, is shown in Figure 9.8.

FIG. 9.8
Some features are common
across all response types.

Click this button to access the
Response Type dialog box.

Automatic erase options

Automatic judgment options

Branching options

To access the Response Options dialog box, simply double-click the response type symbol for the specific response.

TIP In many cases, when you open the Response Options dialog box, the Presentation Window will also open. To prevent the Presentation Window from opening, hold down the Option key (Macintosh) or the Alt key (Windows) when double-clicking the response type symbol.

Shortcuts for Displaying the Response Options Dialog Box

To open the Response Options dialog box without the Presentation Window opening, hold down the Option key (Macintosh) or the Alt key (Windows), and double-click the response type symbol for the response path you want to change. You will notice that the Response Options dialog box opens, but the Presentation Window does not.

When a piece that uses hot spots is running, you can change the response options without jumping to the icon level then opening the Response Options dialog box by following these steps:

1. Hold down the Command (⌘) and Option keys (Macintosh only) to see the clickable areas for each available hot spot.
2. Double-click the border of the clickable area to open the Response Options dialog box.

Understanding the Branching Types

One of the greatest advantages of using the Interaction icon is the capability to enable the user to control the flow, or branching, of the piece. Branching can be used to establish menu schemes, to develop feedback for questions, or to simply present content for which the user has demonstrated a need. In any case, it is the branching characteristics of the interaction that provide this functionality.

Once the user has interacted with the piece and the piece has completed the journey down the response path, it must be assigned a direction to proceed along the Flowline. This assignment, shown as an arrow along the Flowline, which indicates the direction the piece will flow and which follows the response path, is known as the *response branch symbol.*

Within Authorware, there are four response branching types, each of which will be described next.

Try Again   Upon completion of a response path with *try again* branching, as shown in Figure 9.9, Authorware loops around and returns to the Interaction icon with which the response path is associated.

This branching type is most commonly used when the user has responded incorrectly to a question and gets another chance, or when the user has completed a section of the piece and is required to select another section.

Exit Interaction   Upon completion of a response path with *exit interaction* branching, as seen in Figure 9.10, the piece leaves the interaction loop and continues to the next icon on the Flowline.

FIG. 9.9

Try again branching returns the user to the Interaction icon.

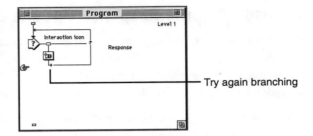

This branching type is most commonly used when the user has responded correctly to a question and the piece continues, or when the user has completed a section of the piece and the user is returned to a main menu.

FIG. 9.10

Exit interaction branching takes the user out of the interaction loop to continue down the Flowline.

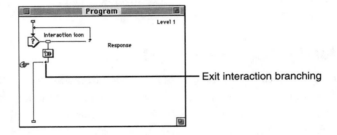

Continue   Upon completion of a response path with *continue* branching, as seen in Figure 9.11, the piece leaves the response and continues to evaluate other responses in the interaction loop. Only responses located to the right of the response with the continue branching are evaluated.

FIG. 9.11

Continue branching enables Authorware to evaluate for more than one possible response match.

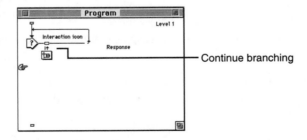

N O T E   The sequence of the responses is critical to the success of a piece using continue branching. Because the piece will have the opportunity to select more than one branch, you must be sure that the icons are sequenced from left to right from the Interaction icon in the order you want them judged. ▪

Part
III

Ch
9

This branching type is most commonly used when the piece is providing very specific judgment or feedback, such as in a performance support tool or when true interactivity is being developed.

Return   When a response path is set to Perpetual, its branching can be set to Return. Perpetual responses, as discussed later in the section "Using Perpetual Interactions," allow a response to be acted upon from anywhere within the piece, as opposed to only from within the interaction loop.

Return branching, as shown in Figure 9.12, enables the piece to return to the point on the Flowline from where the perpetual response was called once all of the icons in the response have been executed.

 TIP   When return branching is used, automatic erasing via backwards leaping will not occur.

Return branching is particularly helpful if you are creating context-sensitive Help or if you have provided tools, such as a notepad or glossary, that you want to appear without the content being automatically erased. As we will discuss in Chapter 18, "Erasing Media," whenever the piece flows backwards along the Flowline, known as backwards leaping, all of the icons that are encountered, or leaped over, are automatically erased. Automatic erasing is prevented when return branching is used.

FIG. 9.12
Return branching returns the user to the point in the piece from where the response was called.

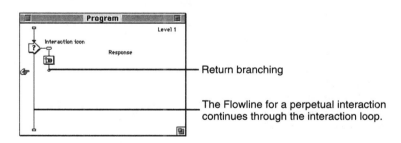

Return branching

The Flowline for a perpetual interaction continues through the interaction loop.

▶ For more information of backwards leaping, **see** "Backwards Leaping," **p. 362.**

Shortcuts Changing the Response Branching

Perform the following steps to change the branching without opening the Response Options dialog box:

1. Hold down the ⌘ key (Macintosh) or the Ctrl key (Windows), and click the response branch path just below the icon for that path.

2. Continue to click this path to cycle through all the branching options.

Erasing Interaction Responses Automatically

Within Authorware, you can erase information from the Presentation Window by implementing the Erase icon (see Chapter 18, "Erasing Media"); by implementing the Erase Icon function; by backwards leaping; and through options associated with the Decision, Framework, and Interaction icons.

Each response path of an interaction can be uniquely set to automatically erase all of the contents presented in that path. Using this feature saves great amounts of time authoring because you do not need to establish Erase icons. Additionally, there is an efficiency of the code because there will be fewer icons altogether.

Automatically erasing the contents of an interaction path can be established by selecting one of the automatic erase options from the pop-up list in the Response Options dialog box, described next.

Before Next Entry   Upon completion of the response path and prior to the user selecting another option, all of the objects in the response path will erase if the Before Next Entry automatic erase type is selected (see Fig. 9.13).

If the branch path type is set to Exit Interaction, the contents will erase upon completion of the branch path while exiting the interaction loop.

FIG. 9.13
The Before Next Entry automatic erasing erases all the contents of a response upon exiting the response path. The After Next Entry automatic erasing erases all the contents of a response after the user's next response with the interaction.

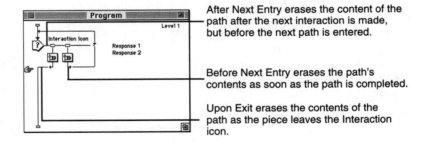

After Next Entry erases the content of the path after the next interaction is made, but before the next path is entered.

Before Next Entry erases the path's contents as soon as the path is completed.

Upon Exit erases the contents of the path as the piece leaves the Interaction icon.

This feature is commonly used when the user does not need any of the previous content that was presented in the path while making another selection from the interaction. For example, if the interaction is a menu of options, the user would not need content from the previous section to make another menu choice.

TROUBLESHOOTING

Why does my response flash on the screen then go away? If your response is set to Before Next Entry, and you are simply displaying a single graphic or block of text, Authorware will automatically erase the objects as soon as the piece exits the response. Be sure you select one of the other automatic erase options.

After Next Entry   If After Next Entry automatic erasing is selected, and the branching is set to either Continue or Try Again, the contents of the response path will not erase until the user has made another interaction (refer to Fig. 9.13).

If the response path type is set to Exit Interaction, the contents will erase upon completion of the response path while exiting the interaction loop.

The After Next Entry option is commonly used if you are providing an interaction in which the user can explore something. For example, the user can click various locations on a graphic of a control panel, and after his response, a definition for that part of the control panel is given. The response will remain in the Presentation Window until after the user's next entry, when it will automatically be erased and the new response will be presented.

Upon Exit   When Upon Exit is specified, the contents of the response will not erase until the piece exits the interaction loop (refer to Fig. 9.13). The Upon Exit automatic erasing erases all the contents of a response upon exiting the interaction loop.

Don't Erase   With the Don't Erase option specified, the contents of the response will not erase, even after the piece has exited the interaction loop.

N O T E   Selecting this option forces you to use an Erase icon, or for the contents of the interaction branch to be included in a higher level automatic erase. ■

Changing the Automatic Erasing Types

Each response path of an interaction can be set with a different automatic erase option. To change the automatic erase type of a path, follow these steps:

1. Double-click the response type symbol for the path you want to change. When the response type symbol is double-clicked, the Response Options dialog box will appear. Keep in mind that each Response Options dialog box is unique, depending on the type of interaction that has been selected.

2. When the Response Options dialog box opens, use the Erase Feedback pop-up list, as shown in Figure 9.14, to select the desired automatic erase type.

FIG. 9.14
Use the Erase Feedback pop-up box to select an automatic erase option.

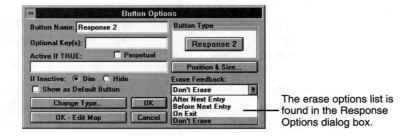

The erase options list is found in the Response Options dialog box.

 TIP In many cases, when you open the Response Options dialog box, the Presentation Window will also open. To prevent the Presentation Window from opening, hold down the Option key (Macintosh) or the Alt key (Windows) when double-clicking the response type symbol.

3. Click the OK button to save the settings in the Response Options dialog box.

Using Automatic Judging

Authorware was originally conceived by educators for educators. Therefore, at the heart of Authorware is an engine that automatically tracks the user's responses to questions, or interactions, as well as a variety of scoring mechanisms.

To have a user's performance automatically tracked by Authorware, however, you must identify which of the responses for an interaction are to be judged as well as how they are to be judged. This is called setting the Automatic Judging type.

Each response path of an interaction can be automatically judged by Authorware. Setting a path to be a correct or an incorrect response will cause the entire interaction to be counted as a judged interaction. All scoring and the tabulation of student records, therefore, will take this interaction into account. A response's judgment can be defined as described next.

Correct Response   By selecting this path, the user will be credited with making a correct response. Authorware places a plus sign (+) to the left of the icon title for any response that is set to be a Correct Response, as shown in Figure 9.15.

Wrong Response   By selecting this path, the user will be credited with making an incorrect response. Authorware places a minus sign (–) to the left of the icon title for any response that is set to be a Wrong Response (refer to Fig. 9.15).

FIG. 9.15
Authorware places a plus sign (+) to the left of the icon title for any response path set to Correct Response and a minus sign (−) to the left of the icon title for any response path set to Wrong Response.

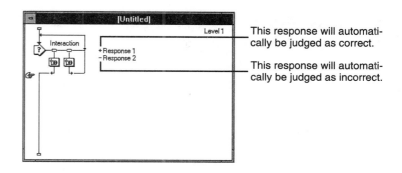

This response will automatically be judged as correct.

This response will automatically be judged as incorrect.

Not Judged   No judgment is applied if the user selects a response that is set to Not Judged. Not Judged is the default setting for each response path.

> **N O T E**   If you are not keeping scoring records, there is no need to set the judgment for a response path. ■

Changing the Judgment Types

Each response path of an interaction can be set with a different automatic judgment option. To change the automatic judgment type of a response, follow these steps:

1. Double-click the response type symbol for the path you want to change. When the response type symbol is double-clicked, the Response Options dialog box appears (see Fig. 9.16). Keep in mind that each Response Options dialog box is unique, depending on the type of interaction that has been selected.

FIG. 9.16
Use the pop-up menu to select an automatic judgment option.

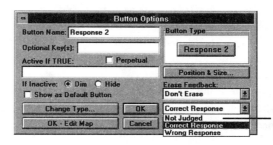

The Automatic Judgment List is found in the Response Options dialog box.

T I P   In many cases, when you open the Response Options dialog box, the Presentation Window will also open. To prevent the Presentation Window from opening, hold down the Option key (Macintosh) or the Alt key (Windows) when double-clicking the response type symbol.

2. Click the OK button to save the settings in the Response Options dialog box.

Part III

Ch 9

Shortcuts for Changing the Automatic Judging

Perform the following steps to change the automatic judging without opening the Response Options dialog box:

1. Hold down the ⌘ key (Macintosh) or the Ctrl key (Windows), and click just to the left of the title for the response you desire to change.

2. Continue to click in this location to cycle through all the automatic judgment options.

Using Perpetual Interactions

One of the greatest opportunities we have with interactive multimedia is to allow the end user to go anywhere they desire within the piece. To accommodate this type of navigation, Authorware supports perpetual interactions. When an interaction is perpetual, it may be responded to at any point within the piece.

N O T E Perpetual responses are most commonly used for such features as: an option to exit the piece; online Help; or glossary/dictionary functions. ■

To build a perpetual interaction, begin by creating an interaction as described in the section "Building an Interaction Loop," earlier in this chapter. The next step is to set the responses that you want to be available throughout the piece to Perpetual. To set a response to Perpetual, open the Response Options dialog box by double-clicking the response type symbol, as described in the section "Understanding the Response Options," previously in this chapter.

When all of the responses within an interaction loop are set to Perpetual, the Flowline will continue through the Interaction icon as opposed to stopping at the interaction, as seen in Figure 9.17. When this is the case, Authorware will activate each of the responses within the perpetual interaction, then continue on to execute other icons on the Flowline.

T I P If all of the responses in an interaction are not set to Perpetual, then the Flowline will not continue through the Interaction icon. Without this visual clue, it is difficult to determine which responses are perpetual. I recommend using the Icon Color palette to set perpetual responses to a color. This allows them to be easily recognized on the Flowline.

FIG. 9.17
Perpetual interactions appear
differently on the Flowline.

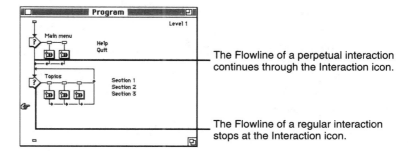

The Flowline of a perpetual interaction
continues through the Interaction icon.

The Flowline of a regular interaction
stops at the Interaction icon.

Understanding the Interaction Options

The Interaction icon comprises features like those from a Display icon, a Wait icon, a
Decision icon, and an Erase icon. A dialog box associated with the Interaction icon controls each of these aspects.

The Interaction Options dialog box (see Fig. 9.18) contains the options described next. To
access this dialog box, double-click the Interaction icon.

FIG. 9.18
The Interaction dialog box is
used to control elements of
the interaction.

Pause Before Exiting   When Pause Before Exiting is selected, the piece will
automatically pause before exiting the interaction loop. This automatic pause works much
like the Wait icon, except that the Time Limit option is not available.

If you elect to use the Pause Before Exiting feature, I recommend that you either also elect to
show the button or provide some type of directions on the screen. If the piece stops without
warning, the user will become confused.

Keep in mind that the pause happens when piece exits the interaction loop. Exiting the interaction loop happens when piece encounters an exit branch type. For more information on branch types, see "Understanding the Branching Types," earlier in this chapter.

Show Button   If the Pause Before Exiting option is selected, you can also select the Show button check box. Selecting this option causes the default pause button to appear in the Presentation Window. The user must click the button to resume the piece.

▶ For guidance on where to define the default pause button, **see** "Wait Button," **p. 49**.

Erase Interaction   The Erase Interaction choices enable you to determine when, or if, the contents of the interaction display will be automatically erased. The automatic erase options shown on the pop-up list (see Fig. 9.19) in the interaction dialog box are discussed in the next sections.

FIG. 9.19
There are three automatic erase options associated with the Interaction icon.

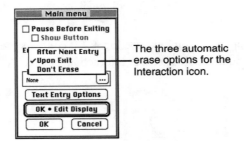

The three automatic erase options for the Interaction icon.

After Next Entry   Selecting this option causes all the contents of the interaction display to be automatically erased after each response entry by the user. If the branch path of the response made by the user returns the user to the Interaction icon, the display contents will be re-displayed.

Upon Exit   Selecting this option causes all the contents of the interaction display to be automatically erased upon exiting the interaction loop. This option is the default setting.

Don't Erase   Selecting this option causes all the contents of them interaction display to remain on the screen, even after exiting the interaction.

N O T E   Choosing Don't Erase forces you to use an Erase icon, or for the contents of the Interaction icon to be included in an automatic erase. ■

▶ For more information on how the contents of an Interaction icon are automatically erased, **see** "Automatically Erasing the Contents of an Interaction Icon," **p. 361**.

Erase Transition   Like the Erase icon, this option in the interaction dialog box enables you to select a transition that will be applied to the interaction display contents if they are automatically erased. For example, you may elect to have all of the content contained in the Interaction icon slide off one side of the Presentation Window, or to slowly fade out.

Text Entry Options   Clicking the Text Entry Options button presents an additional dialog box that is an extension of the Interaction dialog box. This extension is used to establish guidelines for text entry responses (that is, responses that the user enters into on-screen text boxes).

OK-Edit Display   The OK-Edit Display command button saves any selections you have made in the Interaction dialog box, then opens the interaction display, which is described next.

Editing the Interaction Display

The Interaction icon contains a display in which you can place text and graphics. To open the display if it isn't already open, simply double-click the Interaction icon. When the Interaction dialog box appears, click the OK-Edit Display button. The Interaction display can be edited just as any open Display icon can. That is, you can draw or place objects in the Presentation Window that appears and move and position those objects as needed. See Chapter 3, "Presenting Text," and Chapter 4, "Working with Graphics and Objects," for more information.

T I P   If you hold down the ⌘ (Macintosh) key or the Ctrl (Windows) key when opening the Interaction icon, the Interaction Options dialog box will not appear. Rather, you will go right into the Presentation window.

Shortcuts for Opening the Interaction Display   To open the Presentation Window for an Interaction icon without opening the Interaction Options dialog box, hold down the Command ⌘ key (Macintosh) or the Ctrl key (Windows), and double-click the Interaction icon.

Changing the Interaction Options from the Interaction Display   To change the interaction options from the Presentation Window (interaction display), double-click the picture of the Interaction icon located on the left-hand side of the toolbox (see Fig. 9.20). Then make your changes in the Interaction Options dialog box, and click OK.

FIG. 9.20
Double-click the picture of
the Interaction icon located
in the toolbox to open the
Interaction Options dialog
box.

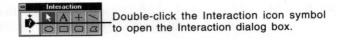

Double-click the Interaction icon symbol
to open the Interaction dialog box.

Changing the Response and Branching Options from the Toolbox

To change the branching and response options from the Presentation Window, hold down
the shortcut keys and double-click the respective symbols as shown in Figure 9.21.

Hold down the shortcut keys and double-click the Response
Type symbol to access the Response Options dialog box.

FIG. 9.21
Change response options
using the toolbox and the
shortcut key combinations.

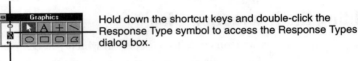

Hold down the shortcut keys and double-click the
Response Type symbol to access the Response Types
dialog box.

Hold down the shortcut keys and click the branching
symbol to change the branching.

N O T E   Automatic judgment cannot be changed from the Presentation Window. ▪

CHAPTER 10

Creating Buttons

The introduction of graphical user interfaces (GUI) into computing has changed the world forever. In a matter of a few years we went from systems that required programmers, capable of converting everyday thoughts into languages foreign and confusing to most of us, to home computers that could be operated by our children (but not by all adults).

The tools used to build these systems have changed at the same pace as the systems themselves. What once took hours to build, and may still take this long using authoring tools based on a scripting language, may now be built in a matter of seconds using icons and objects. These efficiencies are recognized not only in the creation of graphics and animation, but in the generation of interactivity as well.

Creating an interaction that uses a button response

The button response is one of the most common elements in an interactive piece, and one of the easiest to build within Authorware.

Using the Button Options dialog box

The Button Options dialog box is used to set parameters for the button interaction, including the button name, optional action keys, when the button is active, and what to do if the button is inactive. Additionally, the button may be defined as a default button.

Working with the Button Library

Authorware allows you to create custom buttons, then store them in a library. The Authorware Button Library initially contains a variety of system-like buttons.

Positioning and sizing buttons

Buttons can be positioned and sized just as regular objects are or adjusted using variables and expressions.

Using the Button Editor

The Button Editor is used to create custom buttons by importing graphics and sounds, adjusting the button label, and defining each state of the button.

Authorware allows the user to interact with the system in a variety of ways, and this chapter focuses on one of the most common means to communicate with the system—buttons. ■

Building Buttons

Buttons are possibly the most common mechanism used in a graphical user interface (GUI). They are used to create menus and navigation schemes and to provide a way for the user to interact with the application content.

Traditionally, buttons are rectangular in shape and convey a sense of dimension through their slightly beveled edges. This is certainly true for the default button which is used within Authorware when a running piece encounters either the Wait icon which causes the flow to pause; an automatic pause associated with a Decision icon or Interaction icon; or an Interaction icon that has a response using the button response type.

▶ For more information on how the Pause button functions in association with the Wait icon, **see** "Show Button," **p. 158**.

▶ For instruction on setting automatic pausing using the Interaction icon, **see** "Pause Before Exiting," **p. 231**.

▶ For guidance on establishing automatic pausing using the Decision icon, **see** "Taking Advantage of Automatic Pausing," **p. 349**.

Today, however, buttons are being redefined through the creation of irregularly shaped objects, many of which are 3-D in nature. To accommodate this shift in design practices, Authorware allows you to change the default button, which is used for either an interaction or when the flow of the piece pauses (See "Using the Button Editor," later in this chapter.)

N O T E One of my objectives is to make a button not look like a button, but to encourage the user to interact with it because it simply looks clickable, or even touchable. For example, consider the shape and functionality of a pull tab, light switch, cup handle, or a handshake. Each of these items looks like it can be interacted with simply because of its shape. ■

Building a Button Response

Aside from buttons that are automatically created by Authorware in order to pause the flow of the piece, buttons can also be used in association with the Interaction icon. To set up the Interaction icon with a button response, follow these steps:

1. Drag an Interaction icon to the Flowline.

2. Drag another icon to the Flowline and place it to the right of the Interaction icon, as shown in Figure 10.1. The icon that you place to the right of the Interaction icon is called the response. Responses can be created using the Display, Motion, Erase, Wait, Navigate, Calculation, Map, Digital Movie, Sound, or Video icons.

   To add subsequent button responses to the interaction, simply drag additional icons to the Flowline and continue to place them to the right of the Interaction icon.

   ▶ To refer to the introduction of the Interaction icon, **see** "The Interaction Icon," **p. 15**.

   ▶ For step-by-step instruction on creating an interaction, **see** "Building an Interaction Loop," **p. 215**.

FIG. 10.1
Place an icon to the right of the Interaction icon to build a button response.

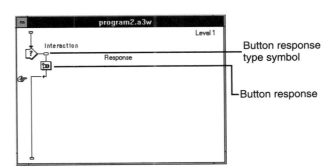

3. Upon releasing the first response on an Interaction icon, the Response Type dialog box appears. Select the button response type, then click OK, or press the Return (Macintosh) or Enter (Windows) key to save your selection.

4. Make additional adjustments to the functionality of the button using the Response Options dialog box. Click OK or press the Return (Macintosh) or Enter (Windows) key when finished to save your settings.

5. Choose Run from the Try It menu to see the button in the Presentation Window. Click the button to initiate the interaction.

 TIP The shortcut keys for Run are ⌘+R (Macintosh) and Ctrl+R (Windows).

Setting the Button Response Options

In Chapter 9, "The Fundamentals of Interactions," I discussed characteristics common across all interactions, such as automatic erasing, branching, and judging. The following features, while they may be found in other response types, are used to establish the functionality of buttons. To apply these options, you must open the Button Options dialog box, as seen in Figure 10.2.

To access the Button Options dialog box, follow these steps:

1. Build a button response as discussed in the previous section.

2. Double-click the response type symbol located just above the icon on the Flowline that was used to create the response.

The key options available in this dialog box are described next.

▶ For an overview of the commonalities for all interaction types within Authorware, **see** "Introducing Interactions," **p. 212**.

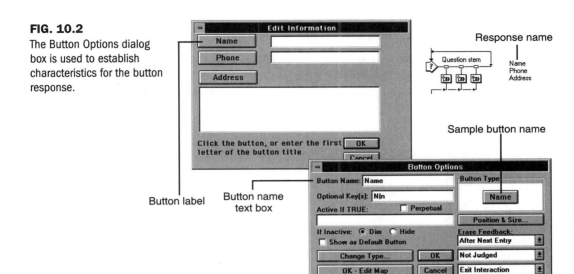

FIG. 10.2
The Button Options dialog
box is used to establish
characteristics for the button
response.

Defining the Button Name

Only occasionally within Authorware is the naming of an icon critical to its functionality, and this is one of those cases. The name that you give to the response icon on the Flowline will appear in the Button Name area of the Button Options dialog box, and vice versa.

Most importantly, if you are using the default button style, the name that you give the response icon will also appear on the button itself, as shown in Figure 10.3.

▶ For more information on naming the Response icon used to create a button, **see** "Button Responses," **p. 202**.

N O T E The size of the button automatically adjusts to accommodate the name you give it. ▪

Establishing an Optional Key

If you enter a key name in the Optional Key text box, you provide an additional means by which the user can interact with the button (see Fig. 10.3). Authorware automatically executes the button response whenever the ⌘ key (Macintosh) or Ctrl key (Windows) is used in conjunction with the key you've assigned. The user can simply press the specified key combination to choose that button.

In the example shown in Figure 10.3, the optional key is "N." To allow for both uppercase and lowercase characters, I entered the uppercase "N" as well as the lowercase "n" in the text box. I then separated the two entries with a vertical bar ("|"), which is read by Authorware as "or." Therefore, the entry in the text box is read as: uppercase N or lowercase n.

N O T E You can use combination keys such as ⌘+1 or Ctrl+7. Keep in mind, however, that the end users will not know that these alternative key options exist unless you notify them within the piece. ■

The user clicks this button to match the response.

FIG. 10.3
If the standard button style is used, the name of the Response icon will also appear on the button, in the sample button type window, and in the button name text box.

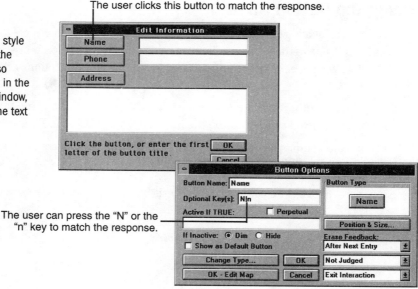

The user can press the "N" or the "n" key to match the response.

Using the Active If TRUE Text Box

You can activate or deactivate a button with a variable or expression in the Active If TRUE text box. Whenever the contents of the Active If TRUE text box evaluate to True, the response will be active, and when it evaluates to False, the response is inactive. To see how the button may change when the response is inactive, refer to the next section.

▶ To learn more about using the Active If TRUE box, **see** "Turning Responses On and Off," **p. 446**.

> **N O T E** When a button is inactive, you can elect to dim it, hide it, or treat it all together differently if you have created a custom button using the Button Editor. ∎

Determining What to Do If the Button Is Inactive

When a button is inactive, you can select to either hide the button (have it erased from view) or dim the button. The default selection for the If Inactive option in the Button Options dialog box is Dim.

▶ To learn more about inactivating a button, **see** "Turning Responses On and Off," **p. 446**.

Making a Button the Default Button

If the button style for the interaction response button is the standard system button, checking this option places a black border around the button, as shown in Figure 10.4. As in most applications, this graphical treatment implies that the button may be responded to by pressing the Return (Macintosh) or Enter (Windows) key.

> **CAUTION**
>
> Be careful not to assume that the Default Button option is simply a graphical treatment. According to interface guidelines, the dark border is reserved for buttons that the piece suggests you select. For example, in most applications, it's assumed you will click the OK button to accept dialog box settings, and continue with, say, a print job. Start watching how this treatment is used within the Authorware piece itself to get a better idea about its implementation.

FIG. 10.4
Default buttons have a black border. You can respond to them with an action key on the keyboard.

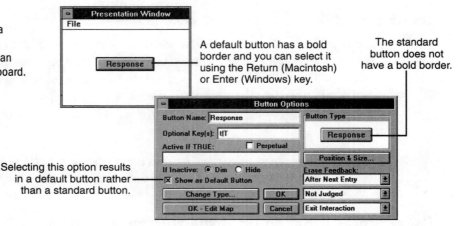

A default button has a bold border and you can select it using the Return (Macintosh) or Enter (Windows) key.

The standard button does not have a bold border.

Selecting this option results in a default button rather than a standard button.

Selecting a Button Type

The Button Type example in the Button Options dialog box shows the currently selected button type. Clicking the example allows you to change the button type by selecting a new type from the Button Library, shown in Figure 10.5.

FIG. 10.5
Authorware provides a variety of button types from which to select.

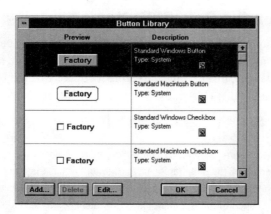

Authorware provides a variety of design styles for buttons, as well as a means for you to create custom button styles. To switch from one button type to another, follow these steps:

1. After you have opened the Button Options dialog box, click the Button Type area to activate the Button Library.

2. Scroll through the list of options available in the library.

TIP Most of the options are fairly standard, and may be more appropriate for creating pieces or performance support tools. Try your hand at creating a more natural button using the Button Editor.

3. Click the button type you desire.

4. Click the OK button or press the Return (Macintosh) or Enter (Windows) key to save your selection.

The button type you selected appears in the Button Type area of the Button Options dialog box.

Defining the Button's Position and Size

The most efficient way to position and size a button is to simply treat the button like a graphic object, as shown in Figure 10.6. From the Presentation Window, you can drag the button to any location on the screen, or you can use the object handles to size the object in any direction after the piece has been paused by choosing Pause from the Try It menu.

FIG. 10.6
Standard buttons can be positioned and sized in the Presentation Window.

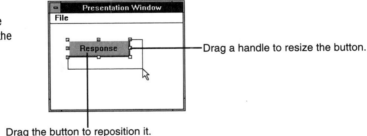
Drag a handle to resize the button.

Drag the button to reposition it.

To adjust the size or position of a button in the Presentation Window while running the piece, choose Pause from the Try It menu, then click the button you want to modify. Handles will appear that allow you to make the modifications. When completed, simply choose Proceed from the Try It menu and the piece will continue.

 TIP The shortcut keys for Pause and Proceed are ⌘+P (Macintosh) or Ctrl+P (Windows). This option is a toggle, so when the piece is running, the Pause option is available, and when the piece is paused, the Proceed option is available.

Buttons can also be positioned and sized using the options which appear after selecting the Position and Size button in the Button Options dialog box. Controls that can be set within the dialog box, which appears after selecting the Position and Size button, are discussed in the following sections.

Setting the Button's Position   A button's position in the Presentation Window can be determined either by providing values representing the desired pixel location, or by entering a variable or expression, which allows the button's position to change dynamically. Controls for the position of a button include the following:

■ Left Side—Determines how many pixels from the left side of the Presentation Window the button will be placed, as shown in Figure 10.7.

FIG. 10.7
A button can be precisely positioned based on its distance from the left side of the Presentation Window.

The button is positioned based on the value entered.

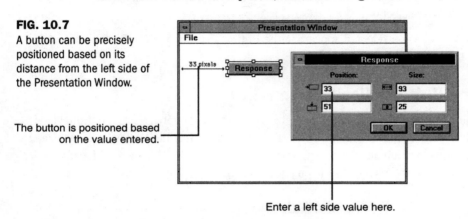

Enter a left side value here.

■ Top—Determines how many pixels from the top of the Presentation Window the button will be placed, as shown in Figure 10.8.

FIG. 10.8
A button can also be precisely positioned based on its distance from the top of the Presentation Window.

The button is positioned based on the value entered.

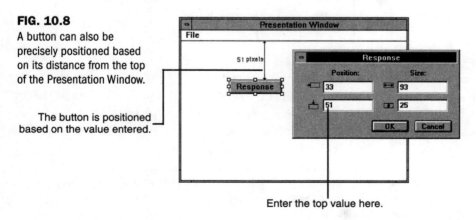

Enter the top value here.

▶ For step-by-step guidance on using variables and functions to position response areas, **see** "Positioning Buttons and Fields," **p. 452**.

Setting the Button's Size   A button's width can be set either by providing values representing the desired width expressed in pixels, or by entering a variable or expression, which allows the size of the button to change dynamically. Controls for the size of the button include the following:

- Horizontal—Determines how wide the button will be. This value is expressed in pixels.

- Vertical—Determines how tall the button will be. This value is expressed in pixels.

    ▶ For step-by-step guidance on using variables and functions to position response areas, **see** "Positioning Buttons and Fields," **p. 452**.

Using the Button Editor

Part
III

Ch
10

While Authorware provides a library of button styles, you may find that none of the options meet your design needs. In such a case, you can design a custom button using the Button Editor, as shown in Figure 10.9. You can access the Button Editor by choosing Buttons from Libraries menu, or by clicking the Button Type area of the Button Options dialog box.

FIG. 10.9
Authorware's Button Editor allows you to create custom buttons.

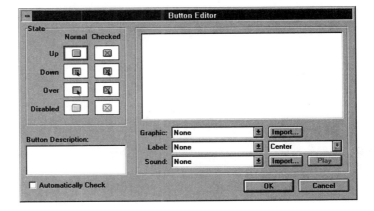

The Button Editor dialog box contains the options described next, which enable you to specify just what form your custom button should take.

Defining Button States   As shown in the State area of the Button Editor dialog box, a button, including radio buttons and check boxes, has four normal states—Up, Down, Over, and Disabled. The following is a description of the button states:

- Up—Shows the button as it normally will appear in the Presentation Window.

- Down—Shows the button as it will appear when the user clicks the button. Additionally, selecting Down plays any sound associated with the button.

- Over—Shows how the button will look when the user positions the cursor over the button.

- Disabled—Shows what the button will look like when it is inactive.

Those states may be categorized as either normal or checked. The following list describes what happens to a button when it is either Normal or Checked:

- Normal—Illustrates how a button will appear in the Presentation Window when the button is active, as shown in Figure 10.10. For radio buttons and check boxes, it illustrates how the button will appear in an unselected mode.

FIG. 10.10

Normal shows how the button will be displayed in the Presentation Window.

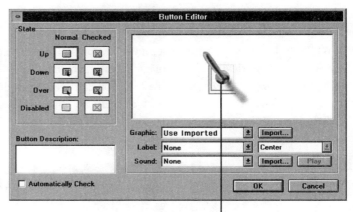

Shows the normal state of the button

- Checked—Illustrates how radio buttons and check boxes will appear in the Presentation Window when they have been selected, as shown in Figure 10.11.

FIG. 10.11

Checked shows how a radio button or check box will appear in the Presentation Window once it has been selected by the user.

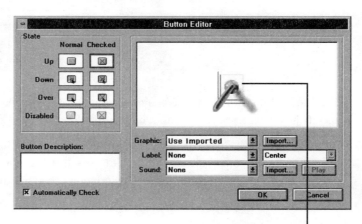

Shows the checked state of the button

The steps for changing the characteristics of the button, such as the button graphic, its label, or the sound it produces, are described in the next few sections.

Leaving a Button Description

You can enter up to 80 characters that describe the button in the Button Description text box of the Button Editor dialog box. This may help in describing where the button is to be used, or how it was originally created.

> **N O T E** These button descriptions are for your use only and have no impact on the final piece. Be as descriptive as possible to make maintenance easier. ■

What Happens When a Button Is Automatically Checked?

Select the Automatically Checked check box in the Button Editor dialog box to create buttons that toggle between selected and unselected, as shown in Figure 10.12.

> **N O T E** This is a great way to create a switch. For example, the Off position may be unchecked, and the On position may be checked. By treating the switch as an Authorware button, you do not have to worry about erasing or determining if it is on or off. ■

FIG. 10.12
Toggle buttons are easy to create using the Button Editor by selecting Automatically Check.

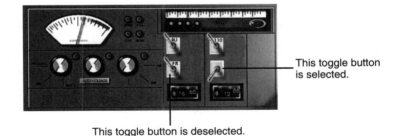

This toggle button is selected.

This toggle button is deselected.

Creating Your Own Button Graphic

Buttons can be created using a variety of graphics tools, then saved in any of the following formats: .BMP, .DIB, .RLE, .EPS, .WMF, .PCX, .TIF, .PIC, or PICT. Once a button has been created, it may be imported into Authorware by following these steps:

1. Once the Button Editor is open, select the state (Up, Down, Over, or Disabled) and the mode (Normal or Checked) to which you want to add the imported button graphic.

2. Click the Import button located adjacent to the Graphic drop-down list.

N O T E You can also import a graphic into the Button Editor by copying a graphic located in an external graphic program, then pasting it into the Button Editor. ■

3. Browse your hard disk, network, or any attached volume to locate the graphic to be used for the button.

4. Once a graphic has been located using the Import dialog box, click the Open button to load the graphic.

5. Repeat these steps for each state and each mode of the button.

▶ For further information on importing, **see** "Using the Import Function," **p. 108**.

Labeling the Button

The label is the name that you gave the response icon when constructing the Flowline, or that you entered into the Button Options dialog box. You can elect to show the label using the Label drop-down list in the Button Editor dialog box, or you can have no label appear.

If you elect to show the label, use the second drop-down list beside the Label option in the Button Editor dialog box to adjust the justification of the text within the button.

Clicking the example picture of the button while using the Button Editor causes handles to appear on the text, as shown in Figure 10.13. When the text is selected, you can use the Text and Attributes menus to adjust font, size, style, and color.

▶ For guidance on changing font, size and style, **see** "Changing Text Characteristics," **p. 79**.
▶ For hints on changing color, **see** "Using the Color Palette," **p. 119**.

FIG. 10.13
Button labels can be customized within the Button Editor.

To edit the text, select it so that the handles appear.

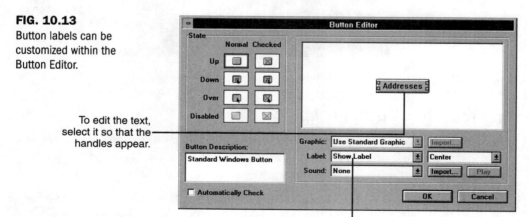

The label can be edited if you elect to show the label.

Adding Sound to the Button

Buttons can also be assigned a sound for each state. If a sound is assigned to the Normal state, it is not played when the button is first displayed; however, it is played whenever the button returns to a Normal state, such as after being deselected.

To associate a sound with a button, follow these steps:

1. Once the Button Editor is open, click the Import button located adjacent to the Sound drop-down list and then click the Play button.
2. Browse your hard disk, network or any attached volume to locate the sound to be used for the button.
3. Once a sound has been located using the Import dialog box, click the Open button to load the sound.
4. After the sound has been loaded, click the Play button to test the sound.

   ▶ For further information on importing, **see** "Using the Import Function," **p. 108**.

CHAPTER 11

Using Hot Spots and Hot Objects

As graphical user interfaces grew in popularity, they also began to evolve in sophistication—for example, interfaces began to reflect realistic, 3-D environments. Additionally, designers began to create interactions that required the end user to explore portions of an illustration by clicking its various components. To create such interfaces, rectangular-shaped, beveled buttons no longer met the design requirements, and an alternative method for triggering a response had to be developed.

Clickable areas, or hot spots as they are commonly referred to, quickly replaced traditional buttons in multimedia-based pieces. While in many cases they were used much like buttons, more creative methods for implementing clickable areas were also implemented. For example, there were several popular children's pieces that allowed end users to click areas of the screen that they felt contained the hidden treasures.

One of the challenges with using clickable areas, however, was that they were typically rectangular-shaped. Therefore, if the user selected an irregularly

Building with hot spot responses

Creating hot spots, like creating other interaction types, requires that specific steps be followed.

Taking advantage of the response options

Hot spot options include defining a title for the response, assigning an optional key, using the Active if TRUE text box, selecting a custom cursor, and electing to have the hot spot automatically highlight when selected.

Positioning and sizing hot spots in the Presentation Window

The position and size of a hot spot is set during authoring or is based on variables and expressions, enabling it to change while the final piece is running.

Adding cursors to the cursor library

Authorware contains a Cursor Library from which you can select a custom cursor.

Building hot objects

When an irregularly shaped area must be selectable by the end user, then the hot object interaction response is the right tool.

shaped object, several clickable areas had to be used to cover the object without covering areas outside of the object. To circumvent this, hot objects were created as a response option in Authorware. With hot objects, an irregularly shaped object, or an object in motion, could be designated as the selectable item.

This chapter focuses on creating clickable areas, as well as using hot objects. ■

Using Hot Spots

With the introduction of multimedia came the movement away from traditional graphical user interface widgets toward a more free-flowing environment. In this type of environment, the user is not prompted to interact with buttons, but rather, with elements that are naturally a part of the environ ment.

To support this type of interface, Authorware provides an invisible boundary that can be placed over any object (movie, graphic, and so on) that the user can click to activate the response. These invisible boundaries are known as *hot spots*.

Building a Hot Spot Response

The creation of a hot s pot response is most like the creation of a button within Authorware, except that you are not defining a physical object to be interacted with, but rather a portion of the Presentation Window.

To set up an interaction with a hot spot response, follow these steps:

1. Drag an Interaction icon to the Flowline.

2. Drag another icon to the Flowline and place it to the right of the Interaction icon (see Fig. 11.1). The icon you place to the right of the Interaction icon is called the response. Responses can be created using the Display, Motion, Erase, Wait, Navigate, Calculation, Map, Digital Movie, Sound, or Video icons.

To add subsequent hot spots to the interaction, simply drag additional icons to the Flowline and continue to place them to the right of the Interaction icon.

▶ To refer to the introduction of the Interaction icon, **see** "The Interaction Icon," **p. 19**.

▶ For step-by-step instruction on creating an interaction, **see** "Building an Interaction Loop," **p. 215**.

FIG. 11.1
Place an icon to the right of the Interaction icon to build a response.

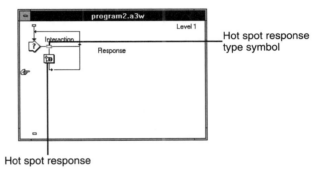

Hot spot response

3. Upon releasing the first response on an Interaction icon, the Response Type dialog box appears. Select the hot spot response type.

4. Click the OK button, or press the Return (Macintosh) or Enter (Windows) key to save your selection. When the Response Type dialog box closes, the Hot Spot Options dialog box will appear.

5. Make additional adjustments to the functionality of the hot spot using the Hot Spot Options dialog box. Click OK, or press the Return (Macintosh) or Enter (Windows) key when finished to save your settings.

6. Select Run from the Try It menu.

 The shortcut keys for Run are ⌘+R (Macintosh) and Ctrl+R (Windows).

7. Select Pause from the Try It menu to see the hot spot on-screen.

TIP The shortcut keys for Pause or Proceed are ⌘+P (Macintosh) and Ctrl+P (Windows).

8. Select Proceed from the Try It pull-down menu.

9. Click within the hot spot boundary to initiate the interaction.

Setting the Hot Spot Response Options

In Chapter 9, "The Fundamentals of Interactions," I discussed characteristics common across all interactions, such as automatic erasing, branching, and judging. The following features, while they may be found in other response types, are used to establish the functionality of hot spot responses. These features are applied using the Hot Spot Options dialog box, as shown in Figure 11.2.

To access the Hot Spot Options dialog box, follow these steps:

1. Build a hot spot response as discussed in the previous section.

2. Double-click the response type symbol located just above the icon on the Flowline that was used to create the response.

The key options available in the Hot Spot Options dialog box are described next.

▶ For an overview of the commonalities for all interaction types within Authorware, **see** Introducing Interactions," **p. 212**.

FIG. 11.2
The Hot Spot Options dialog
box is used to establish
characteristics for the hot
spot response.

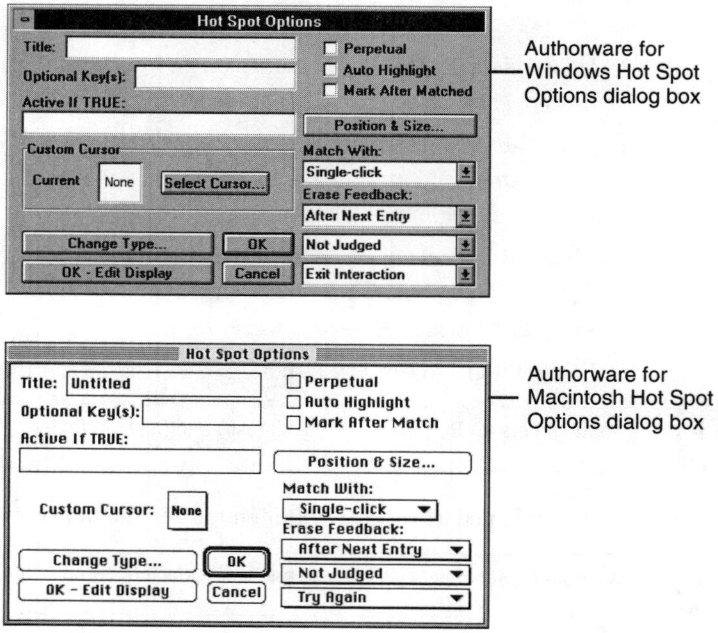

Authorware for
Windows Hot Spot
Options dialog box

Authorware for
Macintosh Hot Spot
Options dialog box

Giving the Response a Title

The name that you give the icon on the Flowline appears in the Title text box of the Hot Spot Options dialog box, and vice versa. Unlike button responses, however, the name is not critical to the functionality of the response.

 TIP Naming the response descriptively makes editing of the hot spot in the Presentation Window much easier.

Assigning an Optional Key

If you enter a key name in the Optional Key text box, you provide an additional means by which the user can interact with the hot spot (see Fig. 11.3). Authorware automatically executes the hot spot response whenever the ⌘ key (Macintosh) or Ctrl key (Windows) is used in conjunction with the key you've assigned. The user can simply press the specified key combination to choose that hot spot.

To allow for several optional keys, separate the two entries with a vertical bar ("|"), which is read by Authorware as "or." For example, the entry in the text box could be "1|2."

FIG. 11.3
Users can click within the designated region of the hot spot or press a designated key (1 in this case) on the keyboard.

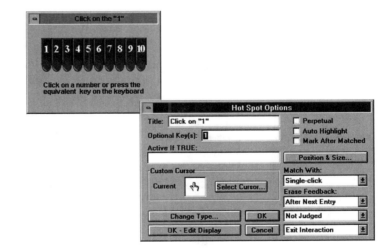

Part
III

Ch
11

NOTE You can use combination keys; however, keep in mind that end users will not know these alternative key options exist unless you notify them within the piece. ■

Using the Active If TRUE Text Box

You can activate or deactivate a hot spot with a variable or expression in the Active If TRUE text box. Whenever the contents of the Active If TRUE text box evaluate to True, the response will be active, and when it evaluates to False, the response is inactive.

▶ To learn more about using the Active If TRUE box, **see** "Turning Responses On and Off," **p. 446**.

Selecting a Custom Cursor

When the user moves the mouse pointer over the hot spot boundary, the mouse pointer will change shape. This visual change helps the user identify what portions of the Presentation Window are selectable, and which are not. Within Authorware there are a variety of cursor styles, as well as a means for you to create custom cursors.

> **N O T E**   You can either create cursors or import them from any other piece. In any case, custom cursors are a great indicator to the end user that something is selectable or clickable. Examples of custom cursors include an I-beam, which indicates text entry; a crosshair, which indicates precision; or a magnifying glass, which suggests enlarging. ▪

To switch from one custom cursor type to another on the Macintosh, follow these steps:

1. Once you have opened the Hot Spot Options dialog box, click and hold down the mouse on the custom cursor pop-up window, as shown in Figure 11.4.

2. Move through the palette of options available in the library by dragging the mouse.

FIG. 11.4
Only the Macintosh has a pop-up window for custom cursors.

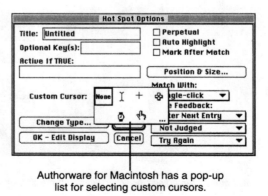

Authorware for Macintosh has a pop-up
list for selecting custom cursors.

3. To save a selection, release the mouse button when the desired selection is highlighted. The cursor type you selected now appears in the custom cursor pop-up box.

To switch from one custom cursor type to another in Windows, follow these steps:

1. Once you have opened the Hot Spot Options dialog box, you must access the Cursor Library, as seen in Figure 11.5, by clicking the Select Cursor button.

FIG. 11.5
Authorware provides a variety of cursor types for you to select from.

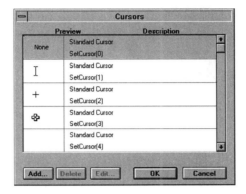

N O T E You can also access the Cursor Library for either Macintosh or Windows by selecting the Cursors option from the Libraries pull-down menu. ■

2. Scroll through the list of available cursors. Click a cursor to select it.
3. To save that selection, click OK when the desired selection is highlighted. The cursor type you selected now appears in the current cursor window in the Hot Spot Options dialog box.

Causing the Hot Spot to Automatically Highlight

When an on-screen button is selected (clicked) by the end user, he can see the button depress. With a hot spot, however, this visual clue is absent unless the Auto Highlight option in the Hot Spot Options dialog box is selected. Selecting this check box causes the entire hot spot region to inverse in color when selected, as seen in Figure 11.6.

> **CAUTION**
> Because inversing results are unpredictable, I either create a button based on the background graphic, or I simply place a highlight in an icon somewhere on the Flowline to provide the same visual clue that is provided when Auto Highlight is selected.

Part
III

Ch
11

FIG. 11.6
The region that inverses is defined by the boundary of the hot spot.

Auto highlight causes the entire clickable region to inverse in color when it is clicked.

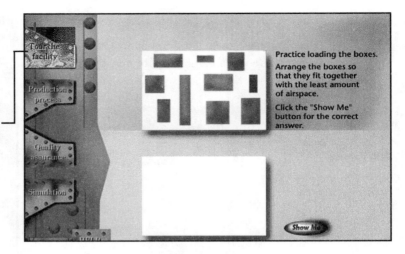

Using the Mark After Match Option

Keeping track of which responses have been selected may be necessary for a given interaction. When Mark After Matched is selected in the Hot Spot Options dialog box, Authorware provides a visual prompt for the user by placing a small empty square alongside the hot spot region. When the user selects the response, the box fills in, as shown in Figure 11.7, and remains filled until the user leaves the interaction loop.

FIG. 11.7
Selecting the Mark After Match option places a small check box in the upper-left corner of the hot spot region.

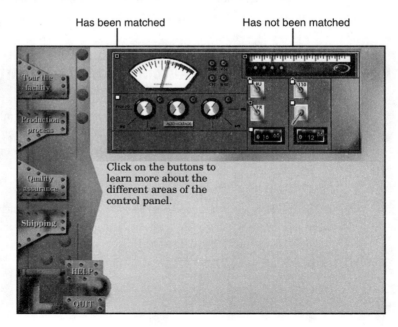

CAUTION

I find that this little box rarely fits into a custom interface, therefore, I have a tendency to not use this option. If the mark were definable, much like a button, this option may be more valuable.

Defining a Hot Spot's Position and Size

You can position and size hot spot in the Presentation Window just as you do graphical elements. Alternatively, you can position and size them using variables or expressions representing pixel values in the dialog box that appears after you click the Position & Size button in the Hot Spot Options dialog box.

▶ For step-by-step guidance on using variables and functions to position response areas, **see** "Positioning Buttons and Fields," **p. 452**.

Controls that can be set within this dialog box are described next.

Setting the Position   A hot spot's position in the Presentation Window is determined either by providing values representing the desired pixel location, or by entering a variable or expression that allows the hot spots' position to change dynamically. Controls for the position of a hot spot include:

- Left Side—Determines how many pixels from the left-hand side of the Presentation Window the hot spot is placed.

- Top—Determines how many pixels from the top of the Presentation Window the hot spot is placed.

Setting the Size   A hot spot's width can also be set either by providing values representing the desired width expressed in pixels, or by entering a variable or expression that allows the size of the hot spot to change dynamically. Controls for the size of the hot spot include:

- Horizontal—Determines the width of the hot spot. This value is expressed in pixels.

- Vertical—Determines the height of the hot spot. This value is expressed in pixels.

To adjust the size or position of a hot spot in the Presentation Window while running the application, choose Pause from the Try It menu, then click the hot spot you want to modify. Handles appear that allow you to make the adjustments. When completed, simply choose Proceed from the Try It menu and the piece continues.

TIP The shortcut keys for Pause and Proceed are ⌘+P (Macintosh) and Ctrl+P (Windows). This option is a toggle, so when the piece is running, the Pause option is available, and when the piece is paused, the Proceed option is available.

N O T E   Variables or expressions are helpful if the position or size of a hot spot might change as a result of the user's interactivity with the piece. ■

Verifying How the User Will Match the Response

Hot spot responses can be matched with any one of the following options shown in the Match With drop-down list of the Hot Spot Options dialog box, shown in Figure 11.8:

- Single-click—This default option requires the user to click once in the designated hot spot area to make the selection.

- Double-click—This option requires the user to click twice within the designated hot spot area to make the selection.

> **CAUTION**
>
> When authoring, the piece will pause when you double-click any object in the Presentation Window, including hot spots.
>
> If your interaction requires a double-click, you can use a single-click while authoring, but name the response with a special word. Then, when you are ready to deliver your piece, you can conduct a search for all icons containing the special note, and change the single-click to a double-click.

- Cursor in Area—This option requires that the user simply move the cursor into the hot spot area to make the selection. When this response type option is selected, the Auto Highlight option is not available.

FIG. 11.8
You can designate how the user must respond to a hot spot interaction.

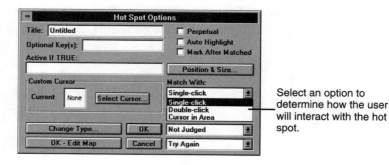

Select an option to determine how the user will interact with the hot spot.

Adding Cursors to the Library

While Authorware provides a library of cursor styles, you may find that none of these options meet your design needs. In this case, you can import a custom cursor.

To open the Cursor Library in Authorware for Windows, choose the Cursors option from the Libraries menu, or click the Select Cursor button in the Hot Spot Options dialog box (Windows only.)

The Cursor Library contains the following options:

- Add—This button opens the standard Open File dialog box, as seen in Figure 11.9, which allows you to search for the file containing the desired cursor to import. Files that can be identified must contain a cursor resource, and are more often than not created with a traditional programming tool.

FIG. 11.9
Authorware enables you to import cursors from other pieces, or that you have created with a graphics editor.

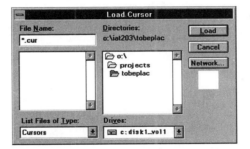

- Delete—An imported custom cursor can be deleted by first selecting the cursor in the Cursors Library list, then clicking the Delete button. Cursors provided by Authorware cannot be deleted.

- Edit—An imported cursor can be overwritten by first selecting the cursor in the Cursors Library list, then clicking the Edit button. Cursors provided by Authorware cannot be edited.

N O T E One of the most aggravating and time-consuming aspects of using custom cursors is the need to set the cursor for each interaction. After you create a custom cursor for an interaction, Authorware is smart enough to assume you want all hot spots to contain that cursor. It would be really helpful to be able to set a global default for custom cursors just as you do for font or color. ■

The Benefit of Hot Objects

As graphical user interfaces evolve further away from traditional widgets, such as buttons, designers are creating pieces that allow the user to interact with objects.

To accommodate this design, Authorware allows you to designate a hot object. When the user selects the object, the response is considered matched. For example, if you designate a piece of Swiss cheese to be the hot object, and the user selects the cheese, then the response is matched. If the user selects a hole in the cheese, however, then the response is not matched.

To set up an interaction with a hot object response, follow these steps:

1. Drag a Display icon to the Flowline.
2. Open the Display icon and create an object with which you want the user to interact. When you're finished, close the Display icon by clicking the Close button in the upper left-hand corner of the Graphics toolbox.
   ▶ To refer to the introduction of the Display icon, **see** "The Display Icon," **p. 15**.
   ▶ For guidance on creating an object within a Display icon, **see** "Drawing Objects," **p. 98**
3. Drag an Interaction icon to the Flowline.
4. Drag another icon to the Flowline and place it to the right of the Interaction icon, as shown in Figure 11.10. The icon you place to the right of the Interaction icon is called the response. Responses can be created using the Display, Motion, Erase, Wait, Navigate, Calculation, Map, Digital Movie, Sound, or Video icons.

   To add subsequent hot objects to the interaction, simply drag additional icons to the Flowline and continue to place them to the right of the Interaction icon.
   ▶ To refer to the introduction of the Interaction icon, **see** "The Interaction Icon," **p. 19**.
   ▶ For step-by-step instruction on creating an interaction, **see** "Building An Interaction Loop," **p. 215**.
5. Upon releasing the first response on an Interaction icon, the Response Type dialog box appears. Select the hot object response type.
6. Click the OK button, or press the Return (Macintosh) or Enter (Windows) key to save your selection.
7. Choose Run from the Try It menu.

FIG. 11.10
Place an icon to the right of
the Interaction icon to build
a response.

Hot Object Response
Type symbol

Hot Object
Response

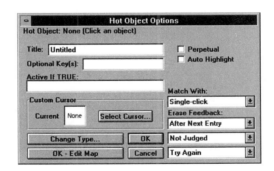

 TIP The shortcut keys for Run is ⌘+R (Macintosh) and Ctrl+R (Windows).

8. Authorware automatically pauses to display the Hot Object Options dialog box, as seen in Figure 11.11, when it hits the Interaction icon with the undefined hot object. The message in the upper-left corner of the dialog box instructs you to click the object in the Presentation Window that you want to be the hot object. Click the object you created in Step 2.

FIG. 11.11
The Hot Object Response
Type Options dialog box.

9. Click the OK button, or press the Return (Macintosh) or Enter (Windows) key to save your selection.

10. Click the hot object to initiate the interaction.

 TIP If you have several hot objects, each located in separate display icons, you can create an icon that contains all of the objects and place it before all of the icons containing the single objects. This prevents the user from seeing the objects appear one by one.

The hot object and the hot spot options are nearly identical. The options for the hot object do not include Mark After Match and Position and Size. For an overview of the remaining options, see "Setting the Hot Spot Response Options," earlier in this chapter.

▶ For an overview of the commonalities for all interaction types within Authorware, **see** Introducing Interactions," **p. 212**.

Building Pull-down Menus

Pull-down menus are a graphical user interface (GUI) feature found within almost every software application in the Macintosh and Windows environments. The benefit of a pull-down menu is that it allows the end user to access functions performed by the application—or to access areas of the application—through a menu that is continually available yet requires very little screen space. For some reason, however, pull-down menus are rarely used in the creation of an interactive multimedia-based piece. Let's consider why some people avoid this popular interface feature.

One reason that pull-down menus are becoming less common is that they distract from the visual appearance of a GUI. For many applications, setting the graphical theater is key to communicating the intended message. When a natural environment is replaced by a sterile, standard pull-down menu, the intended message—the primary motivation for using the piece—might be at risk.

In addition to their concern with a piece's visual aspect, developers need to consider the usability of the piece. As many multimedia applications are aimed at the novice computer user, developers are drifting away from having users interact with objects such as pull-down menus and scrolling windows. Pull-down menus can make a piece difficult to use for several reasons: they show no indication that a selection has been made other than the menu closing; the user does not have a constant reminder of which selection has just been made, or which ones have been made throughout the piece; and the dexterity required to manipulate a pull-down menu can be difficult for beginners.

This chapter explores the process of creating pull-down menus with Authorware, and suggests practical uses for these menus. ■

Creating Pull-down Menus

One of the most common methods of interacting with a computer program is through the use of pull-down menus. While scripting a pull-down menu in a traditional programming tool was tricky, Authorware has made this task unbelievably simple.

Despite the ease of developing pull-down menus, however, you must determine when it's appropriate to use pull-down menus, and when it's more appropriate to use a GUI. Keep in mind that navigating pull-down menus comes naturally for the computer aficionado, but does not come as naturally for the novice user.

To set up the Interaction icon with a pull-down response, follow these steps:

1. Drag an Interaction icon to the Flowline. What you title the Interaction icon is very important when building pull-down menus, because this icon title is the header name for the pull-down menu, as shown in Figure 12.1.

▶ To refer to the introduction of the Interaction icon, **see** "The Interaction Icon," **p. 19.**

▶ For step-by-step instruction on creating an interaction, **see** "Building an Interaction Loop," **p. 215.**

▶ For more information on naming the Interaction icon used to create a pull-down menu, **see** "Pull-down Menu Responses," **p. 202.**

Naming the interaction creates the title of the pull-down menu header.

Naming the interaction responses creates the menu items.

FIG. 12.1

The name of the Interaction icon becomes the header for the pull-down menu.

The name of the menu header is based on the name of the Interaction icon.

The menu items that can be selected are based on the pull-down menu response paths.

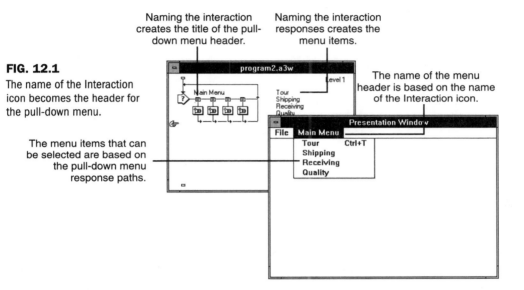

N O T E The number of pull-down menus across the top of the Presentation Window is based on the length of the names assigned to the menus. ▨

2. Drag an icon to the Flowline and place it to the right of the Interaction icon, as shown in Figure 12.2. Any icon placed to the right of the Interaction icon is called a *response*. Responses can be created using the Display, Motion, Erase, Wait, Navigate, Calculation, Map, Digital Movie, Sound, and Video icons.

To add subsequent menu choices to the pull-down menu, simply drag additional icons to the Flowline and continue to place them to the right of the Interaction icon. The order that the items appear in the pull-down menu is based on their sequence along the Flowline within the interaction loop. Items that are closer to the Interaction icon (further to the left in the sequence) will appear on top of those responses to their right.

FIG. 12.2
Place an icon to the right of the Interaction icon to build a response.

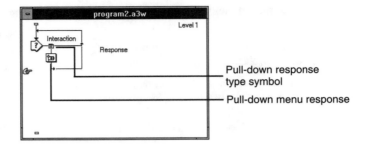

Pull-down response type symbol

Pull-down menu response

3. When you release the first response on an Interaction icon, the Response Type dialog box appears. Select the Pull-Down Menu response type.

4. Click OK to save your selection.

5. Name the icon that you just brought to the Flowline. For example, if you name the response icon **Circles**, a response option titled Circles would be created in the pull-down menu.

6. Choose Run from the Try It menu to test your piece.

 The shortcut key combination for Try It, Run is ⌘+R (Macintosh) or Ctrl+R (Windows).

7. Notice that Authorware has created a pull-down menu with its header the same as the name of the Interaction icon. Click this header to activate the menu, then click the item in the pull-down menu. Using our example again, the menu choice would be Circles.

N O T E Authorware creates a default File menu that contains a Quit command. You can replace this version of the File menu with your own by titling an Interaction icon **File**. If you do this, be sure to provide a means for the user to exit the piece. ▪

 Consider using pull-down menus to hold tools during development, then deleting those menus before final packaging. For example, you might create a menu containing a style guide. Each time you need the guide, access the menu. You might even build another menu to erase the style guides.

Setting the Pull-down Menu Options

In Chapter 9, "The Fundamentals of Interactions," I discuss characteristics common across all interactions, such as automatic erasing, branching, and judging. The following features, while they might be found in other response types, are used to establish the functionality of pull-down menu responses. To apply these options, you must open the Pull-down Menu Options dialog box shown in Figure 12.3.

To access the Pull-down Menu Options dialog box, follow these steps:

1. Build a pull-down menu response as discussed in the previous section.

2. Double-click the response type symbol located just above the icon that was used to create the response.

The key options available in this dialog box are described next.

▶ For an overview of the commonalities for all interaction types within Authorware, **see** "Introducing Interactions," **p. 212.**

FIG. 12.3
The Pull-Down Menu Options dialog box is used to set specific parameters for the functionality of the pull-down menu.

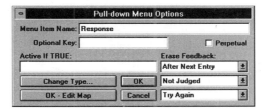

Setting the Menu Item Name

The name that you give to the response icon on the Flowline will appear in the Menu Item Name text box of the Pull-Down Menu Options dialog box, and vice versa. This name also appears in the pull-down menu as a selectable item.

▶ For more information on naming the Interaction icon used to create a pull-down menu, **see** "Pull-down Menu Responses," **p. 202.**

Enter the following special codes in the Menu Item Name text box to customize the pull-down menu:

Code	Result
(Text	This presents the text as dimmed and unselectable.
(Space	This produces an unselectable blank line, or gap, in the menu.
(-	This produces a line separator across the menu that is not selectable as a response. If you only used the hyphen, a line would be created but it would be selectable by the end user.

Part
III

Ch
12

Defining an Optional Key

If you enter a key name in the Optional Key text box, you provide an additional means by which the user can interact with the pull-down menu (see Fig. 12.4). Authorware automatically executes the associated menu command whenever the ⌘ key (Macintosh) or Ctrl key (Windows) is used in conjunction with the key you've assigned. The user can simply press the specified key combination to choose that menu command.

FIG. 12.4
As a shortcut, users can press a designated key sequence on the keyboard instead of selecting the pull-down menu command.

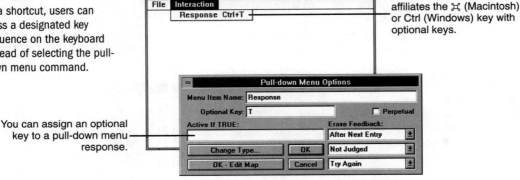

Authorware automatically affiliates the ⌘ (Macintosh) or Ctrl (Windows) key with optional keys.

You can assign an optional key to a pull-down menu response.

  I have often built pull-down menus that contain contents such as a glossary or note cards so that these contents can be accessed easily via shortcut keys. I then turn off the menu bar so that it does not interfere with the GUI. Although the menu bar is inactive, the menu options are still available by using the key combinations.

Using the Active If TRUE Text Box

You can activate or deactivate a pull-down menu with a variable or expression in the Active If TRUE text box. Whenever the contents of the Active If TRUE text box evaluate to True, the response will be active, and when it evaluates to False, the response is inactive.

▶ To learn more about using the Active If TRUE box, **see** "Turning Responses On and Off," **p. 446.**

CHAPTER 13

Setting Up Text-Entry Boxes

Computers were originally built to do advanced calculations based on information provided by the end user, and the most common method of inputting that information was the keyboard. Within a few short years of their creation, these systems evolved into massive containers storing countless pieces of information used by governments, corporations, and individuals. Despite the evolution of the computer, the means for inputting information has changed little since its inception.

Most people look at the computer keyboard as a glorified typewriter. In their eyes, it's simply a way to create letters—or, today, to respond to e-mail. In terms of computer-based learning, the keyboard, in association with the text-entry box, is often used in the creation of tests or exams. You will soon see, however, that text-entry boxes may be used to create a variety of interactions.

This chapter explores the options that Authorware provides for establishing a text-entry box, and for evaluating each entry made by the end user. Later in the chapter, you'll learn how to use the text-entry

Steps to creating text-entry boxes

Creating text-entry boxes requires that specific steps be followed.

Taking advantage of the response options

Text-entry box options include judging what the user enters, matching a set number of words, allowing incremental matching, and defining which characteristics should be ignored.

Using wild cards

Wild cards allow you to accept an unknown character or a string of characters in a user's entry.

Allowing for multiple anticipated responses

You can create a piece that responds to a range of unanticipated responses as well as multiple anticipated responses.

Using the text-entry options

Text-entry options allow you to determine how the entry box will function, including setting the character limit, defining an action key, and determining to ignore null entries.

Positioning text-entry boxes

Text-entry boxes can be positioned manually, or using variables and functions.

response options to create entry boxes for such interactions as logon routines, forms, or user notes. ■

Creating Text-Entry Boxes

One of the most popular ways to collect data from the user is to have the user enter the information into the computer. Text-entry boxes are used to collect answers to test questions, to allow the user to take notes throughout a piece, or to have the user log on to or out of the piece.

In such examples, you can use a text-entry interaction for a single text area or reposition it to accommodate several text areas. In either case, Authorware provides a simple way for the user to enter information and an even easier way for Authorware to judge or interpret the information once it has been entered.

▶ To create a piece with multiple text-entry areas, **see** "Positioning Buttons and Fields," **p. 452**.

To set up the Interaction icon with a text-entry response, follow these steps:

1. Drag an Interaction icon to the Flowline.
2. Drag another icon to the Flowline and place it to the right of the Interaction icon, as shown in Figure 13.1. The icon placed to the right of the Interaction icon is called a *response*. Responses can be created using the Display, Motion, Erase, Wait, Navigate, Calculation, Map, Digital Movie, Sound, and Video icons.
3. When you release the first response on an Interaction icon, the Response Type dialog box appears. Select the text-entry response type.
4. Click OK to save your selection.

FIG. 13.1
Place an icon to the right of the Interaction icon to build a response path.

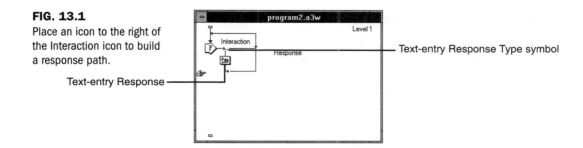

Text-entry Response

Text-entry Response Type symbol

5. Fill in the Match if User Enters box with the anticipated response. This is the entry you expect the user to make in order to match this response path.

6. Make additional adjustments to the functionality of the text-entry response using the Response Options dialog box. Click OK to save your settings when you're finished.

7. Choose Run from the Try It menu to see the text-entry box on-screen. Type the anticipated response; then press Return (Macintosh) or Enter (Windows) to initiate the interaction.

 The shortcut key combination for Run is ⌘+R (Macintosh) or Ctrl+R (Windows).

▶ To refer to the introduction of the Interaction icon, **see** "The Interaction Icon," **p. 19**.

▶ For step-by-step instruction on creating an interaction, **see** "Building an Interaction Loop," **p. 215**.

Setting the Text-Entry Response Options

In Chapter 9, "The Fundamentals of Interactions," I discussed characteristics common across all interactions, such as automatic erasing, branching, and judging. The following features, while they may be found in other response type options, are used to establish the functionality of text-entry responses. Text-entry response options are set using the Text Entry Response Options dialog box, shown in Figure 13.2. The key options in this dialog box are described next.

▶ For an overview of the commonalities for all interaction types within Authorware, **see** "Introducing Interactions," **p. 212**.

Part
III

Ch
13

FIG. 13.2
The Text Entry Response Options dialog box is used to set parameters for defining the text-entry response and what information will be considered to judge that response.

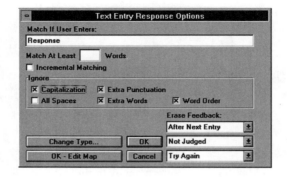

Judging What the User Enters

As with other interaction response types, the title you give to the icon along the Flowline also appears in the Match if User Enters text box and vice versa. Most importantly, however, the name that you give to this icon is what the user must enter for the running piece to encounter this response. For example, if you title the response icon "Dog," then the user must type "Dog." If the user enters "Cat," then the response will not be matched.

Using Match At Least _ Words

Make an entry in the Match At Least _ Words text box if the user does not need to match the anticipated response exactly but should match at least a few of the anticipated words. Enter a number to pinpoint the number of words the user must match in order to match this response.

For example, if the anticipated response—and the title of the response icon—is "Using Macromedia Authorware," and you placed a 2 in this text box, then the user could match the response with "Using Macromedia," "Using Authorware," or "Macromedia Authorware."

Understanding the Incremental Matching Option

Select the Incremental Matching check box if the user can match part of the anticipated response on one try and the remainder of the anticipated response on another try.

For example, the correct response to an interaction regarding total quality management might be "Continuous Improvement." If the user responds with "Improvement," this response is not matched. If incremental matching has been selected, however, Authorware will remember that this response has been partially matched; then if the user responds a second time with "Continuous," the response path for "Continuous Improvement" is matched.

Ignoring Text Characteristics or Elements

The check boxes in the Ignore area of the Text Entry Response Options dialog box give you a greater amount of control when judging a response entered by an end user. The Ignore options include the following:

- Capitalization—Select this option to ignore capitalization. Authorware will judge the user's entry against the anticipated response but will ignore any variance in capitalization.

  For example, if the anticipated response is "ISO" but the user enters "iso," the response is a match as long as the option to ignore capitalization has been selected.

- All Spaces—Select this option to strip out all the spaces in the user's response before comparing it to the anticipated response. Authorware will treat the user's entry, even if it contains spaces, as a single word.

  For example, if the anticipated response—and the title of the response icon—was "Multimedia," and the user entered "Multi media," then the response would be matched.

- Extra Punctuation—Select this option to have Authorware ignore any punctuation contained in the user's entry prior to comparing that entry to the anticipated response.

- Extra Words—Select this option to have the application ignore extra words that the user enters. Authorware will seek out the keywords indicated in the anticipated response, ignoring any additional words.

- Word Order—Select this option to allow the user to enter the correct words in a different order than you established in the anticipated response.

  For example, if the anticipated response is "Income Tax" and the user enters "Tax Income," this response is a match as long as the option to ignore word order has been selected.

Part
III

Ch
13

 T I P The best way to learn what each of these options does is to prototype and experiment with them. If you plan to build a piece that tests your user's typing skills, then you should spend time working with these options.

Working with Wild Cards

In many cases, you will not have a specific anticipated response, but the user will be able to enter any possible response. For example, if you create a logon screen that asks the user to enter his or her last name, the anticipated response for this text-entry response has to be every possible last name.

To get around the need to establish an unreasonable number of anticipated responses, Authorware accepts *wild cards*. The asterisk (*) is used as a wild card throughout Authorware to replace a set of characters. In our previous example, then, instead of listing every possible last name, you simply title the Response icon with an asterisk by typing the asterisk in the Match if User Enters text box of the Text Entry Response Options dialog box (see Fig. 13.3).

FIG. 13.3
Use the question mark as a single-character wild card, and use the asterisk for multiple characters.

This wild card accepts any entry.

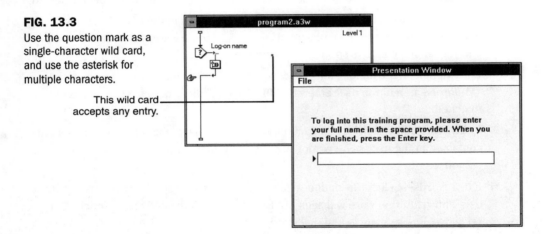

Authorware also accepts the question mark (?) as a wild card to replace a single character. For example, if you want the user to enter "Authorware," but you anticipate that he might spell it incorrectly, you can insert question marks in the anticipated response, such as "Auth?rware" to allow for a misspelling.

Looking for Multiple Responses

You occasionally might desire that a response match more than one answer or that several anticipated responses match the path. For example, your interaction might request that the user enter one color found on the German flag. The user would be correct by entering red, gold, or black.

To create this anticipated response, use the vertical bar (|) to separate the various acceptable responses as follows: **red|gold|black** when naming the response icon. Authorware reads this as "red or gold or black."

T I P The vertical bar is used to separate multiple possible responses, each of which can independently match the user's entry.

Opening the Text Entry Options Dialog Box

Authorware automatically provides a box into which the user can enter a response, and allows you to establish a key that signals the completion of the text entry. Additionally, the text-entry box has a default font, size, style, color, and several other attributes. To change any characteristics of the text-entry box, you must open the Text Entry Options dialog box.

N O T E The name across the top of the Text Entry Options dialog box is based on the name that you have given the Interaction icon. ■

To open the Text Entry Options dialog box, follow these steps:

1. Double-click the Interaction icon containing the text-entry response.
2. Click the Text Entry Options button in the center of the Interaction Options dialog box (see Fig. 13.4).

FIG. 13.4
Double-clicking an Interaction icon opens the Interaction Options dialog box.

Part
III

Ch
13

T I P Text-entry box characteristics including font, size, style, and color may be adjusted without opening the Text Entry Options dialog box. When running, simply pause the flow of the piece using the shortcut keys—⌘+P (Macintosh) or Ctrl+P (Windows)—then use the Text and Attribute pull-down menus to make the adjustments. Use the same shortcut keys to proceed with the piece once the adjustments have been made.

You can also open the Interaction Options dialog box or the Text Entry Options dialog box from the Presentation Window. To do so, follow these steps:

1. If the piece is running, pause the piece by choosing Pause from the Try It pull-down menu.

 TIP The shortcut key combinations for Pause are ⌘+P (Macintosh) or Ctrl+P (Windows).

2. Once the piece is paused, double-click the center of the text-entry box to open the Interaction Options dialog box.

 TIP On the Macintosh, you can hold down the Command and Option keys while the piece is running to see the text-entry box. Double-clicking this box causes the piece to act as though it had been paused before you double-clicked the text-entry border.

3. Click the Text Entry Options button in the center of the Interaction Options dialog box to access the Text Entry Options dialog box.

Several options are adjustable within the Text Entry Options dialog box shown in Figure 13.5; they are described in the following sections.

FIG. 13.5
The Text Entry Options dialog box is used to establish parameters regarding the functioning of the text-entry box.

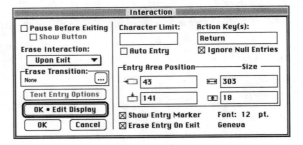

Setting a Character Limit

In the Character Limit text box, enter the maximum number of characters that you want the user to be able to enter in the text-entry box. Keep in mind that spaces, punctuation, and special characters all count as characters.

Using an Automatic Entry

Select the Auto Entry check box if you want Authorware to act as though the user has pressed Return or Enter as soon as the number of characters specified in the Character Limit box is entered.

Defining the Action Key

For Authorware to judge the user's response, the user must signal completion of the text entry by pressing an action key. By default, this is Return (Macintosh) or Enter (Windows). To specify a different key, simply overwrite the default key name in the Action Key(s) text box. To allow for multiple names, separate the various options with a vertical bar ("|"). For example, Tab|Return|RightArrow could be entered to allow any of the three keys to signal the end of the text entry.

TIP Setting a custom action key allows you to simulate any software package or proprietary piece of equipment that's operated by a keyboard.

Learning to Ignore Null Entries

Select the Ignore Null Entries check box if you want Authorware to ignore the pressing of the action key if the user has not typed anything in the text-entry box. For example, if you are asking the user to enter information that would be used in a logon routine, you would not want the user to be able to leave a field blank; therefore, you would elect to not ignore null entries.

Positioning Text-Entry Responses

You can position and size a text-entry box in the Presentation Window just as you do graphical elements. Alternatively, you can position and size it using variables or expressions in the Text Entry Options dialog box.

▶ For step-by-step guidance on using variables and functions to position response areas, **see** "Positioning Buttons and Fields," **p. 452**.

Part
III

Ch
13

Controls which may be set within this dialog box are described next.

Setting the Position of a Text-Entry Box   A text-entry box's position in the Presentation Window may be determined either by providing values representing the desired pixel location or by entering a variable or expression that allows the text-entry box's position to change dynamically. Controls for the position of a text-entry box include

■ Left Side—Determines how many pixels from the left side of the Presentation Window the text-entry box will be placed (see Fig. 13.6).

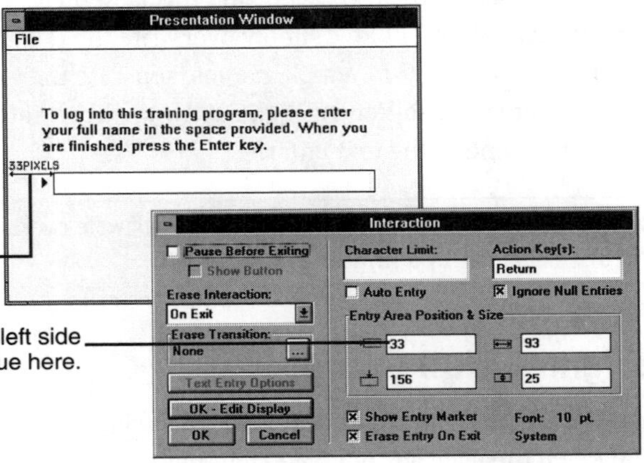

FIG. 13.6
A text-entry box can be precisely positioned based on its distance from the left-hand edge of the Presentation Window.

The text-entry area will be positioned based on the provided value.

Enter a left side value here.

■ Top—Determines how many pixels from the top of the Presentation Window the text-entry box will be placed (see Fig. 13.7).

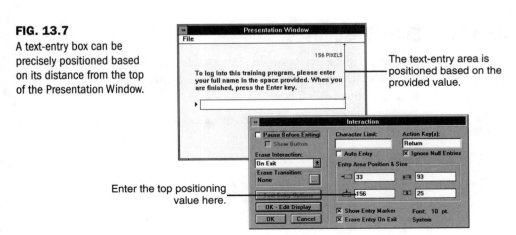

FIG. 13.7
A text-entry box can be precisely positioned based on its distance from the top of the Presentation Window.

The text-entry area is positioned based on the provided value.

Enter the top positioning value here.

Setting the Size of a Text-Entry Box   A text-entry box's width may also be set either by providing values representing the desired width expressed in pixels or by entering a variable or expression that allows the size of the text-entry box to change dynamically. Controls for the size of the text-entry box include

- Horizontal—Determines how wide the text-entry box will be. This value is expressed in pixels.
- Vertical—Determines how tall the text-entry box will be. This value is expressed in pixels.

To adjust the size or position of a text-entry box in the Presentation Window while running the application, choose Try It, Pause and then click the text-entry box. The handles that appear allow you to make adjustments. When you're finished, choose Try It, Proceed and the piece continues.

 TIP The shortcut key combination for Try It, Pause is ⌘+P (Macintosh) or Ctrl+P (Windows). This is a toggle—when the piece is running, Pause is available, and when the piece is paused, Proceed is available.

On the Macintosh, you can see the placement of text-entry boxes without pausing the piece by pressing ⌘+Option.

Determining Whether to Show the Entry Marker

Select the Show Entry Marker check box in the Interaction dialog box to place a small marker to the left of the text-entry box, as shown in Figure 13.8. This marker helps the users identify where to enter their responses.

N O T E This marker is small and fairly inconspicuous. I suggest using your own marker—or building a custom interface—to clearly identify where text is to be entered.

Part

III

Ch

13

Erasing the Entry on Exit

Selecting the Erase Entry on Exit check box in the Text Entry Options dialog box causes the last entry made by the user to be automatically erased when the interaction loop is exited.

FIG. 13.8
You can display a marker
next to the text-entry box.

Text-entry marker

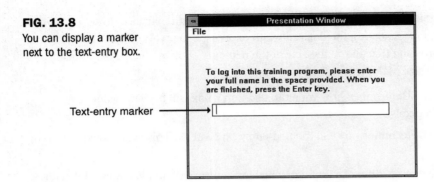

Changing the Entry Box Characteristics

While the Text Entry Options dialog box is open, or while the piece is paused and the text-entry box is selected, you can change the input font, size, style, color, or mode by using the Attributes and Text menus. The currently selected font and size are displayed in the lower-right corner of the Text Entry Options dialog box.

▶ For information on using the text characteristics, **see** "Changing Text Characteristics," **p. 79**.

CHAPTER 14

Using Target Areas

See the steps for creating a target area

Creating target areas, like creating other interaction types, requires that specific steps be followed.

Taking advantage of the response options

In addition to those options that are common to all interaction responses, target area options include defining a title for the response, establishing an object destination action, allowing the target area to match any movable object, specifying an Active If TRUE statement, and determining the position and size of the target area using variables and expressions.

As the graphical user interface (GUI) became standard, new ways to interact with the computer made their way onto the screen. Traditional beveled push buttons, pull-down menus, and scrolling windows gave way to new forms of interaction. The ability to move an object along a path or within a given area is one form of interactivity with the computer that has grown in popularity.

The first use of this form of interactivity was the creation of simulators. Simple markers could be dragged to adjust settings or slide gauges could be used to control equipment operations. Later, these sliders made their way into GUI standards for adjusting such options as speaker volume, system performance, and monitor brightness.

Today, movable objects are taking on much more of a free form than in traditional applications. Students are asked to assemble lab experiments, and employees are asked to organize daily tasks or the steps in a manufacturing process using movable objects.

This chapter explores the features provided in Authorware for designating that an object is movable, and for determining the point to which it can be moved. ■

Creating Target Areas

Target areas are possibly the greatest of all tools for creating *interactivity*, not only when interactivity is defined as allowing the user to participate or respond to elements in the Presentation Window, but also when interactivity is defined as the creation of a dialogue between your piece and the end user.

Target area responses consist of two primary components; the object which is being moved by the end user, and the area to which the user is to move that object. For example, a gauge handle may be the object which is being moved along a scale, and there may be several points, each representing a value for the scale, to which the user can move the handle.

Target areas may also be constructed in such a way that the user is given a broad range of combinations—just like they'd have in the real world—from which they must construct a viable solution to a problem. Based on their responses, or their selection of a combination, you can offer specific feedback or guidance.

N O T E One of my constant challenges is to create a piece that allows a seemingly endless array of options, therefore simulating the real world. I have found that target areas greatly accommodate designs that allow this freedom of choice on the part of the end user, yet provide enough control for me to make a judgment and provide specific feedback to the user. ■

To set up the Interaction icon with a target area response, follow these steps:

1. Drag a Display icon to the Flowline.

2. Open the Display icon and create an object which you want the user to move to a defined position within the Presentation Window. When you're finished, close the Display icon by clicking the close button in the upper left-hand corner of the graphic toolbox.

   ▶ To refer to the introduction of the Display icon, **see** "The Display Icon," **p. 15**.

   ▶ For guidance on creating an object within a Display icon, **see** "Drawing Objects," **p. 98**.

3. Drag an Interaction icon to the Flowline.

4. Drag another icon to the Flowline and place it to the right of the Interaction icon, as shown in Figure 14.1. Any icon placed to the right of the Interaction icon is called a *response*. Responses can be created using the Display, Motion, Erase, Wait, Navigate, Calculation, Map, Digital Movie, Sound, and Video icons.

   ▶ To refer to the introduction of the Interaction icon, **see** "The Interaction Icon," **p. 19**.

   ▶ For step-by-step instructions on creating an interaction, **see** "Building an Interaction Loop," **p. 215**.

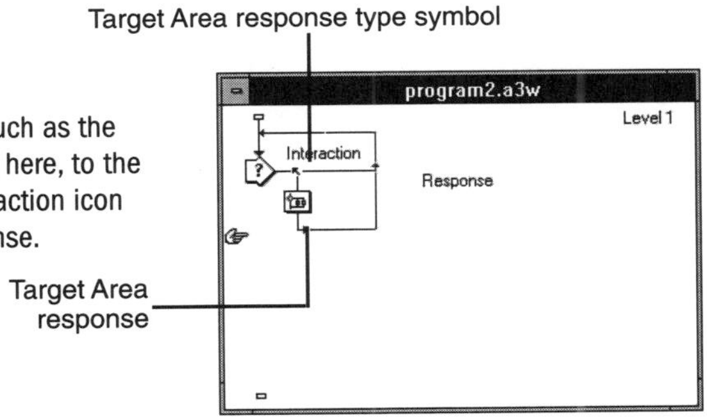

Target Area response type symbol

FIG. 14.1
Place an icon, such as the Map icon shown here, to the right of the Interaction icon to build a response.

Target Area response

5. When you release the first response on an Interaction icon, the Response Type dialog box appears. Select the Target Area response type.

6. Click OK to save your selection.

7. Choose Run from the Try It pull-down menu.

TIP The shortcut key combination for Try It, Run is ⌘+R (Macintosh) or Ctrl+R (Windows). You can also select the Run button from the tool bar.

Part
III

Ch
14

8. Authorware automatically pauses when it hits an Interaction icon with an undefined target area. At this point, the Target Area Options dialog box appears, and the message in the upper-left corner of the dialog box instructs you to drag the object to the position in the Presentation Window that you desire to be the target area.

CAUTION

In their excitement to create a target area, many people ignore the directions and drag the target area into place without ever identifying the object that's to be moved to the target area. Be sure to follow the prompt located at the top of the dialog box.

9. As soon as you release the object that is to be matched by Authorware, the target area moves so that its position is centered above the object. Use the handles on the target area to resize the target area in any direction, or click and drag one of the edges of the target area to reposition it.

When positioning and sizing the target area, keep in mind that Authorware will only match this response when the center of the object being moved is within the boundary you establish. If an outer edge of the object being moved is within the area, but the center of the object is outside of the target area, the response will not be matched.

10. Once you've positioned and sized the target area, click OK to save your selections. Clicking OK will return your piece to run mode.

11. Drag the object to the target area to initiate the interaction.

Setting the Target Area Response Options

Target areas are unlike any other response type in terms of response options, except for those commonalities discussed in Chapter 9, "The Fundamentals of Interactions." The response options for target areas are more specific to the definition of the movable object, as well as to the anticipated landing area.

▶ For an overview of the commonalities for all interaction types within Authorware, **see** "Introducing Interactions," **p. 212**.

You can set each of these options using the Target Area Options dialog box, shown in Figure 14.2. The options in this dialog box are described in the following sections.

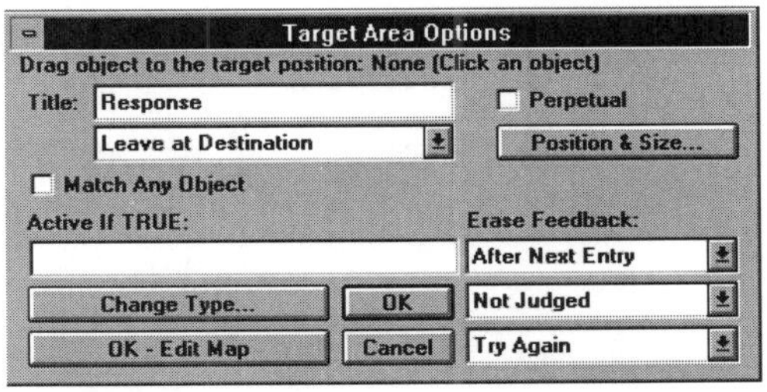

FIG. 14.2
The Target Area Options dialog box is used to set parameters for defining the target area and what action will be taken if an object is moved to it.

Target Area Options

Drag object to the target position: None (Click an object)

Title: Response

Leave at Destination

☐ Match Any Object

Active If TRUE:

Change Type...   OK

OK - Edit Map   Cancel

☐ Perpetual

Position & Size...

Erase Feedback:

After Next Entry

Not Judged

Try Again

Completing the Title Text Box

The name you give to the icon on the Flowline appears in the Title text box, and vice versa. Like hot spots and hot object responses, however, the name is not critical to the response.

TIP Naming the response descriptively makes later editing of the target area in the Presentation Window much easier.

Establishing an Object Destination Action

When you move an object into a target area, Authorware takes one of the following actions, which you specify using the drop-down list shown in Figure 14.3:

- Leave at Destination—When an object is moved into a target area that has been set to Leave at Destination, the object that has been moved is left at its resting position in the Presentation Window.

- Put Back—When an object is moved into a target area that has been set to Put Back, Authorware moves the object from the position where it was dropped by the user to the position where the object was positioned in the Presentation Window prior to being dragged by the end user.

- Snap to Center—When an object is moved into a target area that has been set to Snap to Center, Authorware snaps the object so that the center of the object aligns with the center of the target area.

Allowing the Target Area to Match Any Object

A target area response typically is matched when the contents of a specific icon are moved into the target area. For example, you may have five tiles and five target areas. Each tile would be assigned to a specific target area, and if a tile is placed in the incorrect position, an action such as returning the tile to its starting position would occur.

Part
III

Ch
14

FIG. 14.3
You can designate how Authorware responds when an object is moved into the target area using the three pre-defined actions.

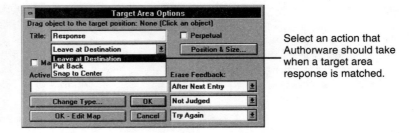

Select an action that Authorware should take when a target area response is matched.

If you select the Match Any Object check box in the Target Area Options dialog box, then *any* object moved into the target area triggers the response. This option is very useful if you want the user to be able to place any of the five tiles into any of the five positions. The order in which the tiles were placed may then be judged using functions and variables.

Using the Active If TRUE Text Box

Target areas can be activated or deactivated using a variable or expression, just as push buttons can. Whenever the contents of the Active If TRUE text box evaluate to True, the response will be active, and when they evaluate to False, the response is inactive.

▶ To learn more about using the Active If TRUE box, **see** "Turning Responses On and Off," **p. 446**.

Determining the Target Area Position and Size

You can position and size target areas in the Presentation Window just as you do graphical elements. Alternatively, you can position and size them using variables or expressions representing pixel values in the dialog box that appears after you click the Position & Size button in the Target Area Options dialog box.

▶ For step-by-step guidance on using variables and functions to position response areas, **see** "Positioning Buttons and Fields," **p. 452**.

▶ To see how button responses are positioned using this same method, **see** "Defining the Button's Position and Size," **p. 243**.

Controls that can be set within this dialog box are described next.

Setting the Position   A target area's position in the Presentation Window can be determined either by providing values representing the desired pixel location or by entering a variable or expression that allows the target area's position to change dynamically. Controls for the position of a target area include

- Left Side—Determines how many pixels from the left hand side of the Presentation Window the target area will be placed.

- Top—Determines how many pixels from the top of the Presentation Window the target area will be placed.

Setting the Size   A target area's width can also be set either by providing values representing the desired width expressed in pixels or by entering a variable or expression which allows the size of the target area to change dynamically. Controls for the size of the target area include

- Horizontal—Determines how wide the target will be. This value is expressed in pixels.

- Vertical—Determines how tall the target area will be. This value is expressed in pixels.

To adjust the size or position of a target area in the Presentation Window while running the application, choose Pause from the Try It menu and then click the target area you want to modify. Handles will appear that allow you to make the adjustments. When completed, simply choose Proceed from the Try It menu and the piece will continue.

T I P The shortcut keys for Pause and Proceed are ⌘+P (Macintosh) or Ctrl+P (Windows). This option is a toggle, so when the piece is running, the Pause option is available, and when the piece is paused, the Proceed option is available.

N O T E Variables or expressions are helpful if the position or size of a target area might change as a result of the user's interactivity with the piece.

Part

III

Ch

14

Hyperlinking and Branching

CHAPTER 15

Building Interactive Documents

In recent years, the proliferation of technology and the complexity of information has caused end users to demand simple computer-based training tutorials, and even simpler interactive multimedia applications. To accommodate this demand, the use for Authorware has grown from a tool for the creation of interactive learning to a tool for the creation of a wide variety of electronic performance support and online documentation products.

As these more sophisticated uses of technology for the presentation of information arrived, the need to consider how the user would navigate through the mountains of information became even more crucial than before. Building on a common structure for the presentation of information—a linear sequence, as in a book—Authorware grew to support several features to make the organization, development, and navigation through such information easy for both the developer and the end user.

What comprises a framework?

A framework consists of a Framework icon, a page, and a navigation scheme.

Exploring the Framework icon

The Framework icon is the heart and soul of establishing hyperlink, as well as linear structures.

Changing the framework transition effect

Transition effects are used for frameworks, in the same way they are used with Display icons.

Working with Rich Text Format documents

Rich Text Format documents can be incorporated into Authorware. To assist in the process, Authorware automatically creates pages based on the Rich Text Format document.

Changing the default Framework icon

The setup of the Framework icon is stored external to Authorware and can be modified as need be.

Although the linear book model does not promote a dialogue between the end user and your piece—even with the introduction of hyperlinking—and therefore is not highly beneficial to the learning process, this model does greatly support reference-based material. Much as a dictionary, a phone book, or a technical reference, the capability to quickly get to the information is the benefit of such a model.

In this chapter, we will explore how Authorware enables you to quickly build and maintain information using a linear or hyperlinked model, as well as some practical applications for such a model. ■

Understanding Frameworks

The structure that Authorware uses to support the organization and development of content when it is to be accessed in either a linear (page turning) manner or non-linear hyperlinking, is called a framework. A framework consists of the following three main components:

■ The Framework Icon—The Framework icon is the core of the framework, much like the Interaction icon is the core of the interaction loop. The primary purpose of the Framework icon is to establish content branching and organization.

▶ For an introduction to the Framework icon, **see** "The Framework Icon," **p. 18**.

■ Pages—Content within a framework is organized into pages. Unlike a page in a book that denotes text, or even a certain layout, a framework page is simply the term given to the branch of a framework that acts as a holder for content. A page may contain a single icon, such as a Display icon containing text, or it may contain several Flowline levels of interactive media.

■ Navigation—Authorware has provided a variety of options for navigating from page to page within a framework. When a framework is first created, a default navigation scheme is created. This default navigation scheme may be modified, and a new default may be created.

In the remainder of this chapter, I will discuss these three components in greater detail, but let's first look at creating a framework structure.

TROUBLESHOOTING

When a running piece encounters a framework, it automatically defaults into the first page. How do I get around this so that the content of the first page is not displayed? There are a couple of things that can be done. First, you can place a Navigate icon within the Framework icon just below the Interaction icon. The Navigate icon forces the piece to navigate to a page other than the first. Another solution is to place an empty Map icon as the first page. When the piece runs, the first page (the empty Map icon containing nothing) is displayed.

Building a Framework Loop

Building the framework, complete with content, can be simple. As you will see in the next chapter, "Applying Advanced Interactivity and Searching," however, navigation within a framework can grow to be quite complex depending on the requirements for interactivity and searching.

To create a basic framework, follow these steps:

1. Drag a Framework icon to the Flowline, as seen in Figure 15.1.

2. Drag another icon to the Flowline and place it to the right of the Framework icon, as shown in Figure 15.2. Any icon that you place to the right of the Framework icon is called a page. Pages can be created using the Display, Motion, Erase, Wait, Navigate, Calculation, Map, Digital Movie, Sound, or Video icons.

   At any point in the development process, you can add additional pages to the framework by dragging an icon from the Icon palette and placing it to the right of the Framework icon.

FIG. 15.1
The Framework icon is the
heart of a Framework loop.

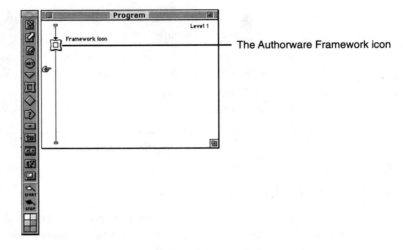

The Authorware Framework icon

FIG. 15.2
Place an icon to the right of
the Framework icon to build
a page.

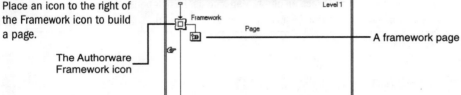

A framework page

The Authorware
Framework icon

Exploring the Framework Icon

The Framework icon, like the Map icon, can be used to hold other icons. That is, the Framework icon contains a Flowline level on which other icons may be placed (see Fig. 15.3). To access the framework Flowline, double-click the Framework icon.

The default framework Flowline includes a Display icon containing a background graphic on which eight push buttons rest, and an Interaction icon that is used to create the eight buttons (see Fig. 15.3 and Fig. 15.4). I will discuss each of the default push buttons in greater detail in the next chapter, "Applying Advanced Interactivity and Searching."

The framework Flowline is divided into two windows: the entry pane and the exit pane. These windows can be used as described next.

Entry Pane

The entry pane contains information that effects every page. For example, the default controls will be displayed with each page, and they can be interacted with at any time while within the framework.

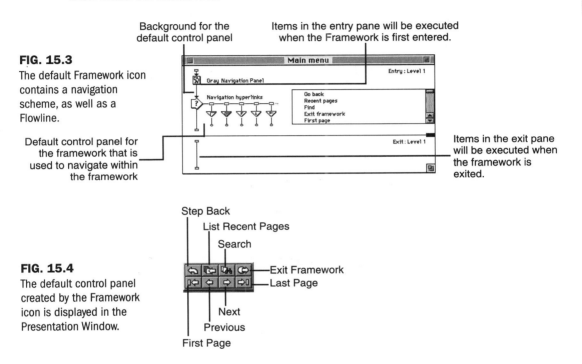

FIG. 15.3
The default Framework icon contains a navigation scheme, as well as a Flowline.

FIG. 15.4
The default control panel created by the Framework icon is displayed in the Presentation Window.

In one case, I used a framework for a main menu (modules), and then placed another framework inside each of the pages to create submenus (topics), as seen in Figure 15.5. In the entry pane for each of the submenus, I placed the graphic containing the highlight showing which module was active, which would be true for each topic.

N O T E When a page in a framework is accessed through a hyperlink, as you will see in Chapter 16, "Applying Advanced Interactivity and Searching," all the icons in the entry pane are executed before the page is entered. ■

Exit Pane

Just as you can place icons in the entry pane, you can also place icons in the exit pane (refer to Fig. 15.3.) The icons will be executed after the user has elected to exit the framework and prior to continuing down the Flowline at the next highest level.

Contains navigation for movement between modules

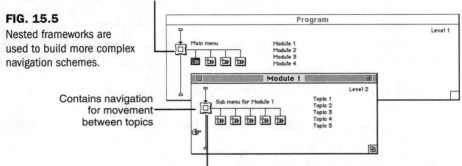

FIG. 15.5
Nested frameworks are
used to build more complex
navigation schemes.

Contains navigation
for movement
between topics

The entry pane contains the highlight to show which module was selected

N O T E   The items in the exit pane are also executed if the program encounters a hyperlink
that directs them to a location outside of the current framework. ■

All of the objects encountered in the exit pane—including sound—are executed; then
when the piece exits the Framework icon and the exit pane, they are erased.

Setting Up the Framework Transition Effect

As the piece moves from page to page within a framework, each page may be automatically erased using a transition (for more information on using transitions, see Chapter 5,
"Working with Display Effects and Transitions"). The transition can be applied to the
entire framework or to a single page.

Setting a transition for a Framework icon is done using the same steps as I provided in
Chapter 5, "Working with Display Effects and Transitions." To set the transition for the
framework, follow these steps:

1. Select the Framework icon on the Flowline for which you want to establish a
    transition.

2. Select the Transition option from the Attributes pull-down menu.

 The shortcut keys for selecting the Transition option are ⌘+Shift+E (Macintosh) and Ctrl+Shift+E
(Windows).

3. Use the Page Transition dialog box, as seen in Figure 15.6, to select a transition for
    the framework. Keep in mind that the selected transition will be used for the
    transition between each page in the framework.

FIG. 15.6
Use the Page Transition
dialog box to set a transition
for the framework.

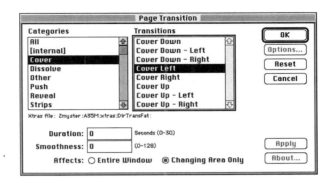

4. Once a selection has been made, click OK button to exit the Transition dialog box.

▶ For more information on setting the erase transition for a Framework icon, **see** "Erasing a Framework Page," **p. 363**.

The automatic erase transition that has been set for the framework as a whole can be overridden by setting a transition that is unique to a single page. For example, if the transition for the framework is set so that objects are displayed by sliding in from one side of the screen, but if, you set the transition of a single page (a single Display icon rather than a map of icons) to fade in, the transition to fade in will be the transition used when the objects are displayed.

If you notice a flash from page to page, select the Smooth Change transition from the Internal category.

From this point on, I will refer to building the framework and setting the transition as *creating the framework*.

Creating Pages Automatically

As previously mentioned, a page is a branch of content that hangs off of a Framework icon in the framework loop. A page can consist of a single display or be as complex as an entire module of content. Pages can even contain other frameworks that contain more pages.

If you are using pages to simulate the actual pages of a document or a book, Authorware makes the development of this structure really easy. To automatically build a page-turning application based on an electronic document created with a word processor, follow these steps:

1. Create page breaks in your external text file to indicate how much information should be presented on one screen. When your document is formatted as you want it to appear on the screen, save it as an RTF (Rich Text Format) file.

T I P Keep in mind that text can appear in scrolling windows on the screen, where it only appears in single blocks on the printed page. Therefore, determine how much information you want on each screen, rather than in a single block.

2. Create a framework with one page comprised of a Display icon, as seen in Figure 15.7.

FIG. 15.7
The Display icon contains the content of the electronic document.

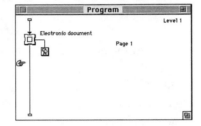

3. Open the Display icon that is the page of the framework by double-clicking it.
4. Select the Import option from the File pull-down menu.
5. Use the dialog box to locate and select the RTF file you just created.
6. Once the RTF file has been selected, the RTF Import dialog box appears, as shown in Figure 15.8.

FIG. 15.8
The RTF Import dialog box allows you to set options for importing an RTF formatted document.

7. The Hard Page Break area of the RTF Import dialog box enables you to select how Authorware treats the occurrence of a hard text break found in the external RTF file. Make your selection from the following options:
   - Ignore—When you select this option, all of the information in the external RTF document will be imported into the current screen.

- Create New Display—When you select this option, Authorware creates as many pages on the framework as necessary to accommodate the number of pages identified by hard returns in the RTF document.

> **CAUTION**
>
> If the amount of text on the printed page is more than the screen can hold, be sure to select the Scrolling option as defined below; otherwise, the text block will run out of the Presentation Window.

8. The Text Object area enables you to select how Authorware treats text that is contained in the RTF document. Choose one of the following options:

   - Standard—When you select this option, all of the text will be imported as a standard text object. Keep in mind that this object may not fit in the Presentation Window once it is imported.

   - Scrolling—When you select this option, Authorware will create a scrolling window sized to accommodate all of the text for that page of the external document.

9. To see how Authorware automatically creates pages in a framework, select the Create New Display option. It does not matter which Text Object selection is made: Authorware will either create a scrolling window or a text object on each new page.

10. Click OK to save your settings. Authorware then begins importing the contents of the RTF document. When you return to the Flowline, you will see that pages have been created and are attached to the framework, as seen in Figure 15.9.

   In addition to creating the new page icons, Authorware also assigns these new icons a name based on what you named the first page icon. The new name is comprised of the name of the first page icon, followed by a colon, and then followed by a number representing the page number. Pages are numbered in consecutive order from left to right.

FIG. 15.9
Authorware has automatically created and named the number of icons required to build the framework.

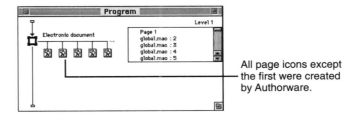

Changing the Default Framework

The default Framework icon contains a graphic background upon which eight buttons will rest and an Interaction icon that is used to set up those eight buttons. Together, the graphic background and the eight buttons provide a control panel that is used to navigate through the framework.

Although the default control panel is certainly a great tool for creating electronic documentation, you may find it desirable to customize either the physical appearance of the control panel or the functionality of the buttons or to create an entirely new default for the Framework icon.

TIP Customizing the Framework icon takes far less time than editing the default features of the icon if you plan on using a large number of Framework icons in your piece.

For example, if you have designed a graphical interface in which the elements of control rest, you may not want the Framework icon to contain the default background graphic because it would not fit the graphic style of your piece. Additionally, you may not want all of the default buttons to be provided for your end user. For these examples, you could create a new default Framework icon.

> **CAUTION**
>
> Before modifying the default Framework icon, I recommend that you make a backup copy of the current default. The settings for the default Framework icon are stored as a file titled Default Framework Icon (Macintosh) or FRAMEWRK.MOD (Windows), which is located in the same folder or directory in which Authorware was initially installed.

The Framework icon is actually an Authorware model. Models are pieces of a Flowline structure that are saved as external files. Rather than creating a Flowline structure that will be used extensively throughout your piece from the beginning each time it is required, you may simply paste the model that contains the icons you need. Steps for creating and using models are presented in detail in Chapter 26, "Building Models."

To create a new default Framework icon, perform the following steps:

1. Drag a Framework icon to the Flowline.

2. Open the Framework icon and make modifications to meet your custom requirements, such as eliminating one of the default push buttons or changing the location of the buttons within the Presentation Window.

3. Close the Framework icon that contains your modifications.

4. Click to select the Framework icon that contains your custom modifications.

5. Select the Create Model option from the Libraries pull-down menu.

6. Enter a description for the model in the Model Description dialog box, as seen in Figure 15.10. This description is for your use to help assist in recognizing the functionality of the model. When a description is set, click the OK button.

7. Save the Model using the Save dialog box in the same location in which Authorware was initially installed and using the title Default Framework Icon (Macintosh) or FRAMEWRK.MOD (Windows).

FIG. 15.10
You can give a model a description.

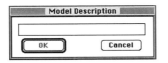

FIG. 15.11
The model must be saved so that it replaces the original model for the framework.

CAUTION
The name of the new Model must be spelled exactly the same as the default, including capitalization.

From this point in development, whenever you bring a Framework icon onto the Flowline, it will contain your modifications.

Becoming familiar with the framework—complete with pages—is the first half of knowing how to build interactive documentation. In Chapter 16, "Applying Advanced Interactivity and Searching," we will explore how to link pages together as well as search among the pages. ●

Applying Advanced Interactivity and Searching

Moving through the pages of frameworks

When Authorware encounters a hyperlink, it can either jump to the defined destination, or it can call the information contained at the destination, then return to the point from which the call was made.

Using the Navigate icon

The navigate icon is the icon used to initiate the hyperlink. There are five destination types for hyperlinking, including Recent, Nearby, Anywhere, Calculate and Search.

Using keywords in your piece

Keywords are established so that your end user can more efficiently identify content, or you can more efficiently create and maintain the piece.

Using navigation in a text style

Just as you can determine text characteristics in a style, you can also define navigation using any of the destination types.

As the need to access greater amounts of information grew, the technology known as *hyperlinking* became a part of everyday jargon for most application developers. As a result, today's user can browse databases full of information at hyper speeds using hypertext and hypermedia.

The American Heritage Dictionary defines *hyper* as "over, above, or in great amount," or "in abnormal excess." The terms *hypertext* and *hypermedia,* therefore, make a great deal of sense in light of the amount of information available to us today. The technologies created to access and link this data are quite appropriate.

As soon as you move away from providing a tool to access information, however, to a tool that is meant to instruct or teach, the application of hyperlinking becomes less appropriate. Recent studies are even beginning to suggest that hyperlinking does not aid in the learning process and can even result in reduced retention. This coincides with similar studies showing that the attention span of today's students has dramatically decreased from those of past students.

In this chapter, we focus on constructing hyperlinks within an Authorware piece. These links can be used for navigation purposes or they can be used for creating hypertext. Before commencing with development, I suggest that you determine the purpose of your piece, then determine an appropriate strategy for implementing hyperlinks. ■

Navigating Through Frameworks

In Chapter 15, "Building Interactive Documents," you discovered how to create a framework. As you may recall, a framework consists of a Framework icon from which branches—known as pages—are arranged. Each page can contain further interactivity or content.

In this chapter, I explain how the user can move between frameworks and pages, as well as practical applications for using pages in a multimedia piece.

Moving Between Pages

When Authorware encounters a hyperlink, it responds in either of two ways: Jump to Page or Call and Return. In either case, the destination for a hyperlink is always a page of a framework. Each of these hyperlink responses is described next.

▶ For an introduction to frameworks and pages, **see** "Understanding Frameworks," **p. 294**.

Jumping to a Page (One-Way Trip)   If the hyperlink is set up as a one-way trip, Authorware simply leaps off of the Flowline and proceeds directly to the destination page. For example, the World Wide Web uses this type of linking for navigation.

When a one-way trip, or jump, is encountered, all of the information in the current page is automatically erased and Authorware proceeds to the destination page. If the destination page is outside of the current framework, Authorware will execute all of the icons in the Exit Pane of the Framework icon after the current page is erased and before leaping to the destination page.

Defining Call and Return (Round Trip)   If the hyperlink is set up as a round trip, or a call, the content of the current page will not be erased as the destination page is displayed. When the piece has completed executing everything in the destination page, it returns to the page from which the destination page was called.

One application of round-trip hyperlinks I like to use is the creation of a glossary of terms. Users can link to the destination page, which contains the glossary interaction, but when they complete the interaction, they will return to the page from which they called the glossary.

CAUTION

Implementing hyperlinking breaks the Authorware Flowline metaphor, resulting in a piece that is much more difficult to maintain. Although using calls rather than jumps reduces maintenance efforts, I suggest only using Framework icons and Navigate icons when a high degree of hyperlinking is required by the design of your piece. Simple navigation is much easier to maintain when constructed with the Interaction icons and Decision icons.

In most cases, you will be able to determine whether a link uses the Call or the Jump option. In some cases, however, this setting is predetermined by the type of link that is being created.

Now that we have looked at the types of links that can be created in Authorware, let's look at how the links are created.

Introducing the Navigate Icon

The Navigate icon, as seen in Figure 16.1, is used to define the links used for either navigation or for hypertext. Additionally, the Navigate icon is used to create one-way and round-trip links, and should be used together with the Framework icon in all cases. As mentioned earlier, the Navigate icon is the only icon within Authorware that breaks the Flowline metaphor. When reading the graphic Flowline, you will be unable to tell where the piece will go next—or what it will be doing—without first opening the Navigate To dialog box within the Navigate icon.

▶ To refer to the introduction of the Navigate icon, **see** "The Navigate Icon," **p. 17**.

FIG. 16.1
The Navigate icon is similar to a traditional Go To function because the Flowline is not followed.

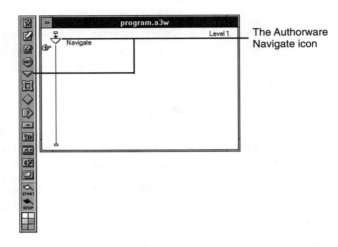

The Authorware Navigate icon

N O T E Navigation via the Navigate icon is more like scripting than authoring because it does not take advantage of the Flowline. ■

Although using the Navigate icon does have its drawbacks as far as maintainability is concerned, its ease of use and powerful searching capabilities make it a great tool for the creation of certain applications.

To set up the Navigate icon, follow these steps:

1. Drag a Navigate icon to the Flowline. Navigate icons can be placed directly on the Flowline or they can be attached to an Interaction icon, Decision icon, or Framework icon.

2. Open the Navigate To dialog box, as seen in Figure 16.2, by double-clicking the Navigate icon on the Flowline.

FIG. 16.2
The default Navigation To dialog box is set with the Anywhere destination type.

The default Navigate To settings are Anywhere and Jump to Page.

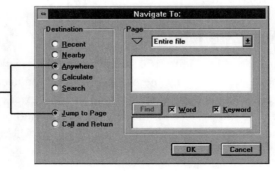

3. Determine the Destination type you want to create, then make the appropriate adjustments. There are five Destination types within Authorware that are discussed in greater detail throughout the remainder of this chapter.

4. Click OK to save your selections.

Using the Recent Destination Type

The Recent destination link is most commonly used to either link the current page back to the previous page, or to present a list of previously encountered pages to the end user so that a destination page can be selected.

Creating a Recent Destination Link

Once you have brought a Navigate icon to the Flowline and have opened the Navigate To dialog box by double-clicking the Navigate icon, follow these steps to create a Recent Destination link:

1. Select the Recent option from the Destination area of the Navigate To dialog box.

2. When this selection is made, the Navigate To dialog box will change to reveal the Recent settings, as seen in Figure 16.3.

FIG. 16.3
The default destination page setting is Go Back, which forces the piece to return to the previous page when this Navigate icon is encountered.

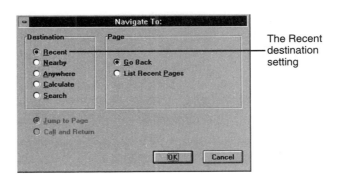

The Recent destination setting

> **NOTE** The Recent destination type uses the Jump option; the Call option is not available. ▪

The Recent settings contained in the Navigate To dialog box are Go Back and List Recent Pages. These options work as described next.

Selecting the Go Back Option   Select this option if you want the user to step backwards, one page at a time, through all of the pages previously encountered. Each time this Navigate icon is encountered, it returns the user to the previous page.

To provide a hint as to the settings made within the Navigate To dialog box, the Navigate icon located on the Flowline, which has the Recent destination option selected, changes to that shown in Figure 16.4.

FIG. 16.4
This icon is typically used in conjunction with a "go back one page" icon in the Presentation Window.

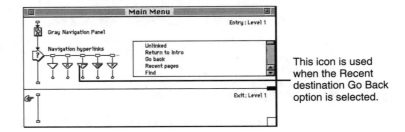

This icon is used when the Recent destination Go Back option is selected.

TIP If you are creating a piece that fully supports hyperlinking for navigation, provide your end users with the capability to step backwards through content because they may have no other way to readily access that information.

Listing Recent Pages   Selecting this option provides your end user with a floating window that contains the list of visited pages, as seen in Figure 16.5, when the Navigate icon is encountered. The names of the pages appear with the most recent pages placed at the top of the list and the first page seen placed at the bottom of the list. As the user continues to use the piece, the list will continue to update.

Use this box to close the window.

FIG. 16.5
Pages listed in the floating window get their name from the name of the icon used to create the page.

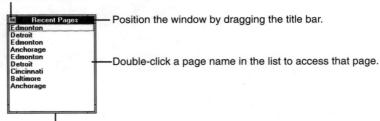

Position the window by dragging the title bar.

Double-click a page name in the list to access that page.

Resize the window just as you would any other window.

> **CAUTION**
>
> The names that appear in the list are based on the names you assign to the pages—the icons attached to the Framework icon. Be sure that these names are spelled correctly and are descriptive enough to be meaningful for the end user.

When the floating window of recent pages is present, the end user can double-click a listed page to immediately go to that page. The end user can also reposition or resize the window or close the window.

> **N O T E**   The floating window containing the scrolling list of recently seen pages adheres to either Macintosh or Windows standards. If you want to create your own look and feel, you can create a custom window to contain the list of recent pages using the Authorware variables `IconLogTitle` and `IconLogID`. ▨

When the List Recent Pages option is selected in the Navigate To dialog box, the Navigate icon changes to that shown in Figure 16.6.

FIG. 16.6
This icon is typically used in conjunction with a "show history" icon in the Presentation Window.

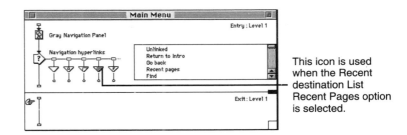

This icon is used when the Recent destination List Recent Pages option is selected.

Customizing the Recent Pages Window

If you plan to use the List Recent Pages option, consider the settings available in the Navigation Setup dialog box, as seen in Figure 16.7. To access this dialog box, select the Navigation Setup command in the File menu.

The Navigation Setup dialog box contains three settings that apply to the List Recent Pages option, as follows:

■ Window Title—You can overwrite the default for this field, Recent Pages, with a title that will be positioned across the top of the List Recent Pages floating window.

FIG. 16.7
The Navigation Setup dialog box can be used to set parameters for the List Recent Pages option.

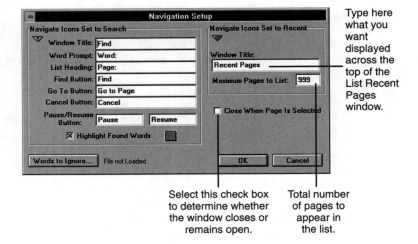

Type here what you want displayed across the top of the List Recent Pages window.

Select this check box to determine whether the window closes or remains open.

Total number of pages to appear in the list.

N O T E The maximum number of characters that can be used in the floating-window title is 40. If the window is resized so that all the characters are not able to fit, Authorware will truncate (shorten) the title. ■

■ Maximum Pages to List—You can overwrite the default for this text box, 999, with a value representing the maximum number of pages you want to be listed in the floating window for your piece.

N O T E The maximum number of pages that can be listed in the floating window is 32,000. ■

■ Close When Page Selected—If you select this check box, Authorware will close the floating window once the user has selected to go to a recent page listed in the window.

N O T E The List Recent Pages settings found in the Navigation Setup dialog box are global settings. This means that all instances of the List Recent Pages function have the same settings. ■

Using the Nearby Destination Type

As we saw in Chapter 15, "Building Interactive Documents," the Framework icon is used to establish pages of content. These pages can actually be imported from external text documents or they can consist of interactions and other media constructed in Authorware.

In any case, the Nearby destination link is most commonly used to link the current page to either the next, previous, first, or last page of the framework. The Nearby destination link is also used, however, to allow the end user to exit the framework.

N O T E The Nearby destination type uses the Jump option; the Call option is not available. ▩

As a general note, if you plan to create a linear content structure in which you use the Nearby navigation options, I recommend that you display the current page, as well as the total number of pages, somewhere on the screen so that the user can get a sense of how much content is left.

Creating a Nearby Destination Link

Once you have brought a Navigate icon to the Flowline and have opened the Navigate To dialog box by double-clicking the Navigate icon, follow these steps to create a Nearby destination link:

1. Select the Nearby option from the Destination area of the Navigate To dialog box.
2. When this selection is made, the Navigate To dialog box will change to reveal the Nearby settings, as seen in Figure 16.8.

FIG. 16.8
The Nearby settings include Previous, Next, First, Last and Exit Framework/Return

The Nearby destination setting

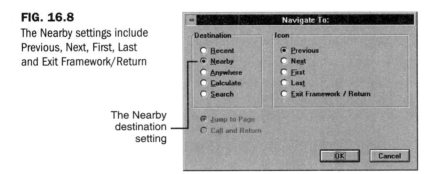

There are five Nearby settings contained in the Navigate To dialog box. These are described next.

Linking to the Previous Page   Select this option if you want the piece to leap to the page directly to the left of the current page of the framework when the Navigate icon is encountered. If the current page is the first page of the framework, then the piece will leap to the last page of the framework, thus creating a loop. When this option is selected, the Navigate icon changes to that shown in Figure 16.9.

FIG. 16.9
This icon is typically used in conjunction with a "page backwards" icon in the Presentation Window.

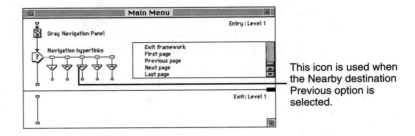

This icon is used when the Nearby destination Previous option is selected.

Next   Select this option if you want the piece to leap to the page directly to the right of the current page of the framework when the Navigate icon is encountered. If the current page is the last page of the framework, then the piece will leap to the first page of the framework. When this option is selected, the Navigate icon changes to that shown in Figure 16.10.

FIG. 16.10
This icon is typically used in conjunction with a "page forward" icon in the Presentation Window.

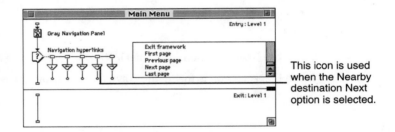

This icon is used when the Nearby destination Next option is selected.

First   Select this option if you want the piece to leap directly to the first page of the framework when the Navigate icon is encountered. When this option is selected, the Navigate icon changes to that shown in Figure 16.11.

FIG. 16.11
This icon is typically used in conjunction with a "go to the beginning" icon in the Presentation Window.

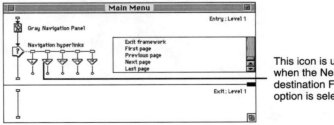

This icon is used when the Nearby destination First option is selected.

Last   Select this option if you want the piece to leap directly to the last page of the framework when the Navigate icon is encountered. When this option is selected, the Navigate icon changes to that shown in Figure 16.12.

FIG. 16.12
This icon is typically used in conjunction with a "go to the end" icon in the Presentation Window.

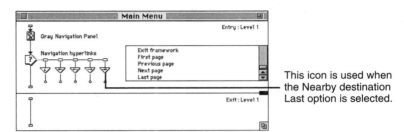

This icon is used when the Nearby destination Last option is selected.

Exit Framework/Return   Select this option if you want the piece to exit the framework when the Navigate icon is encountered. Keep in mind that the current page will be erased, then all of the icons in the exit pane will be executed before the framework is exited. When this option is selected, the Navigate icon changes to that shown in Figure 16.13.

▷ For information regarding the use of the exit pane, **see** "Exit Pane," **p. 297.**

FIG. 16.13
This icon is typically used in conjunction with an "Exit" icon in the Presentation Window.

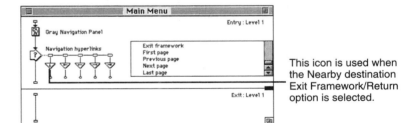

This icon is used when the Nearby destination Exit Framework/Return option is selected.

Using the Anywhere Destination Type

One of the greatest benefits of hypermedia is the capability to link related or unrelated content topics together. In the linear content structure, which we explored in the last section, the content was organized in a contiguous manner. In many cases, however, content will not be structured in such an orderly manner. In those cases, the navigation must be able to link to any point in the piece. (See "Using the Recent Destination Type," earlier in this chapter.)

Creating an Anywhere Destination Link

The Anywhere destination option enables the piece to jump directly to any page of any framework in your piece. Once you have brought a Navigate icon to the Flowline and have opened the Navigate To dialog box by double-clicking the Navigate icon, follow these steps to create an Anywhere destination link:

1. Select the Anywhere option from the Destination area of the Navigate To dialog box.

2. When this selection is made, the Navigate To dialog box will change to reveal the Anywhere settings, as seen in Figure 16.14.

FIG. 16.14
This icon is typically used for main menu navigation, or when navigation will not occur in a linear manner.

The Anywhere destination setting

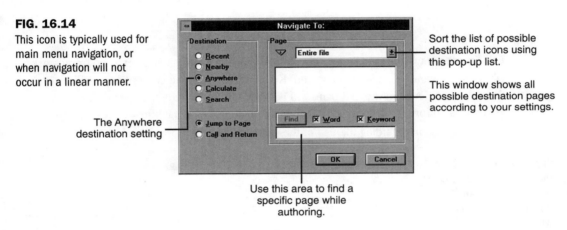

Sort the list of possible destination icons using this pop-up list.

This window shows all possible destination pages according to your settings.

Use this area to find a specific page while authoring.

N O T E   The Anywhere destination link is the default setting for the Navigate icon. ▉

3. Use the drop-down list to select the Framework icon that contains the page to which you are linking.

4. Select the page to which you are linking from the scrolling list. If you are unable to find the page, and you know either a keyword or content that has been assigned to the page, use the Find options to help locate the page.

The options contained in the Anywhere Navigate To dialog box are discussed next.

Selecting a Destination Page   The pop-up menu contains a list of all of the Framework icons in your piece, as well as an option to display all of the pages in the entire piece. Once you have made a selection from this list, the scrolling window located just under the pop-up menu will populate with the names of the pages attached to the selected Framework icon.

To define the destination for the link, simply select a page from the scrolling list so that it highlights.

Finding a Specific Page You can control the scrolling list of page names that appears by using the Find option. To use this option, enter information for which you want to search into the Find field, then click Find. The search for the entered information will be limited to the framework that you have selected using the pop-up menu.

You can further control the search by using either of the following filters:

- Text Filter—Selecting this option causes Authorware to search for matching text contained in text objects found in the pages of the framework that has been identified in the pop-up list.

- Keyword Filter—Selecting this option causes Authorware to search for matching keywords for the pages of the framework that have been identified in the pop-up list. You see how to create keywords later in this chapter.

When the Anywhere destination type is selected, the Navigate icon changes to that shown in Figure 16.15.

FIG. 16.15
The Anywhere destination link links to one specific page, no matter which page it is called from.

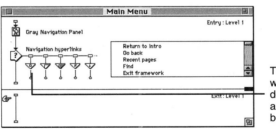

This icon is used when the Anywhere destination is selected and a destination has been established.

N O T E The Anywhere destination link can function using either the Jump or the Call option. Be sure that you are familiar with the rules for these settings, as discussed earlier in this chapter.

If the Anywhere destination page is later deleted, the Navigate icon changes to that shown in Figure 16.16. This icon, which is the default for the Navigate icon, is used when no link is established for the Navigate icon.

 Because the Anywhere destination link breaks the Flowline metaphor, I suggest that you give special attention to naming the Navigate icon. Its name can be used to identify where the piece will jump.

FIG. 16.16
When a Navigate icon is first added to the Flowline, it uses the Anywhere Destination type, however, a destination page must be identified.

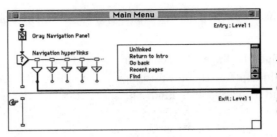

This icon is used when the Anywhere destination is selected and no destination is established.

Using the Calculate Destination Link

The Calculate destination link is used to navigate to a page that has not been predetermined by you, but that is a result of how the user has been interacting with the piece. When the end user runs your piece, and a Navigation icon using the Calculate destination type is encountered, the piece jumps to the page containing a unique ID (address), which has been identified by a variable or expression placed in the Navigate To dialog box.

▶ For more information on using the Calculation destination type, **see** "Calculating Navigation Based on Data," **p. 442**.

▶ For an overview of working with variables and expressions, **see** "Working with Variables and Functions," **p. 366**.

For example, you may want to create a bookmarking feature for the end user. At any point within the piece, the user can set a bookmark, then at any later point he can view the list of bookmarks, select an item from the list, and navigate directly to that page.

Creating a Calculate Destination Link

Once you have brought a Navigate icon to the Flowline and have opened the Navigate To dialog box by double-clicking the Navigate icon, follow these steps to create a Calculate destination link:

1. Select the Calculate option from the Destination area of the Navigate To dialog box.

2. When this selection is made, the Navigate To dialog box will change to reveal the Calculate settings, as seen in Figure 16.17.

3. Enter a variable or expression into the Icon Expression text box that will return the unique ID for the destination page. If the ID is not for a page—an icon attached directly to a Framework icon—then the Navigate icon will be ignored and the piece will continue down the Flowline.

FIG. 16.17
The Calculate option provides a window in which a variable or expression must be entered.

The Calculate destination setting

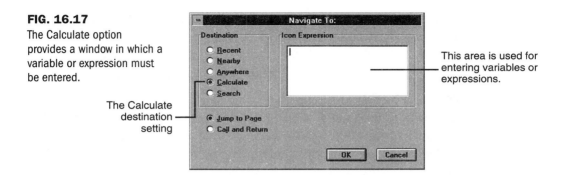

This area is used for entering variables or expressions.

Part
IV
Ch
16

T I P Having a firm understanding of how Authorware functions and variables work is critical to successfully implementing the Calculate navigation type.

N O T E The Calculate destination links can function using either the Jump or the Call option. Be sure that you are familiar with the rules for these settings. For more information, see the sections, "Jumping to a Page (One-Way Trip)" and "Defining Call and Return (Round Trip)," earlier in this chapter.

If the Calculate option is selected, the Navigate icon changes to that shown in Figure 16.18.

FIG. 16.18
This icon is typically used in conjunction with bookmarking, or a similar function in which a specific icon address is identified.

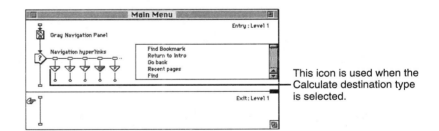

This icon is used when the Calculate destination type is selected.

Building Bookmarks

Since I have piqued your interest with the bookmarking example, I will finish teaching you how I implemented this functionality. To do so, I must first warn you that a thorough understanding of Authorware functions and variables is necessary. If you do not have this background yet, to skip to Chapter 19, "Using Variables and Functions."

As you may recall, the user is able to set a bookmark at any point within the piece, then at any point later, view a list of bookmarks and select a page to which the piece jumps. To create such functionality, follow these steps:

1. Place a Calculation icon on the Flowline at the point reached when the user selects to place a bookmark.

2. Place the name of the current bookmark—one that you create— in a list (let's call it MarkNameList), as well as the current page's ID (Authorware variable CurrentPageID) into a second list (let's call it MarkNumberList).

3. Create a scrolling list that contains MarkNameList.

4. Create an interaction that allows the user to click the scrolling list.

5. Place a Navigate icon on the Flowline at the point reached when the user selects a bookmark to jump to.

6. Place an expression that returns that page's ID, such as the one seen in Figure 16.19, into the Icon Expression field.

FIG. 16.19
The expression shown in the Navigate To dialog box returns a page's ID that has been stored in the list named MarkNumberList.

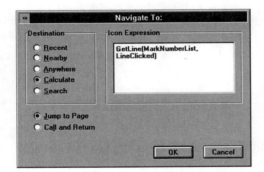

Using the Search Destination Type

Search engines are typically used when creating a performance support tool, such as a technical reference guide. These engines provide a means by which the user can search for specific words or phrases in the content, or search for keywords that you have established.

Like the Recent navigation type, the Search navigation type provides a floating window, the Find window, as shown in Figure 16.20, with which the user interacts to navigate through the content. The Find window is displayed as soon as the piece encounters a Navigate icon set to the Search destination type. For more information, see the sections, "Using the Recent Destination Type" and "Listing Recent Pages," earlier in this chapter.

Enter the content or keyword to
be searched for in this area.

FIG. 16.20
Pages listed in the floating
window get their name from
the name of the icon used to
create the page.

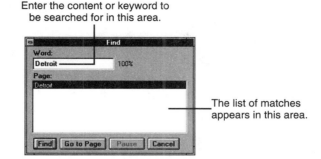

The list of matches
appears in this area.

Creating a Search Destination Link

Once you have brought a Navigate icon to the Flowline and have opened the Navigate To
dialog box by double-clicking the Navigate icon, follow these steps to create a Search
destination link:

1. Select the Search option from the Destination area of the Navigate To dialog box.

2. When this selection is made, the Navigate To dialog box will change to reveal the
   Search settings, as seen in Figure 16.21.

FIG. 16.21
This feature is most
commonly used for text-
intensive applications.

The Navigate To
Search setting

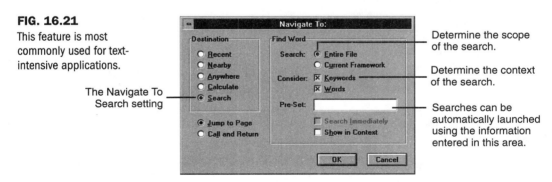

Determine the scope
of the search.

Determine the context
of the search.

Searches can be
automatically launched
using the information
entered in this area.

The Search settings contained in the Navigate To dialog box, and how to use them, are
described next.

Search   The Search portion of the dialog box contains two options that specify the scope
of the search, as follows:

■ Entire File—Selecting this option causes Authorware to search all of the frameworks in the entire file in order to find the specific match.

> **CAUTION**
>
> Searching the entire file can take quite a long time, and even though the user is able to continue using the piece while the search is taking place, you may want to limit the scope of the search.

- Current Framework—Selecting this option causes Authorware to conduct the search within the current framework only.

Consider   Because searching can take quite a long time, you can further limit the scope of the search using the following options:

- Keywords—Select this option to have your piece search for keywords that have been established for the pages of the frameworks you have determined to search. We look at defining keywords later in this chapter.
- Words—Select this option to have the piece search for content text contained in the pages of the framework you have determined to search. (For more information, see Chapter 3, "Presenting Text.")

> **CAUTION**
>
> Searching for both keywords and words will result in slower performance, especially if you have selected to search the entire file.

Pre-Set   If you enter a word, phrase or variable in this field, the entry will appear in the Find field of the Find floating window with which the user will interact. The end user can elect to either overwrite this entry or begin the search.

 T I P   If you are not entering a variable, you must enclose the Pre-Set word or phrase in quotes.

This option is very useful if you are providing the type of hyperlinking in which the end user can click a word, then see a list of places where that word or keyword is used throughout the piece. In such a case, enter a variable (LastWordClicked) containing the word that has been clicked into the field.

Search Immediately   If an entry has been made in the Pre-Set field, then this option becomes available. If this check box is selected, Authorware will begin to search for the value in the Pre-Set field as soon as the piece encounters the Navigate icon and the Find window is placed in the Presentation Window.

In our previous hyperlinking example, we would more than likely want to begin the search for related content areas as soon as the user clicks the hypertext word. Therefore, we would select the Search Immediately option.

Show in Context   If this option is selected, results of the search will be displayed with words surrounding the text that is being searched for. To accommodate this additional text, the Find window may become larger. This option only applies to content text, not to keywords.

> **N O T E**   The Search destination links can function using either the Jump or the Call option. Be
> sure that you are familiar with the rules for these settings. For more information, see
> the sections, "Jumping to a Page (One-Way Trip)" and "Defining Call and Return (Round Trip)," earlier in this chapter. ■

Customizing the Find Window

When the piece encounters a Navigate icon that is set to Search, the Find window, as seen in Figure 16.20, is placed in the Presentation Window for the end user to interact with. The settings available in the Navigation Setup dialog box, as seen in Figure 16.22, can be used to customize many of the items in the Find window, such as the window title or the names of the buttons it contains. To access this dialog box, select the Navigation Setup command available in the File menu.

FIG. 16.22
The Navigation Setup dialog box can be used to set parameters for the Search option.

The left side of the Navigation Setup dialog box is used to set options for the search function.

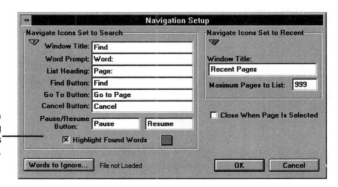

The Navigation Setup dialog box contains several settings that apply to the Find window. You learn what each of these options does next.

Window Title   The default value, Find, can be overwritten with any word or phrase you want placed along the top of the floating window.

> **N O T E**   The maximum number of characters that can be used in the floating-window title
> is 39. ■

Word Prompt   The default value, Word:, can be overwritten with any word or phrase you want placed above the entry field in the floating window.

List Heading The default value, Page:, can be overwritten with any word or phrase you want placed above the scrolling list of pages, containing the matched keywords, words, or phrases in the floating window.

N O T E The maximum number of characters that can be entered in the Navigation Setup dialog box is 40; however, Authorware will only display five characters in the floating window. ■

Find Button The default value, Find, can be overwritten with any word or phrase you want placed in the button located in the lower left-hand corner of the floating window.

N O T E The maximum number of characters that can be used for any of the buttons in the floating window is 40. The button is automatically sized to accommodate your label. Additionally, the Find window is sized based on the dimension of the buttons. Therefore, if you use a very large label for each button, the Find window may extend off of the screen. ■

Go To Button, Cancel Button, and Pause/Resume Button The default values for each of these buttons can be overwritten with any word or phrase you want placed in the buttons respectively.

Highlight Found Words If you select this check box, Authorware will highlight the found word or phrase with the selected color after the user clicks the Go To button.

Words to Ignore When you click this button, Authorware presents the Open File dialog box where you can identify an ASCII file containing values that you want Authorware to ignore in its search if the user enters such a value in the Find window.

When constructing this external file, each value should be written on a separate line. Additionally, because this file is not packed with your piece, be sure it is stored together so that it is not forgotten during distribution.

Implementing Keywords

Now that you have seen how to build a Search engine and how to customize the Find window with which the user will interact, let's look at how to build one more level of sophistication into your piece by implementing keywords.

When developing the capability for the end user to do searching, there are two sides of the functionality that must be created. In the last section we looked at the first side: building the search engine. In this section, we look at the second side of searching: creating text objects and implementing keywords.

When Authorware conducts a search, it can search for either content, which is contained in text objects, or it can search through predefined keywords. In Chapter 3, "Presenting Text," we explored creating text objects, so let's now look at implementing keywords.

▶ For further instruction on creating content text, **see** "Using the Text Tool," **p. 76**.

N O T E If text has been made into a graphic, it will not be found in a search. Only text objects from the Presentation Window are included in a search. ■

Keywords or phrases are additional, hidden "labels" you apply to icons, so that there will be more detailed information for which the piece can search, without the piece having to search the entire icon contents. For example, if you are building a product catalogue, you may want to incorporate the product identification number, the product name, and the various configurations in which the product can be ordered as keywords. When users conduct a search on any of these items, they will be directed to a specific page of content.

Using Keywords

Keyword searching can be used either during authoring or while the end user is running your piece. Although assigning keywords for either of these purposes is nearly the same, let's explore each situation in closer detail.

Keywords for Authoring In some instances, it can be helpful to identify who from the production team worked on a particular graphic or interaction; what the original source for certain media was; or where embedded information or calculations are stored. In such a case, you can assign a keyword to the icon to identify those portions of the Authorware code.

For example, I am just finishing a piece that uses the current tax rate to perform several calculations. Unfortunately, as we crossed into a new year, all of these calculations had to be revised based on adjusted tax tables. By assigning each of the Calculation icons that contain the tax calculations a keyword, however, I could quickly search through the very large piece for the few instances where the tax tables existed.

Keywords for the End User Although keywords can be used for authoring, they are more commonly used to establish search criteria for the end user. This is especially true when you have created an electronic performance support tool or a tool that will be used when performing a specific task, through which the user must navigate in order to find related material.

Whether you are implementing keywords for authoring or for the end user, there is one critical point to know. Although keywords can be attached to any icon located on the Flowline, only keywords associated with a page of a framework will be identified in a search.

Setting Up Keywords

Creating a keyword for an icon is rather simple. Perform the following steps:

1. Select the icon to which you want to associate the keyword by clicking it in the Flowline.

2. Choose the Keyword command from the Attributes menu. Once this selection is made, the Keywords dialog box appears (see Fig. 16.23).

3. Enter a keyword for the selected icon into the Keyword text box at the bottom left-hand corner of the dialog box.

FIG. 16.23
The Keywords dialog box can be used to define keywords for a page of a Framework icon, which will be considered when the user initiates a search.

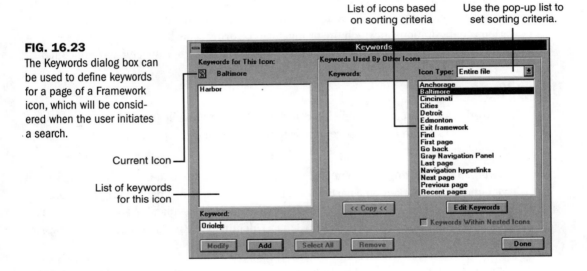

List of icons based on sorting criteria

Use the pop-up list to set sorting criteria.

Current Icon

List of keywords for this icon

N O T E Authorware will only accept single words as keywords. If you attempt to assign a phrase, only the first word of the phrase is entered. It is possible to string words together with underscores or other characters but it's not likely that the end user will do the same. Using underscoring may, however, be a way to "hide" keywords that have been entered to facilitate the authoring process.

4. Click the Add button once you have entered a keyword. Continue adding keywords to the list or select a keyword to be modified or deleted.

5. Click Done when finished to save your settings.

The Keywords dialog box has several buttons and fields that can be used in the setting of a keyword for an icon. Some of these fields are used to actually define the keyword, and some are used to reference other keywords used throughout your piece. Let's look at each of these fields in greater detail, beginning with the ones used to create a keyword.

■ Keywords for This Icon—This list, located along the left of the Keyword dialog box, contains all of the keywords for the currently selected icon. You can modify this list by clicking a keyword to select it, or clicking the Add, Modify or Delete buttons.

 To select more than one keyword from the list, hold down the Shift key while dragging over the list. To select or deselect single keywords, hold down the ⌘ (Macintosh) or Ctrl (Windows) key while clicking.

■ Keyword Field—It is in this text box that you enter the desired keyword for the currently selected icon. Although you can enter a seemingly unlimited number of characters, try to anticipate what your end user will be entering.

The remainder of the dialog box is used to identify keywords used for other icons or to switch to another icon to update keywords without jumping back to the Flowline and selecting a new icon. The remaining selections are as follows:

■ Keywords—This scrolling list contains all of the keywords for the icon that has been selected in the scrolling list of icon titles located on the right-hand side of the Keywords dialog box.

■ Icon Type—This pop-up list enables you to sort the list of icon names according to their type, or you can select to see the name of the icons for the entire file.

■ Edit Keywords—If an icon has been selected from the list of icons along the right-hand side of the Keywords dialog box, click this button to switch from the current icon to the highlighted icon.

This feature is very helpful if you are implementing keywords for several icons at one time. For example, if you are creating a product catalogue in which each page represents a unique product and the page's name is the same as the product's, you can simply switch from page to page to implement all of the keywords at once.

■ Keywords with Nested Icons—Selecting this check box enables you to see all of the keywords associated with the current icon as well as the icons attached to the current icon (if it is a Framework, Interaction, Map, or Decision icon).

More About Hyperlinking

Now that we have explored creating keywords, let's move on to complete a topic that we started in Chapter 3.

In Chapter 3, "Presenting Text," we began looking at how hyperlinks are created using text styles. We defined a style, then explored in detail how that style could be applied to text in the Presentation Window. When defining the style, however, we skipped over setting the Navigate To field. In this section, we define the style so that it incorporates navigation.

▶ To refer to the introduction of hyperlinks, **see** "Building Hyperlinks," **p. 91**.

▶ To learn how to define a style, **see** "Defining a Style," **p. 88**.

Setting Navigation to a Text Style

Just as you define whether the user single-clicks or double-clicks the text that has been identified as *hot text,* you can also identify what type of navigation will be used when the end user clicks (see Fig. 16.24).

FIG. 16.24
The Define Styles dialog box enables you to define navigation criteria for a style.

Set the attributes for launching navigation.

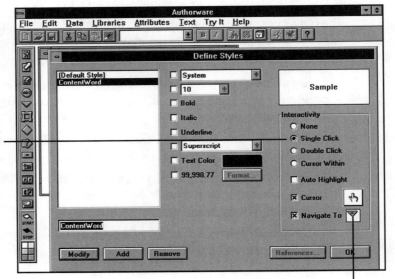

Double-click this icon to determine the destination type.

 TIP The World Wide Web has instituted the convention that a single-click is used for linking. Because this expectation is established in many users, I recommend that you follow it and reserve double-clicking for such things as opening a graphic or showing an animation.

To set the navigation for a style, follow these steps:

1. Choose the Define Style command from the Text menu.

2. Select the style for which you want the navigation defined.

3. Select the check box labeled Navigate To. As we discussed in Chapter 3, you can either set the navigation as a part of the style, or you can set it uniquely for each application of the style.

   ▶ For more information regarding using navigation as a part of a style, **see** "Including Navigation in the Style," **p. 94**.

4. If you plan to identify the navigation as a part of the style, click the Navigation icon symbol located to the right of the check box. When you click this icon, the standard Navigate To dialog box appears.

   If you wait to define the navigation so that it is unique to each application of the style, the Navigate To dialog box will appear the first time you run the piece and select the text.

5. Use the Navigate To dialog box just as we discussed throughout this chapter to set the link. (For more information, see "Introducing the Navigate Icon," earlier in this chapter.)

Part
IV

Ch
16

CHAPTER 17

Setting Up Branching

Most commonly, we see the computer used as a presentation device for multimedia. It displays text, graphics, video, animation, and audio that the designer has prepared and over which the end user has control of the pace of presentation. But rarely do we see the computer contributing to the sequence in which content is presented.

Early attempts were made at giving the computer such control. Educators and entertainers alike used the computer's capability to generate randomness. This function was used for everything from selecting the order in which test questions would be asked, to determining the reward given for the completion of a level in a game.

As our designs for interactive learning and performance support become more complex, however, the computer must evolve to assume the role of guide, mentor, or coach. As the user demonstrates a need for one type of information, the computer must be able to interpret that need and make the decision to branch to that content without the user being aware of the action.

Use decision loops to establish branching along the Flowline

Just as Interaction icons and Framework icons allow you to create branching, so does the Decision icon.

Creating the decision loop

The decision loop is comprised of three parts: the Decision icon, the branch path, and the branching.

Understanding the branching types

A Decision icon may use one of four branching types: Sequentially, Randomly to Any Path, Randomly to Unused Path, and To Calculated Path

Applying the Repeat options

A Decision icon may also incorporate one of five Repeat options: Times, Until All Paths Used, Until Click/Keypress, Until TRUE, and Don't Repeat.

Using time-based decisions

Time can be used to determine how long the end user will be held in the decision loop.

Working with the dialog box attached to each branch

Each attached dialog box allows you to determine parameters for automatic erasing, automatic pausing, and editing the branch.

In this chapter, I will explain how the Authorware Decision icon is used to construct a linear presentation controlled by the end user, to create a series of branches that could then be randomly executed or to build a system in which the computer can branch based on its recognition of the end user's need. ■

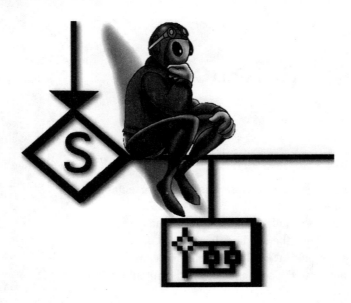

Defining the Decision Loop

The Decision icon, like both the Interaction icon and the Framework icon, is used to set up branching within Authorware. With the Interaction icon, the end user interacts directly with the Interaction loop to select which branch the piece will take. With the Decision icon, the end user does not interact with the decision loop; rather, you—the designer— establish parameters that determine the path taken. The determination of which path to take is made by the system, not by the end user.

▶ To refer to the introduction of the Decision icon, **see** "The Decision Icon," **p. 18**.

▶ To refer to the introduction of the Interaction icon, **see** "The Interaction Icon," **p. 19**.

▶ To refer to the introduction of the Framework icon, **see** "The Framework Icon," **p. 18**.

▶ To see how Interaction loops are created, **see** "Introducing Interactions," **p. 212**.

N O T E   The most common decision structure is one where the branching is based on data that is collected in a previous interaction. In this case, the end user is indirectly interacting with the decision. ▨

Introducing the Decision Icon

The Authorware Decision icon, shown in Figure 17.1, is the core tool used to develop system level branching; that is, branching that does not result from the user's interaction. One of the more common uses of the Decision icon, however, is to establish a specific path of content following a user's response to a series of interactions.

FIG. 17.1
The Decision icon is used to create branching based on pre-set options rather than user interaction.

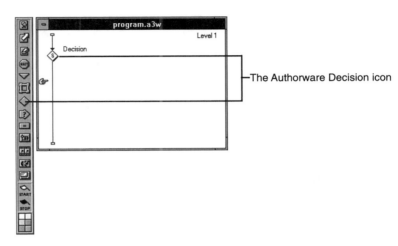

The Decision icon, unlike the Interaction icon, does not contain a Display icon. Therefore, the Decision icon cannot be used to create text or graphics in the Presentation Window. Branches associated with the Decision icon, however, can contain icons that display text and graphic objects like those of a framework or Interaction loop.

▶ For guidance on using the display associated with an Interaction icon, **see** "Editing the Interaction Display," **p. 233**.

▶ To refer to the introduction of the Display icon, **see** "The Display Icon," **p. 15**.

 It has helped me to think of the Decision icon as the brains of the operation. It is with this icon that you can create a learning application that is individualized to the end user or a performance support tool that is smart enough to make product recommendations. Whenever you envision the opportunity, use the Decision icon to determine which content should be presented.

Recognizing the Decision Loop

Much like the Interaction icon is the center of the Interaction loop, the Decision icon is the center of the decision loop, and just as the interaction would be nothing without the responses, the decision serves no purpose without its branch path. To fully understand how the decision loop functions, it is important to understand the parts that make up the decision loop.

The Decision Icon   The Decision icon is the core to the decision loop. Based on parameters that you establish in the Decision dialog box, shown in Figure 17.2, the piece follows the Flowline through the Decision icon and along a defined branch path.

FIG. 17.2
The Decision dialog box enables you to determine what criteria the piece will use for selecting a branch.

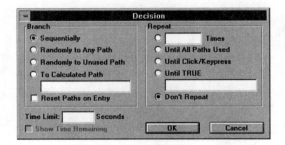

The Decision Branch Path   To the right of the Decision icon, you can develop a number of decision branch paths. Decision branches can consist of any icon except another Decision icon, a Framework icon, or an Interaction icon. Decision, Framework, and Interaction icons can, however, be placed inside of a Map icon used as a decision branch path.

▶ To refer to the introduction of the Map icon, **see** "The Map Icon," **p. 20**.

 To have more than one item within a branch, place the items in a Map icon and then place the Map icon on the decision loop.

Decision Branching   The final component of the decision loop is the decision branching. The branching is the portion of the Flowline located under the branch path. The branching illustrates which direction on the Flowline the piece will go once the branch path is completed, as shown in Figure 17.3.

Building a Decision Loop

Now that we have explored the individual pieces of the decision loop, let's look at how to set up the decision. Simply follow these steps:

1. Drag a Decision icon to the Flowline.

2. Drag another icon to the Flowline and place it to the right of the Decision icon, as shown in Figure 17.4, to create a branch path.

FIG. 17.3

The decision loop is made up of the Decision icon, the branch path, and the branching.

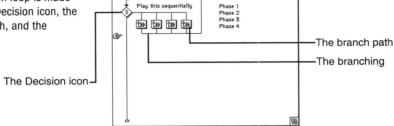

The Decision icon

The branch path

The branching

FIG. 17.4

A branch on a Decision icon can be any icon except another Decision icon or an Interaction or Framework icon.

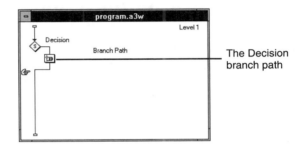

The Decision branch path

Part
IV
Ch
17

3. Drag additional icons to the Flowline and continue to place them to the right of the Decision icon to create more branches.

4. You may now create the content for each branch. Keep in mind that content can be as simple as a single Display icon or as complex as an entire level of interactions and decisions.

Once you have created the first branch path to the right of the Decision icon, you can continue placing icons in the decision loop. You can place additional branches to either the left or to the right of the first icon. Additionally, you can move the icons to adjust their position.

After you create a sixth path, if there is one, Authorware will build a scrolling window, as shown in Figure 17.5, which presents only five branches at a time. To view icons located closer to the decision icon, scroll up; to see icons further from the Decision icon, scroll down. This scrolling window functions just like the one used in an interaction loop.

When you select an icon, its title will highlight in the scrolling list, and vice versa.

▶ To see how branches are presented in a scrolling list in an interaction, **see** "Building an Interaction Loop," **p. 215**.

FIG. 17.5
Decision loops can contain
more than one branch path.

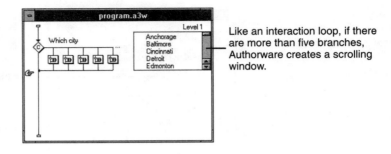

Like an interaction loop, if there
are more than five branches,
Authorware creates a scrolling
window.

Recognizing the Branching Types

There are several ways in which Authorware can branch when a Decision icon is encountered. Although a few of these result in something as straight forward as a sequential or random presentation, others enable you to create a more "intelligent" piece.

As we begin to explore the branching types, you will discover that in some instances the piece will proceed through all of the branch paths before exiting the decision loop and going on to the next icon on the Flowline. In other cases, the flow of the piece will only go through one branch path before exiting the decision. The number of times that the piece will pass through the Decision icon, or the number of paths which may be selected, is based upon the Repeat options, which I will discuss in the "Using the Repeat Options," section later in this chapter.

Both the Branch options and the Repeat options may be set using the Decision dialog box (refer to Fig. 17.2) which is opened by double-clicking the Decision icon.

The five options for branching using the Decision icon are described next.

Defining Sequential Branching

When the Sequentially option is selected in the Decision dialog box, Authorware will present the branches associated with the Decision icon in sequential order, beginning with the branch farthest to the left and working to the branch farthest to the right.

If the sequence is interrupted part way through, Authorware will pick up the sequence when it next returns to the decision loop. When a Decision icon is set to Sequentially, the icon changes to that shown in Figure 17.6.

Rather than using a Display icon followed by a Wait icon and an Erase icon when building a linear, slide show like presentation, the Decision icon can be used if the Branch option is set to Sequentially. The benefit of using the Decision icon is that it can be set to automatically pause the presentation as well as erase the contents of each branch path, therefore eliminating the need for the Wait and Erase icons. (See "Working with Branches in a Decision Loop," later in this chapter.)

FIG. 17.6
When a Decision icon is set to Sequentially, as small *S* appears within the icon.

This icon is used when the Sequentially decision type is selected.

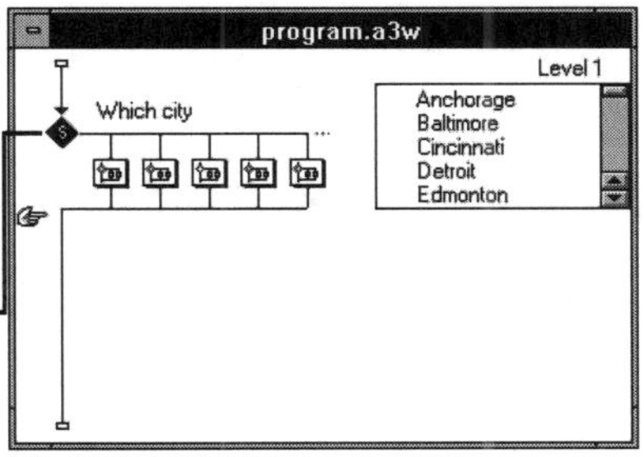

For example, you can have a series of animations that reflects how a specific process works. Rather than stringing the icons vertically on the Flowline, you can arrange them horizontally using the Decision icon set to Sequentially.

Using the Randomly to Any Path Option

When the Randomly to Any Path option is selected in the Decision dialog box, Authorware will randomly select from any of the branch paths in the decision loop. It is possible that Authorware will select one of the paths more than once before it has selected all of the paths.

When a Decision icon is set to Randomly to Any Path, the icon changes to that shown in Figure 17.7.

FIG. 17.7
Authorware changes the Decision icon on the Flowline to reflect that the branches will be selected using the Randomly to Any Path option by placing an *A* in the Decision icon.

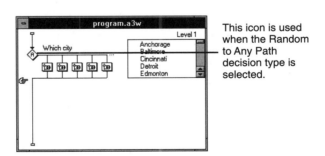

This icon is used when the Random to Any Path decision type is selected.

Creating a Randomly to Unused Path Decision

When this option is selected, Authorware will randomly select one of the branches in the decision loop. However, all branches must be selected before a branch is repeated.

Part
IV

Ch
17

T I P   This option is great for creating banks of test questions that will be presented uniquely for each user.

When a Decision icon is set to Randomly to Unused Path, the icon changes to that shown in Figure 17.8.

FIG. 17.8
Authorware changes the Decision icon on the Flowline to reflect that the branches will be selected using the Randomly to Unused Path option by placing a *U* in the Decision icon.

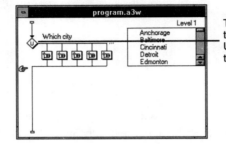

This icon is used when the Randomly to Unused Path decision type is selected.

Defining a To Calculated Path Decision

When the To Calculated Path option is selected in the Decision dialog box, you can enter a value, variable, or expression with the text box that results with a number representing the path that is to be taken by Authorware. Each icon connected to the Decision icon is numbered from left to right, beginning with 1 and ending with the total number of icons attached to the Decision icon.

If the resulting path is less than or equal to zero, no path will be taken and the piece will exit the decision loop. Likewise, if the result is a number greater than the amount of paths in the decision loop, no path will be taken and the piece will exit the Decision loop.

Using variables and expression in conjunction with the To Calculated Path decision will be discussed at length in Chapter 22, "Working with Data."

▶ For step-by-step instructions on using variables and expressions, **see** "Working with Variables and Functions," **p. 366**.

N O T E   I find the To Calculated Path response to be the most commonly used of all the branching types. As you begin to design applications with which the end user enters into a dialogue, you will also see the benefit of this branching type. ▪

When a Decision icon is set to Calculated Path, the icon changes to that shown in Figure 17.9.

It is possible that a decision loop may be interrupted before all of the paths are selected. By default, Authorware remembers which paths had and had not been selected the next time that the piece returns to the decision loop.

FIG. 17.9
Authorware changes the Decision icon on the Flowline to reflect that the branches will be selected using the To Calculated Path option by placing a *C* in the Decision icon.

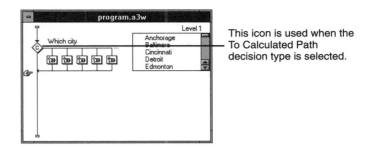

This icon is used when the To Calculated Path decision type is selected.

For example, if you have ten branches that are to be executed sequentially and the loop is interrupted after path six was selected, when the piece returns to the decision loop, it will begin the sequence with path number seven.

Although in many cases this would not affect the presentation; in other instances, it would. In the case of our previous example, if you have an animated sequence that explains how a process works, you would not want to start the animation at step number seven. In this case, you would use the Reset Paths on Entry option found in the Decision dialog box.

Reset Paths on Entry

When the Reset Paths on Entry check box is selected in the Decision dialog box, Authorware will forget what it had done previously and will treat the Decision loop as if it were the first time it had been encountered.

 TIP Be sure to select the Reset Paths on Entry check box if you are using the Sequentially branch option and the sequence of events is critical to the piece.

Using the Repeat Options

Setting the Branch options is the essence to how the Decision icon functions. In addition to the Branch setting, however, you must also consider the Repeat options. Both the Branch options and the Repeat options may be set using the Decision dialog box (refer to Figure 17.2), which is opened by double-clicking the Decision icon.

As we saw in the previous section, the Branch options determine what criteria will be used to select a branch path in the decision loop. (See "Recognizing the Branching Types," earlier in this chapter for more information.) In support of the Branch options, the Repeat options let you specify whether the piece will pass through a single branch of the decision,

Part
IV
Ch
17

or multiple branches. In other words, you could have the piece go through all of the branches before exiting the decision or only a specified number.

While each Repeat option can be defined by itself, the effect that the Repeat option has on the final piece is dependent on which Branch option has been selected. Let's take a close look at each of the Repeat options and how each Branch option impacts the Repeat options.

Times

When the Times option in the Decision dialog box is selected, you can enter a value, variable, or expression into the text box to define how many times the piece will pass through the Decision icon. Each time the piece passes through the Decision icon, a "counter" that Authorware automatically controls is increased by one. Once the number in the Times field is the same as the number of times the piece has passed through the decision icon, it will exit the decision loop.

When a Decision icon is set to Times, the branching changes to that shown in Figure 17.10.

▶ For step-by-step instruction on using variables and expressions, **see** "Working with Variables and Functions," **p. 366**.

FIG. 17.10
Authorware changes the Flowline branching to reflect that the Authorware mites will return to the Decision icon each time a branch is selected.

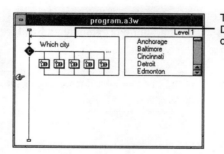

This Flowline returns to the Decision icon; therefore, more than one branch path can be selected.

Because each of the Branch options impacts how the Times Repeat option will be treated, let's look at an example for each variation of options.

■ Sequentially—If you have ten branches in a decision loop that are set to play Sequentially, you can enter a number less than ten, equal to ten, or greater than ten in the Times text box of the Decision dialog box.

   If you enter a seven in the Times text box, for example, only the first seven branches—from left to right beginning after the Decision icon—will be executed by Authorware. If you enter a ten, then all of the branches will be executed in order.

If you enter a thirteen in the Times text box, all ten branches will be executed, but then Authorware will return and play the first three branches again before exiting the decision loop.

- Randomly to Any Path—If you again have ten branches in a decision loop that are set to play Randomly to Any Path, you can enter a number less than ten, equal to ten, or greater than ten in the Times text box of the Decision dialog box. No matter what number you enter in the Times text box, Authorware will randomly pick that many branches to be executed before exiting the decision loop.

N O T E   It is possible that when this option is chosen not all of the branches would be selected because Authorware can repeat branches that have already been selected. If you want to select each branch, consider the Randomly to Used Path, which is described next. ■

Part

IV

Ch

17

- Randomly to Unused Path—If you have ten branches in a decision loop that are set to play Randomly to Unused Path, you can enter a number less than ten, equal to ten, or greater than ten in the Times text box of the Decision dialog box. No matter what number you enter in the Times text box, Authorware will again randomly pick that many branches to be executed before exiting the decision loop.

  Unlike the Randomly to Any Path scenario, however, Authorware will not repeat a branch until all of the branches have been selected. Therefore, all of the branches will be selected at least once if the number is greater than or equal to ten.

- To Calculated Path—In this scenario, Authorware will pick the path identified by the value, variable, or expression that has been entered into the To Calculated Path text box. If this value does not change while the piece is running, Authorware will select the same field the number of times you have identified in the Times field.

  ▶ For step-by-step instruction on using variables and expressions, **see** "Working with Variables and Functions," **p. 366**.

Until All Paths Used

When the Until All Paths Used Repeat option in the Decision dialog box is selected, Authorware will pass through the Decision icon until all of the branches have been selected. As soon as each of the branches has been selected at least once, the piece will exit the decision loop.

When a Decision icon is set to Until All Paths Used, the branching changes to that shown in Figure 17.10.

Because each of the Branch options impacts how the Repeat option will be treated, let's look at an example for each variation.

■ Sequentially—If you have ten branches in a decision loop that are set to play Sequentially, each of the branches will be executed before the piece exits the decision loop.

■ Randomly to Any Path—If you again have ten branches in a decision loop that are set to play Randomly to Any Path, each of the branches will be executed before Authorware exits the decision loop. Keep in mind that it may take quite some time to complete this, especially if you have a large number of branches attached to the Decision icon. Although there are only ten branches, a single branch can be selected more than once, therefore, the end user will more than likely encounter more than ten branches.

■ Randomly to Unused Path—If you have ten branches in a decision loop that are set to play Randomly to Unused Path, Authorware will randomly pick a branch until all ten of the branches have been executed before the piece exits the decision loop.

■ To Calculated Path—In this scenario, Authorware will pick the path identified by the value, variable, or expression that has been entered into the To Calculated Path text box. If this value does not change while the piece is running, Authorware will select the same branch path continuously, and the piece will never exit the decision loop.

▶ For step-by-step instruction on using variables and expressions, **see** "Working with Variables and Functions," **p. 366**.

Until Click/Keypress

When the Until Click/Keypress Repeat option is selected in the Decision dialog box, Authorware will pass through the Decision icon indefinitely unless the mouse button is clicked or a key is pressed. When a Decision icon is set to Until Click/Keypress, the branching changes to that shown in Figure 17.10.

Because each of the Branch options impacts how the Repeat option will be treated, let's look at an example for each variation.

■ Sequentially—If you have ten branches in a decision loop that are set to play Sequentially, each of the branches will be executed in order from left to right repeatedly until the mouse button is clicked or a key is pressed. As soon as this action is taken, the sequence will stop and Authorware will exit the loop.

■ Randomly to Any Path—If you again have ten branches in a decision loop that are set to play Randomly to Any Path, the branches will be executed randomly until the mouse button is clicked or a key is pressed.

■ Randomly to Unused Path—If you have ten branches in a decision loop that are set to play Randomly to Unused Path, Authorware will randomly pick a branch until all ten of the branches have been executed, then Authorware will begin again. This will continue until the mouse button is clicked or a key is pressed.

■ To Calculated Path—In this scenario, Authorware will pick the path identified by the value, variable, or expression that has been entered into the To Calculated Path text box. If this value does not change while the piece is running, Authorware will select the same field continuously, and the piece will never exit the decision loop. This will continue until the mouse button is clicked or a key is pressed.

▶ For step-by-step instruction on using variables and expressions, **see** "Working with Variables and Functions," **p. 366**.

Until TRUE

Part

IV

Ch

17

When the Until TRUE option is selected in the Decision dialog box, the piece will pass through the Decision icon indefinitely until the specified condition becomes TRUE. For example, you could pass through a Decision icon containing test questions until the user's score is 70 percent and at least 10 questions have been responded to.

Using the Until TRUE option requires an understanding of variables and functions. Therefore, I will cover using this option in greater detail in Chapter 22, "Working with Data."

▶ For step-by-step instruction on using variables and expressions, **see** "Working with Variables and Functions," **p. 366**.

When a Decision icon is set to Until TRUE, the branching changes to that shown in Figure 17.10.

Because each of the Branch options impacts how the Repeat option will be treated, let's look at an example for each variation.

■ Sequentially—If you have ten branches in a decision loop that are set to play Sequentially, each of the branches will be executed in order from left to right repeatedly until the condition becomes TRUE.

■ Randomly to Any Path—If you again have ten branches in a decision loop that are set to play Randomly to Any Path, the branches will be executed randomly until the condition becomes TRUE.

■ Randomly to Unused Path—If you have ten branches in a decision loop that are set to play Randomly to Unused Path, Authorware will randomly pick a branch until all ten of the branches have been executed, then Authorware will begin again. This will continue until the condition becomes TRUE.

■ To Calculated Path—In this scenario, Authorware will pick the path identified by the value, variable, or expression that has been entered into the To Calculated Path text box. If this value does not change while the piece is running, Authorware will select the same field continuously, and the piece will never exit the decision loop. This will continue until the condition becomes TRUE.

▶ For step-by-step instruction on using variables and expressions, **see** "Working with Variables and Functions," **p. 366**.

 TIP Putting FALSE in this field causes the decision to loop indefinitely.

Don't Repeat

The Don't Repeat option in the Decision dialog box is different than the other Repeat options in that only one branch will be selected each time the piece encounters the Decision icon. How the piece branches in consecutive encounters with the Decision icon should be considered, however.

- Sequentially—If you have ten branches in a decision loop that are set to play Sequentially, the first branch will be selected for the first encounter, then the second for the following, and so on until all of the branches have been selected.

- Randomly to Any Path—If you again have ten branches in a decision loop that are set to play randomly to Any Path, a unique branch will be selected with each encounter.

- Randomly to Unused Path—If you have ten branches in a decision loop that are set to play Randomly to Unused Path, Authorware will randomly pick a branch for each encounter until all ten of the branches have been executed; then Authorware will begin again.

- To Calculated Path—In this scenario, Authorware will pick the path identified by the value, variable, or expression that has been entered into the To Calculated Path text box.

  ▶ For step-by-step instruction on using variables and expressions, **see** "Working with Variables and Functions," **p. 366**.

When a Decision icon is set to Don't Repeat, the icon changes to that shown in Figure 17.11.

FIG. 17.11
Authorware changes the
Flowline branching to reflect
that the Authorware mites
will only select a single
branch before exiting the
decision loop.

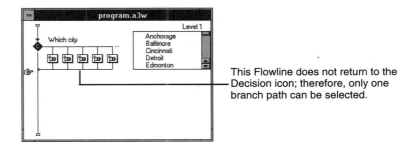

This Flowline does not return to the
Decision icon; therefore, only one
branch path can be selected.

Creating Time-Based Decision Loops

The final setting in the decision dialog box enables you to place a time limit determining how long the decision loop will run. For example, if you have created a random test bank, you can provide a challenge to see how many questions the user could respond to correctly within a given period of time.

If you have entered a value (in seconds) into the Time Limit text box, you can select the Show Time Remaining check box, which displays a small clock in the Presentation Window that counts down the time remaining. This is the same clock used for a timed pause with the Wait icon as well as that used for a timed response to an Interaction icon.

▶ To refer to how Authorware presents a small time clock, **see** "Time Limit," **p. 159**.

T I P If time is not a critical part of your content, I suggest that you avoid this option to create a more relaxed environment for your end user.

Working with Branches in a Decision Loop

The decision loop consists of the Decision icon as well as the branches attached to it. The last section focused on the Decision icon and setting parameters in the Decision dialog box. Just as important to the functionality of the decision loop are options associated with each branch. (See "Introducing the Decision Icon," earlier in this chapter for more information.)

Displaying the Decision Options

Each branch of the decision loop contains an attached dialog box, as shown in Figure 17.12, which is used to set automatic pause and erase options. To access the attached dialog box, simply double-click the branch icon.

FIG. 17.12

Use the attached dialog box to control each decision branch uniquely.

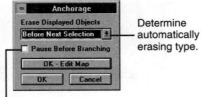

Determine automatically erasing type.

Set automatic pausing.

The icon that was used to create the branch can not be directly opened from the Flowline as icons are normally opened. When a branch icon is double-clicked, the attached dialog box opens.

When the attached dialog box opens, the name across the top of the dialog box is based on the name that you gave to the icon on the Flowline. Additionally, Authorware recognizes what kind of icon was used to create the path and uses that name in the OK-Edit button located within the dialog box. To open the branch icon, you must click the OK-Edit button located within the attached dialog box.

 When you double-click a branch in the decision loop, the attached dialog box will open. To prevent this dialog box from opening, hold down the ⌘ (Macintosh) key or the Ctrl (Windows) key when double-clicking the branch.

Defining the Automatic Erasing Types

Within Authorware, there are four ways to have information erased from the Presentation Window: by implementing the Erase icon (see Chapter 18, "Erasing Media"), by implementing a functon that erases objects in the Presentation Window, by backwards leaping, and through automatic erasing options associated with the Decision, Framework, and Interaction icons.

As you have seen in earlier chapters, the contents of the Interaction icon as well as the pages of a Framework icon can be automatically erased. In addition to this, all the information located in a decision branch path can also be automatically erased.

▶ To refer to how Authorware presents a small time clock, **see** "Automatically Erasing the Contents of a Decision Path," **p. 362**.

Each branch path of a decision can be uniquely set to automatically erase all of the contents presented in that branch path. Using this feature saves great amounts of time authoring in that you do not need to establish Erase icons. Additionally, you will realize an efficiency of the code because there will be fewer icons altogether.

You can specify three kinds of automatic erasing for the contents of a decision branch using the options of the Erase Displayed Objects drop-down list in the branches options dialog box. Each of the list selections is described next.

Before Next Selection When you choose Before Next Selection, upon completion of the branch path and prior to the selection of another branch path, all of the objects in the branch path will erase. If the piece exits the decision loop after the current branch path is executed, the contents will erase upon completion of the branch path and while exiting the decision loop, as shown in Figure 17.13.

This feature is commonly used if the user does not need any of the previous content that was presented in the path when the next branch is selected. For example, if the decision loop is being used to present a series of test questions and each branch represents a unique question, then the user will not need content from one branch as the next one is executed.

Part
IV

Ch
17

FIG. 17.13
The Before Next Selection automatic erasing erases all the contents of a response upon exiting the branch path.

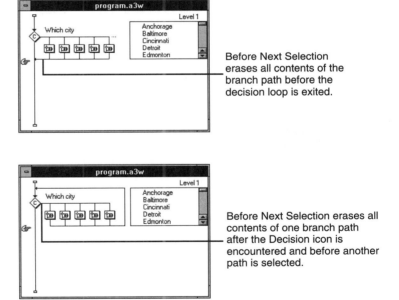

Before Next Selection erases all contents of the branch path before the decision loop is exited.

Before Next Selection erases all contents of one branch path after the Decision icon is encountered and before another path is selected.

Upon Exit When Upon Exit is chosen from the Erase Displayed Objects drop-down list in the branch options dialog box, the contents of the branch path will not erase until the piece exits the decision loop, as shown in Figure 17.14.

For example, if you have six branch paths in a decision loop—each representing a bullet point in a presentation—and the branches are set to erase Upon Exit, then the bullets will build on the screen as each branch is executed. When the piece exits the decision loop, all six bullets will erase at once.

FIG. 17.14

The items are not erased when the piece exits the branch path.

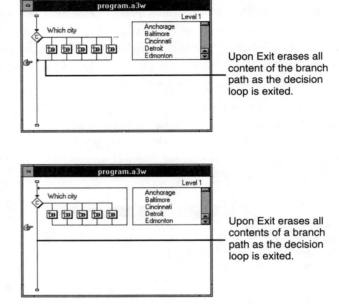

Upon Exit erases all content of the branch path as the decision loop is exited.

Upon Exit erases all contents of a branch path as the decision loop is exited.

Don't Erase   When you choose Don't Erase from the Erase Displayed Objects drop-down list, the contents of the branch will not erase even after the piece has exited the Decision loop. For these items to be erased, an Erase icon or higher level automatic erase must be encountered.

 Learning what the automatic erase options do and where they are located is key to mastering Authorware.

Changing the Automatic Erasing Types

Each branch path of a decision can be set with a different automatic erase option. To change the automatic erase type of a branch, follow these steps:

1. Double-click the icon representing the branch you want to change.
2. When the options dialog box opens, use the pop-up list, as shown in Figure 17.15, Erase Displayed Objects, to select the desired automatic erase type.

▶ To learn about similar automatic erase options for an interaction response, **see** "Changing the Automatic Erasing Types," **p. 227**.

3. Click the OK button to save the settings.

FIG. 17.15
The decision branch automatic erase options are similar to those used for an interaction response.

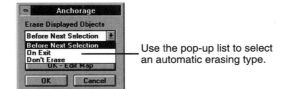

Use the pop-up list to select an automatic erasing type.

Taking Advantage of Automatic Pausing

Just as each branch of the decision loop has an automatic erase option, it also has an option to cause the piece to pause before exiting the branch. To establish this pause, you must select the Pause Before Branching check box in the options dialog box for the desired decision branch.

Unlike the Wait icon, the Decision icon does not give you an option to not display the pause button. If Pause Before Branching is selected, the pause button appears. There are also no options for providing timed waits or to show the time remaining.

Finally, Authorware will use the default pause button as it has been defined in the File Setup dialog box. You can edit this button using the Button Editor, which is discussed in Chapter 10, "Creating Buttons."

▶ To refer to the introduction of the Wait icon, **see** "The Wait Icon," **p. 17**.

▶ For guidance on using the Wait icon, **see** "Building Pauses," **p. 156**.

▶ To learn how to set the default pause button, **see** "Wait Button," **p. 49**.

Creating Media Rich Programs

CHAPTER 18

Erasing Media

The design of a multimedia piece typically assumes one of two metaphors. The more traditional metaphor is that of a slide show, or presentation. In this scenario, the Presentation Window fills with media—text, sound, video, animation, and graphics—and the user passively absorbs it. At a point designated by either the computer or the user's interaction, the entire Presentation Window clears, except maybe for a control panel, and is regenerated with an entirely new set of content.

An alternative to the slide show metaphor is the theater metaphor. In this scenario, the Presentation Window is designed like a stage. There is a backdrop or even elements in the foreground. As the story unfolds, characters come onto the stage, play their role, then gracefully depart.

Authorware provides the functionality to clear the Presentation Window according to either metaphor. For the slide show metaphor, all elements can be erased, leaving space for new elements. Characters can also be erased one at a time as they leave the stage of the theater metaphor.

Erasing objects from the Presentation Window

Objects, such as text, graphics, and video, can be erased from the Presentation Window using the Erase icon.

Working with the erase options

The Erase Options dialog box allows you to control several erase features, including the transition, preventing cross-fading, and erasing all icons except those that have been selected.

Erasing buttons and menus using the Erase icon

Objects created by you and by Authorware can be erased using the Erase icon.

There are several alternatives to using the Erase icon

While the Erase icon is certainly valuable, there are several alternatives to using it, such as automatically erasing Interaction icons, text entries, interaction responses, the contents of a decision path, and pages within a framework.

Defining backward leaping

Whenever Authorware is forced to travel up the Flowline, or backwards, all of the contents along the portion of the Flowline covered by the leap are erased.

This chapter introduces you to the features used to erase elements from the Presentation Window, as well as providing some practical suggestions for their application. ▪

Erasing Objects

Authorware displays objects in the Presentation Window as the running piece encounters icons along the Flowline. Icons that can contain displayable objects include the Display, Interaction, and Digital Video icons. Once objects have been displayed in the Presentation Window, they will reside there until erased. If previously displayed objects are not erased, new objects will simply overlay them.

Within Authorware, there are several ways to erase an object: by using the Erase icon; by using a function that causes objects in the Presentation Window to be erased; or by specifying an automatic erasure. Automatic erasure is discussed later in this chapter and throughout the book.

▶ To explore how automatic erasure is established for an interaction, **see** "Erasing Interaction Responses Automatically," **p. 226**.

▶ To learn how to set automatic erasure for an Interaction icon, **see** "Erase Interaction," **p. 232**.

▶ To learn how to set automatic erasure for a Decision loop, **see** "Defining the Automatic Erasing Type," **p. 346**.

Introducing the Erase Icon

The Authorware Erase icon, shown in Figure 18.1, is the mechanism used to erase objects from the Presentation Window. Objects typically consist of text, graphics, and digital video. You also see, however, that the Erase icon can be used to erase buttons, pull-down menus, and other elements.

When erasing objects, all of the objects in an icon are erased simultaneously. For example, if you have both text and a graphic in a Display icon, both objects will be erased by the Erase icon. To erase only one of the items, it would have to be contained in a separate icon.

The Erase icon can also be used to erase the contents of more than one icon at a time. So if you have objects in separate Display, Interaction, or Digital Video icons, and you want them to erase together, you can use a single Erase icon.

FIG. 18.1
The Erase icon is used to erase media elements, such as text and graphics, from the Presentation Window.

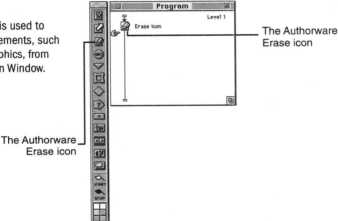

The Authorware Erase icon

The Authorware Erase icon

Part
V

Ch
18

To use the Erase icon, follow these steps:

1. Open the Presentation Window for a Display, Interaction, or Digital Video icon.

2. Create an object or import a digital movie, so that it appears in the Presentation Window.

   ▶ For step-by-step instructions on creating text in the Presentation Window, **see** "Placing Text On-Screen," **p. 68**.

   ▶ For guidance on creating objects in the Presentation Window, **see** "Drawing Objects," **p. 98**.

   ▶ To learn how to load digital movies into Authorware, **see** "Getting Started with Digital Movies," **p. 394**.

3. If an Erase icon directly follows the icon it is to erase, the object will be displayed and erased so quickly that the user will not see the object displayed. Therefore, place a Wait icon or other additional icons on the Flowline to separate the Erase icon and the object it is to erase.

4. Drag an Erase icon to the Flowline and place it following the Wait icon, as shown in Figure 18.2.

FIG. 18.2

The Erase icon must be executed after the icon that contains the object to be erased.

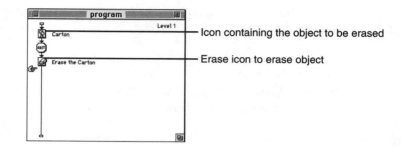

Icon containing the object to be erased

Erase icon to erase object

5. Open the Erase icon by double-clicking. The Presentation Window contains what-ever was last displayed on the screen, as well as the Erase Options dialog box. If a single icon was last opened, the contents of that icon will be shown. If the piece was running, however, the entire Presentation Window will be displayed.

   The title of the Erase Options dialog box contains the name you gave the Erase icon on the Flowline. By clearly naming the Erase icon, you will be reminded of what is to be erased.

6. Follow the directions located on the top of the Erase Options dialog box, instructing you to click the object(s) to erase. Keep in mind that all objects in an icon will be erased simultaneously, and that you can erase the objects of more than one icon with a single Erase icon.

   As objects are selected within the Presentation Window, a picture and the name of the icon that held those objects appear in the lower portion of the Erase Options dialog box. As objects from more than one icon are selected, a scrolling list is cre-ated.

7. Once you have selected the object(s) you want to be erased and specified any of the desired erase options, click OK to save your selection. The Erase Options dialog box closes.

We take a closer look at the erase options in the next section.

Understanding the Erase Icon Options

The Erase Options dialog box, as seen in Figure 18.3, contains several options that make development more efficient or provide special effects when the erase is applied. These options include setting the erase transition, preventing cross-fade, selecting icons not to erase, opting to remove an item from the list of icons to be erased, and replaying the currently selected transition.

When an Erase icon that has not been shown which objects to erase is encountered by the running piece, the Erase Options dialog box will automatically open. Once the erase options have been defined, this dialog box will no longer automatically open. You can open the Erase Options dialog box, however, at any point of authoring to redefine the erase options.

FIG. 18.3
The Erase Options dialog box allows you to set specific options for erasing.

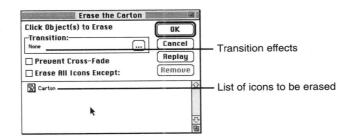

Transition effects

List of icons to be erased

Part
V

Ch
18

These erase options are described next.

Selecting an Erase Transition   When Authorware removes an object or a collection of objects from the Presentation Window, you can select to apply a transition to this erase action. To select a transition, click the "..." button in the Transition area of the Erase Options dialog box to open the Transitions dialog box, as seen in Figure 18.4.

▶ For information on how transitions work, **see** "Setting Transitions," **p. 148**.

FIG. 18.4
Select an erase transition from the Erase Transition Options dialog box.

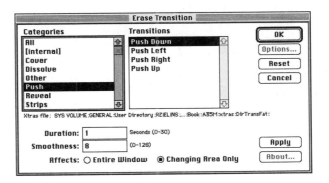

To choose an erase transition, simply select a category, then select a transition from that category. Click the Apply button to see that transition applied to the objects you have selected to be erased. When you have selected the desired erase transition, click the OK button to return to the Erase Options dialog box.

 TIP Try to select transitions that enhance the content. For example, if something is vaporizing, select Fade Out, or if you want a line to disappear as if it is sliding off the right-hand side of the screen, select Remove Right.

N O T E Be careful using erase transitions. While they may be fun initially, a wide variety of transitions used too often quickly becomes annoying to the end user. Using erase transitions to enhance the content, however, will continue to hold the end user's interest. ■

Prevent Cross—Fade   If you have selected the Fade In transition for one icon that is adjacent to an Erase icon using the Fade Out transition, the erasing objects will disappear at the same time that the displayed objects appear. This effect is referred to as cross-fading.

▶ For guidance on selecting a display effect transition, **see** "Setting Transitions," **p. 148**.

When the Prevent Cross-Fade option is selected in the Erase Options dialog box, the action of the objects being erased and the objects being displayed will not occur at the same time. Rather, either the display or the erase action will take place, followed by the other action.

Erase All Icons Except   The normal action of an Erase icon is to erase the objects in the selected Display, Interaction, and Digital Video icons only. When the Erase All Icons Except option is selected in the Erase Options dialog box, however, all objects in the Presentation Window, other than those that have been selected, will be erased.

CAUTION

Use of the Erase All Icons Except option must be carefully thought out. I have seen many cases where the developer selected this option, only to find later that not everything needed to be erased after all. Additionally, erasing everything on the screen will more than likely cause end users to become disoriented and frustrated because they need to become familiar with each screen as it flashes into view.

Remove As you select objects in the Presentation Window that are to be erased by a particular Erase icon, a picture and the name of the icon containing those objects appear in the lower portion of the Erase Options dialog box (see Fig. 18.5).

FIG. 18.5
Click the Remove button to remove icons from the list of those that have been selected to be erased.

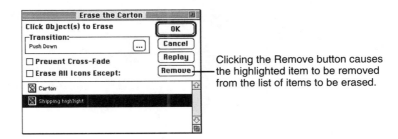

Clicking the Remove button causes the highlighted item to be removed from the list of items to be erased.

If you determine that an object you have selected to erase should not be erased, you can select the icon from the list at the bottom of the Erase Options dialog box, then click the Remove button. Clicking the Remove button removes the icon from the scrolling list of icons to be erased and places the objects contained in that icon back onto the Presentation Window.

Replay Click the Replay button in the Erase Options dialog box to see how all the objects you have selected to be erased will erase. If a transition has been selected, it will be applied when the Replay button is clicked.

Erasing Buttons and Menus

Just as Authorware allows you to erase displayed objects, such as text, graphics, and movies, with the Erase icon, you can also erase objects such as buttons and menus.

For example, you may have created a series of pull-down menus or buttons. At some point you then elect to eliminate these options (see Fig. 18.6) rather than simply making them inactive.

▶ For guidance on building a button response, **see** "Building Buttons," **p. 236**.
▶ For guidance on building a pull-down menu response, **see** "Creating Pull-Down Menus," **p. 266**.

Part
V

Ch
18

FIG. 18.6
Erase icons can be used to
erase buttons and pull-down
menus.

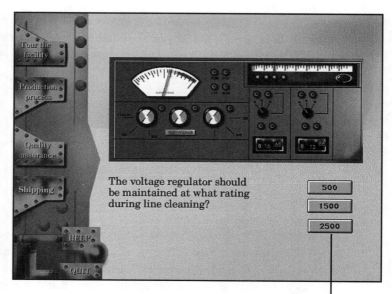

These buttons can
be erased using
the Erase icon.

Selecting to erase the buttons or pull-down menu works just like selecting text or graphics. When the Erase Options dialog box is open, select the button or pull-down menu by clicking it in the Presentation Window. Once a button or pull-down menu is selected, a symbol for the button or pull-down menu appears in the scrolling list in the Erase Options dialog box (see Fig. 18.7).

FIG. 18.7
When a button or pull-down
menu is selected, a symbol
for the button or menu will
appear in the scrolling list of
the Erase Options dialog box.

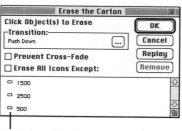

A symbol for the button or pull-
down menu appears in the list of
items to be erased.

You can also select an erase transition; however, the transition doesn't apply to pull-down menus.

N O T E The need to erase pull-down menus and buttons using the Erase icon is more often than not a sign of poor design. Backwards leaping and perpetual navigation, both of which will be discussed later, should eliminate the need for this functionality. ▪

Exploring Alternatives to the Erase Icon

Aside from using the Erase icon, Authorware provides several means by which displayed objects can be automatically erased. Automatic erases were designed to make development more efficient by requiring fewer icons. For example, rather than using an Erase icon to remove all of the objects displayed in an entire module of a piece, Authorware can automatically erase all of those items as another module is selected in an interaction.

The alternatives to using the Erase icon are described next.

Automatically Erasing the Contents of an Interaction Icon

You can determine when or if the contents of an Interaction icon will be automatically erased. To have the contents of an Interaction icon automatically erase, double-click the Interaction icon on the Flowline to access the Interaction Options dialog box, then select the Automatic Erase option from the pop-up or drop-down list. This procedure is discussed in detail in Chapter 9, "The Fundamentals of Interactions."

▶ To explore how automatic erasure is established for an interaction, **see** "Erasing Interaction Responses Automatically," **p. 226**.

Automatically Erasing a Text Entry

An entry made by the end user in a text-entry response can be automatically erased when the user exits the interaction. To have the text entry automatically erase, double-click the Interaction icon used to create the text-entry response, then click the Text Entry Options button. When the Text Entry Options dialog box appears, select the Erase Entry On Exit option. This procedure is discussed in detail in Chapter 9.

▶ To learn how to set automatic erasure for an Interaction icon, **see** "Erase Interaction," **p. 232**.

▶ To learn how to set automatic erasure for an Interaction icon, **see** "Erasing the Entry On Exit," **p. 281**.

Part
V

Ch
18

Automatically Erasing the Contents of an Interaction Icon Response

Just as the contents of an Interaction icon can be automatically erased, the contents for each branch of an interaction can also be automatically erased. To select from the automatic erase options for an interaction branch, double-click the small symbol representing the type of interaction required to encounter the branch (called the *response type symbol*). The symbol is located just above the icon used to create the branch.

▶ To explore how automatic erasure is established for an interaction, **see** "Erasing Interaction Responses Automatically," **p. 226**.

The Response Options dialog box for that branch appears. Use the pop-up or drop-down menu to select an automatic erasure type. The automatic erasure types are discussed in detail in Chapter 9.

Automatically Erasing the Contents of a Decision Path

Like each branch of an interaction, the contents for each branch of a decision can also be set to erase automatically. To have the contents for a decision branch automatically erase, double-click the icon used to create the decision branch, then select an automatic erasure type from the pop-up or drop-down list. This procedure is discussed in detail in Chapter 17, "Setting Up Branching."

▶ To learn how to set automatic erasure for a decision loop, **see** "Defining the Automatic Erasing Types," **p. 346**.

Backwards Leaping

Another feature within Authorware is the ability to erase objects on the screen automatically by moving backwards along, or up, the Flowline. This occurs when an interaction response is set to Perpetual, and is then acted upon from further down the Flowline.

▶ To learn how to set automatic erasure for a decision loop, **see** "Using Perpetual Interactions," **p. 230**.

For example, Figure 18.8 shows a Flowline with a Display icon labeled "Background"; a perpetual menu with three buttons labeled "Dining," "Hotels," and "Entertainment"; and under that, a Decision icon with three paths labeled "Dining information," "Hotel information," and "Entertainment information."

If the user is viewing "Dining," then selects one of the buttons for another topic, all of the content for "Dining" will be automatically erased as Authorware moves backwards up the Flowline to the Interaction icon.

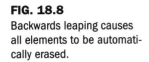

FIG. 18.8
Backwards leaping causes
all elements to be automatically erased.

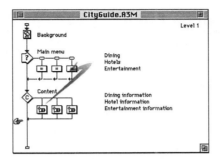

In this example, however, the Display icon labeled "Background" will not be erased, because Authorware did not leap back over it as it moved up the Flowline. Only the items
from the current position to the point to where Authorware leaps will be erased.

 TIP Not only does backwards leaping erase displayed elements, including buttons and pull-down
menus, but non-displayed elements, such as sound, are also erased.

Erasing a Framework Page

As the Authorware program moves from page to page within a framework, the currently
displayed page will automatically erase as the next page is displayed. If you do not want a
page to erase, I suggest building this structure using other icons such as the Decision and
Interaction icons. Avoid setting the Prevent Automatic Erasing option in the Effects dialog
box for each page icon.

▶ To learn how to set the automatic erase transition for a Framework icon, **see** "Setting Up
the Framework Transition Effect," **p. 298**.

Erasing with Navigate/GoTo

The Navigate icon, like the GoTo function, causes Authorware to leap off the Flowline and
proceed to a specifically identified icon. If this jump causes a backwards leap, displayed
elements will erase following the same guidelines as backwards leaping.

▶ To learn more about implementing the Navigate icon, **see** "Navigating Through Frameworks," **p. 306**.

Erasing Sound with the Erase Icon

As strange as it may be, Sound icons can actually be erased, causing the sound to stop playing, using the Erase icon. In a few cases this may prove to be advantageous, but in most cases it is accidental and problematic.

Accidentally erasing sound most commonly occurs when the Erase All Except option is selected in the Erase Options dialog box, as seen in Figure 18.9. When the Erase All Except option is selected, every icon currently being executed or displayed in the Presentation Window will be erased, including Sound icons.

FIG. 18.9
Sound can be erased using the Erase icon.

The sound erases causing it to stop playing.

All of the icons except the background are erased by the Erase icon.

Selecting this option causes all items, except those listed, to be erased.

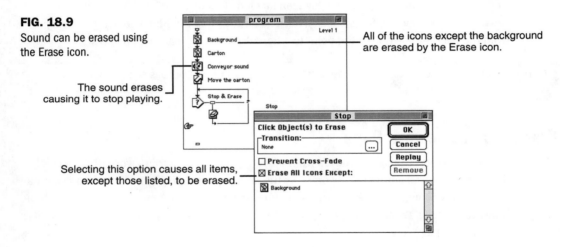

CHAPTER 19

Using Functions and Variables

In high school and college I studied German as a foreign language. I attended classes, read books, and I was even the president of the German club. Although the order in which the words had to appear and their pronunciation was a little awkward at first, German eventually became second nature to me. After enough study, I was even having dreams in German.

Learning to use Authorware variables and functions is much like learning a foreign language. Once you learn a few keywords and understand the order in which the words must appear, the awkwardness will begin to go away. Unfortunately, most people are as uncomfortable with using Authorware variables and functions as they are with a foreign language.

In this chapter, you will not learn to become fluent in this new language. Rather, you will simply explore the "travelers" version of Authorware and a few places where variables and functions can be "spoken." Keep in mind that many tourists never learn the native

Using variables and functions

Variables and functions allow you to collect and manipulate data as the piece runs.

A quick tour of the Calculation icon

The Authorware Calculation icon is the primary location for using functions and variables in the development of expressions.

What are variables?

Variables are holding tanks for information that is collected as the end user runs the piece.

What are functions?

Functions are tasks performed by Authorware such as exiting the program or writing external data files.

language before their trip. With Authorware, you can still have a wonderful journey without speaking the language. ■

Working with Variables and Functions

So far in this book you have seen how to build pieces using text and graphics, how to apply visual effects, and how to introduce interactivity into the piece. To this point, however, the final piece has been little more than a high-priced presentation in which the end user could control the sequence of events or the pace of the piece. Although I have suggested high-level interactivity throughout this book, I have not explored how to construct it. This chapter begins that exploration.

If our goal is to create a dialog between the end user and the piece, then we must equip the piece with enough intelligence to remember information about the end user and to make decisions based on that information. To give an Authorware piece intelligence, you will need to understand variables and functions.

As you become more comfortable with using functions and variables, your piece will take on a greater level of interactivity and efficiency.

Variables and functions are used to give Authorware the capability to remember certain information, as well as the capability to act on that information. The use of variables, functions, and expressions in Authorware is called *scripting*.

Variables

An Authorware variable is simply a place to store information. To help understand this, I often picture one of the Authorware mites as a bookkeeper and his ledger as the variable (see Fig. 19.1).

FIG. 19.1
Entries in the ledger are variables.

Every time a piece of information is to be remembered, the information is entered into the ledger. As the end user runs the piece, Authorware refers to the ledger as it requires information.

N O T E Authorware automatically keeps track of over 170 predefined variables. ▪

Entries made in the ledger are called strings. *Strings* are words, sentences, numbers, or phrases. Like regular sentences, Authorware strings can be separated with spaces, tabs, carriage returns, or special characters.

Functions

An Authorware function completes a specific job task. For example, a task that requires a function is writing an external file, talking to a database, adding a list of numbers, or quitting the application. To help envision the purpose of a function, I imagine an Authorware mite equipped for the specific task (see Fig. 19.2).

Part
V

Ch
19

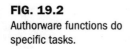

FIG. 19.2
Authorware functions do
specific tasks.

In most cases, the item on which the task is performed, and the result of the task, are
stored in a variable. For example, if you took the math expression 2+3=5, the 2 and 3 are
the items on which the task—addition—is being performed; 5 is the result. In this example, 2, 3, and 5 can all be stored in variables.

N O T E   Authorware can automatically perform over 160 predefined functions. ■

Expressions

An Authorware expression is the combination of values, variables, and functions that have
a definite result. Authorware expressions work much like simple math expressions. For
example, a math expression is 1+2=3. The 1 and the 2 are values; the + and the = are functions; and the 3 is a value known as the result.

In Authorware, this expression can be written as result:=1+2, and result is a variable into
which the value 3 is placed. The expression can also be used for purposes other than
tabulation. For example, the expression variable1+variable2 can be used to select which
path is taken in a decision loop.

TROUBLESHOOTING

**When I try to close the Calculation icon after entering an expression, I get an error message
stating that the syntax is incorrect. How can I prevent that?** Expressions within Authorware

must be scripted in a particular manner, otherwise, they are not recognizable. To make sure that the syntax is correct, try pasting the functions into the Calculation icon window, by highlighting the desired function in the Functions dialog box, clicking the Paste button, then simply replacing the description portions of the script. This eliminates your need to memorize complex code and lessens the possibility for error.

Introducing the Calculation Icon

The Authorware Calculation icon, shown in Figure 19.3, is typically where Authorware scripting takes place. Authorware scripting is also used, however, in the dialog boxes that control other Authorware features such as interactions, digital movies, and animation. I will discuss using variables and functions for these purposes in Chapter 22, "Working with Data."

FIG. 19.3
The Calculation icon contains variables, functions, and expressions.

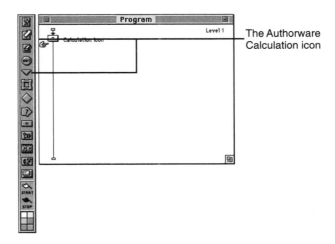

The Authorware Calculation icon

▶ To refer to the introduction of the Calculation icon, **see** "The Calculation Icon," **p. 19**

The Calculation Icon—like the Decision icon and the Framework icon—does not contain a Display icon. The Calculation icon is simply a container for expressions, variables, and functions.

To set up a Calculation icon, follow these steps:

1. Drag a Calculation icon to the Flowline. Calculation icons can be placed anywhere on the Flowline, including next to Interaction, Decision and Framework icons.

2. Double-click the Calculation icon on the Flowline to open the Calculation Icon window, as seen in Figure 19.4.

Part
V

Ch

19

3. Enter the Authorware scripting.

4. Close the Calculation icon when finished.

While working in the Calculation icon, you may find it helpful to understand and use the Calculation Icon window. Next, you learn more about working with that window.

FIG. 19.4
The Calculation icon contains the Calculation Icon window, which is used for scripting.

Enlarges/reduces the Calculation window

Prompt to enter Authorware scripting

Closing the Calculation Icon Window

To close a Calculation icon window, click (Macintosh) or double-click (Windows) the box in the upper left-hand corner of the Calculation window.

 N O T E   You can have several Calculation icon windows open at one time.   ■

When you close the Calculation icon window, Authorware will ask if you want to save the changes you made before closing. Press Enter or click Yes to save your changes. Clicking No will ignore any changes and clicking Cancel will return you to the Calculation icon window.

 T I P   The shortcut for closing the Calculation icon window without saving any changes is to press Esc key. The shortcut for closing the Calculation icon window and saving changes is to press the Enter (Windows) or the Return (Macintosh) key on the numeric keypad.

◆
TROUBLESHOOTING

I entered information into the Calculation icon window, but it did not seem to have an effect when the piece was run. What might have caused this? Be sure that you close the Calculation icon window before running the piece. Leaving the window open can result in the changes being overlooked.

Changing the Window Size and Position

You can resize and reposition the Calculation icon window just as you would any word processing window. To resize the window, drag the resize box (Macintosh) or any of the window's sides (Windows). To reposition the Calculation icon window, simply drag the window by the title bar.

Adjusting the Display Font and Size

You can change the font and size of the text in the Calculation icon window just as you do in the Presentation Window.

▶ For more information on changing the characteristics for text, **see** "Changing Text Characteristics," **p. 79**

N O T E The Calculation window font and size are global settings. The font and size you selected are used for all lines in every Calculation icon. The size and font are selected merely for ease of use. They have no affect on the variable, function, or expression. ■

Attaching Ornaments to Icons

Authorware scripting can either be placed in a Calculation icon, or it can be attached directly to any other icon. When scripting is attached to an icon other than the Calculation icon, Authorware creates an *ornament,* as seen in Figure 19.5.

FIG. 19.5
A Calculation window can be attached to any icon except the Calculation icon.

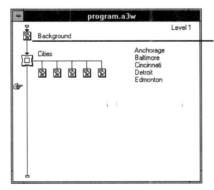

An *ornament* appears on the icon when calculations are attached.

Part
V

Ch
19

To attach scripting to an icon, follow these steps:

1. Select an icon on the Flowline.
2. Select the Calculations Option from the Data pull-down menu.

T I P The shortcut keys for opening the Calculation window for either a Calculation icon or an ornament are ⌘+= (Macintosh) or Ctrl+= (Windows).

3. Enter the Authorware scripting.
4. Close the Calculation icon window when finished.

In most cases, it does not matter whether a script is in a separate icon or attached as an ornament. The benefit of using the Calculation icon, however, is that you can give a descriptive title to it. The benefit of using ornaments, however, is that your program uses fewer icons. If an icon has an ornament attached, the piece will execute the ornament slightly before the icon.

N O T E   If an ornament is attached to a Decision icon or an Interaction icon, the script will be executed each time the piece passes through the icon. If you do not want the calculation to be executed each time, you must place it in a Calculation icon located elsewhere on the Flowline. ■

Using Comments in the Calculation Icon

Another popular use of the Calculation icon is to leave comments to other members of the development team, or for future use when making revisions. For example, I often place a Calculation icon as the first icon on the Flowline and fill it with comments regarding the date the piece was completed, who worked on the team, the target delivery platform, and other tools used in the development of the piece.

Because these comments become a part of the piece, I do not have to worry about losing them or maintaining some type of recording system external to the piece. To mark an item as a comment so that it is ignored as the piece is executed, place two hyphens in front of the characters to be ignored, as seen in Figure 19.6. Comments will not impact the performance of your piece.

▶ For additional information on using comments, **see** "Including Comments in an Icon Name," **p. 203**.

  If I need to make a change to complex scripting, I first make a copy of that script within the Calculation icon window, then comment it out. I then make the changes to the original script. If I need to revert to a version before the changes, I can simply remove the comments. If the scripting was deleted, I would not be able to do this.

FIG. 19.6
Comments can be left in a Calculation icon.

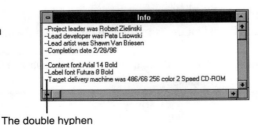

The double hyphen
indicates a comment.

Exploring Variables

As we have seen, Authorware predefined variables are used to store pieces of information that can be used throughout the program. To help determine how an Authorware variable is to be used or to determine what type of information the variable can contain, they have been organized into nine categories.

How Authorware Variables Are Organized

Authorware variables have been separated into nine categories listed alphabetically. In addition to the nine categories, Authorware enables you to view all of the variables listed together, as well as variables that you may have created uniquely for this piece, by using the Variables dialog box.

To open the Variables dialog box, as seen in Figure 19.7, select the Show Variables command from the Data menu.

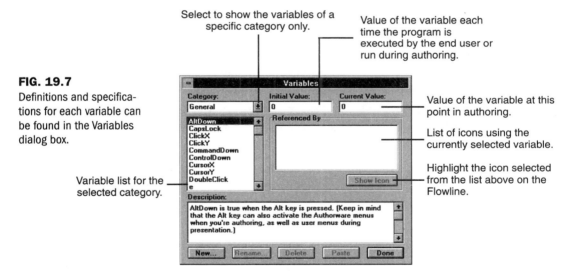

Select to show the variables of a specific category only.

Value of the variable each time the program is executed by the end user or run during authoring.

FIG. 19.7
Definitions and specifications for each variable can be found in the Variables dialog box.

Value of the variable at this point in authoring.

List of icons using the currently selected variable.

Highlight the icon selected from the list above on the Flowline.

Variable list for the selected category.

TIP The shortcut keys for opening the Variables dialog box are Option+⌘+V (Macintosh) and Ctrl+Alt+V (Windows).

When using the Variables dialog box, you will want to be familiar with each of its text boxes and options. These are described next.

Category   Use the Category drop-down list to select from the following variable categories:

- Decision—These variables contain information regarding the Decision icon, such as how many times the piece has passed through the Decision icon, which path was last selected, and how much time has expired if the decision is time based.
- File—These variables contain information regarding your program, such as the name of the file, its location on the hard drive, and the location of student records.
- Framework—These variables contain information regarding the framework loop, such as the current page number, which hot text was selected, or the location from which the piece has jumped if a Navigate icon was selected.
- General—These variables contain information regarding your program, such as the type of machine the end user is running, where the user clicked on the screen, or what keys are currently being pressed.
- Graphics—These variables contain information regarding graphics in the Presentation Window such as what layer they are displayed in.
- Icons—These variables contain information regarding the current icon, such as its ID number, its position along a path that has been established in the Display Effects dialog box, or whether it is movable or not.
- Interaction—These variables contain information regarding the interaction loop, such as which branch of the Flowline was the last one taken, how many judged responses have been matched correctly, and how much time it took the end user to respond to the interaction.
- Time—These variables contain information regarding the program in general, such as the current time and date, the amount of time the end user has been working on the program, and the number of days since this program was last used.
- Video—These variables contain information regarding the playing of video via a laserdisc player, such as whether the player is responding and whether the video is currently playing.

In addition to the nine categories of variables listed in the Category pop-up menu, there are two other selections:

- All—This option lists all of the Authorware variables in alphabetical order.
- Custom—The custom variables list is labeled with the name of your file. The list contains all of the variables that you have created. (See "Creating Custom Variables," later in this chapter.)

Variable List   Once you select a category, the scrolling list just below the category menu changes to reflect all of the variables that are contained in that category. Click a variable name to select it. When a variable is selected, all other information in the dialog box changes.

Initial Value   Many of the Authorware variables have a value as soon as the piece runs such as the current date or time. This value appears in the Initial Value text box. Other variables don't have an initial value but are given a value after the piece has been used. For example, the variable that shows which path of a decision loop was taken does not have a value until the first decision loop is encountered.

Current Value   As your piece runs, the value of many variables changes. To see what the current value of a variable is, open the Variable dialog box, select the variable you want to examine, and look at the Current Value field.

The Current Value field is helpful for debugging your piece. Use this field to be sure that the variables are being set as you intended when using a Calculation icon.

Referenced By   When a variable has been selected, the scrolling Referenced By field fills with the names of all the icons that use the variable. Variables can either be in Calculation icons or ornaments, embedded within the Presentation Window, or used in dialog box fields.

Show Icon   When a referenced icon has been selected from the Referenced By scrolling window, the Show Icon button activates. Clicking the button causes Authorware to open all of the Flowline levels necessary to reveal the position of the selected icon within the entire Flowline.

The Show Icon button can also be activated by double-clicking the icon name in the Referenced By list.

Description   A variable's Description tells why the variable can be used; it clearly defines how the variable should be used if it is a variable that can be changed by the author.

New   Clicking the New button opens the New Variable dialog box (see Fig. 19.8), which enables you to define new or custom variables. In addition, when you are defining a new variable, you should also provide a detailed description of the variable, including when and how it should be used. This description helps you maintain the program, as well as allow others to assist in the development efforts more efficiently. For more information on creating new variables, see "Creating Custom Variables," later in this chapter.

Rename   When a custom variable is selected, click the Rename button to change the name of that variable everywhere it is used in the piece.

Delete   When a custom variable is no longer used anywhere in the piece, you can delete it. To delete an unused variable, select it from the scrolling list of variables, then click the Delete button.

Paste If a Calculation Icon window is open or the insertion bar is in a dialog box text field that will accept variables, you can select a variable from the scrolling list in the Variables dialog box, then click the Paste button to paste the variable directly into the piece.

Although I do not suggest that you spend a great deal of time trying to memorize each of the variables available in Authorware, I do suggest that you quickly read through the list of Authorware variables just to become familiar with the type of information Authorware is keeping track of.

Creating Custom Variables

Although Authorware provides variables that keep track of just about everything you can imagine, there are times when you will want to create your own variables to keep track of certain items. For example, if you are creating an interaction in which the users are asked to enter their names and employee ID numbers, you can use the Authorware variable UserName to keep track of the names, but you would have to create a variable to keep track of the employee ID numbers.

To create a custom variable, choose New Variable from the Data menu. When this option is selected, the New Variable dialog box appears, as shown in Figure 19.8.

FIG. 19.8
Provide a meaningful name and a general description for all new variables.

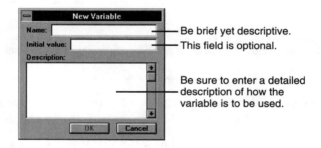

Be brief yet descriptive.

This field is optional.

Be sure to enter a detailed description of how the variable is to be used.

 T I P The shortcut keys for opening the New Variable dialog box are Option+⌘+N (Macintosh) and Ctrl+Alt+N (Windows).

The New Variable dialog box also opens if you have entered an unrecognizable variable into a Calculation window, the Presentation Window, or a field within a dialog box. Additionally, the New Variable dialog box can be accessed by clicking the New button in the Variables dialog box.

When the New Variable dialog box opens, you need to enter information about the variable into three text boxes, as described next.

Name   Be sure that you give your custom variable a descriptive name in the Name text box. Temp and x1 are not good names for variables because they do not provide direction as to their purpose. For example, UserID is a good name for the variable that will hold the information regarding an employee's ID number.

 Try to keep the name of the custom variable as short and concise as possible because you will need to remember the variable's name, and be required to type it, many times throughout the remainder of development.

Initial Value   The optional Initial Value text box can be used to assign an initial value to your variable. Like Authorware variables, the variable is set to the value assigned in this field each time the piece is launched.

Description   The Description text box, also optional, is commonly ignored, even though it is probably the most important field when defining a custom variable. Although a variable can make perfect sense to you during authoring, it is not uncommon to find that the variable's name and purpose do not make sense to others on the development team, or even to you months after you have created it. To best understand the purpose and use of the custom variable, be as descriptive as possible in this field.

 There is no limit as to the number of custom variables that you can create. I suggest, however, that you try to limit the number by reusing variables whenever possible. The fewer the variables, the easier an application is to maintain. For example, create a string with four lines rather than creating four custom variables.

Assigning a Value to a Variable

Because the key purpose of a variable is to store information, you must be able to assign a value to a variable. As you already know, many of the Authorware variables have a value assigned to them as the piece runs.

To assign a value to a variable that does not automatically have its value updated, follow these steps:

1. Open a Calculation icon window.
2. Enter the name of the variable to which you want to assign a value. For example, if you want to assign a value representing the employee ID number to the variable UserID, then enter **UserID.**
3. Follow that entry with the equal sign.

N O T E   Authorware actually expects a colon then an equal sign (i.e., :=). If you do not put the
colon in, Authorware will do it for you automatically when the Calculation window
closes. ■

CAUTION

A colon is used when you are assigning a value to a variable. Be careful not to include the colon when
you are making judgments in an expression.

---

4. Finally, enter the value you want assigned to the variable, UserID.

   Values can be any of the following formats:

   • Literal—By placing the value in quotes, the value of the variable will be exactly
     what you enter. For example, the value of the variable UserID will be literally
     012345, as shown in Figure 19.9.

FIG. 19.9
Values placed in quotes are
assigned literally to the
variable.

The quotes are used to set a literal
value. The variable value will be
exactly what is contained in the
quotes.

   • Variable—One variable can be assigned the value represented by another
     variable. For example, if you want to capture what the user entered in a text-
     entry interaction, use the calculation shown in Figure 19.10.

FIG. 19.10
Variables can be set equal to
one another.

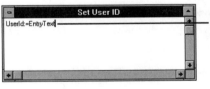

EntryText is an Authorware
variable that captures the entry
made by the user at a text-entry
response.

   • Expression—A variable can also be assigned the result of an expression. For
     example, if you need the user's name set in all capital letters, use the expres-
     sion shown in Figure 19.11.

FIG. 19.11
The result of an expression is
stored in a variable.

The value of UserName is set to
the result of this function.

My Top Ten Favorite Variables

Although I am not able to go into detail for every Authorware variable available, I have selected the ten variables that I use the most often. Becoming familiar with these is like learning the top ten phrases of a foreign language before going on vacation. You cannot expect to be fluent, but you will certainly survive.

ChoiceNumber

The ChoiceNumber Authorware variable contains the number of the last response matched by the user in the current interaction loop. Response paths are numbered from left to right, beginning with one.

I use this variable to determine whether I should display specific feedback. For example, if the user responds to either of the first two responses in an interaction, then I show the feedback; otherwise, I don't. This expression, possibly used in a conditional response type, is written ChoiceNumber<3, as seen in Figure 19.12.

FIG. 19.12
ChoiceNumber is being used in a condition response in this example.

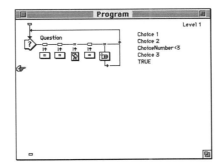

> **CAUTION**
> Be sure to keep track of where ChoiceNumber is used. If edits are made by adding or deleting paths from the interaction loop, this expression may also have to change.

ClickX and ClickY

ClickX contains the number of pixels from the left edge of the Presentation Window to the position of the mouse pointer, and ClickY contains the number of pixels from the top of the Presentation Window to the position of the mouse pointer, when the user last clicked the mouse button.

I use this option in conjunction with one large hot spot interaction as opposed to many small hot spot interactions to determine where the user has clicked. I used the example in Figure 19.3 when the Presentation Window was divided into squares that were 20 pixels wide, and I needed to know on which square the user clicked.

FIG. 19.13
ClickX and ClickY are used to find the position of the user's last click.

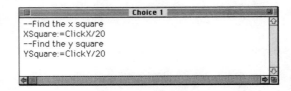

```
                        Choice 1
--Find the x square
XSquare:=ClickX/20
--Find the y square
YSquare:=ClickY/20
```

Date

The Date Authorware variable contains the current date in numerical format (for example, 7/15/65). The format is automatically set to local standards using localization settings for the computer. I often use this variable in conjunction with recording student data in an external text file, as seen in Figure 19.14.

FIG. 19.14
Date is one of the variables being recorded in the external text file.

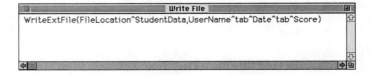

```
                        Write File
WriteExtFile(FileLocation^StudentData,UserName^tab^Date^tab^Score)
```

EntryText

EntryText contains the text that was entered at the last text-entry interaction. I use this variable almost every time I create a text-entry interaction in order to capture what the user has entered, as seen in Figure 19.15.

FIG. 19.15
EntryText is used to set either the variable UserName, or the variable UserID.

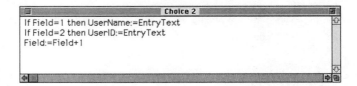

```
                        Choice 2
If Field=1 then UserName:=EntryText
If Field=2 then UserID:=EntryText
Field:=Field+1
```

FileLocation

The FileLocation variable contains the path, including subdirectories, to the location of the running piece. I often use this variable when writing external data files to ensure that the data files will be placed in the same location as the piece. Refer to Figure 19.14 to see how this variable is used.

HotTextClicked

HotTextClicked contains the hot text that a user has clicked when you selected single-clicking or double-clicking as the action that triggers the hot text.

I most recently used this variable to create hyperlinking in an electronic product catalogue. When the user clicked hot text, I used the Navigate icon to search for the HotTextClicked value in the keyword for each page in a framework. If the value was found, the piece jumped to that page.

FIG. 19.16
HotTextClicked updates every time the user clicks text that has interactivity associated with it.

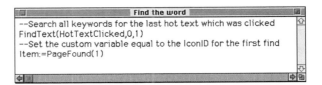

```
                          Find the word
--Search all keywords for the last hot text which was clicked
FindText(HotTextClicked,0,1)
--Set the custom variable equal to the IconID for the first find
Item:=PageFound(1)
```

IconID

IconID contains the unique numerical identifier for a specified icon. This identifier is critical when using the Navigate icon with a calculate destination. It can also be used in conjunction with other variables or functions. For example, you can erase the contents of an icon using a function based on the value of IconID, as seen in Figure 19.17.

FIG. 19.17
Authorware returns the unique ID for the named icon.

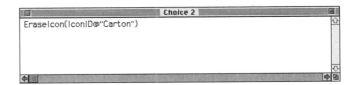

```
                          Choice 2
EraseIcon(IconID@"Carton")
```

Part
V

Ch
19

LastLineClicked

LastLineClicked contains the number of the line the user clicked in a text object. A line is defined by a carriage return.

I use this feature to help create a book-marking scheme. When the user clicks a line of text in a list of bookmark names, I am able to identify which line was clicked. I then use that value to retrieve another value from a list containing corresponding IconID values so that the Navigate icon can be used, as seen in Figure 19.18.

FIG. 19.18
Authorware uses
`LastLineClicked` to
retrieve a value from the
custom variable
`MarkNumberList` that
stores a list of icon address
numbers.

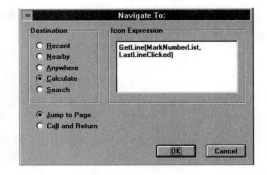

ObjectMatched

The `ObjectMatched` Authorware variable contains the name of the icon that is used to create the object last moved by the end user and matched by a target area interaction. As variables can be placed in a variety of text boxes, I use this variable to determine which path of a decision icon should be taken based on which selection the user has made.

When I use this variable, I like to name the icon containing the object with a number or letter, then compare that value with a list of possible values that can be matched. Figure 19.19 illustrates another example in which I use a value taken from the name of the object that was matched in order to specify a path in a decision loop.

FIG. 19.19
The first number contained in
the icon's name will be used
to determine which path of
the decision loop is taken.

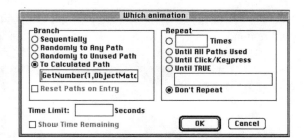

TimeOutLimit

`TimeOutLimit` is used to specify the amount of time, in seconds, that the piece waits for user activity of some kind before jumping to the icon specified in the `TimeOutGoTo` system function.

I like to use this variable to time how long a system will sit idle before an attract loop will engage. This is very popular for trade show exhibits and museum kiosks. Figure 19.20 gives an example which, after 360 seconds, will cause the program to jump to the icon titled Demo Loop.

FIG. 19.20
The amount of time set for `TimeOutLimit` is provided in seconds.

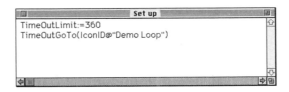

```
TimeOutLimit:=360
TimeOutGoTo(IconID@"Demo Loop")
```

Exploring Functions

Unlike Authorware variables, which are used to store pieces of information, Authorware functions are used to perform special tasks. Like variables, functions have been organized into categories that help communicate how the function is to be used.

Functions can either be in Calculation icons and ornaments, embedded within the Presentation Window, or used in dialog box fields.

By using Authorware functions, your piece can begin to make judgment calls based on information it collects as the end user interacts. As it does this, a dialog is formed between the end user and the computer, and the role of the computer changes from that of a presentation device to one that aids in the learning process.

How Authorware Functions Are Organized

Authorware functions have been separated into fourteen categories and are listed alphabetically within those categories. In addition to the fourteen categories, Authorware enables you to view all of the functions listed together, as well as functions that you may have created uniquely for this piece by using the Functions dialog box.

To open the Functions dialog box, as shown in Figure 19.21, select the Show Functions command from the Data menu.

TIP   The shortcut keys for opening the Functions dialog box are Option+⌘+F (Macintosh) and Ctrl+Alt+F (Windows).

When using the Functions dialog box, you will want to be familiar with its text boxes and options, described next.

Category   Use the Category drop-down list to select from the following function categories:

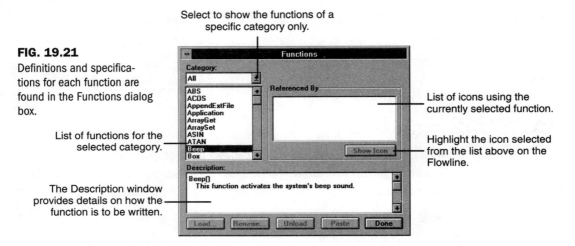

Select to show the functions of a specific category only.

FIG. 19.21
Definitions and specifications for each function are found in the Functions dialog box.

List of functions for the selected category.

The Description window provides details on how the function is to be written.

List of icons using the currently selected function.

Highlight the icon selected from the list above on the Flowline.

- Character—These Authorware functions are used when dealing with text and strings. For example, you can use these functions to count the number of characters in a string, get a specific line of text from a string, or find a pattern of characters in a string.

- File—These functions enable you to create and work with external files. For example, you can create a directory, write a text file in that directory, then catalogue all of the files within that directory.

- Framework—These functions enable you to work within a framework. For example, you can conduct a search for content text or keywords, you can get a list of keywords for a certain icon, or create a list of the past pages visited by the end user.

- General—The General functions often perform general system level tasks. For example, you can press a key, turn off the cursor, or copy text to the Clipboard.

- Graphics—These functions affect how graphics appear in the Presentation Window. For example, you can set a Fill pattern, determine the RGB color, or draw an object, such as a line or box.

- Icons— These functions manage icons from behind the scenes. For example, you can display and erase icons, change the display layer for the objects in an icon, or get the title of a particular icon.

- Jump—The Jump functions enable the piece to leap from one icon to another as well as jump out to external files. For example, you can set Authorware to launch other applications, jump to a specific icon when a determined amount of time passes without any user activity, or to jump from one Authorware piece to another.

- Language—These functions perform specific programming operations, such as If-Then statements, Repeat While statements, and assigning a value to a variable.

- Math—These Authorware functions perform complex math operations. From simple addition to determining the cosine of an angle, Authorware can perform most needed math functions.

- OLE—The OLE functions are used to handle OLE objects within Windows. All standard OLE communications are supported by Authorware.

- Platform—The Platform functions are typically used to get information that will later be used by XCMDs or DLLs. For example, one Platform function will return the creator type to determine if Authorware is the currently running application.

- Time—The Time functions convert aspects of time and date to a numerical format so that they can be used to make comparisons. For example, one function converts today's date to a number representing the number of day's since January 1, 1900.

- Video—The Video functions are used to control the playing of video through video overlay cards via a laserdisc player. The functions seek out specific frames, pause the video, or set the chroma key value.

- Network—The Network functions are used for pieces that will be run over the Internet. Accessing external data or downloading content from the Web to a local hard drive is accomplished through such functions.

In addition to the fourteen categories of functions listed in the Category pop-up menu, there are two other selections:

- All—This option lists all of the Authorware functions in alphabetical order.

- Custom—The custom functions list is labeled with the name of your file. The list contains all of the functions that you have created and imported using XCMDs (Macintosh) or DLLs (Windows).For more information on XCMDs and DLLs, see Chapter 21, "Implementing XCMDs and DLLs."

Function List Once you select a category, the scrolling list just below the category menu will change to reflect all of the functions that are contained in that category. Click a function name to select a function. When a function is selected, all other information in the dialog box changes.

Referenced By When a function has been selected, the Referenced By scrolling field fills with the names of all the icons that use the function.

Show Icon When a referenced icon has been selected from the Referenced By scrolling window, the Show Icon button activates. Selecting the button causes Authorware to open all of the Flowline levels necessary to reveal the position of the selected icon within the entire Flowline.

Part
V

Ch
19

T I P The Show Icon button can also be activated by double-clicking the icon name in the Referenced By list.

Description   A function description not only tells why the function can be used, but it clearly defines how the function should be used. Each function has a specific style as to how it must be written and the fields it requires to perform properly.

Load   Clicking the Load button enables you to locate and import external functions. These functions can be stored as XCMDs (Macintosh), DLLs or UCDs (Windows) or other applications that contain user code.

N O T E   The Load Button is only active when the Custom Functions category is selected. ▪

N O T E   You can also access the Load Function window by choosing the Load Function command in the Data menu. ▪

Rename   When a custom function is selected, you can click the Rename button to change the name of that function everywhere that it is used in the piece.

Unload   When a custom function is no longer used anywhere in the piece, you can un-load, or delete, it. To delete an unused function, select it from the scrolling list of func-tions; then click the Unload button.

Paste   If a Calculation window is open or the insertion bar is in a field or text block that will accept functions, you can select a function from the scrolling list, and then click the Paste button to paste the function directly into the piece.

When a function is pasted in place, it contains placeholders for all the fields that it re-quires to perform properly. Fields that appear in brackets are optional.

Like variables, I recommend that you become familiar with a few functions, then learn the remainder as you go. First determine what you want the piece to do; then find a function to do it. Too many people build pieces based on what the authoring tool can do rather than what the end user needs the tool to do.

My Top Ten Favorite Functions

To continue with our basic language preparation before you begin authoring with vari-ables and functions, let's explore a few functions that I find very helpful.

ArrayGet/ArraySet

ArraySet places a value into a given position within a linear array, and ArrayGet retrieves a value from a given position within the array. To understand this concept, think of an array as a line of buckets into which you can put either single values or entire strings of information. The fifth bucket is array position five, and the tenth bucket is array position ten.

To place a value into an array position, write:

```
ArraySet(position, value)
```

To retrieve the contents of the array position, write:

```
result:=ArrayGet(position)
```

I occasionally use arrays to temporarily store many pieces of information. Be careful, however, not to replace the use of variables with array positions. Trying to remember what content is in each array position is much worse than scrolling through lists of variable names.

In the example shown in Figure 19.22, I am placing a value in array position number 1. This value is used to determine if audio is to play throughout the piece.

FIG. 19.22
The value in the array position number 1 determines if audio will play throughout the piece.

Part
V

Ch
19

DisplayIcon

The DisplayIcon function is used to display the contents of an icon just as if the piece had run through the icon on the Flowline. To display the contents of an icon, write:

```
DisplayIcon(IconID@"IconTitle")
```

The DisplayIcon function is great if you are running through a calculation that is to determine when certain highlights or graphics will be displayed, such as the one shown in Figure 19.23.

FIG. 19.23
Rather than using a Display icon, or even a Library icon, DisplayIcon displays an icon that already exists on the Flowline.

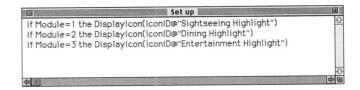

CAUTION
The icon that is being called by the `DisplayIcon` function will act just as if the original icon was located on the Flowline in the same position as the function that called it. This means that automatic erasing will work just as if you were using a Display icon.

EraseIcon

`EraseIcon`, shown in Figure 19.24, works just as the `DisplayIcon` function, except that the icon is erased rather than displayed. To use the `EraseIcon` function, write:

```
EraseIcon(IconID@"IconTitle")
```

FIG. 19.24

Rather than using an Erase icon, the function `EraseIcon` erases an icon that has been displayed in the Presentation Window.

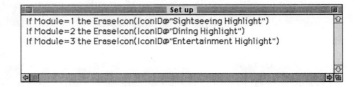

```
Set up
If Module=1 the EraseIcon(IconID@"Sightseeing Highlight")
If Module=2 the EraseIcon(IconID@"Dining Highlight")
If Module=3 the EraseIcon(IconID@"Entertainment Highlight")
```

Find

The `Find` function searches for a pattern of characters within a stated string. When the pattern is found, Authorware returns the character position of the first character. To use this function, write:

```
result := Find(pattern, string)
```

I like to use the `Find` function to locate a user's response in a list of anticipated responses to determine if the response was correct. For example, the user has seven tiles and four empty boxes to which the tiles could be dragged. As the user drags the tiles, I will build a string representing which tile was dragged to which spot. If tile five was in position one, tile three in position two, tile one in position three, etc., I would end up with a string that looked like 5 3 1 4.

I would then look for the pattern 5 3 1 4 in a list of possible sequences to see if this is an acceptable response.

FIG. 19.25

If the user gets an acceptable combination, one message is given, but if they get an unacceptable combination, a different message is given.

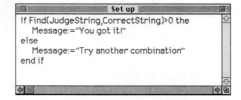

```
Set up
If Find(JudgeString,CorrectString)>0 the
    Message:="You got it!"
else
    Message:="Try another combination"
end if
```

N O T E Unfortunately, this function only returns the character position of the pattern found. It would be much more helpful if you could locate the character, the word, or the line position in which the pattern occurred. For example, if you could locate the line in which the pattern occurred, you could then use another Authorware function to extract that specific line. ◼

GetLine

This is probably my favorite and most used function. Because I like to use character strings as miniature databases, I am continually pulling information out of the string using GetLine.

For starters, a string can contain lines—by default defined by carriage returns. Lines can also be delineated, or separated, by tabs or special characters. Therefore, you will have five lines if you have a list of five numbers written as follows:

1

2

3

4

5

This string is created in Authorware as shown in Figure 19.26.

FIG. 19.26
Strings are created in Authorware using variables, functions, literal values, and operators.

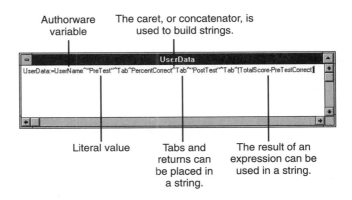

Authorware variable

The caret, or concatenator, is used to build strings.

UserData

UserData:=UserName^"PreTest"^Tab^PercentCorrect^Tab^"PostTest"^Tab^(TotalScore-PreTestCorrect)

Literal value

Tabs and returns can be placed in a string.

The result of an expression can be used in a string.

Using the GetLine function, you can retrieve any of the lines in the string. The GetLine function is formatted as follows:

```
result:= GetLine("string", from which line [, to which line, using what as a delimiter])
```

N O T E The items in brackets are optional. ■

Therefore, if I want the third line, I write:

```
result:= GetLine("string", 3)
If I wanted the third and fourth lines, I would write:
result:= GetLine("string", 3, 4)
```

If the line is delimited with tabs rather than returns, and I want the third and fourth lines, I write:

```
result:= GetLine("string", 3, 4, tab)
```

If-Then

Making a decision is one thing, but being able to reason is another. By using If-Then functions, you can begin to give your program a sense of intelligence that simple page turning applications never reach.

Once you get the hang of them, If-Then functions are fairly simple. See if you can read the following example:

```
if (it is raining)then
(I will take an umbrella)
else
(I will drive with the top down)
end if
```

This string is created in Authorware as shown in Figure 19.27.

FIG. 19.27

If-Then statements can be used to make decisions.

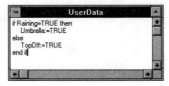

The portions of the script in parentheses are statements that must be completed by you during authoring. The beauty of scripting is that it enables you to take several actions based on a simple condition. Look at the change I made to our If-Then statement.

```
if (it is raining)then
(I will take an umbrella)
(I will jump in all the puddles)
(It will be cloudy)
else
(I will drive with the top down)
(I will go for a walk in the park)
end if
```

This string is created in Authorware as shown in Figure 19.28.

FIG. 19.28
If-Then-Else statements
are used to make more
complex decisions.

InsertLine

As I previously mentioned, I like to use character strings as miniature databases. To retrieve information from a character string, I use GetLine, but to place information into the string, I use InsertLine. As the name implies, the InsertLine function will insert a line into a specified position in a character string.

To use the InsertLine function, write:

```
result:= InsertLine("string", position, "additional string"[, delimiter])
```

> **N O T E** Use ReplaceLine if you will be overwriting a line that already exists. ∎

Quit

In most of the applications I build, I turn off the user menu bar and use a graphical interface. When I do this, however, I eliminate the capability for the user to exit the program using the default Quit command in the File menu that is created by Authorware.

So that the user will be able to exit the application without rebooting the computer, I use the Quit function in a Calculation icon associated with an icon on the interface. To use the Quit function, simply write Quit().

> **CAUTION**
> All scripting that occurs after the Quit function will be ignored because Authorware immediately exits the program when it encounters the Quit function.

Repeat While

The `Repeat While` function is similar to the `If-Then` function in that it gives Authorware the capability to analyze information based on conditions that you set. See if you can read the following script:

```
Repeat While (it is raining)
If (the sky is blue)then
(it is not raining)
end if
end repeat
```

In this example, the loop will continue to repeat until it is no longer raining. Each time it repeats, it checks to see if the sky is blue. If it is, then it is no longer raining and the loop stops. If the sky is not blue, however, the loop repeats.

WriteExtFile

Writing external text files can be used for such things as collecting student records, building an itemized order list, or creating a file that will be read by a database. To write an external text file, write:

```
WriteExtFile("filename", string you want written to the file)
```

N O T E You can use the Authorware variables `FileLocation` and `RecordsLocation` to help place or locate the file to be read or written. ■

CAUTION

If you write to a file with a file name that already exists, the existing file will be overwritten.

CHAPTER 20

Working with Digital Movies

As computer technology continues to advance, our expectations for on-screen realism also increase. Only a few years ago, people were willing to continually feed quarters into an arcade machine to control PacMan as he gobbled up dots while avoiding the terrible ghosts.

Today, however, arcades are filled with virtual reality systems that allow you to feel, see, hear, and believe the experience with which you are interacting. Characters are either created by computers with such a sense of realism that it's hard to tell that the characters aren't real, or else they are actors who have filmed hundreds of responses that, when linked together, create a realistic dialog with the end user.

This expectation of reality has also found its way into interactive learning programs. Today's learner does not want cartoon-like animation of a manufacturing process or a surgical procedure. Animation and simulations are being replaced by three-dimensional characters and virtual experiences. Video has begun to play a much greater role than simply mimicking a television screen on the computer. Digital video now provides opportunities for characters to walk through and interact with the content and the end user.

Digital movies come from a variety of places

Authorware can take advantage of several digital video file formats for use in your multimedia piece, including QuickTime, Video for Windows, Macromedia Director, Autodesk Animator, and MPEG.

Realistic animation has several characteristics

Unlike path animation, realistic animation can be characterized as being rotational/relational, pivotal, or z-axis.

Adding the digital movie icon to the multimedia piece

When a Digital Movie icon is added to the Flowline, Authorware prompts you to locate the externally created digital movie file.

Working with the digital movie options

Authorware can be used to control a variety of presentation characteristics, such as playback speed, concurrency, mode, interactivity, and a variety of options that determine when the movie will play.

Taking advantage of the various digital video types

Knowing when to use each of the various digital video types is key to the success of your multimedia piece.

While Authorware does not have the functionality to create such animation or video, Authorware does allow you to import and control them. This chapter explores how to import and use realistic animation and digital video within Authorware. ■

Getting Started with Digital Movies

As I explained in Chapter 7, "Making Objects Move," there are two basic types of movement within Authorware: path animation and realistic animation. The Authorware Motion icon is used to create path animation in which objects move two-dimensionally across the Presentation Window without changing any of their physical characteristics.

Throughout this chapter we explore the second type of animation—realistic animation. Realistic animation is played within Authorware using the Digital Movie icon, however, the actual animation, or movie must be created with an application other than Authorware. A few of the applications that I use to create realistic animation, and the type of files that they output, are listed in Table 20.1.

Table 20.1	Applications That Create Realistic Animation		
Platform	**Creator**	**Movie Format**	**Extension**
Macintosh	Macromedia Director	Director movie	.DIR
	Macromedia Director	PICS movie	
	Adobe Premiere	QuickTime	
	Movie Editor	Movie Editor files	.MVE

Platform	Creator	Movie Format	Extension
Windows	Macromedia Director	Director Movies	.DIR
	Macromedia Director	Sequenced Bitmaps	.DIB
	Adobe Premiere	Video for Windows	.AVI
	Adobe Premiere	QuickTime for Windows	.MOV
	AutoDesk Animator		.FLC, .FLI, .CEL
	MPEG		.MPG

When incorporating digital movies, I recommend that you spend some time experimenting with the various movie formats. As you will discover, each type has its advantages in terms of performance or compression, as well as its drawbacks in terms of development time or cross-platform compatibility.

As you begin to rely on this type of media, don't forget the importance of interactivity. While the user may initially be drawn to the movie, this interest will quickly fall away if there is no opportunity to interact with the piece.

Introducing the Digital Movie Icon

The Digital Movie icon shown in Figure 20.1 is the tool used to import or control realistic animation and digital video. As you will see, sometimes animation and video are imported into Authorware (PICS movies, for example), becoming a part of the Authorware piece. At other times Authorware creates a link or pointer to the piece and the digital movies remain external (Macromedia Director, QuickTime, and Video for Windows, for example). In either case, digital movies are commonly used to create animated logos for introduction screens, animated icons for menus, and simulations throughout the piece.

▶ To refer to the introduction of the Digital Movie icon, **see** "The Digital Movie Icon," **p. 20**.

> **N O T E** Digital movies that remain external to Authorware must be distributed along with your final multimedia piece. I recommend trying to keep all external media in a single location so that it can be easily located. ▨

The Digital Movie icon, unlike other icons that allow you to place objects in the Presentation Window, does not allow you to create or edit the content of the files it controls. All files controlled by the Digital Movie icon must be created and edited using external applications such as Macromedia Director or Adobe Premiere.

FIG. 20.1

The Digital Movie icon is used to import or control realistic animation and digital video.

The Authorware Digital Movie icon

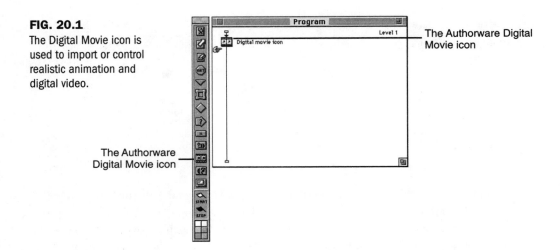

The Authorware Digital Movie icon

Understanding the Characteristics of Digital Movies

Digital movies, unlike animation created with the Motion icon, can be extremely realistic. Unlike path animation, digital movies can posses three characteristics common to real motion: rotational/relational, pivotal, and z-axis. Each of these motion characteristics is described next.

Rotational/Relational   *Rotational/Relational animation* allows an object to rotate or move in relationship to other objects. A wheel on a piece of equipment, a blood cell moving through an artery, and the lifting of a load with a forklift are all examples of *rotational/relational animation*. Figure 20.2 was created using rotational motion.

Pivotal   *Pivotal animation* is characterized by one end of an object remaining static while another end moves. A pendulum, the hands on a clock, and the needle on a speedometer, as shown in Figure 20.3, are examples of pivotal animation.

Z-axis   *Z-axis animation* creates the illusion of depth. For example, if you are looking down a road, a car driving away from you becomes smaller and smaller, and finally disappears. In the example shown in Figure 20.4, the animation simulates zooming in and out, as in the operation of a video camera.

FIG. 20.2
The helicopter blades are an example of rotational motion.

> **CAUTION**
>
> It is common among novice developers to attempt to construct these same animations using a series of Display icons and Erase icons. While this may suffice for prototyping, a Motion icon is a much better solution for the final piece in that it requires only a single icon, and you have finite control over the timing and playback rate of the movie.

FIG. 20.3
The needle gauge in the control panel is an example of pivotal motion.

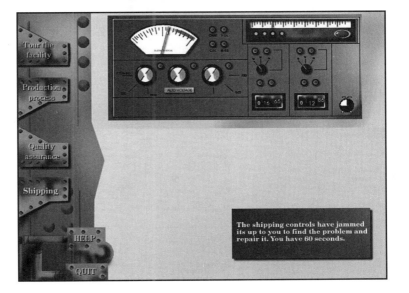

Part
V

Ch
20

If you require animation that involves any of these characteristics, you should use the Digital Movie icon to import or control the animation.

FIG. 20.4
The series of pictures demonstrates Z-axis motion.

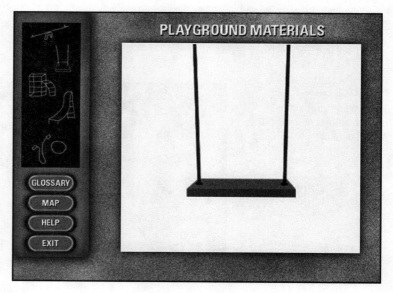

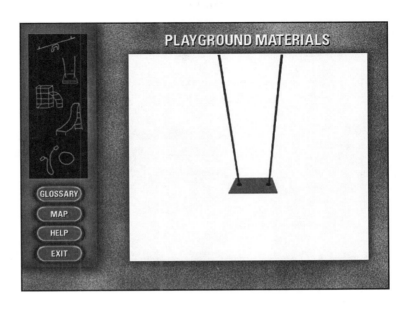

Adding a Digital Movie to Your Piece

While it is easy to import or reference a digital movie, there are several options that must be considered for controlling how the movie will play. Follow these steps to use the Digital Movie icon and to apply the various options:

1. Drag a Digital Movie icon to the Flowline.

2. Open the Digital Movie icon on the Flowline by double-clicking it. Once the Digital Movie icon is opened, the Load Movie dialog box appears as shown in Figure 20.5.

3. The Load Movie dialog box works just like the Import dialog box that you use to import text and graphics. As you locate and highlight a piece, a preview of it is displayed in the preview window, as long as the Show Preview check box is selected. If a preview is not showing, click the Create button (if it's available).

4. Select the movie you want to use in your multimedia piece. If you selected a piece to be imported into Authorware rather than stored externally, the Options button becomes available. You can set two options when loading a PICS movie into Authorware.

   - Use Full Frames—Selecting the Use Full Frames option creates a unique, full frame for each frame of the movie, rather than simply a frame that contains the portion of the movie that has changed from the previous frame.

Part
V

Ch
20

For example, if you have a bird flying through the forest, and the only thing that changes as you move from frame to frame is the bird's wings, then not selecting this option results in frames containing only the changes (that is, the area around the bird's wings). The remainder of the movie (the forest) would not be displayed in any frame other than the first, as shown in Figure 20.6.

FIG. 20.5
The Load Movie dialog box allows you to locate a digital movie to be imported into or controlled by Authorware.

This is the Authorware for Windows Load Movie dialog box.

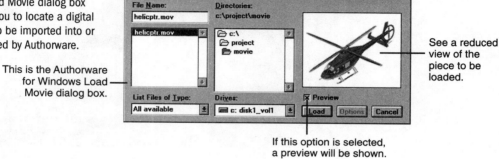

See a reduced view of the piece to be loaded.

If this option is selected, a preview will be shown.

See a reduced view of the piece to be loaded.

This is the Authorware for Macintosh Load Movie dialog box.

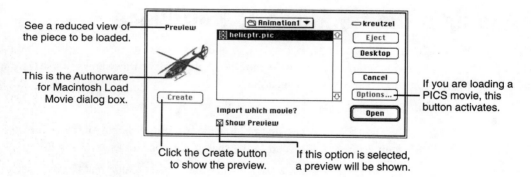

If you are loading a PICS movie, this button activates.

Click the Create button to show the preview.

If this option is selected, a preview will be shown.

If you select the Use Full Frames option, then each frame of the movie contains all elements in the movie, whether or not they differ from the previous frame; this is shown in Figure 20.7.

N O T E   One benefit of selecting this option is that the movie can be played one frame at a time; another is that you can play the movie backward much faster. If you plan to play the movie only forward, and only from start to finish, then there is no need to select this option. ▪

CAUTION

Selecting the Use Full Frames option increases the piece's size and might negatively impact performance. Additionally, high RAM and processor speeds may be required to run the movie.

FIG. 20.6
Not selecting the Use Full
Frames option creates
frames where each frame
contains only changes from
the previous frame.

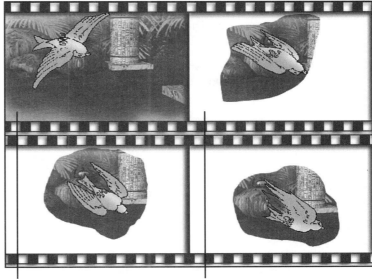

The first frame of the
movie contains the
complete image.

Subsequent frames contain only
the portions of the movie that
differ from the previous frame.

FIG. 20.7
Selecting the Use Full
Frames option creates
frames that each contain all
elements in the movie.

Each frame of the movie
contains a full image.

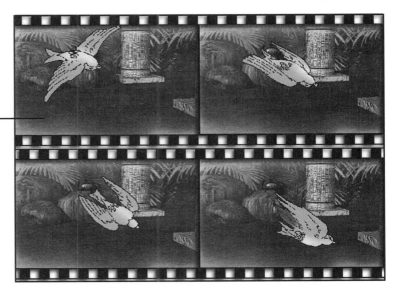

- Use Black as the Transparent Color—When a PICS movie is loaded into
  Authorware, the background color is white by default. Selecting the Use Black
  as the Transparent Color option changes the background color to black.

5. Once you have selected a movie to load—and have adjusted the options if it's a PICS movie—click the Open button, or press Return or Enter (Macintosh) or Enter (Windows) either to import or to create the reference to the movie file.

6. Adjust the controls for playing the digital movie using the Digital Movie icon dialog box. Each option is described in detail in the next section of this chapter.

7. Once you have set all the desired options in the dialog box, click OK to save your changes and return to the Flowline, or click Load to access the Load Movie dialog box to select a different movie.

▶ To refer to the steps for importing graphics, **see** "Using the Import Function," **p. 108**.

Setting Options for a Movie

When a movie has been loaded or referenced, the Digital Movie icon dialog box, shown in Figure 20.8, becomes available. This dialog box also appears when you double-click the Digital Movie icon after a movie has been loaded or referenced.

When this dialog box is open, you can see the movie in the Presentation Window. You can reposition the movie by dragging it to a new location.

The Digital Movie icon dialog box offers numerous settings to adjust how the digital movie plays. These options, and how to work with each, are described next.

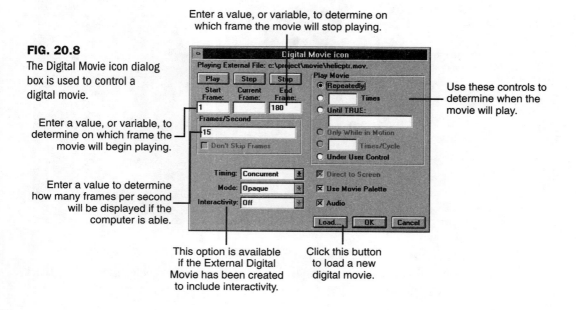

FIG. 20.8
The Digital Movie icon dialog box is used to control a digital movie.

Enter a value, or variable, to determine on which frame the movie will stop playing.

Enter a value, or variable, to determine on which frame the movie will begin playing.

Enter a value to determine how many frames per second will be displayed if the computer is able.

Use these controls to determine when the movie will play.

This option is available if the External Digital Movie has been created to include interactivity.

Click this button to load a new digital movie.

N O T E The best way to understand what the options in the Digital Movie icon dialog box do is to practice using them. I suggest loading each movie type, and then selecting and de-selecting each option.

Controlling Playback

In the upper-left corner, the Digital Movie icon dialog box offers three command buttons for controlling movie playback:

- Play—Starts playing the movie from the beginning frame to the ending frame, based on any other settings you have adjusted.
- Step—Advances the movie one frame at a time.
- Stop—Stops the movie that's playing (obviously, this button is useful only if the Play button has been clicked earlier).

Working with Frames

Four text boxes and a check box option for working with frames are located below the playback buttons in the Digital Movie icon dialog box:

- Start Frame—When a movie is first loaded, this text box defaults to 1. You can enter a new value, or a variable, to start playing the movie at a frame other than the first. I often use a variable to control the starting frame of a movie, as I explain in Chapter 22, "Working with Data."
- Current Frame—This field contains the frame of the movie currently displayed in the Presentation Window. This field only contains information as you click the Step button.
- End Frame—When the movie is first loaded, this field defaults to the total number of frames contained in the movie. You can enter a new value, or a variable, to stop the movie at a frame other than the last. I often use a variable to control the ending frame of a movie, as I explain in Chapter 22.

Part
V

Ch
20

N O T E A movie that has been loaded into Authorware can be played backward by entering a higher value in the Start Frame field than in the Stop Frame field. Movies stored externally cannot be played backward (except for Director movies controlled by Lingo scripting), and audio does not play when a movie is played backward.

TROUBLESHOOTING

I want the movie to play in reverse, but the performance seems much slower. How can I get around this? I often create a movie, for example one with 20 frames, where the first 20 frames are the movie playing forward. I then copy those 20 frames, flip or reverse them, and append them to the original 20 frames. The result is a 40-frame movie that looks like it is playing forward then backward, but in reality is always playing forward. While performance increases, so does the piece's size, so you need to determine if this trick will work for you.

- Frames/Second—You can enter a value, or a variable, to control the rate at which frames of externally stored movie files are displayed. Leaving this field blank causes movies to play as quickly as possible.

  To understand the impact that frame rates have, it is helpful to know that "real life" seems to happen at 30 frames per second. Television and videotapes interpret 30 unique images, or frames, per second to achieve realistic quality. As soon as fewer than 30 frames per second are displayed, the end user begins to see jerkiness from frame to frame.

  The original digital video compression formats were only capable of showing about 15 frames per second, if the computer was able to process that many images. This is part of the reason why desktop video used to look so chunky.

  Today, however, faster computers and better compression techniques are able to achieve almost TV-quality video for smaller video windows. As these technologies continue to progress, they will soon be able to handle the greater amounts of data required to produce larger windows of video running at a higher quality.

N O T E If a given computer is unable to process the number of frames you have set to be played per second, Authorware skips some frames. Hindrances to processing video frames include slower processor speeds, insufficient RAM, inadequate compression techniques, or throughput if the video is being played over a network or from a CD-ROM. ▣

- Don't Skip Frames—Selecting this option overrides Authorware when it attempts to skip frames to play a movie within the period of time set in the Frames/Second field. Selecting this option might cause the movie to play slower on some machines, but usually results in a better quality presentation.

N O T E This option is not available for QuickTime. Video for Windows or Director movies; it's available only for PICS movies. ▣

Working with Movie Timing

The Timing drop-down list in the Digital Movie icon dialog box contains options that function just as the Concurrency options for the Motion icon do. The Timing options are used to determine what the piece does while a digital movie is playing. They work as follows:

- Wait Until Done—This option causes the movie to play completely before the next Authorware icon on the Flowline is executed.
- Concurrent—This option determines that as soon as the digital movie begins, the next Authorware icon on the Flowline is executed.
- Perpetual—The Perpetual option allows the play of a Digital Movie icon to be controlled from anywhere within the program, as long as it has not been erased from the Presentation Window. The digital movie will begin and end playing whenever a defined condition is True.

N O T E The default option is Concurrent. ▓

For example, you might have a manufacturing line set to play perpetually whenever the variable PlayIt is True. If the program begins and the value of PlayIt is True, the digital movie begins playing.

If the user clicks a Stop button, setting the value of PlayIt to False, the movie pauses until the value of PlayIt is again set to True.

Controlling the Mode, or Appearance

Just as you can set the mode for a graphic or a block of text, you can set the mode for a digital movie. Since the digital movie is not treated as an object in the Presentation Window like text or graphics are, control of the mode is accomplished using the Mode drop-down list in the Digital Movie icon dialog box. Here are the possible choices, and how each affects the movie's appearance during playback:

N O T E These Mode options are not available for digital video QuickTime and Video for Windows movies or Director movies; they are available only for PICS movies. ▓

- Opaque—Selecting this option when importing PICS movies causes all white pixels to be displayed as white rather than invisible. This option is not available for Director or digital video files.

T I P Opaque, the default option, plays faster and results in a smaller size when imported.

Part
V

Ch
20

■ Transparent—Selecting this option makes all white pixels—even those that are a part of the graphic—invisible.

> **CAUTION**
>
> If your movie contains any white pixels that you want to remain white, be aware that setting the Mode to Transparent makes them see-through. I suggest using the lightest gray instead of white for these pixels.

■ Matted—Selecting this option makes all white pixels outside the colored border of an object invisible. When you change a movie's mode to Matted, Authorware builds a unique image for each frame.

■ Inverse—Setting a colored movie to Inverse has the same unpredictable results that setting a graphic to Inverse does.

Setting the Interactivity Option

If you are using the Digital Movie icon to reference a Macromedia Director file that contains interactivity, you can use the Interactivity drop-down list to turn the interactivity on or off.

Working with the Play Movie Options

The settings in the Play Movie area of the Digital Movie icon dialog box allow you to adjust how the movie performs once it is loaded.

■ Repeatedly—This option causes the movie to play over and over until it is erased, or paused using variables and functions.

■ Times—The value, or variable, you enter in this field determines how many times the movie plays. If the value is zero, then only the first frame of the movie is displayed.

■ Until True—This option causes the movie to play as long as the variable or expression you have entered in the field evaluates to True.

For example, you might have a control panel with On and Off buttons. When the user clicks On, you can set a variable that causes the movie to play, and when the user clicks Off, you can reset the variable so that the movie stops playing.

■ Only While in Motion—This option is used to control the playing of a PICS movie that has been loaded into Authorware. The PICS movie then plays only when it is being moved around the Presentation Window by the Motion icon, or when it is being moved by the end user.

■ Times/Cycle—This setting is used to synchronize a movie that is playing using the Digital Movie icon while it is being animated by the Motion icon. For example, if you want all the frames of the digital movie to play in the same amount of time it takes to animate that movie across the Presentation Window, enter **1** here.

N O T E   If you set Times/Cycle, the Don't Skip Frames option is ignored. ■

■ Under User Control—If the movie being played is a QuickTime movie, selecting this option displays the controller bar that allows the user to play, pause, and step through the movie.

■ Direct to Screen—This option causes the movie to be played on top of all other objects in the Presentation Window. If you want the movie to play behind other objects, deselect this option, then assign the movie a layer value lower than every object you want it to play behind.

N O T E   The Direct to Screen option is available only when the mode is set to Opaque, and externally stored movies are always played Direct to Screen. ■

■ Use Movie Palette—This Windows-only feature allows you to use the palette that was created with the digital movie, as opposed to using the Authorware palette. Keep in mind that a palette is used for the entire monitor, so you could get some discoloring for the remainder of the Presentation Window when the digital movie is playing.

■ Audio—When this option is selected and the external movie contains audio, the end user is able to hear the audio. PICS movies can't contain audio, so this option is unavailable if you have loaded a PICS movie.

T I P   When developing cross-platform solutions, I often place audio in QuickTime files since a single QuickTime file can be played on both Macintosh and Windows platforms. This gives me the advantage of QuickTime compression without having to load the audio file into Authorware.

Part
V

Ch
20

Using the Different Movie Types with the Digital Movie Icon

The Digital Movie icon is used to import or control a variety of digital movie types. Each type of digital movie has special characteristics, and Authorware treats them in a unique way. The next sections introduce you to the most common digital movie types.

Macromedia Director Movies

Macromedia Director is the leading tool for the creation of interactive animation and presentations. Additionally, Director allows you to create realistic animation that can incorporate each of the motion characteristics described earlier. Therefore, using Director movies in Authorware results in an interactively rich, media-intensive piece.

Director movies can contain only animation or interactivity and audio as well. In any case, once a Director file has been created, it can be controlled from within Authorware. Unlike graphics and text, Director movies cannot be imported into Authorware. They remain as external files that are called from Authorware.

The program shown in Figure 20.9 demonstrates how an interactive Director movie can be utilized within an Authorware program. In this example, the user is able to rotate the three-dimensional piece of equipment by clicking the mouse pointer, which is shaped like a hand, and then dragging.

This virtual type of interaction is impossible using Authorware alone, but by incorporating an interactive Director movie into Authorware, you can achieve the desired effect.

FIG. 20.9
Interactive Director movies can be played within Authorware.

This Director movie includes interactivity that can be used in Authorware.

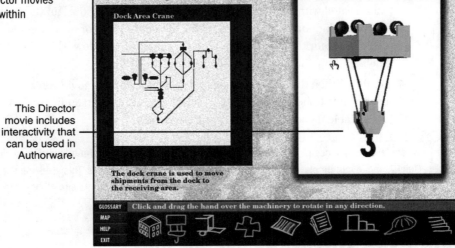

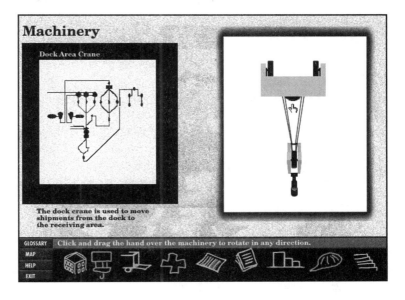

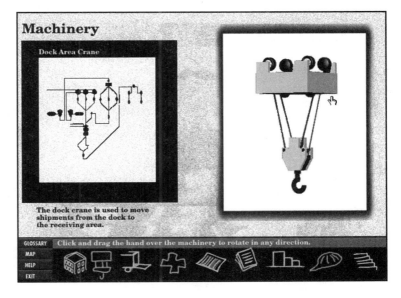

QuickTime and Video for Windows

Digital movie files, whether stored in a QuickTime or Video for Windows format, must also be saved externally and are then called by the Authorware Digital Movie icon. Additionally, in order for either of these digital movie formats to play within Authorware, the

QuickTime or Video for Windows software must be loaded on both the development and the delivery systems.

There are a variety of applications that export to the QuickTime or Video for Windows formats. Adobe Premier is one popular application, however, Macromedia Director and other animation programs are used to export to these digital movie formats.

N O T E   Externally controlled movies are advantageous in that they do not increase the Authorware file size, and performance for executing the files is typically better. On the other hand, there is an increased amount of effort required to keep track of the external files since they may not be packaged with your multimedia piece for final distribution. Losing a single file can ruin an entire multimedia piece. ■

Here are a couple of ways I've found digital video to be useful.

Displaying in a Video Window   In most cases, digital video is presented in a rectangular area overlaid on the Presentation Window, as shown in Figure 20.10, a project that was completed for Toyota Motor Manufacturing of America. This type of digital video assumes the characteristics of *television-like video*. Although this technology got off to a bad start because slow processor speeds resulted in jerky performance, better compression techniques and faster processors now are resulting in very high-quality images.

FIG. 20.10
Digital video often occurs in a small rectangle located in the Presentation Window.

A traditional video window

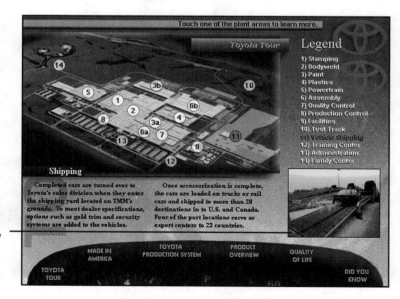

In this form, you can elect to show or hide a playback controller bar. Additionally, you can use the one-eighth screen window, as I did here, or you can make the video window larger. To create a traditional video window, follow these steps:

1. Drag a Digital Movie icon to the Flowline.

2. Open the Digital Movie icon on the Flowline by double-clicking it. Once the Digital Movie icon is opened, the Load Movie dialog box appears.

3. Locate and select the digital movie you want to load. The digital movie that I used to create the Toyota Motor Manufacturing of America example was saved as a QuickTime file.

4. Select the Under User Control option from the Digital Movie icon dialog box if you want the standard QuickTime controller to be available for the end user, or leave this option unselected to hide the controller. I left this option unselected in the Toyota Motor Manufacturing piece.

5. Close the Digital Movie icon dialog box to return to the Flowline.

6. Choose the Run command from the Try It menu to see the digital movie play.

CAUTION

If you use a larger video window, performance may be negatively impacted; however, additional RAM and a higher speed processor on the final delivery platform can help increase performance.

Using the Blue Screen Technique   As compression technologies and processor speeds continue to improve, we will begin to see video used for more than the traditional mimicry of television or videotape players. For example, we already are beginning to see lifelike computer characters act as guides through content, or actually present the content.

A video trick that's growing in popularity is to shoot the video using a *blue screen* technique. With this process, you shoot video of an actor against a blue background, then replace the blue background via video editing. Steps for creating the digital movie are based on the product you are using to create the movie, and you should consult the user documentation for specific guidance.

During editing, the background can be replaced with any image. In the example shown in Figure 20.11, we used blue screen video to place a live body in the illustrated manufacturing environment.

To incorporate digital video that uses the blue screen process, follow these steps.

1. Drag a Digital Movie icon to the Flowline.

2. Open the Digital Movie icon on the Flowline by double-clicking it. Once the Digital Movie icon is opened, the Load Movie dialog box appears.

3. Locate and select the digital movie you wish to load. The digital movie that I used to create the Toyota Motor Manufacturing of America example was saved as a QuickTime file.

Part
V

Ch
20

FIG. 20.11
You can use common video shooting and editing techniques to create realistic characters in your piece.

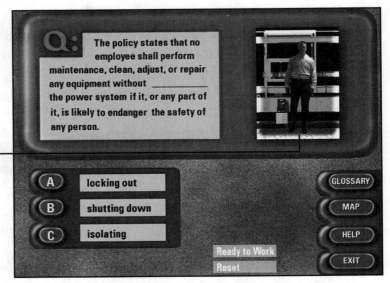

Video is incorporated using blue screen technology.

4. Carefully place the video so that it appears over the top of the scene within which the character is to be incorporated.

5. Close the Digital Movie icon dialog box to return to the Flowline.

6. Choose the Run command from the Try It menu to see the digital movie play.

 QuickTime movies can be played on both Macintosh and Windows platforms. A single movie file can be played on both platforms after it has been "flattened." (For guidance on "flattening" a movie file, refer to the Adobe Premier guidelines for creating QuickTime.) Creating one movie to play on both platforms allows you to reduce the storage requirements for the piece, and possibly to deliver the final piece for both platforms on a single, hybrid CD-ROM.

Motion Picture Experts Group (MPEG)

MPEG is used for the compression of digital movies and synchronous audio, and is supported by the Windows platform only. Like QuickTime and Video for Windows, MPEG files remain external to Authorware.

Creating an MPEG digital movie file requires proprietary hardware and software, which is just becoming cost-effective for mid- to large-sized multimedia organizations. MPEG is available, however, through numerous production facilities around the world.

PICS Movies

PICS movies are similar to Macromedia Director movies, except that they cannot contain interactivity or audio, and are imported directly into Authorware rather than referenced as external files. At the most basic level, a PICS movie is no more than a series of still PICT images assimilated into one file. Like cartoons, these still images are then presented in a sequence to give the illusion of movement.

N O T E   PICS movies can only be loaded into Authorware on the Macintosh. The Macintosh file, however, can then be converted for use with Authorware for Windows. Additionally, the content of a PICS movie cannot be edited using Authorware. ▓

In the example shown in Figure 20.9, we could replace the Director movie with a PICS movie. If we did so, we would also have to change the way the end user interacts with the movie, since PICS movies cannot contain interactivity. For example, we might place click-touch areas on the four sides of the piece of equipment so that whenever the user clicks, the values for the start frame and end frame change.

While the basic functionality thereby can be accomplished, the realistic interactivity provided by Director is missing.

While PICS movies work great when playing forward, they are a bit touchy when played in reverse. If you need a movie to play backward and forward, I suggest using a Director movie that is controlled by Authorware.

TROUBLESHOOTING

When I import a PICS movie, a large white rectangle is placed behind my movie. This rectangle goes away when I set the mode to Transparent, but then I can see through portions of my movie. How do I prevent this? When creating the movie, use the lightest shade of gray rather than white. When the image is then set to Transparent within Authorware, only the white pixels will become invisible.

Part
V

Ch

20

FLC, FLI, and CEL Files

Files created using Autodesk Animator and Autodesk Animator Pro are available for the Windows platform only. Using the same steps as used to import a PICS movie, these files are imported into Authorware.

Referencing External Digital Movie Files

When digital movies are stored external to the Authorware piece and are called by the piece when the Digital Movie icon is encountered on the Flowline, the Authorware piece will locate the external file according to the information entered in the Content Search Path field of the File Setup dialog box. While the search path can be modified using variables and functions when the piece is running, it is generally a good idea to leave all external media elements in a single location so that they are not forgotten when the final piece is distributed.

▶ For more information on the content search path, **see** "Content Search Path," **p. 48**.

CHAPTER 21

Implementing XCMDs and DLLs

We sat around a table in the design room, confident that we could meet our client's request—we just weren't quite sure how. A major telecommunications company in the southeastern United States needed to train new operators in areas of procedure and customer service. Simulating the equipment, teaching vocabulary, and drilling the trainees on processes were standard requests for a training piece. There was, however, one unusual request that had us puzzled.

As part of this piece, the client wanted to digitize a voice representing a customer calling the customer service center. This caller's voice would then be used to create a realistic simulation. Rather than having the trainees type their responses, select the most appropriate response from a list of options, or even digitize the trainees' responses on the computer, the client wanted to record the trainees' voices using a standard audio cassette player. The trick, though, was that this had to happen without the user pressing any buttons on the player.

When to use external code

Use external code as a last resort when developing a piece in Authorware.

Understanding how external code works

External code can work in one of two ways: as a function or a command.

Tips to using external code

External code can be created using a variety of programming languages and compilers. Once it is created, however, it must be linked to the Authorware piece.

Dealing with external code that does not follow Authorware conventions

When Authorware recognizes that a Dynamic Link Library (DLL) that does not follow conventions is being loaded, a few more steps are added to the process.

Knowing when to use external code

Knowing when to use external code is as important as implementing it properly, so I have shared a few of my examples as well as the code.

After some deliberation—and prototyping—we found the solution. Knowing that this was out of bounds for Authorware, we turned to our chief engineer to write some external code that, when operators indicated they were ready to respond to the caller, sent an electrical current out of the computer into the surge protector. At the far end of the surge protector was a standard A/B switch that, when it detected the current, switched either one direction to turn on the player or the other direction to turn off the player.

This chapter explores how to implement external code such as this into Authorware using XCMDs and DLLs. ■

Understanding External Code

The beauty of using Authorware is that you don't need to be a trained programmer to create sophisticated applications. That's true until you run across a functionality that Authorware does not support, or that *could* be built in Authorware were it not for unacceptable time requirements or negative performance impact.

That said, let me warn you against the temptation of relying on external code. In my experience, new authors have a tendency to rely on external code for one of two reasons:

■ Traditional Programming Background—New authors who come from a traditional programming background have a tendency to rely on what they already know—don't we all? So, when they get into the heat of battle and need to perform a complex calculation, make a branching decision, or produce an animation, they quickly fall back on tools that they know can do the job rather than exploring what is possible within Authorware.

- Missing the Spirit—The second group of people who quickly turn to external code rather than using the functionality of Authorware is comprised of those who follow the rules of Authorware rather than the spirit. As we discussed in the opening of this book, there is much more to learning Authorware than simply learning the rules.

  For example, I can tell you that there is one, and only one, function for creating scrolling text within Authorware, which is by applying the Scrolling characteristic to a block of text when editing the Presentation Window. By bending the rules with a little creativity, though, I can tell you that I have created scrolling text that does not use the standard background, that uses standard Authorware buttons or hot spots, and that actually performs faster than the Authorware-provided scrolling text. I did not need to create an external function to do this. I simply had to apply a little creativity to the features that Authorware has.

  ▶ For more information on using the Scrolling text characteristic, **see** "Scrolling Text," **p. 81**.

While your first approach should be to explore all avenues provided by Authorware before turning to external code, there will be times when extending the functionality of the authoring tool is appropriate.

I do not intend to teach C++ Programming 101 for the remainder of this chapter, or to provide the shortcuts to building external code. I am happy to say that this is not my forte. I will, however, give a brief overview of how external code works, and describe a few places where I have elected to use such functionality.

My hope is that you will be able to recognize the best opportunities for implementing external code and that, most importantly, you will quickly acquire the spirit of Authorware.

How External Code Works

External code works essentially the same way within Authorware for Macintosh as it does Authorware for Windows. Understanding what you need the code to do from a systems level helps ensure that when the code is built, it is correct the first time.

Building external code is typically done using either C or C++ programming. Therefore, to participate in creating external code, you must have some experience or training in traditional programming.

When designing external code, or discussing its functionality with a contract programmer, it is helpful to understand that external code is constructed in the two formats—functions and commands—described next.

Part
V

Ch
21

Functions

A *function* typically performs an action that has a returned result. For example, I might need to check an initialization file for the location of a piece of software required by my end user. Once I know the location, I can check that location to see that the software is actually installed. If it is installed in the correct place, I can have the function return one result to Authorware, and if the software is not properly installed, I can return a different result to Authorware.

> **N O T E**   In Chapter 19, "Using Functions and Variables," I introduced how to incorporate scripting into Authorware using variables and functions. When listing Authorware functions, Authorware groups both routine classes (functions and commands) together, although some of Authorware's functions perform according to the rules of the function class, and some of them perform as commands. ▪

Since I require information to be returned, I must use a function. Functions are written in the Calculation icon window according to the following format:

```
CustomVariable:=FunctionName(arguments)
```

Commands

A *command* is different from a function in that a command does not return a result. For example, I might want a pie chart drawn in the Presentation Window, and want the chart to be comprised of three different colors with the amount of each color based on a complex set of calculations. When the command finishes calculating and drawing the chart, I don't need any information returned to Authorware.

Commands are written in the Calculation icon window according to the following format:

```
CustomCommand(arguments)
```

▶ For guidance on scripting within the Calculation icon window, **see** "Working with Variables and Functions," **p. 366**.

TROUBLESHOOTING

I created a DLL to draw a bar chart in the Presentation Window, and that worked fine. As soon as I interacted in Authorware, however, part of the graphs erased. How can I keep this from happening? Unfortunately, objects that are created using external code only take precedence if the Presentation Window redraws and the XCMD or DLL is still active. As soon as Authorware is back in control of the system, the objects created by the external code are erased when something else is drawn in the same area of the Presentation Window.

Using DLLs and XCMDs

External code can be created using a variety of applications. The most popular are C/C++ compilers. Once this code has been written, it must be compiled according to external command (XCMD) for Macintosh or Dynamic Link Library (DLL) for Windows standards.

An external code file can include a single function that you require, or a series of functions to be used throughout the piece. In either case, once the external code is compiled, it must be linked to Authorware.

TROUBLESHOOTING

I need several functions created using external code, but keeping track of all those files is a real maintenance problem. How can I limit the number of DLL files? A single DLL or XCMD file can actually contain numerous functions. Try compiling a new DLL that contains all the needed functions, and then relink the DLL to your piece.

Once external functions are linked to Authorware, they become available throughout the piece just as Authorware functions are. To use an external function, you would open a Calculation icon window, an ornament, or a dialog box and place the external function just as you would a standard Authorware function. Linking external functions is discussed next.

Linking DLLs and XCMDs

To link external code to Authorware, follow these steps:

1. Open the Functions dialog box, shown in Figure 21.1. To open the Functions dialog box, select the Show Functions option from the Data pull-down menu.

The shortcut keys for opening the Functions dialog box are Option+⌘+F (Macintosh) and Ctrl+Alt+F (Windows).

2. Once the Functions dialog box has opened, you must switch to the custom or user category. This category is named according to the title of your piece; therefore, it will be different for every piece. In Figure 21.1, the custom category is named "programx.a3w." Authorware will only load functions into the custom category.

Part
V

Ch
21

FIG. 21.1

Switch the category to show custom functions.

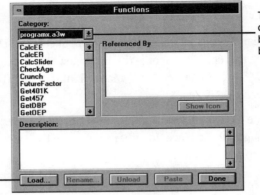

The custom functions category must be selected before the Load button becomes active.

Click the load button to access the Load Function dialog box.

3. Select the Load button to access the Load Function dialog box shown in Figure 21.2. This dialog box operates much like the dialog box for opening an Authorware file.

TIP You can also select the Load Function option from the Data pull-down menu to access the Load Function dialog box without first opening the Function dialog box and then clicking the Load button.

External functions are saved using these extensions.

FIG. 21.2

The Load Function dialog box is used to locate and import externally created code.

Available files are listed here.

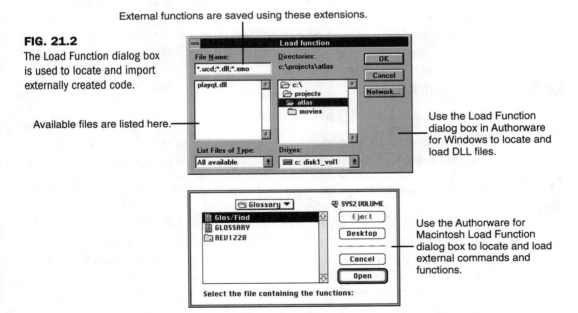

Use the Load Function dialog box in Authorware for Windows to locate and load DLL files.

Use the Authorware for Macintosh Load Function dialog box to locate and load external commands and functions.

4. Use the button options and the pop-up list of directories to locate the DLL or XCMD file containing your functions. Once you have located the file, click the Open (Macintosh) or OK (Windows) button.

5. When the external code file opens, you will see another dialog box, shown in Figure 21.3, containing a list of available functions or commands within the external XCMD or DLL file. Select one of the functions, then click the Load button.

FIG. 21.3
Select which function from the external code file is to be loaded into Authorware.

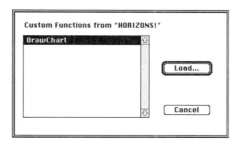

N O T E Even though Authorware uses the term "load," an XCMD or DLL is not actually incorporated into Authorware. Rather, a link is drawn to the file containing that code. When you distribute your final application, therefore, you must be sure to include the external code file. ▨

At this point, Authorware creates a link to the external file containing the code, and the function you have selected becomes available in the custom portion of the Category pop-up menu in the Functions dialog box. The link is shown in the upper-right section of the Functions dialog box, as seen in Figure 21.4.

▶ To refer to the introduction of the Functions dialog box, **see** "How Authorware Functions Are Organized," **p. 383**.

FIG. 21.4
When a link has been created to an external function, the path for that link is displayed in the Functions dialog box.

A list of functions contained in the DLL file appears when the file is loaded.

The path to the DLL file is used to create a link between the file and Authorware.

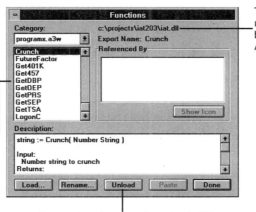

Custom functions can be unloaded if they are not being used.

The function that was created externally can now be used just as if it were a predefined Authorware function.

Loading DLLs that Don't Follow Authorware Conventions

During the loading of a DLL function you might encounter another dialog box, shown in Figure 21.5. This dialog box is presented whenever Authorware attempts to load a DLL function that does not adhere to Authorware's conventions.

Enter a name for the custom function in this field.

Enter the arguments for the custom function. Arguments must be separated by commas.

FIG. 21.5
This dialog box is used to define DLL functions that do not adhere to Authorware conventions.

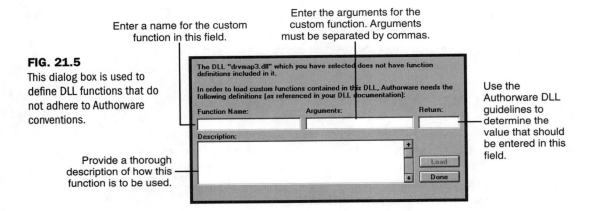

Use the Authorware DLL guidelines to determine the value that should be entered in this field.

Provide a thorough description of how this function is to be used.

When this dialog box appears, enter the requested information described below. Once all this information is provided, click the Done button to continue the load procedure.

Function Name   You can name a function in one of three ways:

- Original Name—When a name is entered in this format (for example, MyFunction), Authorware looks for a function with that specific name within the DLL.
- Variable Name—When a name is entered in this format (for example, MyFunction = AnotherFunction), Authorware looks for AnotherFunction in the DLL, and then loads it into Authorware with the name MyFunction.
- Ordinal—When a name is entered in this format (for example, MyFunction = @112), Authorware looks for the function by its address rather than by its name.

N O T E The Ordinal naming format allows slightly faster access to the function by the piece. However, the scripting is less intuitive so I only recommend using this format when only a limited number of developers will be working to create the piece.

▶ For more information on using variables, **see** "Assigning a Value to a Variable," **p. 377**.

List of Arguments An argument is a piece of information that the function or command needs in order to perform its job correctly. In most XCMDs and DLLs, the number and sequence of the arguments is critical. In a few cases, however, arguments are optional. When describing or documenting the function, be sure to note which arguments are required, and which are optional.

When the dialog box that allows you to define a function appears, you must enter a list of all the arguments required by the function. Separate the items in the list with commas.

T I P Open lines of communication between the person building the external code and the person implementing the external code are necessary to ensure that the arguments are set correctly.

Return Value Just as the function needs to understand how you will be passing information to it via arguments, it also needs to know how you want the information returned. This information is called the *return value*. Knowing how the DLL is constructed helps determine what is entered in this field.

▶ To learn how to assign a return value to a variable, **see** "Assigning a Value to a Variable," **p. 377**.

Description Whenever you get an opportunity to document information for future reference, take advantage of it. Future maintenance of your Authorware application is made much easier if you spend some time now to elaborately define why the function was created, what the function does, and how to script the function in the Authorware Calculation icon window.

Unloading DLLs and XCMDs

If you have loaded a function that is no longer being used, it is best to *unload* that function so that it is no longer residing in memory. To unload a custom function, follow these steps:

1. Open the Functions dialog box by choosing the Show Functions option from the Data pull-down menu.

Part

V

Ch

21

TIP The shortcut keys for opening the Functions dialog box are Option+⌘+F (Macintosh) and Ctrl+Alt+F (Windows).

2. Select the custom function category from the Category pop-up list. The custom function category will be labeled with the same name you used when you named the multimedia piece in which you are working.

3. Select the function you want to unload by clicking it.

4. Click the Unload button.

Applications for External Code

As I mentioned earlier, I am not going to illustrate how to write external code, but rather why and when you should write external code. For the remainder of this chapter, I'll demonstrate a few useful applications for external code. The source code for these example DLL and XCMD files is included on the CD that accompanies this book.

Creating a Glossary

In most cases, I am not a big fan of providing a glossary for the end user. Let's be honest—if you had the choice of interacting with a CD-ROM full of science experiments or scrolling your way through a list of over 500 terms and definitions, where would you spend your time? As we began a project for West Publishing Company, however, I gave in to the notion of a glossary because we were working on an educational piece that would be used for reference.

Based on interviews with students, professors, and subject matter experts, we determined that the end user should be able to scroll through a list of terms and select a term to see its definition. There was no problem building this in Authorware.

We also determined, though, that the user should be able to enter a term into a Find field, and as the user typed, the scrolling list of terms should intelligently narrow in on the desired term. This might be a struggle in Authorware.

By creating an XCMD, all this functionality was provided in an interaction, shown in Figure 21.6, that was quick to respond and took very little time to build.

In addition to the basic functionality we had originally considered, we also constructed the XCMD so that it read from an external text file, allowing quick and easy updates to the content. All the button and title bar labels were based on arguments, as seen in the script placed in an Authorware Calculation icon window shown in Figure 21.7.

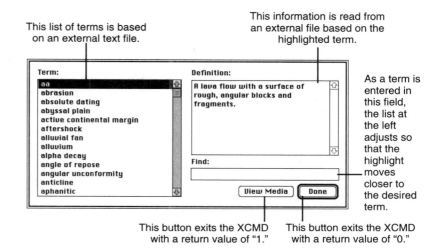

This list of terms is based on an external text file.

This information is read from an external file based on the highlighted term.

FIG. 21.6
The XCMD allows text entry and scrolling to locate a term.

As a term is entered in this field, the list at the left adjusts so that the highlight moves closer to the desired term.

This button exits the XCMD with a return value of "1."

This button exits the XCMD with a return value of "0."

Custom function

Authorware variable to define the location of the piece

Name of the external text file containing the terms and their definitions

Name that appears in the title bar of the glossary window

Variable used to store the return value

Default term to be selected when the glossary opens

FIG. 21.7
The glossary XCMD was incorporated into other Authorware scripting.

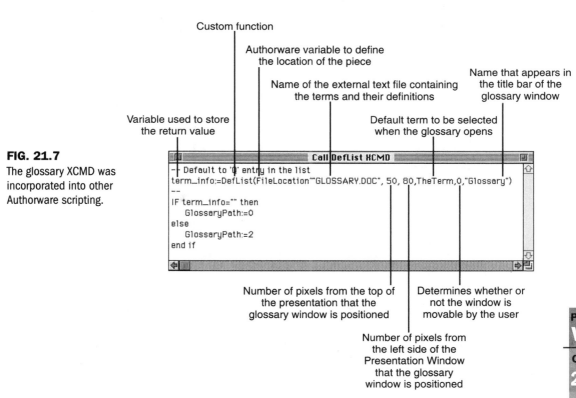

Number of pixels from the top of the presentation that the glossary window is positioned

Determines whether or not the window is movable by the user

Number of pixels from the left side of the Presentation Window that the glossary window is positioned

The final functionality incorporated into the XCMD was to read the external text file, look for a special character, and, if the character was there, activate the Show Media button.

When the user selected the Show Media button, the XCMD returned a value representing the term; we could use this value to branch in Authorware and display the media.

As you can see, creating this type of functionality within Authorware would have taken quite some time, and ultimately would not perform as seamlessly as this XCMD does.

Allowing the Student to Take Notes

A popular extra in many interactive learning pieces is to provide the ability for the end users to take notes as they progress through the piece. You can record a user's entry using a text entry interaction, and can store the notes using external text files.

As part of the Notes feature, I also want the capability for multiple users to store notes, or for a single student to store multiple sets of notes. This goal, coupled with the need to seamlessly print, led me to develop this routine using a DLL.

The resulting DLL, the interface of which is shown in Figure 21.8, responds incredibly quickly. Moreover, because of the technique used to construct it, the end user can keep the DLL open while they work in the learning piece and can toggle between the note cards and the learning piece.

FIG. 21.8
Interface for the Notes DLL.

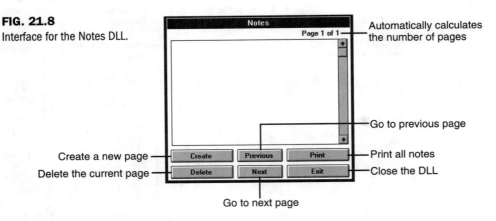

Automatically calculates the number of pages

Go to previous page

Create a new page — Create | Previous | Print — Print all notes
Delete the current page — Delete | Next | Exit — Close the DLL

Go to next page

Using a simple log-on process, I was able to determine where the user stored their notes, and when the note file was written, I embedded the user's name. When the user executed the Notes feature, I could be sure that I had the right set of notes. The user's name and the location of the notes were passed to the DLL through arguments, as shown in the Authorware scripts that were placed in a Calculation icon window as seen in Figure 21.9.

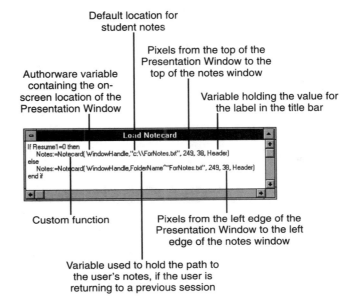

Default location for
student notes

Pixels from the top of the
Presentation Window to the
top of the notes window

Authorware variable
containing the on-
screen location of the
Presentation Window

Variable holding the value for
the label in the title bar

FIG. 21.9
Arguments for the
Notes DLL.

Custom function

Pixels from the left edge of the
Presentation Window to the left
edge of the notes window

Variable used to hold the path to
the user's notes, if the user is
returning to a previous session

Building a Log-on Routine

As you might be required to do at some point, our team was once asked to build a
CD-ROM that could be delivered stand-alone, be installed to a hard drive, or be placed on
a network. This request was not a concern because many third-party installation packages
provide this functionality, and an Authorware file can run in any of those environments.
But when the client asked that the student be allowed to quit a session and return to it at
another time—possibly even at another workstation—we realized that development could
become tricky.

Since this piece could be run essentially anywhere, we needed to allow the students to
determine if they wanted a fresh start, or if they wanted to continue a previous session.
We created a DLL that produced the interface shown in Figure 21.10 to handle this admin-
istrative task.

If the user selects to start fresh, we ask them to define a location to store information
regarding bookmarks and notes taken during the session. If they select to continue a
previous session, we provide a browser that allows them to locate their bookmark information and notes. When a location has been established, or the user has canceled the
routine, the DLL stops and a value is passed back to Authorware. We use this value to
determine the application branching. Figure 21.11 shows how this functionality is scripted
in an Authorware Calculation icon window.

Part

V

Ch

21

FIG. 21.10
Interface for the log-on DLL.

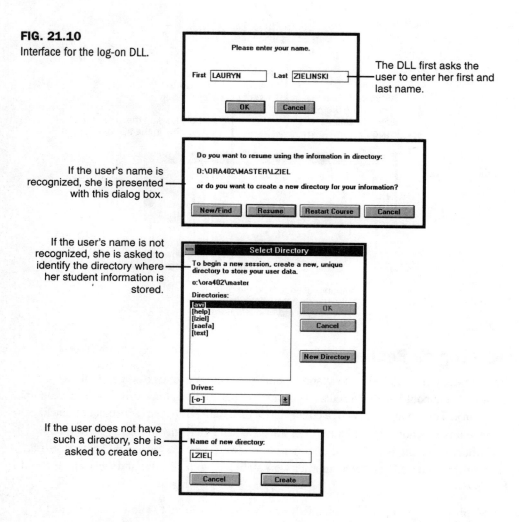

The DLL first asks the user to enter her first and last name.

If the user's name is recognized, she is presented with this dialog box.

If the user's name is not recognized, she is asked to identify the directory where her student information is stored.

If the user does not have such a directory, she is asked to create one.

Custom variable used to hold the string returned by the DLL   The custom function for the log-on routine

FIG. 21.11
Arguments for the log-on DLL.

These custom variables store information taken from the string, which was returned by the DLL

Authorware variable containing values for the Presentation Window's position on the screen

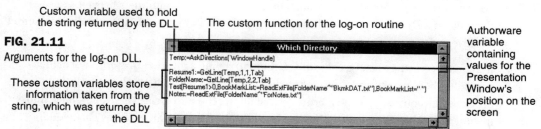

This routine supports multiple users running on any workstation, and performs much faster than what we could build using Authorware. ●

CHAPTER 22

Working with Data

Computer-based training programs are known for their ability to track and record student information. In fact, one of the greatest selling points for this medium is its ability to conduct computer-managed instruction, or to connect to a database that collects information about the user and then makes prescriptions for that user based on the collected data.

It's been said, however, that the important thing is not what you learn but what you do with what you learn. This philosophy pertains to the collection of data within an Authorware piece as well as to the real world.

The computer offers a greater benefit to learning than simply acting as a recording mechanism. More important than what the computer learns about the user is what the computer does with that information. Using the collected information to form an experience unique to a particular end user is one way to act upon what has been learned.

This chapter explores how to use data that has been collected through the use of predefined Authorware variables or custom variables, and how to, based on that collected information, create a piece that reacts to its user. Before entering this chapter, you should have a good understanding of how variables and

Data can impact the Presentation Window

Use data to position the Presentation Window or as content displayed in the Presentation Window.

Using data to control the Motion icon

Data can be used to define where an object is to be displayed, what rate the motion plays, and when perpetual motions begin and end.

Using data for navigation and hyperlinking

The Navigate icon allows you to search for content or keywords or to display a specific page of a framework.

Individualize your piece with data-driven branching

Use data to determine which path of a decision loop should be taken to provide branching that responds to the end user.

Using data in conjunction with the interaction loop

Functions and variables can be used to activate/deactivate responses, establish conditional responses, and to position button and entry fields.

Produce simulations using data and the digital movie icon

Digital movies are controlled with data, resulting in an interaction that emulates the operating experience.

functions work and be comfortable with creating custom variables. (See Chapter 19 "Using Functions and Variables.") This chapter also revisits each of the Authorware icons where data can be used to control the piece. ■

Data and the Presentation Window

You can use data in relation to the Presentation Window in one of two ways. You can use it in the Effects dialog box to control the position of displayed objects within the Presentation Window, or you can use it as content within the Presentation Window.

As you learn to use data in the Presentation Window, keep in mind that the Display and Interaction icons each allow you to create displays. Therefore, the processes covered in this section apply to development using either of these icons.

Positioning a Display Using the Display Options

When an Authorware piece encounters an icon that contains a display, it determines where that display is to be placed in the Presentation Window based on the settings within the Calculate Initial Position area of the Effects dialog box (see Fig. 22.1). If the None option is selected, Authorware places the display according to how you placed the objects when the display was created. If the On Path or In Area option is selected, a variable can be used to control the positioning of the display within the Presentation Window.

Part V

Ch

22

FIG. 22.1
Use the Effects dialog box to position the contents of the Display or Interaction icon.

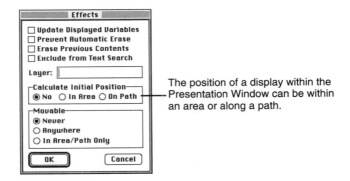

The position of a display within the Presentation Window can be within an area or along a path.

The Effects dialog box is accessed from either the Flowline window or the Presentation Window. To access the Effects dialog box from the Flowline window, follow these steps:

1. Click the Display or Interaction icon on the Flowline for which you want to access the Effects dialog box.

2. Choose the Effects command from the Attributes menu.

To access the Effects dialog box from the Presentation Window, follow these steps:

1. Open the Display or Interaction icon on the Flowline by double-clicking it.

2. Choose the Effects command from the Attributes menu.

TIP
The shortcut keys for opening the Effects dialog box from either the Flowline window or the Presentation Window are ⌘+E (Macintosh) and Ctrl+E (Windows).

▶ To learn more about using the Effects dialog box, **see** "Setting Display Effects," **p. 130**.

To position the display within the Presentation Window using a variable, select either the On Path or In Area option from the Calculate Initial Position area of the Effects dialog box. Since both of the Calculate Initial Position options function similarly, we'll examine the On Path option to see how to control the display position using data.

Let's use a portion of a piece that my company developed for Lutheran Brotherhood, Inc., as an example. As you can see in Figure 22.2, a series of sliders has been created on a path. When the user enters this portion of the piece, the sliders are positioned initially based on information that was entered or calculated in previous sections of the piece.

The position of this object was calculated along a path.

Base point of the path   End point of the path

FIG. 22.2
The sliders in this piece are positioned initially using data collected in another portion of the piece.

Base and End values were dependent on the path's scale.

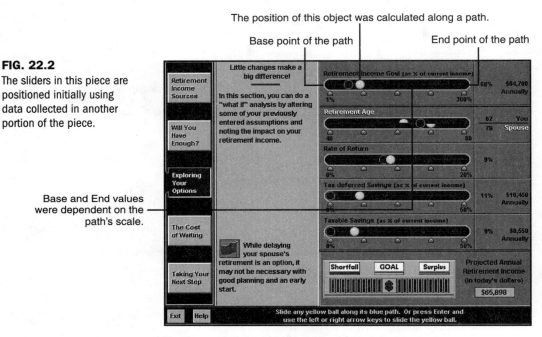

Used by permission from Lutheran Brotherhood, Inc.

To create the functionality that initially positions each slider, as I did to create the example, follow these steps:

1. Drag a Display icon to the Flowline.

2. Open the Display icon by double-clicking it.

3. Create a background graphic by either using the tools in the Authorware Graphics toolbox or importing a graphic created external to Authorware as I did.

4. Once you have created a background, close the Display icon by clicking the close box in the upper left-hand corner of the Graphics toolbox.

5. Drag another Display icon to the Flowline and place it just following the Display icon that contains the background graphic.

6. Open the second Display icon by double-clicking it.

7. Create, or import, an object that will be positioned along the background graphic. In my example, the yellow ball is the object that will be positioned along the path and on top of the background graphic.

8. Open the Effects dialog box by choosing the Effects command from the Attributes menu.

TIP The shortcut keys for opening the Effects dialog box from either the Flowline window or the Presentation Window are ⌘+E (Macintosh) and Ctrl+E (Windows).

9. Select the On Path option from the Calculate Initial Position area of the dialog box. Once this selection is made, the Effects dialog box will expand, as seen in Figure 22.3.

FIG. 22.3
The variable entered in the Variable/Expression text box is used to determine the slider's initial position.

Custom variable used to position the slider.

Base value according to the scale, or range, of the slider.

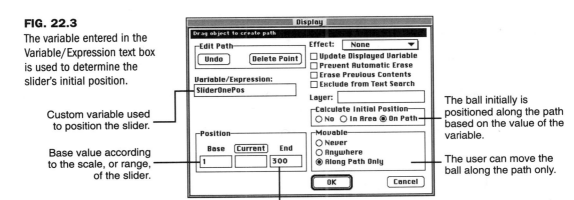

The ball initially is positioned along the path based on the value of the variable.

The user can move the ball along the path only.

End value according to the scale, or range, of the slider.

10. When the dialog box expands, a triangle appears in the center of your object. Drag the object to create a path along which the object will be positioned. Be careful not to drag the triangle.

    Creating a path using the Effects dialog box is the same as creating a path along which an object will animate.

11. Position the path using the base and end triangle markers.

12. Enter a value, or a variable, in the text box for both the Base and End positions.

13. Enter a variable into the Variable/Expression text box. I created a custom variable and named it SliderOnePos.

14. Once the path is established, the Base and End values set, and a variable has been entered in the Variable/Expression text box, click OK to save your changes.

15. Close the Display icon by clicking the close box in the upper left-hand corner of the Graphics toolbox.

> ▶ To refer to the steps for creating a path, **see** "Moving Objects Using the To End Motion Type," **p. 181**.

As the user interacts with portions of the piece, the value of the variable SliderOnePos is set. When the user enters this portion of the piece, that value is used to determine where in the Presentation Window the display should be positioned. Additionally, as the user moves each slider, I am able to determine its relative position on the path, and therefore determine a value to be used in performing a new set of calculations.

Just as I use a custom variable here to control the position of a display along a path, you also can use variables to control the position of a display within an area of the Presentation Window. To do this, of course, you might want to consider having one variable for the horizontal axis and one for the vertical axis.

TROUBLESHOOTING

I am not using a path to position the display, but I am limiting the display's movement by the user to remain along the path. How do I determine where on the path the display should be placed initially? Place a Calculation icon before the Display icon. Open the Calculation icon window and set the variable equal to the value of the position along the path to where you want the display placed. Now use this variable to position the display. You can also simply determine the value of the position along the path, then place the value in the Variable/Expression entry box in the Effects dialog box.

> ▶ For more information on creating objects using the Graphics toolbox, **see** "Drawing Objects," **p. 98**.

> ▶ For guidance on importing graphics into Authorware, **see** "Importing Graphics," **p. 107**.

Embedding Data in the Presentation Window

Just as data can be used behind the scenes in Authorware, it also can be used as part of the display. For example, you might want to show the results of a test, create a user prompt bar, or provide the results of a calculation that teaches a concept.

In the piece shown in Figure 22.4, developed for MSI Insurance, the student can explore the effects of fluctuating interest rates on an investment. Each of the interest rates at the time of investment is randomly generated, then the fluctuating rates are randomly calculated based on that initial rate. Finally, the total value of the investment is determined.

These values are calculated and then displayed using an embedded variable.

FIG. 22.4
The numbers that appear in the chart are the results of a calculation.

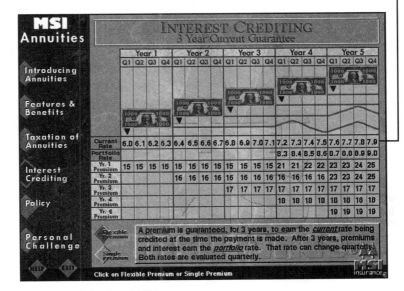

Used by permission from MSI Insurance.

To display the value of the variable, we embed the variable in a Display icon. To embed a variable, follow these steps:

1. Open the display of either a Display icon or an Interaction icon.

2. Using the Text tool, place the I-beam cursor in the display so that the Margin Line appears.

3. Enter the name of the variable that contains the data you want to be displayed. When entering the variable, enclose it in braces ({ }), as seen in Figure 22.5.

   When Authorware encounters a variable contained in braces, the value of that variable is displayed in the Presentation Window. For example, if you placed the Authorware variable Date in braces, rather than seeing the word Date as you do while editing, during running you would see the actual date based on the system clock.

FIG. 22.5

Enclosing a variable name in braces causes the value of that variable to be displayed.

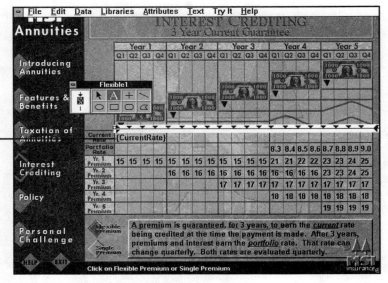

Embed a variable by placing it in braces.

Used by permission from MSI Insurance.

TROUBLESHOOTING

How do I control the formatting of numerical data that is presented in an embedded variable? Select the embedded variable, then select the Number Format option from the Data menu. Use the Number Format dialog box to adjust how the information stored in the embedded variable will be displayed.

4. When you select another tool, or place the I-beam cursor to create another text block, the value of the variable replaces the variable name. If you select the text block to be edited, the variable and braces reappear.

5. Close the Display icon to save your changes.

Embedded data is updated each time the piece executes the icon that contains that data. If you select the Update Displayed Variables option from the Effects dialog box, however, the embedded variables will be updated each time their value changes, whether or not the piece executes the icon.

▶ For step-by-step instructions on using the Text tool, **see** "Using the Text Tool," **p. 76.**

CAUTION

Using the Update Displayed Variables option can have a negative impact on performance. To enhance performance, put as few elements as possible in the icon that contains the data being updated.

 T I P I use embedded variables often for debugging purposes. By placing a variable in a Display icon, then selecting the Update Displayed Variables option in the Effects dialog box, I can see the value of the variables as they change.

Controlling Motion Icons with Data

Just as displayed objects can be controlled using data, objects that are moved on-screen using the Motion icon also can take advantage of collected data. As you will see, data can be used for everything from determining where on a path or in an area an object should be moved to how fast it should move.

▶ For an overview to using the Motion icon, **see** "All About Moving Objects," **p. 166**.

Positioning an Object Using the Motion Icon

Authorware provides three motion types that allow you to establish a scale or grid in which an object can be displayed—To Calculated Point, To Calculated Point on Line, and To Calculated Point on Grid. In each case, a variable or expression can be used to determine the point to which the object will be moved.

▶ To learn how to apply the To Calculated Point motion type, **see** "Moving Objects Using the To Calculated Point," **p. 188**.

▶ To learn the specific steps to using the To Calculated Point on Line motion type, **see** "Moving Objects Using the To Calculated Point on Line," **p. 185**.

▶ For guidance on applying the To Calculated Point on Grid motion type, **see** "Moving Objects Using the To Calculated Point on Grid Motion," **p. 191**.

In the piece shown in Figure 22.6, developed for West Publishing, each slider is positioned using a Motion icon. While I have selected the To Calculated Point motion type as an example of using the Motion icon to position an object, all three motion types work similarly.

FIG. 22.6
The Calculated Point of a Path motion is used to position each slider after the user interacts.

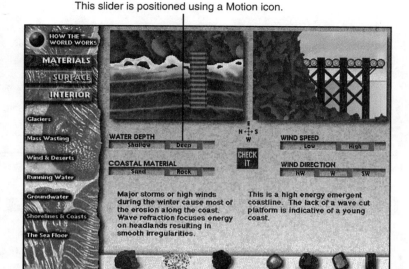

Used by permission from West Publishing.

In this exercise, the user can drag a slider into position or click a label. In either case, as soon as the user makes a selection, the slider is moved into position using a Motion icon.

To create the functionality that positions the slider, as I did to create the example, follow these steps:

1. Drag a Display icon to the Flowline.

2. Open the Display icon by double-clicking it.

3. Create a background graphic. You can either use the tools in the Authorware Graphics toolbox, or you can import a graphic created external to Authorware as I did.

4. Once you have created a background, close the Display icon by clicking the close box in the upper left-hand corner of the Graphics toolbox.

5. Drag another Display icon to the Flowline and place it just following the Display icon that contains the background graphic.

6. Open the second Display icon by double-clicking it.

7. Create, or import, an object that will be positioned along the background graphic. In my example, the gold bar is the object that will be positioned along the path.

8. Close the Display icon by clicking the close box in the upper left-hand corner of the Graphics toolbox.

9. Drag a Motion icon to the Flowline and place it just following the Display icon that contains the object to be moved. In my example, I attached the Motion icon to an Interaction icon so it would be encountered after the user interacted with the sliders.

10. Choose the Run command from the Try It menu to run the piece. When Authorware encounters the undefined Motion icon, the piece will stop, and the default Motion icon dialog box will be displayed.

11. Click the Change type button, then select the To Calculated Point option.

12. Click OK once you have changed the motion type. The To Calculated Point motion dialog box, as seen in Figure 22.7, is displayed. Remember that the name that appears across the top of this dialog box is the same as what you titled the Motion icon.

FIG. 22.7
The variable entered in the Variable/Expression text box is used to determine where the slider will be moved.

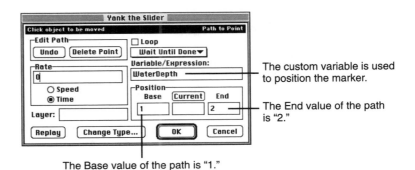

The custom variable is used to position the marker.

The End value of the path is "2."

The Base value of the path is "1."

13. Click the object you want the Motion icon to move along a defined path based on the value of a variable. In my example, this is the gold bar.

14. A triangle appears in the center of your object. Drag the object to create a path along which the object will be positioned. Be careful not to drag the triangle.

Creating a path using the Motion icon dialog box is the same as creating a path along which an object will animate.

15. Position the path using the base and end triangle markers.

16. Enter a value, or a variable, in the text box for both the Base and End positions.

17. Enter a variable into the Variable/Expression text box. I created a custom variable and named it WaterDepth.

18. Enter a Rate at which you want the object to move. Entering a zero will cause the object to jump into place.

19. Once the path is established, the Base and End values set, the Rate set, and a variable has been entered in the Variable/Expression text box, click OK to save your changes.

   ▶ For more information on creating objects using the Graphics toolbox, **see** "Drawing Objects," **p. 98**.

   ▶ For guidance on importing graphics into Authorware, **see** "Importing Graphics," **p. 107**.

   ▶ To refer to the steps for creating a path, **see** "Moving Objects Using the To End Motion Type," **p. 181**.

As the user interacts with the piece, the value of the variable is changed. That value is then used to determine where the display should be positioned with the Motion icon.

Just as I use an Authorware variable here to control the position of a display along a calculated path, you also can use variables to control the position of a display within a grid. Like positioning an object within an area using the Effects dialog box, you might want to consider having one variable for the horizontal axis and one for the vertical axis.

Using Data to Control Rate

In the previous example, I used a variable in the Variable/Expression text box to determine where on a scaled path a display should be positioned. A variable also can be used in the Rate text box to determine the speed at which motion occurs.

For example, I once worked on a project where the user was asked to drag objects out of a palette and place them in a designated area in the Presentation Window. Because we wanted the user to be able to select the same object more than once, we did this: Whenever the user dragged an object to a correct location, we moved the original object back to the palette in zero seconds so that it could be dragged again, and placed a copy of the moved object in the position where the user had moved the object. If the user dragged the object to an incorrect location, however, we wanted the object to take a few seconds to move back to the palette so that the user could see that the object did not belong where he had positioned it.

To avoid having two Motion icons—one for zero seconds and one for two seconds—I create a variable and place it in the Rate text box of the Motion dialog box (see Fig. 22.8). The Motion dialog box can be accessed by double-clicking the Motion icon.

When the user responds incorrectly, I set the value of the variable to 2, and when they respond correctly, I set the value to 0.

FIG. 22.8
The variable entered in the Rate text box is used to determine how quickly the object is moved.

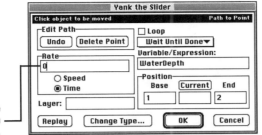

Because the rate is zero, the marker will jump rather than slide into position.

T I P If you are not using a variable to change the Rate setting, you can use the Authorware variable `IconTitle` in the Rate text box, and then title the icon with the required amount of time. Changing the Rate, therefore, only requires that you change the name of the icon rather than opening the dialog box.

▶ To refer to the Rate option contained in a Motion icon dialog box, **see** "Understanding the Rate Settings," **p. 176**.

Using Data to Control Perpetual Motion Icons

One of the Concurrency settings for the Motion icon is Perpetual. When a Motion icon is set to Perpetual, you can use a variable or expression to control its performance, and whenever the variable or expression changes—and the objects being animated have been displayed—the Motion is carried out.

▶ To refer to the Perpetual concurrency option contained in a Motion icon dialog box, **see** "Perpetual," **p. 178**.

For example, you might have a marker showing student performance that is continually present and updated as the user moves through the piece (see Fig. 22.9).

To use the Perpetual setting, set up the Motion icon just as you would any other motion. Once the motion is set up, select Perpetual from the pop-up list of Concurrency options, and then enter the controlling variable or expression in the Variable/Expression text box.

N O T E The Perpetual option is not available with Fixed Point motions.

FIG. 22.9
The progress marker is positioned using a Motion icon with Perpetual as the Concurrency setting.

The position of the marker is updated each time the user completes a question.

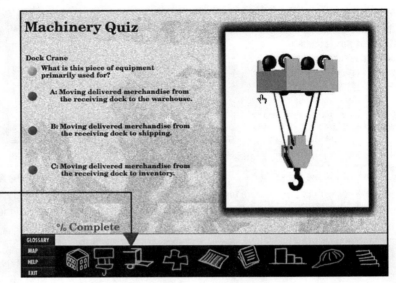

 You can set the rate to something other than zero to draw attention to the motion. For example, one gauge can be movable by the user while a second gauge adjusts automatically, based on the position of the movable slider. As the user moves the first gauge, you slowly reposition the second so that the user can see the change.

Calculating Navigation Based on Data

One of the more sophisticated ways to use data is for navigation. The Navigate icon, you might recall, allows you to link directly to a page of a framework using the unique address of that icon.

▶ For direction on using the Navigate icon, **see** "Introducing the Navigate Icon," **p. 307**.

In the example shown in Figure 22.10, developed for Oracle Corporation, I take advantage of the ability to navigate based on data to create a bookmark functionality. As users move through the piece, they can place a bookmark for any screen. Users can later view the list of bookmarks that have been created and select a bookmark from that list, and the piece jumps directly to that page.

FIG. 22.10

The user can create a list of bookmarks that, when selected later, link directly to the page where the bookmark was created.

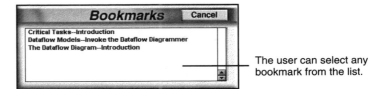

The user can select any bookmark from the list.

The data that has been collected and stored in a variable is the list of bookmark names, as well as the associated IconID for each page for which a bookmark is set. When the user selects a bookmark from the list, the script seen in Figure 22.11 is executed, and the piece displays the appropriate screen based on the collected data.

FIG. 22.11

This calculated link is used to navigate based on data stored in an Authorware variable.

Calculate destinations are used to jump to a specific icon address.

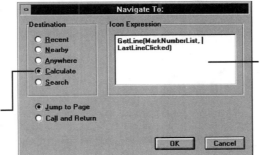

The expression is used to extract an icon address from MarkNumberList based on the value of LastLineClicked.

In addition to linking to an icon with a particular address, you also can employ variables and expressions to conduct searches using keywords and icon content. I suggest that you explore the variables and functions associated with the Navigate icon to invent ways to take advantage of this capability.

Data-Driven Branching

Creating a piece that branches according to information it collects about the user is the key to making it an interactive learning piece. Specific branching based on the user's responses to various interactions, and then the comparison and evaluation of those responses to drive branching, is how a "dialog" with the end user is created.

You can use data in conjunction with the Decision icon in two ways. The first, most prominent way is to determine which branch should be taken based on a variable or expression. The second way is to use data to control the cycling, or repeating, of a decision loop.

▶ For more information on controlling branching in a Decision icon, **see** "Defining a To Calculated Path Decision," **p. 338**.

▶ To learn more about the repeat options in a Decision icon, **see** "Until TRUE," **p. 343**.

N O T E The Authorware function Repeat While can be used in place of a Decision icon if the branch consists of no more than a Calculation icon. ▪

Building Calculated Path Decision Branches

One area in which I frequently use data-driven Decision icons is the creation of complex navigation schemes, such as the one shown in Figure 22.12.

FIG. 22.12
This navigation scheme was developed using a nesting of data-driven Decision icons.

In this example, the user can select one of the products shown along the left-hand side of the Presentation Window, or one of the three sections from across the top of the Presentation Window. When a product is selected, the section button does not change, and when a section button is selected, the product selection does not change. Therefore, the user can explore the content from a product perspective, or explore a section as it applies across all products.

To create this piece, I used one custom variable to represent the product, and another to represent the section. I then created a data-driven Decision icon to determine which product was being requested, and inside each product branch I created another data-driven Decision icon to determine which section was being requested.

Repeating the Decision Loop Until a Condition Is True

Data also can be used to control the repeating of a decision loop. For example, in the same project described in the preceding section, I've included a "Challenge" section to ensure 100 percent mastery of the defined content. In this section, the user is presented with real-world scenarios as well as a variety of responses to those scenarios. As the user responds, the list of scenarios shuffles based on how the user has responded.

As the user demonstrates mastery of a learning objective, that learning objective is retired from the list. When all the learning objectives have been retired, the student receives a special congratulations and an on-screen certificate of completion.

In this example, the piece repeatedly enters the path of the decision loop that contains the exercises, until the list of scenarios, contained in the custom variable TestQ, is empty. To accomplish this functionality, I continually check the value of the variable that contains the list of scenarios yet to be viewed—when that list is empty, the piece exits the loop. This setting is shown in Figure 22.13.

FIG. 22.13
Data can be used to determine how often a decision loop repeats.

As soon as TestQ no longer contains the list of objectives, the piece exits the decision loop.

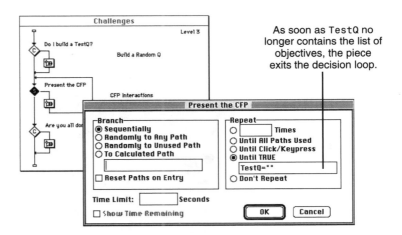

Controlling Interactions with Data

The interaction loop has several aspects that can be controlled using data. These controls can determine if a response option is active, if multiple response paths can be taken by the piece, and where responses are positioned on-screen.

▶ For guidance on creating an interaction loop, **see** "Introducing Interactions," **p. 212**.

Turning Responses On and Off

With most pieces, there's a time when you don't want any of the menu items, or interaction responses, to be active. For example, if the user has selected to view a Help screen, you more than likely should turn off all other on-screen options while the user is working in Help. When the user exits Help, you should then reactivate the other options.

This was the case in a piece, shown in Figure 22.14, that was developed for the IAMS Company.

To control the activation of an interaction response, follow these steps:

1. Drag an Interaction icon to the Flowline.

2. Drag another icon to the Flowline and place it to the right of the Interaction icon to create a response path. Responses can be built using any icon except the Decision icon, the Framework icon, or another Interaction icon.

3. When you release the mouse button to drop the icon next to the Interaction icon, the Response Types dialog box will appear. Select the type of action you want the user to perform in order to match this response, then click OK.

4. Drag a Calculation icon to the Flowline and place it at the point that you want to turn the interaction response off, as seen in Figure 22.15.

FIG. 22.14
You can use particular data to turn menu items on and off.

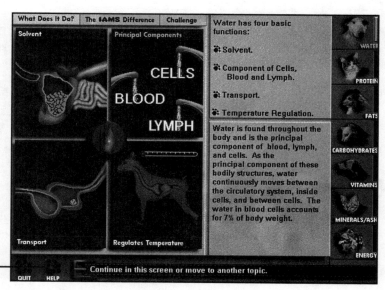

The user can enter a Help section at any time.

Used by permission from the IAMS Company.

5. Open the Calculation icon window by double-clicking the Calculation icon.

6. Create a custom variable named InHelp, for example, and in this Calculation icon place the expression InHelp:=TRUE.

7. Drag another Calculation icon to the Flowline and place it at the point that you want to turn the interaction response on, as seen in Figure 22.15.

The custom variable in this Calculation Icon is used to turn on all menus as soon as the piece exits the Help section.

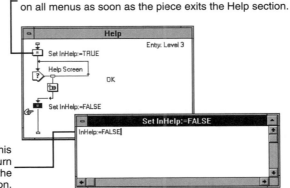

FIG. 22.15

Calculations at the entry and exit points for the Help section set the variable InHelp.

The custom variable in this Calculation icon is used to turn off all menus as soon as the piece enters the Help section.

TROUBLESHOOTING

I used a variable to turn off a response when the user entered the Help section, but after the user exited Help, the response did not reactivate. What happened? Be sure that you have reset the variable in all places where the user exits the Help section. Pressing the Exit Help button is the most obvious, but perhaps there are other menus that are still active. If the user selects one of them, he will bypass the Calculation icon that resets the variable, which activates the response.

8. Open the Calculation icon window by double-clicking the Calculation icon.

9. In this Calculation icon place the expression InHelp:=FALSE.

   Therefore, whenever the user is viewing Help, the variable InHelp is TRUE, and whenever the user is viewing the content for the piece, the value of InHelp is FALSE.

10. Open the Response Options dialog box by double-clicking the response type symbol located just above the icon that was used to create the response path.

11. Place an expression in the Active If TRUE text box. Either of the following expressions can be entered, depending on your desired results:

- `InHelp=TRUE`—If you enter this expression, the piece determines that this interaction response should be active whenever `InHelp` is `TRUE`, which is whenever the user is viewing Help. Therefore, this option is only available when the user is viewing Help, and not during the remainder of the piece.

- `InHelp=FALSE`—If you enter this expression, the piece determines that this response should be active whenever `InHelp` is `FALSE`, which is whenever the user is viewing any part of the piece other than Help. Additionally, this option is inactive when `InHelp` is `TRUE`, which is the case when the user is viewing the Help section.

CAUTION

If you use a colon in the expression used in the Active If TRUE text box, Authorware treats this as an assignment and the value is `TRUE`.

As you can see, therefore, the expression `InHelp=FALSE` is the one to use to inactivate the response option when the user is viewing Help (see Fig. 22.16).

FIG. 22.16
Enter a variable or expression in the Active If TRUE text box of the Response Options dialog box to activate/ inactivate response options.

The expression causes the response to activate and inactivate.

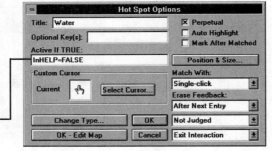

  TIP   You can use the variable `InHelp` rather than the Expression `InHelp=TRUE`, because the value of the text box is based upon the value entered in the text box that equals `TRUE`. Using the expression doesn't cause a problem, but is a bit redundant.

Likewise, you can use `~InHelp` rather than the expression `InHelp=False`. The `~` symbol is read as "not."

Using Conditional Response Types

Conditional responses not only add to the intelligence of your piece, but might also contribute to its efficiency. A conditional response, like other response types, is associated with the Interaction icon. Unlike other response types, however, the user does not directly interact with anything to prompt the selection of the response by the piece. Instead, the piece evaluates a condition that you have established.

For example, you might build a test question in which you want a special hint to be given if the user responds to answer one or answer two, but not to answer three. Rather than placing the same hint in two places—which adds to file size and maintenance efforts—you could use a conditional response to create the path that contains the hint. Let's look at a couple of ways to build this interaction using a conditional response.

Using a Selective Condition   The first method for constructing this interaction is to create a *selective condition*, one that judges all responses and selects only certain ones based on criteria you have established. To build a selective conditional response, follow these steps:

1. Drag an Interaction icon to the Flowline.
2. Drag another icon to the Flowline and place it to the right of the Interaction icon to create a response path. Responses are built using any icon except the Decision icon, the Framework icon, or another Interaction icon.
3. When you release the mouse to drop the icon next to the Interaction icon, the Response Types dialog box will appear. Select the type of action you want the user to perform in order to match this response, then click OK.
4. Place on the Flowline to the right of the Interaction icon as many responses as necessary to create the interaction loop you require.
5. Once you have created the interaction loop, be sure that each of the responses is set with the Continue branch type, as seen in Figure 22.17, so that later branches can be judged. If this isn't done, the piece won't encounter the condition but instead will detour elsewhere.

FIG. 22.17
Each response path's branch type should be set to continue.

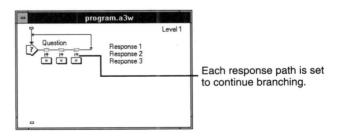

Each response path is set to continue branching.

6. The next step is to add a final branch path.
7. Open the Response Options dialog box (see Fig. 22.18) by double-clicking the response type symbol located just above the icon that was used to create the response path.

FIG. 22.18

The Response Options dialog box is where you enter the condition that must be met for this response path to be matched.

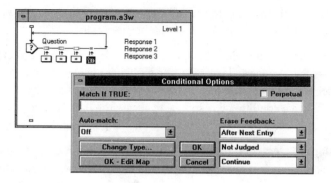

8. Click the Change Type button.

9. Change the response type to Conditional, then click the OK button.

10. Enter a condition into the Match If TRUE text box using a variable or expression that defines when you want the response to be matched.

For example, since we want the response to be matched if the user selects either the first or second response, we can use the Authorware variable ChoiceNumber (see Fig. 22.19). ChoiceNumber is set each time a response is matched, and the result is the number of responses counted left to right beginning at the Interaction icon.

FIG. 22.19

You can use a variable or expression to control the conditional response.

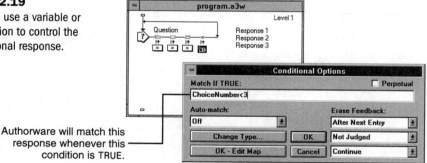

Authorware will match this response whenever this condition is TRUE.

If you set the condition to be matched with the expression ChoiceNumber<3, this response path is matched when ChoiceNumber is 1 or 2, but not when the third choice is selected.

Using an Inclusive Condition   A second method for constructing this interaction is to create an *inclusive condition*, one that is always matched by Authorware. In this scenario, you use the response branches to exclude certain paths from being matched.

Using the same example of an interaction where we want to provide a special hint if the user has selected the first or second response, but not if they have selected the third, follow these steps to create the logic for an inclusive condition:

1. Drag an Interaction icon to the Flowline.

2. Drag another icon to the Flowline and place it to the right of the Interaction icon to create a response path. Responses are built using any icon except the Decision icon, the Framework icon, or another Interaction icon.

3. When you release the mouse to drop the icon next to the Interaction icon, the Response Types dialog box will appear. Select the type of action you want the user to perform in order to match this response, then press OK.

4. Place on the Flowline to the right of the Interaction icon as many response icons as necessary to create the interaction loop you require.

5. Once you have created the interaction loop, be sure that each of the response paths is set with the Continue branch type (see Fig. 22.20).

FIG. 22.20

Begin by setting each response path's branch type to Continue.

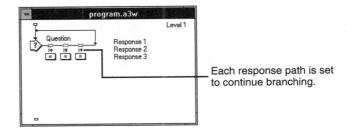

6. The next step is to add a final branch path.

7. Open the Response Options dialog box (see Fig. 22.21) by double-clicking the response type symbol located just above the icon that was used to create the response path.

FIG. 22.21

The Response Options dialog box is where you enter the condition that must be met for this response path to be matched.

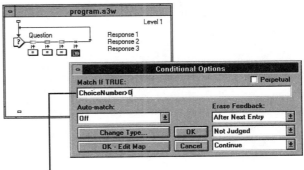

Because this condition is always TRUE, this response will be matched every time.

8. Click the Change Type button.

9. Change the response type to Conditional, then click the OK button.

10. Enter a condition using a variable or expression that defines exactly when you want the response to be matched.

    For example, since we want the response to be matched every time the piece comes to it, we can use the Authorware variable ChoiceNumber again, this time setting the condition to ChoiceNumber>0. This condition is always TRUE, so this response will always be matched.

 T I P   You could simply enter the word TRUE as the condition. Since TRUE is always TRUE, this is another response that will always be matched; however, this option is a little less intuitive.

11. The final step in this process is to adjust the branching so that the user only has the opportunity to match the conditional response if he has entered the first or second response. To do so, set the response branch of the third response to Try Again (see Fig. 22.22).

FIG. 22.22
The Flowline does not direct the piece to the conditional response if the third response has been selected.

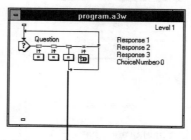

Because this branch is set to Try Again, the conditional response will never be encountered, and therefore never matched.

It's critical that you pay close attention to the Flowline when working with conditional responses. It's very easy to accidentally build a doorway through which the piece can travel even though you don't want it to do so.

Positioning Buttons and Fields

Building an entry form, such as the one for the Lutheran Brotherhood, Inc. shown in Figure 22.23, is a fairly common activity for Authorware developers. Whether these entry forms are for training or performance support, they typically contain several fields that must be completed by the end user.

FIG. 22.23
Entry forms can be con-
structed using a single
Interaction icon with a text-
entry response.

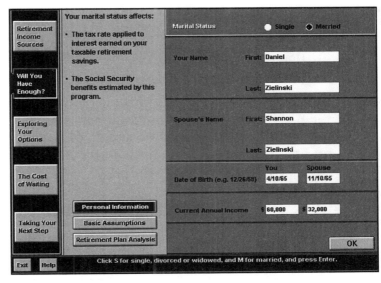

Used by permission from Lutheran Brotherhood, Inc.

The methods for creating the Flowline structure are just as varied as the uses for such
functionality. This development can be made quite efficient, however, if data is used to
drive the text-entry interaction (see Fig. 22.24). Since this functionality is sophisticated, it
stands to reason that the authoring is a bit tricky.

FIG. 22.24
In this example, the text-
entry field must move up
and down the Presentation
Window.

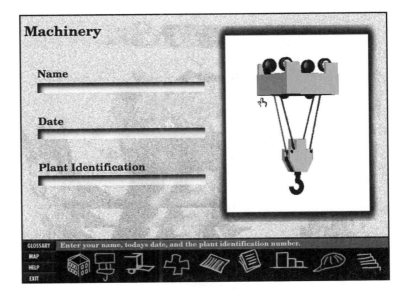

To create a text-entry interaction in which the entry field is used in several locations, such as the example shown in Figure 22.24, follow these steps:

1. Drag an Interaction icon to the Flowline.

2. Drag another icon to the Flowline and place it to the right of the Interaction icon so that it becomes a response branch.

3. When the Response Type dialog box appears, select the Text Entry response type, then click OK to save your changes.

4. Title the Text Entry icon with an asterisk, as shown in Figure 22.25. The asterisk is a wild card that allows any entry to be accepted.

FIG. 22.25
The text entry response must be titled with an asterisk.

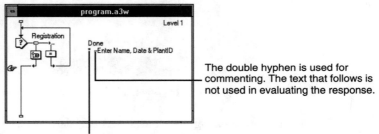

The double hyphen is used for commenting. The text that follows is not used in evaluating the response.

The asterisk is a wild card used to accept any text response.

 T I P You might want to follow the asterisk with a comment to more clearly label the anticipated response.

It is important to accept any entry, because this same interaction will be used for each field in the form. For this piece, we want the user to enter any possible response for each field.

5. Open the Interaction Options dialog box, as shown in Figure 22.26, by double-clicking the Interaction icon. Remember that the name that appears across the top of this dialog box is based on the title that you give the icon.

FIG. 22.26
The Interaction Options dialog box contains the Text Entry Options button.

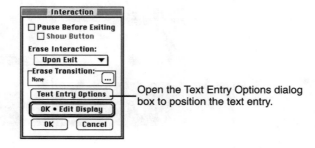

Open the Text Entry Options dialog box to position the text entry.

6. Click the Text Entry Options button in the center of the Interaction Options dialog box to open the Text Entry Options dialog box shown in Figure 22.27. Once again, the name that appears across the top of this dialog box is based on the title that you give the Interaction icon.

7. Drag the entry area to a position over the first field. Click and drag the handles to resize the area so that it covers the entire field.

FIG. 22.27
The Text Entry Options dialog box allows you to set specific controls for the text-entry field.

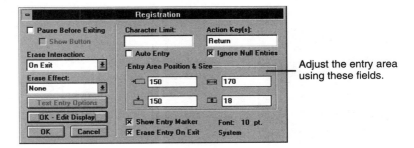

Adjust the entry area using these fields.

T I P   The text-entry area does not work like a hot spot or a normal display object. You cannot drag the object by its border, but instead have to grab the center of the entry area.

8. After the entry area is positioned and sized, notice that the Entry Area Position area of the Text Entry Options dialog box, shown in Figure 22.28, contains the coordinates and dimensions of the area.

Since all our fields will be the same size, as well as the same distance from the left side of the Presentation Window, the only piece of information we must be concerned with is the distance from the top of the Presentation Window. Write down this number so that you can refer to it later.

9. Now, reposition the text-entry area over each of the remaining fields and record the distance from the top of the Presentation Window just as you did for the first area.

10. Once you have created a list of all the necessary coordinates, you can replace these values with variables and expressions that will allow the entry field to dynamically change as the piece runs.

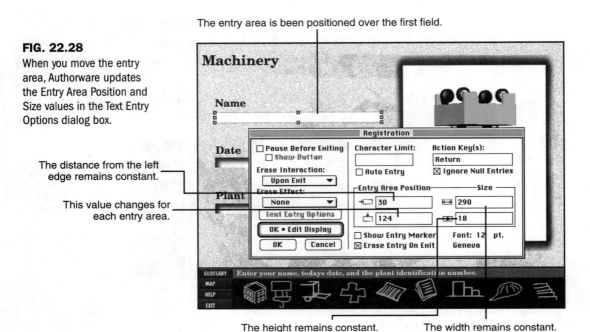

The entry area is been positioned over the first field.

FIG. 22.28
When you move the entry area, Authorware updates the Entry Area Position and Size values in the Text Entry Options dialog box.

The distance from the left edge remains constant.

This value changes for each entry area.

The height remains constant.   The width remains constant.

In our example, we want the vertical position of the entry field to change as the user responds. Therefore, we replace the value in this field with a variable or expression. To do this, we must have two pieces of information, such as:

- Positions—We must have a variable that contains the value used to control the vertical position of the entry field. For this example, we create a custom variable named Positions. This variable contains a line for each of the fields, with each line separated by a carriage return.

- Line—We also must know what entry field we are currently dealing with. To do this, we create another custom variable named Line. When the user enters the piece, we set the value of Line to 1. After the user enters a response for the first field, we increase the value of Line to 2, and so on.

Using these two custom variables, we build an expression that, based on the current value of Line, gets a value from the variable Positions. This expression, which replaces the value for the distance from the top of the Presentation Window in the Entry Area Position of the Text Entry Options dialog box, is GetLine(Positions,Line). Figure 22.29 shows how this expression is placed in the Text Entry Options dialog box.

FIG. 22.29

An expression is used in place of the constant value for the position from the top of the Presentation Window.

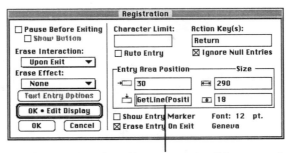

Replace the value with an expression. If the expression is longer than the field, use the arrow keys to scroll.

11. Now that the text entry is set up, it's necessary to establish the value of Positions. To do so, place a Calculation icon prior to the Interaction icon.

12. Open the Calculation icon window by double-clicking the Calculation icon, then construct the value of Positions as shown in Figure 22.30.

Use the caret to build a string.

FIG. 22.30

The string containing the placement coordinates for the text-entry field is written in the Calculation icon window.

The custom variable Positions is used to hold the changing value for the distance of the text-entry field from the top of the Presentation Window.

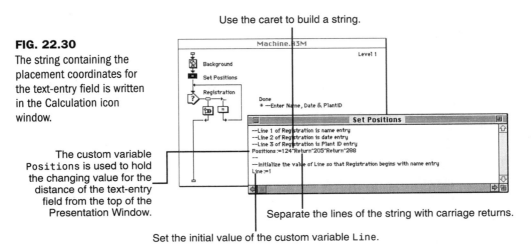

Separate the lines of the string with carriage returns.

Set the initial value of the custom variable Line.

13. Finally, you must increment the value of Line as the user responds to each entry. To do this, place a Calculation icon inside the response path, then implement the variables and functions as shown in Figure 22.31.

The benefit of using a string to control the positioning of the text-entry fields is twofold. First, the text-entry area can be dynamically positioned as the piece runs. The second benefit revolves around maintenance. If, for some reason, the entry areas must change, you can make just one edit to the string to adjust the position of all the entry areas.

FIG. 22.31
You increment the value
of Line as part of the
response.

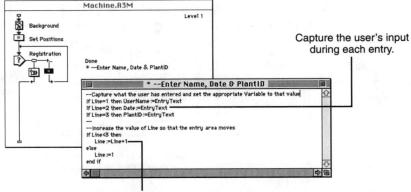

Capture the user's input
during each entry.

Increment the value of the line by 1 unless its current value
is 3, in which case the line is set back to 1.

Working with Data and the Digital Movie Icon

Simulations comprise one of the most common uses for computer-based training.
Whether you are simulating a manufacturing process or a software program, you can use
the Digital Movie icon as you create the simulation.

One benefit to using a single Digital Movie icon rather than several Digital Movie icons—
or even several Display icons and Motion icons—is that you can create a seamless flow
through an animated process. If you tried to create a simulation of an animated process
using Display and Erase icons, timing could be difficult to control and the alignment of the
various objects could be quite tedious.

There is an additional benefit to using the Digital Movie icon. If your simulation is a step-
by-step building process, you can enter the simulation at any point without having to
determine which objects from previous steps need to be displayed in the Presentation
Window.

Starting and Stopping Digital Movies

Once you have created a Digital Movie containing each action that should occur throughout the simulated process, follow these steps to control the Digital Movie with data:

1. Place a Digital Movie icon on the Flowline.

2. Open the Digital Movie icon by double-clicking it. When you first open this icon, the
   Load window appears. Load the correct digital movie by specifying its location and
   name and clicking OK.

3. Once you have loaded a digital movie, the Digital Movie icon dialog box, shown in Figure 22.32 is displayed. Select Perpetual from the Concurrency drop-down list.

When a Digital Movie icon is set to Perpetual, the movie plays from the Start Frame to the End Frame based on their respective values.

4. Place a variable in the Start Frame text box, and a different variable in the End Frame text box (see Fig. 22.32).

The movie ends at the frame
equal to the value of End.

FIG. 22.32
You can use variables to
control the starting and
ending frame values.

The movie begins
playing at the
frame equal to the
value of Begin.

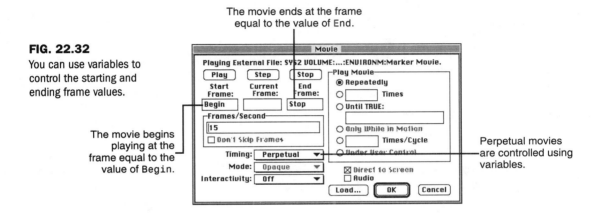

Perpetual movies
are controlled using
variables.

Click OK to close the Digital Movie icon and save your changes.

5. You now can build the interactions of the simulation below the Digital Movie icon on the Flowline, as shown in Figure 22.33.

The movie, and navigation that enables the
user to enter the simulation at any point,
must be located in the Framework icon.

FIG. 22.33
The remainder of the
simulation content is built
beneath the Digital Movie
icon on the Flowline.

This perpetual
movie plays when
the variables
controlling the
Start Frame and
End Frame
settings change.

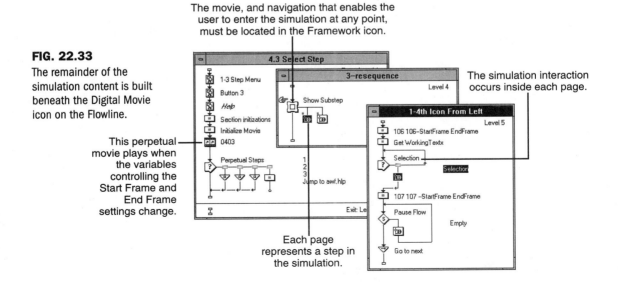

The simulation interaction
occurs inside each page.

Each page
represents a step in
the simulation.

6. Each time you want the movie to advance—such as when a screen changes or a piece of equipment begins running—you must change the values of the variables controlling the movie (see Fig. 22.34).

FIG. 22.34
Changing the value of the variables causes the digital movie to play.

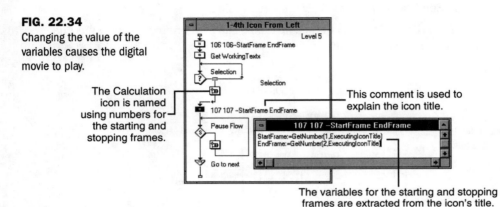

The Calculation icon is named using numbers for the starting and stopping frames.

This comment is used to explain the icon title.

The variables for the starting and stopping frames are extracted from the icon's title.

For example, in the simulation you might begin by setting the value for the variable used in the Start Frame text box—let's call it Begin—as 1, and the value for the variable used in the Stop Frame text box—let's call it End—as 10. When the piece encounters the Digital Movie icon, it will play frames 1 through 10.

The user can then be asked to interact with a Control Panel to determine how the simulation proceeds. Based on how the user interacts, you can adjust the values for Begin and End so that a specific portion of the Digital Movie plays.

The remainder of the simulation is developed by adjusting the values for Begin and End. ●

CHAPTER 23

Importing Audio

One of the last media to be considered in the creation of multimedia is audio. Although all other media—graphics, video, and animation—have gained much attention by development-tool providers, audio has only slowly progressed in terms of compression and overall quality.

This may be due in part to the fact that few multimedia developers have unlocked the real benefit that audio could bring to the interactive experience. Multimedia developers in general rely on audio for narrating content; special sound effects when buttons or menus are interacted with; and emulating the sound of equipment or an environment.

Although multimedia developers have recognized these very practical uses of audio, we have failed to take advantage of audio as a tool to set a tone—much like audio is used in movies. However, until compression or looping technologies become commonplace, and sound cards allow multiple source files to be played at once, continuous use of audio will remain impractical in a computer-based multimedia piece.

Becoming familiar with the sound options

Just as you can control when and how a digital movie will play, Authorware allows you to finitely control the playing of audio within a piece.

Working with the Sound icon

While audio can be created on most Macintosh files, for both Macintosh and Windows pieces, sound is usually imported into a multimedia piece using the Sound icon.

Learning the shortcuts

There are a few tips and tricks that result in a higher-quality piece, lower file size, and cross-platform compatibility.

In this chapter, we explore how to implement audio into an Authorware piece using the Sound icon. Additionally, we explore a few tricks for reducing the size of audio files. ■

Taking Advantage of Audio

Audio is one of those media that, because it is so easy to implement into Authorware, is usually one of the first media to be implemented. Unfortunately, implementing audio too early in the development process can cause significant problems.

The first problem that audio can cause is related to its size. Audio in general takes a great amount of hard drive space. If you are using audio for more than simple beeps and fanfares, your file size will quickly grow. As you use the Save As command throughout the day, the impact on decreasing hard drive space will be multiplied.

There is another valuable resource that will quickly disappear if you implement audio into the piece too early in the development process: your time. Take, for example, a piece that has a 10-second audio introduction to each module. If you practice authoring techniques by which you build the Flowline then run the application and fill in the icons, you will encounter this sound every time you run your piece. How much time is required to listen to that introduction throughout the development process?

It is my recommendation that you build a very small piece to test the feasibility of audio on your delivery platform and demonstrate the effectiveness of the media to your end user. But as soon as this study is over, take that piece, set it aside, and don't use audio again until you are nearing the end of the development process.

TIP

I like to place audio in a decision loop then use a variable to determine whether or not the audio is to play. While I am in development mode, I set the variable so that the audio will not play, but when I am ready to test the piece, or deliver it to the client, I turn the audio back on by adjusting the variable.

The Sound icon, as shown in Figure 23.1, is the tool used to import and control audio.

FIG. 23.1

The Authorware Sound icon is used to play music, provide sound effects, or play the narration of content.

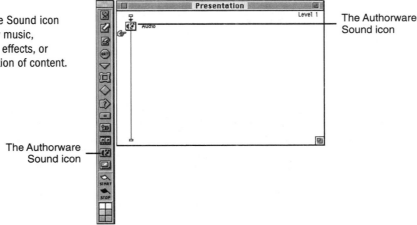

The Authorware Sound icon

The Authorware Sound icon

The Sound Options Dialog Box

The Sound icon and the Digital Movie icon are very similar. The Sound icon, although it can be used for recording through the standard microphone on the Macintosh, was not intended to be an audio recording or editing tool, just like the Digital Movie icon is not an editing tool. Once audio is imported from an external source, it can only be controlled within Authorware. Control of the Sound icon is achieved through the Sound Options dialog box, as shown in Figure 23.2. The title across the top of the Sound Options dialog box is based on the name that you have given the Sound icon on the Flowline.

▶ To refer to the introduction of the Sound icon, **see** "The Sound Icon," **p. 21**.

To access the Sound Options dialog box, simply double-click the Sound icon on the Flowline. Once the dialog box is open, you see that there are several options for controlling sound. (These are described next.) After you've chosen the settings you want, click OK to close the dialog box.

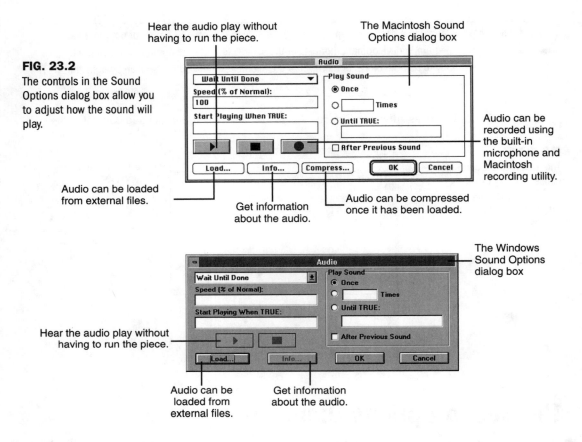

FIG. 23.2
The controls in the Sound Options dialog box allow you to adjust how the sound will play.

Hear the audio play without having to run the piece.

The Macintosh Sound Options dialog box

Audio can be recorded using the built-in microphone and Macintosh recording utility.

Audio can be loaded from external files.

Get information about the audio.

Audio can be compressed once it has been loaded.

The Windows Sound Options dialog box

Hear the audio play without having to run the piece.

Audio can be loaded from external files.

Get information about the audio.

Concurrency Options

The Concurrency options, which you set using the drop-down list in the upper-left corner of the Sound Options dialog box, determine what the piece does while the audio is playing. The Concurrency settings are as follows:

- Wait Until Done—This option causes the audio to play completely before the next Authorware icon on the Flowline is executed. For example, if you want a sound to play completely before a video starts to play, select Wait Until Done.

N O T E The default for this option is Wait Until Done. ▪

- Concurrent—As soon as the current audio begins, the next Authorware icon on the Flowline is executed. For example, if you design audio to accompany a motion, setting the audio to Concurrent will start the audio playing and then the piece will move on to start the motion.

- Perpetual—A perpetual Sound icon plays whenever the stated expression is TRUE. For example, you can have a sound that plays whenever the user changes from one topic to another. Rather than placing a Sound icon within each section, you can simply have one Sound icon that is set to Perpetual, and whenever the value of the section changes, the sound will play.

  ▶ To learn more about setting media to play perpetually, **see** "Using Data to Control Perpetual Motion Icons," **p. 441**.

TROUBLESHOOTING

How can I get two Sound icons to play at the same time? When one Sound icon is playing, then another Sound icon is encountered, the first sound is cut off, or the second waits until the first is done. Therefore, you can't get two Sound icons to play at once. To get two audio files to play at once, however, you can load AIFF-formatted sound files into Digital Movie icons, which you set to play concurrently.

Speed (% of Normal)

The Speed (% of Normal) text box in the Sound Options dialog box enables you to enter a value, variable, or expression to control the playback rate for the sound. The standard playback rate is 100 percent. Anything greater than 100 percent results in a faster sound, and anything lower results in a sound that plays slower.

> **CAUTION**
> Not all Windows audio cards support variable speed playback.

Start Playing When TRUE

The audio begins to play whenever the variable or expression that is entered in the Start Playing When TRUE text box changes from FALSE to TRUE.

Play, Stop, and Record Buttons

Once a sound has been recorded, you can play that sound or stop playing the sound while adjusting the settings in the Sound Options dialog box, as follows:

- Play—Click the Play button to hear the sound play according to the other settings you have made. Playback is dependent on the type of system you are running and the types of audio formats it supports. For example, in Windows you must consider the sound formats that are supported by the sound card.

- Stop—The Stop button stops the sound from playing.

- Record—This feature is available within Authorware on all Macintosh systems capable of recording audio. This feature is not available in Authorware for Windows because most Windows systems do not include a microphone or a standard sound card, and audio recording is not a part of the operating system.

When the button is clicked, a dialog box appears—as shown in Figure 23.3—that is used for recording audio.

FIG. 23.3
The Macintosh Audio Recording dialog box is a standard part of the operating system used for recording audio.

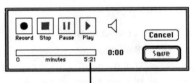

The limit for the amount of audio that can be recorded is based on the available RAM and hard disk space.

The size of the recording is limited by the amount of RAM available. Sound is recorded in Authorware by the Macintosh at 22 kHz and eight bits.

Play Sound Settings

The settings in the Play Sound area of the Sound Options dialog box are used to determine how many times the sound plays, as follows:

- Once—This option causes the sound to play one time only.

N O T E The default for this option is Once. ■

- Times—Enter a value or a variable that determines the number of times the sound will play.

- Until TRUE—If the sound has been set with a Perpetual concurrency, you can use a variable or expression to control the sound. You can elect for the sound to continually play or to stop playing based on the value of the variable.

- After Previous Sound—When a Sound icon is set to have a Concurrent or Perpetual concurrency, it is possible for the piece to encounter another sound icon before the current Sound icon has completed playing. When this happens, the first sound is interrupted and the newly encountered sound begins to play. To prevent this interruption, select the After Previous Sound option, which causes the piece to wait until the previous sound is complete before it executes the new sound.

TROUBLESHOOTING

How can I provide a controller that allows the user to pause the audio, then continue it from the point it stopped playing? The Sound icon does not allow audio to be paused, then restarted. You can, however, import an AIFF audio file into the Digital Movie icon, then use the MediaPause function to pause and continue the audio.

Load

Clicking the Load button in the Sound Options dialog box presents the standard Open dialog box, which enables you to browse for an audio file to be imported into Authorware.

Audio files that have been saved in the WAV, PCM, AIFF, SoundEdit, SoundEdit 16, System 7 sounds, and sound resource files can be loaded into Authorware for the Macintosh. Audio files that have been saved in the WAV, PCM, and AIFF formats can be loaded into Authorware for Windows.

> **N O T E** Once a sound is loaded into Authorware, it can be moved to another platform without reloading. ▣

Info

Once a sound has been either recorded or loaded, you can click the Info button in the Sound Options dialog box to learn valuable information about the sound, including the following:

- Length—This option is more correctly defined as size. It describes how many bytes the sound occupies.

- Compression—This shows the current compression ratio that has been applied to the sound (or None if no compression is being used).

CAUTION
Compressing a sound may have a negative impact on quality.

> **N O T E** In Windows, the Compression option always reads as None because compression is not supported. ▣

■ Channels—This shows whether the audio was recorded in monophonic or stereo.

> **CAUTION**
>
> Although stereo audio files have a much better sound quality than monophonic, they are also twice as big as monophonic audio.

■ Sample Size—This determines how much data was stored about the sound. Sample size can be either 8-bit or 16-bit, with 16-bit being the higher quality.

> **N O T E**   16-bit sample size is used in the production of audio compact discs. ■

■ Sample Rate—Sample rates, which are measured in kilohertz (kHz), define how often the sound frequency was measured when it was recorded: the higher the rating, the better the quality.

> **N O T E**   Audio compact discs have a sample rate of about 44 kHz. ■

■ Data Rate—This shows the rate at which Authorware reads the sound from the disc.
■ Imported From—This shows the path to the point where this audio was imported from. This is very helpful if you need to conduct further edits on the file and have forgotten where the file was stored, assuming of course that the file has not been moved.

Compression

The Compress button, available only in the Sound Options dialog box for the Macintosh version of Authorware, applies file compression routines to the sound as it is loaded into Authorware, reducing the file size by up to one-sixth of its original size. The original sound file, which remains external to Authorware, is not affected.

> **CAUTION**
>
> Compression not only decreases file size, but it also often decreases quality. I must say, however, that the Macromedia sound compression is better than many that I have heard.

When the Compression button is clicked, the Compress Sound dialog box, as shown in Figure 23.4, is presented.

TIP Sound files that are compressed on the Macintosh can be played under Windows, even though you cannot compress files under Windows. Therefore, it makes sense to load sound on the Macintosh then move your Authorware piece to Windows if you are concerned about file size. As a word of warning, however, I would back up the audio files just in case it becomes lost in the conversion process.

FIG. 23.4
The Macintosh Compress Sound dialog box is used to select a compression ratio for audio that is stored internally to Authorware.

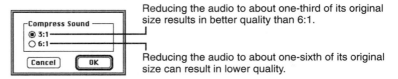

Reducing the audio to about one-third of its original size results in better quality than 6:1.

Reducing the audio to about one-sixth of its original size can result in lower quality.

Using the Sound Icon

Importing sound is much like importing a graphic or a text document. A copy of the audio becomes a part of the Authorware file, while the original source file is left intact.

Importing audio into Authorware is a fairly straightforward activity. To set up a Sound icon, perform the following steps:

1. Drag a Sound icon to the Flowline.
2. When you open the Sound icon for the first time by double-clicking it, the Load Sound dialog box, as shown in Figure 23.5, appears.

FIG. 23.5
When the Sound icon is first opened, the Load Sound dialog box is presented so that a sound file can be identified and imported.

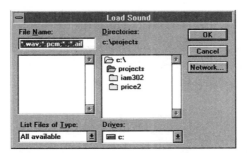

The Load Sound dialog box works somewhat like the Import dialog box, which is used to import text and graphics. On the Macintosh, if the Show Preview check box is selected, an icon and a Play Sound button are displayed in the Preview window as you highlight a file. If you click the Play Sound button, you will hear the sound play before loading it. On either platform, once an audio file is highlighted, click OK to import the audio file.

 TIP I like to play the sound before loading it just to be sure that I have selected the right audio file.

3. Once you have selected a sound to load, click Open (Macintosh) or OK (Windows) or press Return (Macintosh) or Enter (Windows) to import the audio file.

4. When a sound file has been loaded, the Audio dialog box becomes available. This dialog box also appears each time you double-click the Sound icon if a sound file has already been loaded or referenced.

5. Adjust the Audio settings as required.

6. Once you have set all of the desired control options, click OK or press Return (Macintosh) or Enter (Windows) to save your changes, or click the Load button to access the Load Sound dialog box to load a different sound file.

A Few Tricks When Dealing with Sound

Because sound can be large and compressing, it can negatively affect its quality, it is always helpful to pick up a few tricks regarding the use of sound in a multimedia piece.

Copying and Pasting for Better Quality

Some of the best sound programs available are Macromedia's SoundEdit or SoundForge. These tools enable you to record audio at 5 kHz, 11 kHz, and 22 kHz. Although 22 kHz is the best quality, it is also the largest in size. 5 kHz is fine to play with, but the quality is nowhere near what is needed for a professional product. 11 kHz is a great compromise for both size and quality.

 TIP If you can afford the space, I suggest that you use the best quality possible for sound.

Optimally, of course, we want 22 kHz quality at about the 11 kHz size, and by some accident I found a way to make that happen a few years back using SoundEdit. Although there may be better routines available today, the following approach is still a good one to keep in your bag of tricks:

1. Record the sound into a 22 kHz file.
2. Choose Select All, then copy the selected sound with the Copy command.
3. Open a new document set to 11 kHz.
4. Paste the sound you have copied.
5. Save the file, then close it.
6. Open Authorware and import the file into a Sound icon. From my experience, the quality is closer to 22 kHz than 11 kHz, but the file size is closer to 11 kHz.

Trimming to Reduce File Size

When editing sound, it is important that you make the file as condensed as possible. One efficiency, which is commonly overlooked, is the trimming of the lead in and lead out.

As you can see in the sound wave shown in Figure 23.6, there are flat lines on the front end and the back end of the wave. By cutting these tails off of each sound file, you will see a reduction in file size and in start time for the sound.

> **CAUTION**
>
> Before cutting a portion of the sound file that looks like it contains silence, I suggest playing it. Sometimes what looks like silence visually actually contains information. Once you make the cut, play the entire sound, and be prepared to use the Undo command.

A lead out causes a pause after the audio plays and before the next icon on the Flowline is executed. It also increases the file size.

FIG. 23.6
Trim the tails of sound wave files to reduce file size and unnecessary pauses.

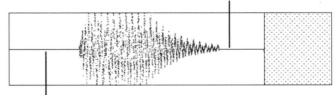

A lead in causes a pause before the audio plays and increases the size of the audio.

Eliminating the lead in and lead out reduces the size of the audio file.

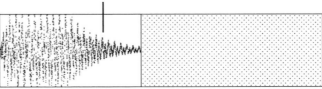

Sharing QuickTime Flat Files

The development of multi-platform CD-ROMs has nearly become the standard. Developing for this medium does have its drawbacks however. The biggest drawback is that the amount of space on the CD-ROM is immediately cut in half when you plan to build a hybrid CD-ROM because you need one executable for the Macintosh and another for Windows.

This hindrance is magnified when you start considering the use of audio. Because these files are typically large to start with, requiring two files for each sound bite in the piece begins to create some real limitations.

In such situations, however, I have a tendency to move away from playing sound using the Sound icon to using the Digital Movie icon instead. To use the Digital Movie icon rather than the Sound icon, perform the following steps:

1. After creating the sound using any sound editing tool, export it to a QuickTime file.
2. Flatten the QuickTime File using Adobe Premiere. Consult the Adobe Premiere user guides for information on flattening a file.
3. Open Authorware and add a Digital Movie icon to the Flowline.
4. Open the Digital Movie icon; when the Load dialog box appears, select the flattened QuickTime file. Authorware will not import the QuickTime file, as it does using the Sound icon, but rather will draw a link to the external file.
5. Save your changes. When you are finished with the piece, you can move it to the second platform.

Because both Authorware for Macintosh and Authorware for Windows can play a flattened QuickTime file, you are now only required to have one audio file for the two executable applications rather than two. This trick enabled me to place over 500 audio clips on a hybrid CD-ROM in addition to the already space-intensive interactive piece. ●

CHAPTER 24

Setting Up Analog Video

It was the first real definition of multimedia. Even though text and graphics had been combined on the computer screen for years, it was not until the introduction of a new technology that permitted video to be a part of a computer program that the term multimedia became commonplace. This exciting new technology, which changed desktop computing forever, was the laserdisc.

Laserdisc video quickly rose as the standard for computer-based instruction; both academic and corporate learning environments made major investments in the technology. The early systems required a touch-screen monitor, a series of extra controller cards for the computer, and a laserdisc player. An external video monitor for end-user viewing was also needed. Around this time popular jokers defined multimedia as having to make more than one trip to the car. This, of course, was due to the large amount of hardware required to use multimedia.

Using the Authorware Video icon

The Authorware Video icon, which is used to incorporate television-quality video into your piece, is placed on the Flowline just like any other icon.

Setting up video overlay

To use video within the Presentation Window, you must have a video overlay card, the video driver software, and the laserdisc player.

Configuring the video overlay system

When using video, several settings must be made so that Authorware will know how to perform, including the type of player, the communication port being used, and which color will be used as the chroma key.

Using the Video Options dialog box

The Video Options dialog box allows you to determine start and end frames for the video sequence; if a controller will be provided to the end user for the video; the timing; the playback speed; and what will remain in the video window when the video sequence has completed.

By the late 1980s, the technology had advanced even further to allow the external monitor to be removed and the video to be overlaid right onto the Presentation Window. Only a few short years later, further advancements brought about the emergence of digital video and people began to question the viability of the laserdisc.

While laserdisc video is beginning to disappear, there are still many developers using this technology. In this chapter, I will briefly discuss how Authorware controls an external laserdisc player and some of the applications for laserdisc video. ■

Using Laserdisc Video

Laserdisc video, whether playing on an external monitor or through a video overlay card, is capable of television-like quality. It's this high quality that has set the standard and made it difficult for digital video to replace the laserdisc. When the quality of the video must be the highest possible, as with certain training applications, laserdisc is still an acceptable solution.

Another reason that laserdisc video continues to capture the attention of developers is its ability to perform on a variety of platforms. For example, a laserdisc can be used on both the Macintosh and in the Windows environment without re-digitizing or going through a conversion process. A laserdisc can even be connected to a television. Of course, interactivity is lost when this is done.

In the last few years, several factors have impeded the growth of laserdisc video use. First, MPEG II compression, complimented by faster processor speeds, has come strikingly close to television quality. Additionally, the need to deliver smaller instructional models to an even broader market via the Internet or CD-ROM has forced developers and users alike to compromise their expectations. I predict that within the next year an acceptable balance between technology, price, and quality will be reached.

Recognizing this, I will only spend a brief amount of time dealing with the control of an external video device and will attempt to point out the areas where I believe the technology will still be appropriate.

Introducing the Video Icon

The Video icon, as shown in Figure 24.1, is the tool used to control laserdisc video. Laserdisc video can be viewed either on an external monitor or in the Presentation Window by using a video overlay card.

FIG. 24.1
The Video icon is used to control an external video device.

The Authorware Video icon

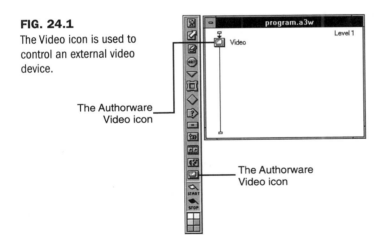

The Authorware Video icon

Like the Digital Movie or Sound icon, the Video icon is used to enhance the Presentation Window by displaying media that has been created external to Authorware. For example, the Video icon is commonly used to play television-quality video to explain a procedure, such as a surgical technique, which requires the high quality image that digital video may not be able to replicate.

When implementing the Video icon into a multimedia piece for purposes such as the example just given, the Video icon can be placed on the Flowline as a response to an interaction, within a decision loop, or in a sequence of icons along the Flowline.

Getting Ready for Video

Before we started authoring, we spent a little time setting up the piece in general using the File Setup dialog box (see "Specifying the Authorware File Setup" in Chapter 2, "Setting Up an Authorware Piece." Likewise, before you spend time using the Video icon, you must set a few general video controls. These controls tell Authorware what hardware will be playing the video, and more specifically, how that video will be controlled.

To set the video controls, open the Video Setup dialog box, as seen in Figure 24.2, by selecting the Video Setup option from the File pull-down menu.

FIG. 24.2
The Video Setup dialog box is used to establish configuration settings used to control external video.

The Windows Video Setup dialog box

The Macintosh Video Setup dialog box

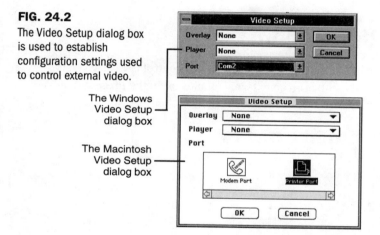

The Video Setup dialog box is used to define which hardware will be used to play the video and through which port Authorware will need to communicate with the video device. It offers three settings (Overlay, Player, and Port). Each of these are described next.

Specifying a Video Overlay

Use a video overlay card whenever you want video to play on the same monitor as your piece. If you are playing video on an external monitor, you will not need to use a video overlay card.

To use a video overlay card, the card, the software to drive the card, and the Authorware drivers to communicate to the card must be properly installed. If all of these items are in place, you should have no problem using video overlay.

NOTE   Each video overlay card has a unique set of drivers to control the video and require-
         ments to install the video card. Refer to the user guide that was included with the
overlay card for specific instructions. ▪

Authorware supports a variety of video cards and drivers. Use the Overlay pop-up list to define which card you are using. Because technologies surrounding laserdisc players continue to evolve, Authorware uses external drivers to create this pop-up list. As new cards and drivers come to market, Macromedia will be able to make the new drivers available without having to upgrade Authorware.

Choosing the Player

Like overlay cards, Authorware supports a variety of laserdisc players. Use the Player pop-up list to define which players will be used by your Authorware piece.

Indicating the Port

You can communicate with a laserdisc player either through the modem port, the printer port (Macintosh), or through a COM port (Windows).

NOTE   If you do not set the Video Setup options, or if the setup options do not match the
         configuration of the end user's system, Authorware will display an error message so
that the new configuration can be specified. This error message occurs both during development
and in the final piece that is distributed to the end user. ▪

Don't Forget the Chroma Key

When using a video overlay card, Authorware requires that you define a certain color, known as the chroma key, through which the video will play. Wherever this color appears in the Presentation Window of the associated Display icon while the video is playing, it will be replaced by the video.

For example, you can create a black background with large bold letters in which you want the video to play. To do this, you would simply set the color of the letters to the chroma key color. Video will play through the letters, but it will not play on the black background.

To set the chroma key, follow these steps:

1. Select the File Setup option from the File pull-down menu to open the File Setup dialog box, as seen in Figure 24.3.

FIG. 24.3

The File Setup dialog box is used for defining the Presentation Window, including which color will be used as the chroma key.

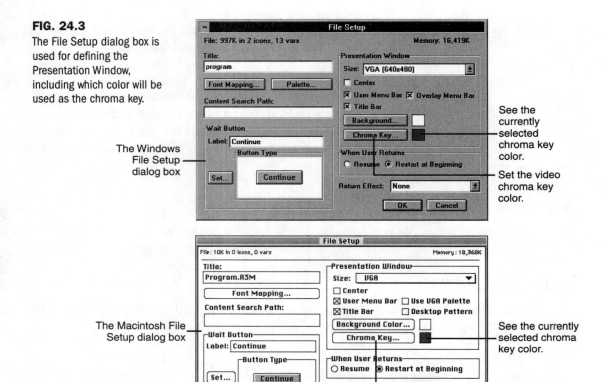

2. Click the Chroma Key button to display the color palette used for your piece, such as the one seen in Figure 24.4.

   When the palette appears, you can identify which color is currently being used as the chroma key by locating the inverse colored "C" (Windows) or the double-box (Macintosh) overlaying one of the colors.

N O T E The default chroma key color is magenta. ■

N O T E You can change the chroma key color while the program is running by using the Authorware function VideoChromaKey. ■

3. Click a new color to change the chroma key setting.

4. Click the OK button, or press the Return (Macintosh) or Enter (Windows) key to save your selection.

FIG. 24.4
The Color palette is used to define the chroma key.

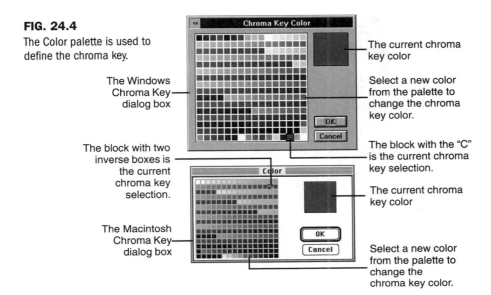

The current chroma key color

The Windows Chroma Key dialog box

Select a new color from the palette to change the chroma key color.

The block with two inverse boxes is the current chroma key selection.

The block with the "C" is the current chroma key selection.

The current chroma key color

The Macintosh Chroma Key dialog box

Select a new color from the palette to change the chroma key color.

Working with the Video Options Dialog Box

You can control the playing of the laserdisc video by implementing variables and functions using Calculation icons or by options that you set within the Video Options dialog box. If you want to control the laserdisc using the Video icon, you must become familiar with the dialog box, as seen in Figure 24.5.

FIG. 24.5
The Video Options dialog box is used to control laserdisc video.

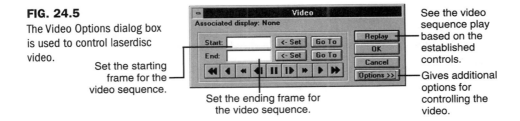

Set the starting frame for the video sequence.

Set the ending frame for the video sequence.

See the video sequence play based on the established controls.

Gives additional options for controlling the video.

To access the Video Options dialog box, double-click the Video icon placed on the Flowline. When the Video Options dialog box opens, it presents the minimum number of options required to play laserdisc video. To display additional options, as seen in Figure 24.6, click the Options button.

 The Options button, once selected, will change to a Collapse button. Click the collapse button to reduce the Video Options dialog box to its original size.

FIG. 24.6
The Extended Video dialog
box provides further options.

> **N O T E**   The Video Options dialog box displays a warning if the configuration defined in the
> Video Setup dialog box does not match the configuration of the system. You can
> bypass this warning to edit the settings in the Video Options dialog box. ▪

Once the Video Options dialog box is open, you can adjust any of the options it contains
before clicking OK to close the dialog box and finish your settings. Each of the options is
described next.

Replay

Click the Replay button to play the video according to the settings that you have specified
in the Video Options dialog box.

Start

In the Start text box, you can enter a value or a variable that will start the video playing at
a specific frame.

End

Use the End text box to enter a value or a variable that will end the video at a specific
frame.

> **N O T E**   You can play video backwards by entering a higher value in the Start field than the
> value in the End field; however, sound will not play. ▪

Set

Click the Set button located next to either the Start field or the End field to enter the value
for the current video frame into the field.

T I P Using the Set button in conjunction with the video controller is much easier than guessing start and end frame values. To do this, simply use the controller to find a starting or ending frame. Once the frame has been identified, click the Set button to place the current frame value into the text box.

Go To

Click the Go To button to skip directly to either the Start or the End frame.

Controller

The Controller portion of the Video Options dialog box is used to play the video during authoring. You can either play the video forward or backward at variable speeds, or you can pause the video. The controller offers several buttons, as shown in Figure 24.7.

Part
V

Ch
24

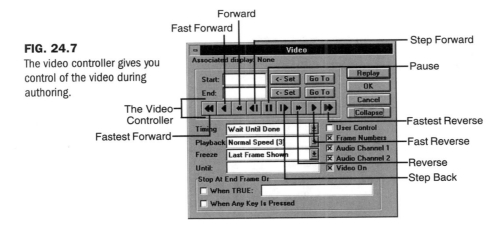

FIG. 24.7
The video controller gives you control of the video during authoring.

Timing

The Timing options for the Video icon function in the same way as the Concurrency options for the Motion or Sound icons. The Timing options are used to determine what the piece will do while the video is playing.

▶ For more information on how the concurrency settings function for the Motion icon, **see** "Setting the Concurrency Options," **p. 178**.

▶ For more information on how the concurrency settings function for the Sound icon, **see** "Concurrency Options," **p. 464**.

■ Wait Until Done—This option causes the video to play completely before the next Authorware icon on the Flowline is executed.

■ Concurrent—Unlike Wait Until Done, Concurrent suggests that as soon as the video begins, the next Authorware icon on the Flowline is executed.

N O T E The default for the Timing option is Wait Until Done. ■

Playback

Use the Playback drop-down list to select the speed at which you want the video to play. This selection is much like the Rate field of a Motion icon or the Frames/Second field of the Digital Movie icon except that you do not specifically set a value. Instead, you select from a pop-up list of speeds as seen in Figure 24.8.

▶ For more information on the Motion icon Rate field, **see** "Understanding the Rate Settings," **p. 176**.

FIG. 24.8
Video can be played forward
or backward at any of the
rates listed in the pop-up
menu.

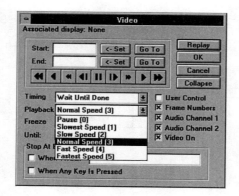

Freeze

The Freeze drop-down list options are used to determine if a video frame will stay in the Presentation Window after the video has stopped playing, and if so, for how long. The Freeze options are as follows:

■ Never—Select this option to remove all video from the Presentation Window when it has stopped playing, or when the controller has been closed.

■ Last Frame Shown—Select this option to leave the last frame shown on the screen. The last frame shown will be the last frame in the sequence if the entire sequence was played, or any frame in the sequence if you closed the control before the sequence was completed.

- End Frame—Select this option to show the frame specified in the End field, whether that was the last frame shown or not. For example, if you closed the controller before the sequence was complete, the piece would jump directly to the end frame.

Until

If a variable or expression is entered in the Until text box in the Video dialog box, the last frame shown according to the Freeze options will remain in the Presentation Window until the condition is TRUE. The video frame can be removed from the Presentation Window if the associated display containing the chroma key is erased, another Video icon is encountered, or the file is exited.

Stop at End Frame Or

These options are used to further control when video will stop playing:

- When TRUE—If the variable or expression that you enter in this field becomes true, whether the video sequence has completely played or not, the video will stop.
- When Any Key Is Pressed—As the title implies, if this selection is made, the video will stop as soon as the end user presses a key.

User Control

If the User Control check box is selected, a Video Controller similar to the one seen in the Video Options dialog box will appear in the Presentation Window. This Controller gives the end user free control of the video. The Controller is movable by the user so that it does not interfere with other content on the screen. It can be closed when the user has finished viewing the video.

NOTE The Controller option is not available with Concurrent Timing. It is only available if the Timing option is Wait Until Done. ■

Frame Numbers

Select the Frame Numbers check box if you want the current frame number to be displayed in the Presentation Window while viewing the video.

Audio Channel 1 and Audio Channel 2

Use these check boxes to turn on and off either of the audio channels.

Part
V

Ch
24

I once used a laserdisc for a training program that was to be distributed in two languages. To make distribution easier, I placed one language in Audio Channel 1, and another language in Audio Channel 2. I then used a Decision icon to determine which Video icon should be encountered; either the one in Audio Channel 1 or the one in Audio Channel 2.

Video On

Check Video On if you want the video image to appear. If you are using the laserdisc for audio only, you will not need to select this option.

N O T E   Sound compression technologies today make the Video On option somewhat obsolete. In many cases, it is worth digitizing the audio rather than fussing with the extra hardware involved with a laserdisc player.   ■

Implementing the Video Icon

Once you have installed the video overlay card and all of its associated software, implementing laserdisc video using the Video icon is not difficult. To set up the Video icon, follow these steps:

1. Select the File Setup option from the File pull-down menu.
2. Click the Chroma Key button to display the color palette. Locate the currently selected chroma key. Select a new chroma key color, or leave the chroma key as the currently selected option.
3. Click the OK button, or press the Return (Macintosh) or Enter (Windows) key to save the chroma key settings.
4. Select the Video Setup option from the File pull-down menu.
5. Set the options that define your hardware configuration.
6. Click the OK button, or press the Return (Macintosh) or Enter (Windows) key to save the Video Setup settings.
7. Drag a Display icon to the Flowline.
8. Open the Display icon and create an object through which the video will be seen. Be sure to color the objects, through which you want video to be displayed, the same color as the chroma key.

N O T E   When you open the color palette to change the color attribute of an object, you will be able to identify the chroma key within the palette by locating the inverse "C" (Windows) or the double-box (Macintosh) overlaying one of the colors.   ■

9. Close the Display icon when you are finished creating the objects through which the video will be displayed.

10. Drag a Video icon to the Flowline. Place the Video icon following the Display icon containing the objects through which the video will be displayed.

11. Double-click the Video icon to open the Video Options dialog box.

12. Click the object in the Display icon through which the video is to be displayed. This selection creates an association between the Display and the Video icons. The name of the associated Display icon appears along the top of the Video Options dialog box.

13. Set the options in the Video Options dialog box required to play the video.

14. Click the OK button when finished setting the video options.

15. Select Run from the Try It pull-down menu to see the piece with video run.

TIP The shortcut keys for Run are ⌘+R (Macintosh) and Ctrl+R (Windows).

TROUBLESHOOTING

How do I avoid the flash of blue that occurs before each video sequence is played? Try calling the first frame of the video sequence that you are going to play prior to encountering the associated Display icon or the Video icon. This prevents a blank screen, or portions of the last video played, to be seen while the laserdisc player is searching for the requested frames. To preset the video, either use the Authorware Video function `VideoSeek`, or place a Video icon that only calls a single frame on the Flowline without an associated Display icon.

Part
V

Ch
24

Becoming Efficient in Development

CHAPTER 25

Controlling Movement Along the Flowline

Fortunately, I joined the computer world just after the era of punch card programming, so I can only imagine the agony and frustration of having to develop something, then having to wait for a long period of time to see how even a slight modification would impact the functionality of the piece.

Multimedia development relies on the precise alignment of animation, the sequencing of interactions, and the choreography of media. The longer it takes to receive feedback regarding the success of programming alterations, the greater the chance that the momentum of creativity will be lost.

With traditional programming, as well as with many authoring tools, there is a great gap between the time a change is made and the first time you get to see the impact of that change. This gap originally existed because of how long it took to compile the code before the piece could be run.

Developing with Start and Stop flags

The Start and Stop flags allow you to control which portion of the Flowline will be executed. This is particularly helpful when you are trying to test the Flowline structure, or when you are searching for a problem.

Placing and moving flags

The Start and Stop flags may be moved onto, or along, the Flowline just like any other icon. Unlike other icons, however, there is only one Start and Stop flag, and the flags may be returned to the Icon palette.

Learning to use the Authorware Trace window

The Authorware Trace window may be used to track which icons are being executed, and the value of variables as they are set. To use the Trace window, you must become familiar with the Step Over feature, the Step Into feature, resetting, and using Pause/Resume.

Interpreting the Trace window information

When the Trace window runs, it produces information including which Flowline level the icon resides on, the type of icon that has been encountered, the title of the icon, and an Enter/Exit message.

With Authorware, this gap is eliminated during authoring because your piece can be run and stopped from any point along the Flowline. In this chapter, we explore how to use the Authorware Start and Stop flags to make development and debugging more efficient. ■

Developing with Start and Stop Flags

Most of the icons in the Icon palette serve some functionality regarding what the end user will see in the Presentation Window. For example, the Display icon is used to place text and graphics in the Presentation Window; the Motion icon is used to animate those objects; and the Sound icon is used to incorporate audio. In each case, the end user's experience will be directly affected by the use of the icon.

Much like the Map icon, however, the Start flag and the Stop flag are not there to serve the end user. Rather, they are there to assist you during authoring. When the piece is completed, the end user will have no idea if, where, or how the flags were used.

▶ To refer to the Icon palette and each of the Authorware icons, **see** "Becoming Familiar with the Icon Palette," **p. 14**.

Introducing the Flags

There are two flags in the Icon palette that may be used during authoring. The first, the Start flag, as seen in Figure 21.1 is used to establish an execution point along the Flowline.

▶ To refer to the introduction of the Start and the Stop flags, **see** "The Start and Stop Flags," **p. 22**.

FIG. 25.1

The piece will begin to execute from the point on the Flowline designated by the Start flag.

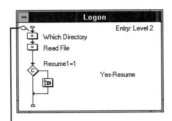

The Start flag designates at which point the piece will begin along the Flowline when the Run from Flag option is selected.

When the Run from Flag command is selected from the Try It menu, the piece will begin at the point designated by the Start flag rather than initiating from the beginning of the Flowline. By using the Start flag, you can continually run a small portion of the piece without having to execute the piece from the beginning each time. This is incredibly helpful if you are working in an area that is buried deep in the piece. If the piece had to be run from the beginning each time an edit was made, large amounts of time would be lost navigating to the point of the change.

CAUTION

In many cases, variables are set at the beginning of a piece, and they are then later used to control another part of the piece for such functions as activating menus or driving Decision icons. (See Chapter 22, "Working with Data.") If you place the Start flag when the piece runs, it will not encounter the location where these variables were set, and the piece will not function as intended. You can, however, use a Calculation icon to temporarily set the value of variables in a location further along the Flowline. Just be sure to delete this icon when you are finished editing.

The second flag available in the Icon palette is the Stop flag. The Stop flag, as seen in Figure 25.2, is used to stop the piece from continuing along the Flowline while authoring.

FIG. 25.2

The piece will stop at the point on the Flowline designated by the Stop flag.

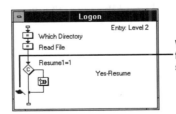

When you are authoring the piece, the Stop flag designates at which point the piece will stop traveling along the Flowline.

When the piece encounters the Stop flag along the Flowline, the piece acts as if you have encountered a Wait icon; however, no interactions are active and no pause button appears.

▶ To understand the characteristics of encountering a Wait icon along the Flowline, **see** "Using the Wait Icon," **p. 157**.

The Stop flag is used like the Start flag to control which part of the Flowline will be executed. I often use this tool to ensure that a certain icon or series of icons is not executed if I'm editing previously executed icons.

For example, I may have an object that is being displayed using the Display icon and is being animated by a Motion icon, which directly follows the Display icon on the Flowline. If I am working to position the object, I do not want the motion to begin until I've had a chance to edit the position of the object. In this case, I would place the Stop flag immediately after the Display icon, so that the piece would pause before the Motion icon was encountered. Then, I could position the object. Once the position of the object has been set, I could either remove the flag and run again, or I could simply choose Proceed from the Try It menu.

 TIP The Wait icon can be used to serve the same function as the Stop flag, and I actually like the Wait icon better—the pause is more obvious because the Pause button is displayed.

The Start flag and the Stop flag are both tools for you to use during authoring. Whether you remove them from the Flowline or not, the flags will be ignored when you create a stand-alone piece for the end user.

Placing, Removing, and Moving Flags

Flags are placed and moved along the Flowline just as any other icon is. The difference, however, is that every other icon is in unlimited supply in the Icon palette. For example, if I drag one Display icon to the Flowline, I can return to the Icon palette and drag another.

There is only one Start flag and one Stop flag available in the Icon palette. Therefore, if I have placed the Start flag or Stop flag on the Flowline, the palette will be empty, as seen in Figure 25.3.

To use the Start flag and Stop flags, follow these steps:

1. Drag the Start flag to the Flowline and place it at the point from where the piece should begin running.

2. Drag the Stop flag to the Flowline and place it at the point at which the piece should pause while authoring.

FIG. 25.3

There is only one Start flag and Stop flag each.

The piece will begin at the Start flag.

The palette is empty if the flags have been used.

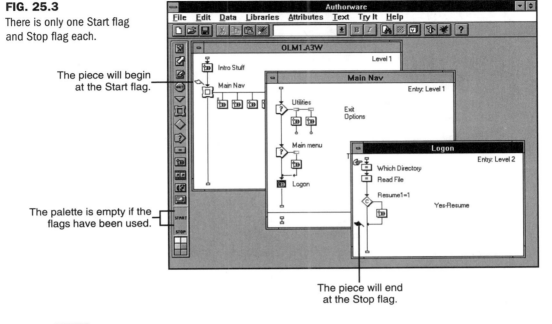

The piece will end at the Stop flag.

N O T E The Start flag and the Stop flag do not have to be used simultaneously. You can use the Start flag to determine the point of execution without determining a stopping point, or you can use the Stop flag to determine the pause point for a piece that was executed from the beginning of the Flowline. ■

3. Choose the Run from Flag command from the Try It menu if the Start flag was used. If the Start flag was not used, choose Run from the Try It menu.

T I P The shortcut key for the Run from Flag option is ⌘+F (Macintosh) or Ctrl+F (Windows). The shortcut key for the Run option is ⌘+R (Macintosh) or Ctrl+R (Windows).

When a piece is executed using the Run from Flag option, the Presentation Window is cleared and all variables are set to their initial value, just as if the piece were being run from the beginning of the Flowline.

4. When the Stop flag is encountered, you can either return to the Flowline for further editing or make edits to the Presentation Window. In either case, you can choose the Proceed command from the Try It menu to continue past the Stop flag once the edits are done.

Part
VI

Ch
25

> **T I P** The shortcut key for the both the Pause and the Proceed option is ⌘+P (Macintosh) or Ctrl+P (Windows).

To remove a flag from the Flowline, you can either drag it back to its position in the Icon palette, or simply click the empty location in the Icon palette and the Flag will return.

To move a flag from one position on the Flowline to another, you can either drag the flag to the new location, or first return the flag to the Icon palette, then place the flag on the Flowline.

Debugging with the Flags

One of my favorite uses for the flags is debugging. Often I find that the flow of the piece has traveled along the Flowline in a way different from how I might have expected, or that objects in the Presentation Window are not behaving as I have anticipated. When this occurs, I use the flags to help isolate the problem.

For example, I can place a Stop flag, as shown in Figure 25.4, along the Flowline to stop the piece before certain icons are reached. I can then place a Start flag in front of the sequence and run the piece from the flag.

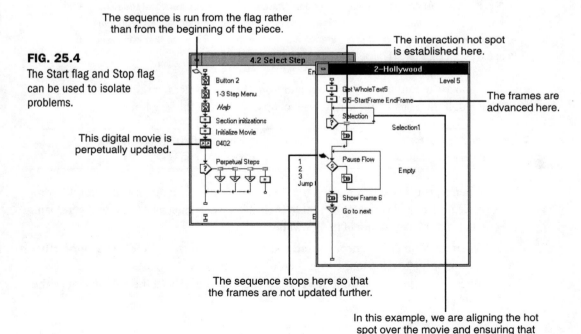

The sequence is run from the flag rather than from the beginning of the piece.

The interaction hot spot is established here.

FIG. 25.4
The Start flag and Stop flag can be used to isolate problems.

The frames are advanced here.

This digital movie is perpetually updated.

The sequence stops here so that the frames are not updated further.

In this example, we are aligning the hot spot over the movie and ensuring that the frames advanced appropriately.

If the piece encounters the Stop flag without error, I can begin to isolate the problem. In any case, I now know the path that the piece took in order to get to the flag.

Using the Trace Window

Throughout this book you have explored the benefit of the Flowline and the flowchart metaphor used by Authorware. As you have seen, development under this metaphor allows you to visually track the sequence of interactivity and branching. The result of using such a metaphor is more efficient development and aid in error-free creation.

Unfortunately, more sophisticated pieces begin to depart from the flowchart metaphor, as well as employing complex branching schemes that make it difficult to track the progress of the piece. For this reason, Authorware contains a feature known as the Trace window, which makes debugging easier.

Introducing the Trace Window

The Trace window, as seen in Figure 25.5, is used to display information about each icon as it is encountered by Authorware. This is particularly helpful if the icons are presented in a unique order because your piece contains several Navigate icons, or if the icons are executed faster than the eye can interpret.

To display the Trace window, choose the Trace command from the Try It menu, or click the button on the tool bar that looks like a little bug.

T I P The shortcut key for Trace is ⌘+T (Macintosh) or Ctrl+T (Windows).

FIG. 25.5
The Trace window is used to track the progress of Authorware along the Flowline.

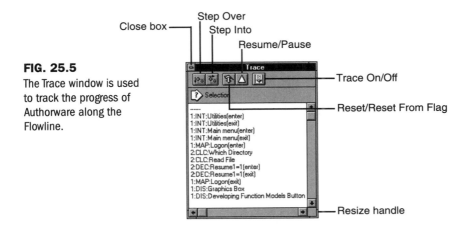

Close box

Step Over
Step Into
Resume/Pause

Trace On/Off

Reset/Reset From Flag

Resize handle

When the Trace window is activated, it appears as a floating window within the Presentation Window. The Trace window can be positioned by dragging the title bar or resized by dragging the lower right-hand corner of the window.

As you are tracing the Authorware piece along the Flowline, icons such as Wait icons, framework or interaction loops (which would require the interaction of the end user) will be encountered. When this happens, the trace will pause until you interact with the piece, just as the end user would, at which point the trace proceeds.

Along the top of the floating Trace window are five buttons, each of which is described next.

Using Step Over Tracing   Clicking the Step Over button, or choosing Step Over from the Try It menu, is used to conduct the highest-level problem-solving.

 The shortcut key for Step Over is ⌘+; (semicolon) (Macintosh) or Ctrl+; (semicolon) (Windows).

In essence, Step Over requires the piece to execute everything contained in Map icons or branching structures all at once, rather than icon by icon. When using the Step Over function, only the picture of the Map icon is shown, and the scrolling list contains the name of the Map icon and a note that the Map icon had been entered or exited.

When using this function, you should watch the Trace window to see that the name of the icons that should have been encountered were. If names of icons found along the wrong portion of the Flowline are shown in the Trace window, you know that the piece has made a wrong turn somewhere along the way.

 The Step Over function is most helpful when you are trying to narrow in on a problem, but not trying to pinpoint it directly.

Using Step Into Tracing   Clicking the Step Into button, or choosing Step Into from the Try It menu, is used to conduct problem-solving at a level much more precise than using the Step Over function.

When using this function, watch the Trace window to see that the name of each icon that has been encountered is situated along the portion of the Flowline that you intended the piece to follow. If the names of icons found along the wrong portion of the Flowline are shown in the Trace window, you know that the piece has made a wrong turn somewhere along the way.

The shortcut key for Step Into is ⌘+' (apostrophe) (Macintosh) or Ctrl+' (apostrophe) (Windows).

Step Into, like running the piece normally, requires Authorware to execute every icon it encounters; however, the icons are executed one at a time as you elect to proceed by pressing the proceed button located along the top of the Trace window. When using the Step Into function, the picture of each icon is shown as it is about to be executed.

 The Step Into function is most helpful when you are trying to pinpoint a problem.

Using Reset   Click the Reset button to reset the trace; that is, to clear the Trace window and start over. The Reset option may be one of two buttons and performs one of two functions:

■ Reset—If you are not using the Start flag, the Reset button starts a new trace from the beginning of the Flowline. You can also choose Run from the Try It menu to reset the trace.

 The shortcut key for Run is ⌘+R (Macintosh) or Ctrl+R (Windows).

■ Reset from Flag—If the Start flag has been placed on the Flowline, the Reset button will reset the trace and start a new trace from the point of the Start flag. You can also choose Run from Flag from the Try It menu.

 The shortcut key for Run from Flag is ⌘+F (Macintosh) or Ctrl+F (Windows).

 Using the Start flag and the Stop flag to control the region of the Flowline for which you are conducting the trace is extremely efficient. Use the Start flag and Stop flag when tracing just as you would when editing a small portion of the piece.

Resume/Pause   The Resume/Pause button toggles between the following functions:

■ Resume—Click this button, or choose Proceed from the Try It menu, to start running the piece either from the beginning or from the Start flag, or to resume tracing if it has been paused. If the Stop flag is encountered or the Pause button is clicked, the piece and tracing will pause.

 The shortcut key for Proceed is ⌘+P (Macintosh) or Ctrl+P (Windows).

Part
VI

Ch
25

■ Pause—Click the Pause button, or select Pause from the Try It pull-down menu, to stop tracing momentarily when the piece is running. Running can also be paused if the Stop flag has been encountered.

 T I P   The shortcut key for Pause is ⌘+P (Macintosh) or Ctrl+P (Windows).

Trace On/Off   The Trace On/Off button is used to turn the display of trace information on and off, even though the tracing continues.

While you may be interested in the trace information for only a certain section of the piece and may therefore opt to turn off the trace information, I suggest that you leave this option on. More information is usually better, and since performance is not affected, you might as well let the trace information be displayed.

Understanding Trace Window Information

Located just under the five buttons along the top of the Trace window is a picture representing the icon that is about to be executed, including its name. When you are tracing in Step Over mode, these pictures are going by as fast as Authorware can encounter them. If you are tracing in Step Into mode, however, the pictures are presented one at a time.

As the piece runs and each icon is encountered by Authorware, detailed information about each icon is displayed as a line in the scrolling list within the Trace window. Pieces of information separated by colons comprise the line.

Recognizing the Flowline Level   The first piece of information shown on a line in the Trace window is a number representing the Flowline level in which the icon resides. Flowline levels are created when icons are grouped together within a Map icon. The initial Flowline level is 1. If a Map icon is placed at level one, the Flowline within that Map icon is level 2, and so on.

▶ For more information on Flowline levels and using the Map icon, **see** "Introducing the Map Icon," **p. 195**.

Identifying the Icon Type   The second piece of information contained within the Trace window is an abbreviation representing the type of icon encountered. The icon types include each of the icons found in the Icon palette except for the Start and Stop flags.

Icon Type	Abbreviation
Display	DIS
Motion	MTN
Erase	ERS

Icon Type	Abbreviation
Wait	WAT
Navigate	NAV
Framework	FRM
Decision	DES
Interaction	INT
Calculation	CLC
Map	MAP
Digital Movie	MOV
Sound	SND
Analog Video	VDO

Using the Icon Title   The third piece of information (after the second colon) making up the line in the Trace window is the title of the icon encountered. In Chapter 8, "Organizing Authorware Logic on the Flowline," I discussed the importance of naming icons descriptively. The name of the icon is not only helpful when trying to interpret the Flowline, but also when using the Trace window. By giving each icon a unique description, you will be able to more efficiently use the Trace window.

Interpreting the Enter/Exit Message   If the trace was conducted in Step Over mode, a fourth piece of information appears in parentheses in the line shown in the Trace window. This information indicates that the Map icon, or branch, was either entered or exited.

Using the Trace Window to Track Variables

The Trace window is not only used to trace where Authorware is traveling along the Flowline; it can also be used to trace the value assigned to a variable. The tracing of variables is a much more complicated process than tracing icons. However, in the more complex pieces it is typically an incorrect value assigned to a variable that causes the largest problems.

To illustrate how the Trace window can be used to track variables, let's look at a very simple example, as shown in Figure 25.6, which incorporates three perpetual pull-down menus set to Exit Interaction branching.

▶ For step-by-step instructions on creating pull-down menus, **see** "Creating Pull-down Menus," **p. 266**.

▶ For guidance on using perpetual menus, **see** "Using Perpetual Interactions," **p. 230**.

Part
VI

Ch
25

FIG. 25.6

The Trace window can be used to trace variables as they change throughout the piece.

All three pull-down menu responses are set to Perpetual.

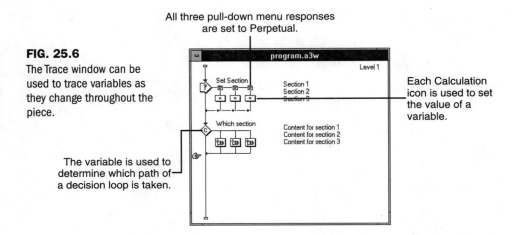

Each Calculation icon is used to set the value of a variable.

The variable is used to determine which path of a decision loop is taken.

Each of the branches of the interaction loop contains a Calculation icon, and in the Calculation icon the custom variable Section is set to a value representing which path of the decision loop should be taken, as seen in Figure 25.7.

▶ To refer to an introduction of the Calculation icon, **see** "The Calculation Icon," **p. 19**.

▶ For guidance on creating variables, **see** "Exploring Variables," **p. 373**.

FIG. 25.7

Custom variables or Authorware variables can be traced.

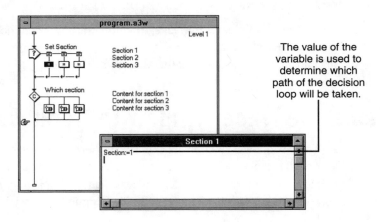

The value of the variable is used to determine which path of the decision loop will be taken.

Below the interaction loop is a Calculated Path decision loop with three branches. The decision as to which path is taken is based on the value of Section, as seen in Figure 25.8.

▶ For more information on using To Calculated Path decisions, **see** "Defining a To Calculated Path Decision," **p. 338**.

FIG. 25.8
The Trace window tracks the value of the custom variable used to drive the Decision icon.

The variable Section is used to determine which path of the decision loop is taken.

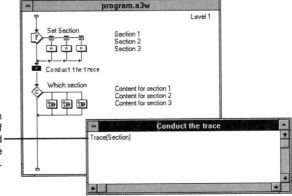

If you want to use the Trace window to track the value of Section before a branch of the decision loop is selected, follow these steps:

1. Place a Calculation icon just above the decision loop. Title the Calculation icon so that you know what the purpose of the icon is. I named my Calculation icon "Conduct the trace."

2. Double-click the newly added Calculation icon to display its window. Enter the Authorware Trace function as shown in Figure 25.9.

   ▶ For guidance using functions, **see** "Exploring Functions," **p. 383**.

Part
VI

Ch
25

FIG. 25.9
The Authorware Trace function can be used to track the value of a variable.

The Trace function displays the value of the variable enclosed in parentheses in the Trace window.

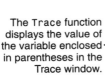

3. Choose Trace from the Try It menu.

TIP The shortcut key for Trace is ⌘+T (Macintosh) or Ctrl+T (Windows).

4. Click the Step Into button. The Trace window will register that the Interaction icon was entered and exited, then the piece will pause at the Calculation icon, right above the decision loop.

5. Click the Step Into button again. The Trace window will place two hyphens followed by the current value for Section in the trace list, as seen in Figure 25.10. It will also place a line detailing the Calculation icon in the Trace window.

FIG. 25.10

When the Trace function is encountered, it places two hyphens in the list, followed by the value of the variable.

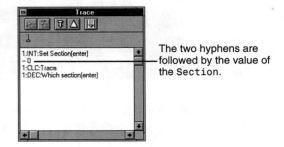

The two hyphens are followed by the value of the Section.

6. Click the Proceed button to continue running the piece.

7. Click the button associated with the interaction loop. The Trace window will register the Calculation icon used to create the response.

The Trace window will also register the value of the variable Section again, as seen in Figure 25.11.

FIG. 25.11

When the Trace function is encountered this time, the value of Section has changed.

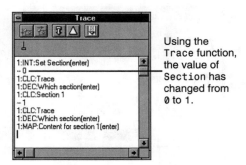

Using the Trace function, the value of Section has changed from 0 to 1.

8. Continue using the Step Into and Step Over buttons to see the effect they have on the Trace window.

If you are tracing only a single variable, the Trace function is very helpful. Unfortunately, I often find the need to track more than one variable. To do this, you must insert the Trace function as many times as you have variables to trace, or you must create a string by patching the variables together. In either case, you must remember the order in which the trace is being registered, since the name of the variable or variables is not displayed in the Trace window.

Another way to trace the value of variables is to embed the variable names into a Display icon using the following steps:

1. Insert a Display icon along the Flowline at the point from which you will execute the piece. If you will run the piece from the beginning, then place the Display icon at the top of the Flowline. If you are running from a flag, however, place the Display icon right below the flag.

2. Open the Display icon and embed the variables you want to monitor as seen in Figure 25.12.

   ▶ To see an overview of placing embedded text in the Presentation Window, **see** "Embedding Data in the Presentation Window," **p. 434**.

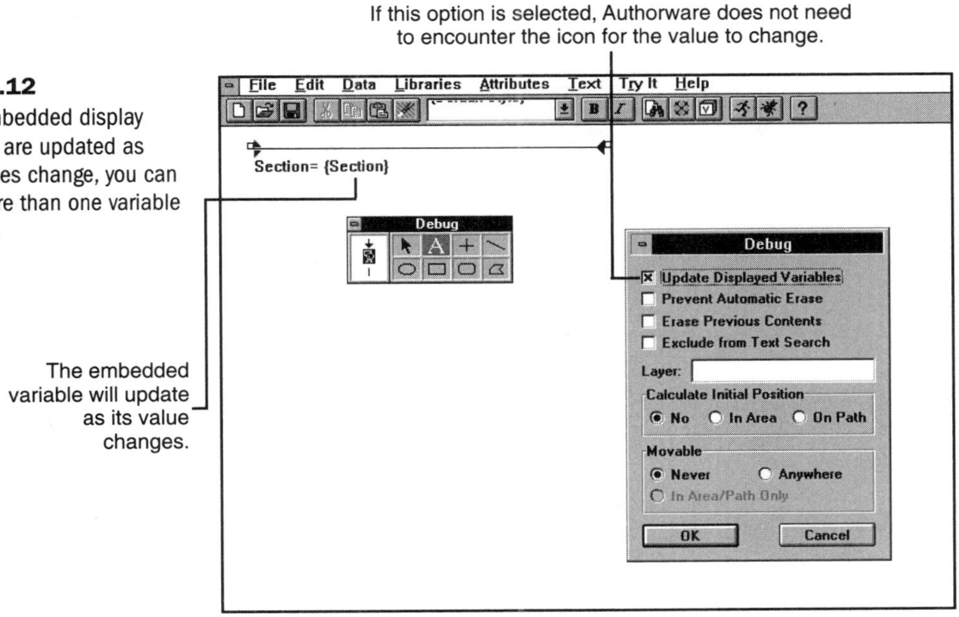

FIG. 25.12
When embedded display variables are updated as their values change, you can track more than one variable by name.

The embedded variable will update as its value changes.

If this option is selected, Authorware does not need to encounter the icon for the value to change.

3. Choose the Effects command from the Attributes menu. The name that appears across the top of the Effects dialog box is based on the title you gave the display icon. I named the Display icon "Debug" so I could recognize it along the Flowline.

TIP The shortcut key for the Effects attribute is ⌘+E (Macintosh) or Ctrl+E (Windows).

4. Select the Update Displayed Variables option. As the value of the variables change, their display values will also change.

Using a Display icon rather than the Trace window allows you to track more than one variable by name, rather than having to remember the order in which the variables are being tracked. ●

CHAPTER 26

Building Models

We have Eli Whitney to either thank (or to blame) for the notion of reusable components. As he perfected the manufacturing of products that used mass produced components, pioneers of the industrial revolution quickly adopted the concept in an attempt to shorten production time and, therefore, produce a standard product more cost effectively.

Unfortunately, many developers of interactive learning applications approach the creation of instruction similarly. They construct a series of standards, or models, into which all content is molded. They then take this cookie cutter of sorts and begin mass producing instruction. The result, as you may imagine, is typically a standard product that—although it may serve the purpose from an instructional perspective—does not take full advantage of the computer as either an interactive or a teaching tool. Additionally, these products commonly have the look and feel of a mass-produced, generic application.

I am happy to say that not all organizations follow this limited view of using models. Last year, for example, one of my clients announced that they were producing four times as much training as two years previously. The amazing part of the story, however, was that they

Implementing models

Models are used to make the development of the Flowline structure more efficient. Before undertaking the development of a model, you should consider the scope of the development and the application of the model.

Working with models

Authorware provides a series of pull-down menus that allow you to quickly create, load, paste, and unload models.

Modifying the default framework

The structure of the Framework icon is based on a model that is provided by Macromedia. Using model development techniques, you can customize the default framework model as needed.

Models can be implemented for a variety of uses

While the list is not all-inclusive, I have found models to be extremely helpful in the creation of logon and startup sequences, navigation schemes, complex interaction and branching scenarios, and the development of test questions.

were achieving this result without increasing their annual budget, and each product had a unique look and feel.

In this chapter, I will focus on how to create Authorware pieces more efficiently—without jeopardizing creativity and quality—by using models. Additionally, I will explore ideas for communicating within a development team. ■

Implementing Models

It is often said that you can work hard or you can work smart. Learning what the icons do, becoming proficient in creating Flowline structures, and even becoming fluent in variables and functions are all valuable. But until you learn to take advantage of models, you will only be working hard—not smart. Working smart involves being able to recognize patterns; that is, how one Authorware structure can be used again somewhere else with either no editing or just enough editing to make the structure or the display objects fit the new location.

A *model* is simply a series of icons on the Flowline that are saved to be used in later development efforts. The model can be a single icon or hundreds of nested icons. In any case, a model is built around functionality—what the icons do—and not the content of the icons.

 Because models are created around functionality and not content, I often replace the content of a model with placeholder text and graphics. This helps limit its size and prevents me from being influenced by its original purpose.

There are two key issues that guarantee the success of using models: scope and application. Each of these is discussed next.

Defining the Scope

The scope or size of the model, as well as its complexity, must be considered before the model is created. You need to avoid the following circumstances, which would make the model less useful than it otherwise could be:

- *The model is too big.* If the model is so large or complex that it takes hours to figure out how to modify it at its new position on the Flowline, then using the model will not be efficient.

  For example, I once had a member of my team who loved to create models. Every model he created, however, was designed to be the end-all model. Although those of us on the team understood what he was doing, there was massive confusion whenever the client tried to take his work and complete it. In most cases, it was easier to rebuild the piece so that it could be explained to the client rather than try to work with his structure.

N O T E The size or number of icons is not necessarily what makes a model unruly. It is the complexity of the structure as it relates to branching and data collection that makes a model unmanageable.

- *The structure is too small.* On the other hand, if the model is so small that it is just as easy to create the Flowline structure from scratch, then there is no need for a model. For example, if the model is a single Wait icon or an interaction with one or two responses that will not be used very often, it may not be worth creating a model.
  - ▶ For an introduction to the Wait icon, **see** "The Wait Icon," **p. 17**.
  - ▶ For guidance on building an interaction, **see** "Building an Interaction Loop," **p. 215**.

T I P If the model is small or even simple in form, it may be easier to copy the Flowline structure to the Clipboard and paste it into the application rather than create a model.

Determining the Application

The second issue that drives the overall success of your piece is the priority that models are given in the design and development phases. That is, you need to consider how a model will be applied in real applications as you're developing the model. The following are a couple of potential scenarios:

Part **VI**

Ch **26**

■ *Create the model first.* In recent years, there have been several companies that have come forward to sell the "ultimate" shell for implementing content. Such shells, consisting of Authorware models, are used to hold content no matter what it is.

When creating interactive learning using this approach, the highest priority is given to the model, with the lower priority given to the need of the user or the uniqueness of the content. The content will be shaped to fit the model.

The result is content that has no life. It does not take advantage of the technology as a teaching tool, so the end user quickly loses interest. Just imagine if everyone had to dress the same; if every house was the same style; and if every movie we watched had the same story line. Sure, the information in the piece and from one piece to another differs; but overall, the structure and actions by the end user would be the same.

■ *Develop the content first.* In contrast to the model-first approach, I encourage you to start with the content. Ask such questions as, "What am I trying to communicate? What can the user do to better understand the concept? How can I use the computer to create a dialog with the end user?"

Through this kind of questioning you, will discover interactivity—interactivity that matches the instructional goal. Once you have discovered how the content should be delivered, then look into your bag of tricks to see if there is anything that you can take advantage of to accomplish your goal and assist in the rapid creation of the Flowline structure. If there is, then you win in the game of using models. If there is not, then don't force another model into place or redesign the content. Build the required structure with its unique functionality, and when finished, make a model of it for next time (if appropriate).

▶ To see how models may fit into the development process, **see** "The New Phases of Multimedia Development," **p. 561**.

▶ For guidance in how to implement true interactivity, **see** "Defining Interactivity," **p. 536**.

Creating a Model

Creating a model is a fairly simple process and one that will save you countless hours of repetitive development. To create a model, perform the following steps:

1. Begin to create your multimedia piece by dragging icons to the Flowline. Once you have created a Flowline structure that you feel could be used as a model, or you have determined that something you have built in the past could be used as a model for what you need next, then stop development.

2. Select the icons on the Flowline, or a portion of the Flowline, that you want for the model. You can either place a marquee around the icons on the Flowline, as shown in Figure 26.1, or you can select them one by one by holding down the Shift key as you click each icon.

▶ For more information on selecting icons on the Flowline, **see** "Grouping and Ungrouping," **p. 197**.

Click here and then drag to
create the marquee.

FIG. 26.1

Select the group of icons
that will become the model.

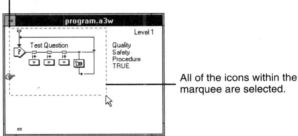

All of the icons within the
marquee are selected.

3. Choose the Create Model command from the Libraries menu.

4. When the Model Description dialog box appears, as shown in Figure 26.2, enter a brief description of the model you are creating.

FIG. 26.2

This description will also
appear in the Authorware
Paste Model pull-down menu
option submenu when it has
been created.

Enter the description
of the model here.

 The model description can be 31 characters long, so be as descriptive as possible. This will make it easier to apply the model in the future.

5. Once you have entered a description, click OK or press the Return (Macintosh) or Enter key (Windows).

N O T E If the model you are creating contains a custom variable stored in a Calculation icon, an icon ornament, or a special field or is embedded in the display, Authorware will present the Variables Used in Model dialog box shown in Figure 26.3. This dialog box enables you to select which variables are to be renamed if you are applying the model to an application that uses the same variable name. ▪

FIG. 26.3

Select the variables to rename before pasting the model into an application.

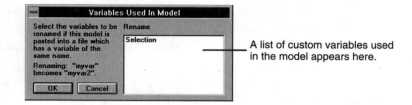

A list of custom variables used in the model appears here.

6. When the Model Description dialog box closes, the Create New Model dialog box appears, as shown in Figure 26.4. Use this dialog box to name, locate, and save the model just as you first saved the piece.

N O T E The name of the model does not have to be the same as the description. ▪

FIG. 26.4

Name, locate, and save the model using the Create New Model dialog box.

Models should be saved using the .MOD extension to accommodate cross-platform development.

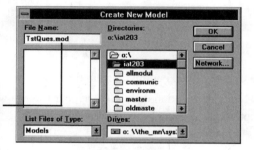

 I have found it helpful to create a central location, or repository, for all of the models my team has created as well as to provide a README document that describes each model. When I am in need of a functionality, I first check the repository for a model that closely meets my requirements. If one exists, I use it; if not, I create a new model for future use.

CAUTION

Be sure to include the .MOD extension when naming a model. This not only helps identify the file as a model, but it enables cross-platform development to go much smoother. Additionally, following the DOS standard of eight characters plus a three letter extension will make cross-platform development more efficient.

7. Once you have named the model and set a location to which it will be saved, click the OK button or press the Return (Macintosh) or Enter (Windows).

When a model is created, a copy of the icons that you have selected are stored in a file external to the Authorware piece. Additionally, a link to the model file is created from the

Authorware application. The description of the model then appears in the Paste Model pull-down menu option.

Using a Model

Once a model has been created, either by you or by someone else, it can be used in the development of your piece. To use a model, it must be loaded into Authorware and then pasted into your piece.

Loading a Model

Because models are stored external to the Authorware application, you can share them with other developers on your team as well as with developers outside of your organization. Over the past few years, several organizations have focused on creating and selling Authorware models.

To use a model, it must first be *loaded* into Authorware. That is, a link must be created between the model and your copy of Authorware. If you created the model, then this link already exists.

To load a model that someone else created and that you have copies of on your hard disk, perform the following steps:

1. Choose the Load Model command from the Libraries menu.
2. When the Load Model dialog box appears, as shown in Figure 26.5, locate the model that you intend to load using the pop-up menu and scrolling list. Once the model you want to load is highlighted, click Open.

Part
VI
Ch
26

FIG. 26.5
Use the Load Model dialog box to locate the model that will be loaded into Authorware.

Models search for .MOD extension by default.

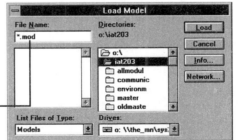

As soon as the model is loaded, a link is drawn between Authorware and the external icons contained in the model.

N O T E   Models created on one platform can be loaded on another platform.

Pasting a Model

After a model has been created or loaded, it can be used to enhance development efficiency. To paste a model onto the Flowline for the piece you're currently working on, perform the following steps:

1. Click the Flowline at the point where you want to paste the icons contained in the model. The Paste pointer—the little hand shown in Figure 26.6—appears on the Flowline where the model is to be pasted.

FIG. 26.6
The Paste pointer indicates where the icons will be pasted.

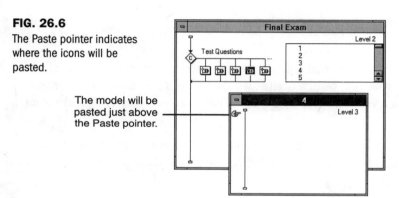

The model will be pasted just above the Paste pointer.

> **N O T E** If you are pasting the model as a branch for an Interaction, Decision, or Framework icon, and the model comprises more than one icon, Authorware will automatically create a Map icon into which the model will be pasted. Authorware will also create a Map icon if the model contains an Interaction, Decision, or Framework icon and is being pasted as a branch. ■

2. Choose the Paste Model option from the Libraries pull-down menu; then select the model to be pasted from the submenu.

Once a model has been pasted onto the Flowline, its icons or contents can be edited.

Unloading a Model

As you create or load more and more models, the list of models within Authorware may become unmanageable. To limit the number of models in the Paste Model list, Authorware provides the capability to *unload* a model. When a model is unloaded, it is not deleted from the repository. Rather, it is removed from the list within Authorware. You can reload the model again if needed. To unload a model, perform the following steps:

1. Choose the Unload Model command from the Libraries menu to display the Unload Model dialog box, as shown in Figure 26.7.

FIG. 26.7
A model can be unloaded from Authorware using the Unload Model dialog box.

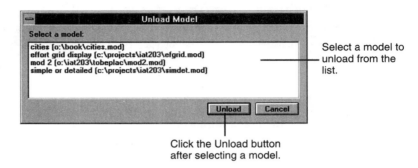

Select a model to unload from the list.

Click the Unload button after selecting a model.

2. Select the name of the model that you want to unload.

3. Click the Unload button, and the name of the model will no longer appear in the list.

N O T E   Only one model can be unloaded at a time. ▪

Changing the Default Framework Model

Part
VI

Ch
26

In Chapter 15, "Building Interactive Documents," I discussed using the Framework icon for creating electronic documents, hyperlinking, and navigation. As a Framework icon is placed on the Flowline, a background graphic on which eight buttons lie—as well as the functionality of the eight navigation buttons—is automatically created. These elements are actually stored externally as a model.

▶ For an introduction to the Framework icon, **see** "The Framework Icon," **p. 18**.

▶ For guidance on using the Framework icon, **see** "Understanding Frameworks," **p. 294**.

Just as you can modify a model that you created, you can also modify the model that is used for the Framework icon. You may want to do this if the default controls or interface do not match the requirements of your piece. For example, I recently completed a project that used the Framework icon extensively. The navigation features that I required (Next, Previous, and a custom search function) did not match those provided by the default framework model.

So that I would not have to modify the default model each time or create my own model that would be added to the Paste Model list, I modified the default Framework icon controls. To change the default Framework icon model, perform the following steps:

1. Drag a Framework icon to the Flowline.

> **CAUTION**
>
> Make a backup copy of the framework model file in the same directory in which Authorware was installed so that it is not lost when you create the new default Framework icon model.

2. Open the Framework icon and edit the framework controls as necessary. You can also add icons to the entry pane, such as Sound icons or highlights.

3. Close the Framework icon.

4. Select the Framework icon and create a model with it following the steps listed in the "Creating a Model," section earlier in this chapter. When naming the model, you must apply a specific name in order for Authorware to locate the model later. On the Macintosh, the file name must be Default Framework Icon, and in Windows it must be framewrk.mod.

5. Choose to replace the existing model when the Authorware Warning dialog box is displayed.

From this point, you can use the custom default Framework icon model each time a Framework icon is brought to the Flowline.

Understanding When to Work with Models

Models are most efficiently used for functionality that is implemented repeatedly throughout a piece or across a variety of pieces. The rest of this section lists opportunities that I have found for creating models. Although the list is by no means exhaustive, I hope that it prompts you to recognize other opportunities for using models.

Logon and Startup Sequences

One of the best opportunities for using a model is for a functionality that seems to make its way into the design of more than one piece or that will be used across several pieces.

For example, we started a series of CD-ROMs for Oracle Corporation. As a requirement, each CD-ROM had to have a logon process. Obviously, we were not going to start from scratch for each CD-ROM in the series; rather, we created a model that could simply be pasted into the beginning of each piece.

After creating this functionality for one client, we quickly found that this was a functionality that other clients were considering. Because we had created it already, it was easy for us to implement the solution for them as well.

Navigation Schemes

A navigation scheme is the main avenue used to move from one part of a piece to another. For example, you might place a button somewhere on the screen that directs the user to a list of topics, or you may have icons continuously available in the Presentation Window for selecting topics.

Over the last eight years of developing interactive learning, I have discovered that there are really only a few forms that a navigation scheme can take for functionality. (Let me clarify that I believe there are an infinite number of graphical interfaces that can be applied to the navigation scheme.)

To expedite the development of prototypes, I have created a general navigation model that employs the functionality of those navigation schemes. When development begins, I simply paste the model and begin with content rather than start from the first icon each time.

Complex Interactions and Branching

As Authorware structures become more interactive, they also become more complex. For example, I have created a model that—based on concepts of adaptive learning—can ensure mastery of the content that it contains. To do this, the piece must keep track of a great deal of information about how the user is progressing with each learning objective, as well as what learning objectives are taught by each part of the piece.

Although this is certainly a powerful tool for instruction, I would not want to re-create it each time it was needed. For this reason, I created a model that simply adds the interactions to a shell that already contains the functionality of record keeping.

Part

VI

Ch

26

Test Questions and Interactions

Questions, whether used for scoring or not, are one of the most common structures within an Authorware piece. Multiple choice questions using hot spot or button responses; challenges to arrange a variety of items; or even interactions that enable the user to explore a matrix of information are commonly the groundwork for the majority of a piece. If you find yourself creating a structure repeatedly, then you have discovered an opportunity to create and implement a model.

Working in a Development Team

I also use the model feature of Authorware to enable several developers to work on the same piece at one time. As sections of the piece are completed, they are saved as models that I load into my copy of Authorware; then paste directly into the master version of the piece.

Alternatively, each person would have to copy the Flowline structure for the section, close his copy of the piece, open a new piece, and paste the copied Flowline structure. I would then have to close the master version of the piece, open the new file, copy the Flowline structure, close the new file, open the master version of the piece, and finally paste the new Flowline structure. All of the opening and closing of files is avoided by using models. ●

CHAPTER 27

Working with Libraries

If one rumor about multimedia is true, it is the fact that multimedia pieces are big in terms of file size. Graphics, digital video, and audio each requires a great amount of disk space, and when these media are combined to create multimedia, the requirement can be even greater.

To account for growing file sizes, the rule has always been to *get twice as much storage space as you can imagine using.* When I started developing multimedia, I followed this principle and doubled my investment to get the never-to-be-filled 40M hard drive. It was full within the year.

Today we are creating multi-volume sets of CD-ROMs to hold single multimedia pieces. As the technology providers promise double-sided, double-density CD-ROMs capable of holding up to 12G, however, we once again wonder what we would ever do with that much space.

What is a library?

Libraries are external files that contain content resources such as graphics and sound. Rather than storing multiple copies of a content element in the piece, you can create a library, then establish links to the content in the library.

Working with libraries

Authorware provides an efficient means for creating a new library, opening existing libraries, using multiple libraries with a single piece, placing icons in the library, or organizing contents of the library.

Editing library icons

Library icons can be edited just like an icon along the Flowline, however, the changes will be seen wherever that icon has been linked to the Flowline.

Working with the Library window

The Library window can be customized to make development more efficient by using the read/write status button, sorting the icons, using the condense/expand button to create notes, or arranging the icons in ascending or descending order.

Although compression techniques can be used to reduce file size, the careful use of media within a piece created with Authorware is the key to size control. In this chapter, you learn how to utilize the Authorware Library for the storage of media, which not only helps to reduce overall file size, but makes the maintenance and organization of the media more efficient. ■

Using Libraries

Just as models are used to make development more efficient, libraries are designed to make the organization of content more efficient and the size of the multimedia piece smaller. For example, if a single piece of content, such as a sound or large graphic, is used several times within your piece, the size of the piece can become quite large. In such a case, you may consider using a library.

▶ To refer to how models are used to make development more efficient, **see** "Implementing Models," **p. 506**.

What Is a Library?

A *library* is a file, external to your piece, in which individual icons containing content can be stored. Rather than placing the content in an icon along the Flowline, the content can be placed in an icon within the library. Whenever you need for that content to occur within the piece, you can link the icon containing the content to your piece.

N O T E Icons that can be placed in a library and linked to a piece include the Display icon, Interaction icon, Navigate icon, Calculation icon, Digital Movie icon, and the Sound icon. ∎

For example, if you have created a graphic, such as a logo, that will be used throughout the piece, you can place that graphic inside a Display icon within the library rather than in a Display icon directly on the Flowline. As you require the use of that graphic, simply drag the Display icon containing the logo to the Flowline from the library instead of bringing a new Display icon to the Flowline. The result would be a single copy of the large graphic within the library and several links to it, as opposed to multiple copies of the large graphic located directly within the piece.

Since libraries are external to the Authorware piece, you must be sure that they are distributed along with the final piece. For distribution, the libraries can either be included as a part of the executable piece or left as separate files. If they are left as separate files, they must be installed in the student records directory, in the same directory as your final piece, or in an area specified in the Content Search Path text box within the File Setup dialog box.

▶ To refer to the requirements of the Content Search Path, **see** "Content Search Path," **p. 48**.

How Are Links Created?

If a piece contains an icon that has been placed on the Flowline from the library, or an icon has been moved from the Flowline to the library, the piece and the library become *linked*, and the icon that references the library is called a *linked icon*.

When a link is created, Authorware leaves the original icon in the library and places a duplicate, or linked icon, on the Flowline. The duplicate, however, does not act like a copy, but like a reference, or alias, to the original. When the piece encounters the linked icon, the piece acts just as if it had encountered a normal icon.

How Do I Use Linked Icons on the Flowline?

The Flowline for your piece can be constructed using icons from the Icon palette as well as icons from the library. When an icon from the library is used, it appears on the Flowline with an italicized label, as shown in Figure 27.1, and the original icon—which remains in the library—is marked with a link symbol.

FIG. 27.1

The Flowline structure can consist of both normal icons and icons linked to a library.

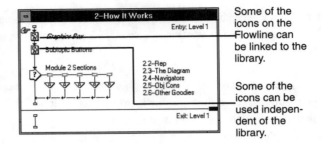

Some of the icons on the Flowline can be linked to the library.

Some of the icons can be used independent of the library.

 TIP You may find it useful to build models using library icons. For example, if you have a variety of test questions, yet each one uses the same background graphic for feedback, the model could use a Display icon from the library for the background.

Creating a New Library

Libraries can either be created before you start authoring the piece, or as you go along. In any case, to create a new library, perform the following steps:

1. Choose the New Library command from the Libraries menu. When this selection is made, the Library window appears, as shown in Figure 27.2.

FIG. 27.2

The Library window contains the scrolling list of icons stored in the library.

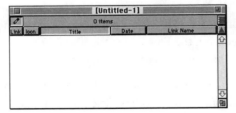

2. Save the library once it has been created and each time modifications have been made to it. (Guidelines for saving the library are the same as those for saving work completed on the piece.) Be sure that the Library window is the active window, then choose Save Library or Save Library As from the File menu.

3. Select a name and location for the library.

4. Click Save.

Once a library has been created or opened, and links have been made between your piece and the library by using a library icon in the piece, the library will automatically open each time your piece is opened.

Opening Libraries

When an Authorware piece containing icons that are linked to a library is opened, the library automatically opens. If the library is closed after it has initially been opened, or if you want to access a library that is not linked to your piece, you can open it using one of the following methods:

■ *Use the Open Library menu option.* Choose Open Library from the Libraries menu, then browse for the library using the Open Library dialog box shown in Figure 27.3.

FIG. 27.3
Use the Open Library dialog box to locate a library to open.

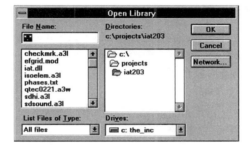

N O T E The library that you open using the Open Library feature does not have to be linked with the piece in which you are currently working. Libraries that are linked to other pieces, or have no links established, can be opened. ■

■ *Use the Libraries option.* Libraries containing icons linked to the piece in which you are working are listed in the submenu for the Libraries command in the Libraries menu. Each line in the submenu shows the name of the library as well as the path to its location, as shown in Figure 27.4.

FIG. 27.4
Linked libraries are listed in the Libraries submenu.

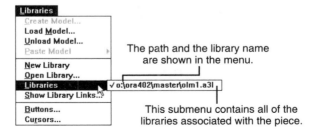

The path and the library name are shown in the menu.

This submenu contains all of the libraries associated with the piece.

Using Multiple Libraries

A piece can contain more than one library, and you can have more than one library open at a time. Additionally, one library can be shared by more than one Authorware piece. There are several reasons why you would use multiple libraries with a single piece or share a single library with more than one piece.

> **N O T E** You can open up to 20 libraries at one time in order to access media stored in those libraries, but an Authorware piece can contain links to only seven libraries. ▪

Separating Objects in Libraries

I often find it beneficial to separate the various types of objects into unique libraries. For example, I might place all digital video in one library, audio in another library, and graphics in yet another library. Doing this limits the size of a single library—both in terms of file size as well as the length of the icon list. Additionally, it enables me to distribute a version of the piece without one of the media, if needed.

> **CAUTION**
> Creating numerous libraries for use in your final piece increases maintenance and distribution efforts. The more pieces you have to keep track of, the greater the chance that you or your end user will lose one of the pieces.

Storing Objects Used for Several Pieces

Because libraries can be accessed by multiple pieces, I could create a library that has elements consistent across a variety of pieces. For example, I may have created a standard startup screen and animation. Rather than use a copy of this structure for each piece I create—thus increasing file storage requirements—I can simply refer to the common library at the beginning of each piece.

This only works if all of your final pieces that share the library are resting on a single delivery medium, such as a CD-ROM or local area network. If the piece does not have direct access to the library, the elements will not be shown, and if you must deliver a unique copy of the library with each piece, the benefit of the library is lost.

Storing Objects for Multiple Authors and Users

It is not uncommon for several authors to work on the same project at the same time. To accommodate this, however, it is necessary to make a unique copy of the piece, or part of the piece, for each person. If the size of the piece is very large—as multimedia pieces have a tendency to be—this could require that each person have a great amount of storage space.

In a networked environment, however, this strain could be eliminated for development as well as viewing the final piece, as follows:

- Development—Although it is not possible for several authors to work on a single Authorware piece at once, it is possible for them to work on copies of the piece that all reference a single, common library. While this is possible, performance may be decreased.

  The library would be stored in a central location, and each author's piece would reference the library for media. For several authors to access a single library, the library must be in read-only mode.

  As each developer worked, they could view media which is stored in the library and linked to their piece, and they could create new links using existing library icons. They could not, however, create new library icons, or save any changes made to linked icons.

  Once they have completed their portion of the development, their changes could be copied from one Authorware piece and pasted together with all of the other edits.

- Final product—Just as several authors can share a single library, end users can also simultaneously share a single library. This is incredibly beneficial because it reduces the overall storage required to run the piece in a networked environment.

  Additionally, end users can also share a single executable Authorware piece. This further reduces the need for storage because a single executable can be used in a networked environment.

Part
VI

Ch
27

> **CAUTION**
> More than one end user running a single piece can negatively impact performance.

Creating Multiple Versions of a Piece

Another benefit of using libraries is that it enables you to create multiple versions of the final piece with minimal effort. For example, you might need to create one version of the piece that contains English text and audio and a second version that contains French text and audio. Both of these versions, however, contain the exact same functionality, graphics, and so on.

To create the two final pieces, perform the following steps:

1. Create the English version, placing all content text icons and audio icons in one library and all other elements that will be used for both versions in another library.

2. When the piece is finished, use Save As to create a copy of both the piece and the library that contains the text and the audio.

3. Translate all contents of the text and audio library, but you do not need to make any changes to the copied piece or to the second library (which you didn't copy).

Placing Icons in a Library

Authorware pieces can be created using a combination of icons from the Icon palette and from libraries. When the piece encounters an icon that references an icon in the library, it continues down the Flowline just as if the icon was not linked to a library. Icons can be added to the library in a number of ways, each of which is described next.

Copying an Icon from the Flowline

If you have defined an icon on the Flowline that you feel belongs in a library, perform the following steps:

1. Create a library using the steps defined in "Creating a New Library," earlier in this chapter.

2. Drag the icon that you want stored in the library to the Library window. When you do this, Authorware actually makes a duplicate image of the icon that is left on the Flowline in its original position—known as the linked icon—and the original icon is moved to the library.

Copying an Icon from One Library to Another

If you have an icon in one library that you want to move to another library, perform the following steps:

1. Open both libraries.

2. Drag the icon from one library to the other. When you do this, Authorware does not leave a copy of the icon in the original library. If the icon is linked to icons on the Flowline, the links remain intact.

If you want to move an icon from one library to another without retaining the link information, hold down the Alt key (Windows) or Option key (Macintosh) while dragging.

If you move an icon from one library to another, Authorware ensures that its name remains unique by appending a number to it.

Cutting, Copying, and Pasting Library Icons

An icon on the Flowline can be copied then pasted into the library. When you paste rather than drag an icon into the library, no link is created.

An icon can also be cut or copied and pasted within the library. When an icon is cut from a library, the icon is removed but the links are retained if the icon is pasted into a library. When an icon is copied, the original icon remains in the library, but no links remain when the icon is pasted into a library.

If more than one icon is cut or copied from the Flowline, Authorware treats them as individual icons when pasted into the library.

N O T E Icons on the Flowline that are already linked to an icon in a library can't be pasted into a library. ▨

Creating a Library Icon with the Tool Palette

If you have a library associated with your piece, you can drag an icon directly to the library from the Icon palette. If you do this, of course, you will still need to open the icon and define its contents.

I typically define an icon on the Flowline the first time that it is used rather than start with it in the library. This enables me to see the icon in context of the other icons. Once the Flowline structure is created and the portion of the piece on which I am working is completed, I then drag the icon to the library.

Editing a Library Icon

Once an icon has been defined and placed in a library, only certain elements can be edited from the Flowline, and others must be edited in the library.

Editing from the Flowline

When an icon is linked to a piece, the only attributes that can be modified for the linked icon on the Flowline are the display effects, the object's position in the Presentation Window, and keywords. The remainder of the attributes, including color, fill, font, size, style, and mode, must be changed in the original icon located in the library.

When a linked icon is opened by double-clicking it on the Flowline, all of the tools in the Graphics toolbox are inactive except for the Pointer tool, as shown in Figure 27.5. This means that you can't, for example, add more objects and text into the icon.

Braces indicate
that this icon is
linked to a library.

FIG. 27.5
Tools in the Graphics toolbox are inactive if you are editing a linked icon on the Flowline.

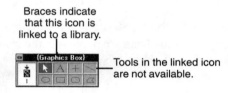

Tools in the linked icon are not available.

When one of the editable attributes is changed for the icon on the Flowline, the changes are not reflected in the original icon in the library.

Editing in the Library

An icon in the library can be edited just as if it were an unlinked icon on the Flowline. If the icon is linked to icons on the Flowline, however, changes made are reflected across all associated icons—whether in the current piece that you are creating or in others that can reference the icon. Changes are not made if they are for display effects or positioning.

> **CAUTION**
> Because edits made to icons in a library apply to all icons linked to that library icon, you must make sure that the edits apply to every linked icon. In some cases, you might need to copy the library icon and create a new set of links so that the edits do not affect other icons.

When a linked icon—either on the Flowline or in a library—is edited on the Flowline, the icon title appears in braces in the title bar of the Graphics toolbox, as shown in Figure 27.6. When a linked icon is edited in a library, the library name appears in brackets followed by the icon name in brackets (Macintosh), or the library name followed by the icon name separated by a vertical bar (Windows).

Braces are used to indicate that this
Flowline icon is linked to a library.

FIG. 27.6
The Graphics toolbox title
bar changes for a library
icon, and a linked icon.

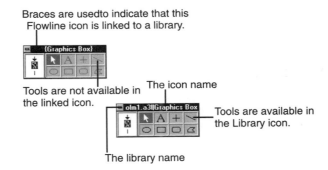

Tools are not available in
the linked icon.

The icon name

Tools are available in
the Library icon.

The library name

Controlling the Library Window

When a library has been opened and icons have been linked to a piece, there are several controls that you can employ to make using the Library window, shown in Figure 27.7, more efficient.

Read/Write status button

Condense/Expand button

FIG. 27.7
The Library window controls
make using the library more
efficient.

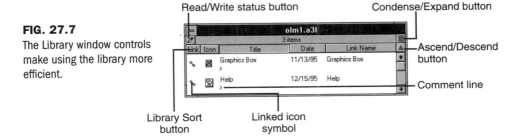

Ascend/Descend button

Comment line

Library Sort
button

Linked icon
symbol

Using the Read/Write Status Button

If a library is set to read/write, then only one author can work with the library at a time. To change the library from read/write status to read-only, click the Pencil button. When a library is read-only, the Pencil button has a diagonal line through it, as shown in Figure 27.8.

NOTE Libraries open in read/write mode by default.

FIG. 27.8
Simply click the Pencil button
to toggle back to read/write
mode.

Symbol for
read-only
mode

Part
VI
Ch
27

A library that is read-only can be used by several authors at a time; however, no changes will be saved to the library.

Working with Sort Buttons

Icons in a library can appear in a variety of ways. By default, the icons are listed alphabetically and sorted by icon type and in ascending order. Use the following sort options to organize the icons according to your needs:

- Link button—Icons in the library that are linked to the piece currently being authored have a link symbol next to their names in the list. Clicking the Link button causes all linked icons to appear first in the list, sorted by icon title.

- Icon button—Click the Icon Button to sort icons by type and in the following order: Display, Interaction, Calculation, Digital Movie, and Sound.

 TIP This option is very helpful if you are making edits to one type of media. For example, you might be replace placeholder audio with the final, professionally recorded version. In this example, listing the icons by type enables you to quickly access each of the Sound icons.

- Title button—Authorware lists the icons in the library in alphabetical order, depending on the status of the Ascending/Descending button. The title of an icon in the library can be edited at any time.

N O T E   If you strategically label icons, this option might be helpful when editing a particular section of the piece. For example, if you label each icon in a section beginning with an abbreviation for the section, then all of the icons for that section will be placed together in the library. ■

- Date button—The library shows the date that the icon was last modified. Click the Date button to organize the icons either from earliest to latest or latest to earliest, based on the state of the Ascending/Descending button.

- Link Name button—The Link Name is the same as the title of the library icon unless you change it. Like sorting by icon Title, Authorware can list the library icons alphabetically by Link Name, depending of the status of the Ascending/ Descending button.

Using the Condense/Expand Button

When the library is in expanded view, an extra line for comments appears for each icon, as shown in Figure 27.9. Use the Condense/Expand button to toggle between the expanded view and condensed view.

FIG. 27.9
Comments can be left in the
library to further define each
icon.

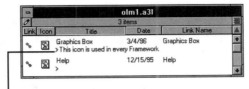

Use comments to increase
maintainability and project
communication.

Using the Ascend/Descend Button

Use this button in the Library window to toggle between viewing the library in ascending
and descending order, based on the sort that has been selected.

Deleting Library Icons

Just as icons can be added to a library, they can also be deleted. If a library icon is linked,
however, Authorware provides a warning mechanism to prevent valuable content from
being erased. To delete an icon from the library, perform the following steps:

1. Select the library icon that you want to delete by clicking it.
2. Choose Clear or Cut from the Edit menu, or press the Delete key.

 The shortcut keys for Cut are⌘+(Macintosh) and Ctrl+X (Windows).

3. When the warning dialog box appears, press the Continue button to remove the
icon from the library.

Working with Library Links

Part
VI

Ch
27

As you are authoring, not all changes made to a library icon are applied to its linked icons.
To update each of the linked icons in the piece, perform the following steps:

1. Select the library icon to which changes have been made by clicking it.
2. Choose the Show Library Links option from the Libraries menu to display the Show
Links dialog box, as shown in Figure 27.10.

FIG. 27.10
Display a list of icons in your piece that are linked to the selected library icon.

Show Library Links
Show
Unbroken Links
Broken Links
Graphics Box
Graphics Box
Graphics Box
Graphics Box
Graphics Box
Help
Help
Help
Help
Help
Close
Show Icon
Select All
Update
An icon is listed each time it is used in the piece.
Use this toggle to change the view of the list.
When an icon from the list is selected, clicking this button will highlight it on the Flowline.

3. Use the dialog box buttons to update the library links. Click the link to update; then click one of the following buttons:

   - Show Broken/Unbroken Links—Use this toggle to either see links that have been broken or to view icons whose links are intact. If a link has been broken, Authorware will ignore the icon when it is encountered on the Flowline. Broken links can be identified, as shown in Figure 27.11.

FIG. 27.11
The broken link symbol is used on the Flowline to identify icons that have lost their association with the library.

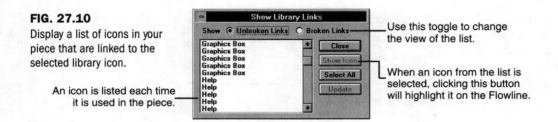

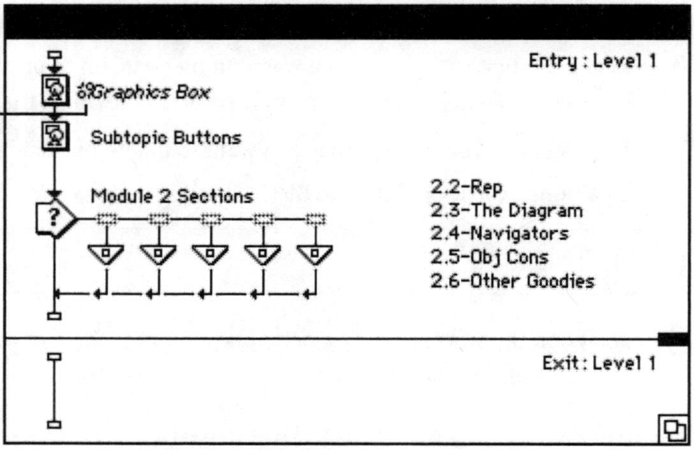

Entry : Level 1
Graphics Box
Subtopic Buttons
Module 2 Sections
2.2-Rep
2.3-The Diagram
2.4-Navigators
2.5-Obj Cons
2.6-Other Goodies
Exit : Level 1
Broken link symbol

   - Show Icon—When a single library icon is selected in the list, you can use this button to pinpoint the linked icon on the Flowline. This is helpful if you are looking for a particular icon, but have forgotten its position on the Flowline.

4. Click the Close button to close the Show Library Links dialog box.

As the size and number of libraries with content grows, it becomes more difficult to keep track of which icons are linked to which libraries. Authorware provides two mechanisms for you to track the links between Flowline icons and their library counterparts.

Tracking Links from the Flowline

Because it is possible to have more than one library associated with a piece, it can become difficult to determine which library a linked icon on the Flowline is associated with. To locate a library for a particular linked icon, perform the following steps:

1. Select an icon on the Flowline that is linked to a library by clicking the icon.

2. Choose Get Info from the Edit menu to display the Get Info dialog box, as shown in Figure 27.12.

FIG. 27.12
The Get Info dialog box reveals information about the selected icon.

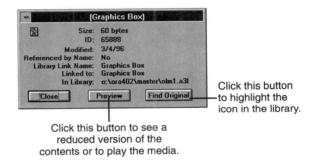

Click this button to highlight the icon in the library.

Click this button to see a reduced version of the contents or to play the media.

3. Use the buttons in the Get Info dialog box to learn more about the icon, as follows:

   ■ Preview—This button enables you to see a reduced version of the contents of the icon. If the icon is a Sound icon, the sound plays; if it is a Digital Movie icon, the movie plays. If the library icon is empty, then the Preview button is not active.

   ■ Find Original—When this button is clicked, the Library window that contains the icon is brought to the front of all the other Library windows, and the linked icon is located and highlighted.

4. Click the Close button to close the Get Info dialog box.

If the Library window is closed, it will be opened when the Find Original button is clicked. If the original library cannot be located by Authorware, a warning dialog box is displayed.

Tracking Links from the Library Window

To get a list of all the icons in a library that are linked to the current piece, perform the following steps:

1. Select an icon in the library that is linked to the piece.

2. Choose Get Info from the Edit menu to display the Get Info dialog box for the library icon, as shown in Figure 27.13.

FIG. 27.13
The Get Info dialog box for the library icon reveals information about the selected icon.

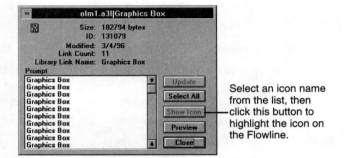

Select an icon name from the list, then click this button to highlight the icon on the Flowline.

This dialog box works just like the one used when working with links, except that it contains a Preview button. The Preview button enables you to see a reduced image, see the digital movie, or hear the sound for the linked icon.

The Select All button selects all of the icons in the list. This option is helpful when you have a large number of broken links.

If you want to update linked icons, select the icons in the library, then click the Update button. Any changes that were made to icons in the library will be applied to their associated icons on the Flowline. When this button is clicked, a confirmation dialog box is displayed, as shown in Figure 27.14.

FIG. 27.14
Use the Update Configuration dialog box to update all linked icons that have been modified in the library.

TIP   A shortcut for updating linked icons is to simply drag the icon that has been changed from the library, and place it on top of its associated icon on the Flowline, or vice versa. Although this updates the link, changes to either icon are not affected.

VII

Exploring Design and Development Methodologies

CHAPTER 28

Thinking Interactively

With public excitement for multimedia growing and now supported by recognized quantitative benefits, more industries are hoping to be included in the multimedia wave. And as the definition of multimedia continues to expand to include such technologies as desktop video-conferencing, CD-ROM recorders, hardware upgrade kits, and even cable television and theater, we must not overlook what has the potential to be the greatest benefit of multimedia: interactivity.

Interactivity is the dialog that takes place between the user and the system. But more than pressing buttons, interactivity is also the personality that drives the dialog. As we look closely at the marketplace definition of interactive, however, we begin to see that a number of products, including CD-ROMs produced for education and training, are only by the lowest definition interactive.

If we continue to focus on the magic of the technology without carefully considering interactivity—real interactivity—we will not be able to recognize the fullest potential multimedia has to offer as an instructional tool. The challenge for us is to design or think

Defining interactivity

Interactivity is a reactionary conversation between two parties, not the activity performed by the end user when using a multimedia piece.

Exploring low-level interactivity

Low-level interactivity is most generally classified as being a linear sequence of events.

Recognizing mid-level interactivity

Pieces that incorporate mid-level interactivity allow the end user to explore content in an undetermined sequence.

Using high-level interactivity

High-level interactivity is characterized by the computer looking into the eyes of the end users and determining what they need based on their demonstration of understanding.

interactively and to produce systems that—although actually having perimeters within which the user can roam—provide a seemingly endless conversation through which the user is carefully and gradually brought to the point of understanding through experience.

This chapter does not focus on the technical uses of Authorware. Rather, it provides some insight into design that you may want to consider when planning an *interactive* piece. ■

Defining Interactivity

Throughout this book I have sought to challenge you to think about interactivity in a way other than in terms of what the user does with the mouse or keyboard. In this chapter, you will not be looking at the functionality of Authorware; rather, I will discuss the end result of using Authorware to create interactive multimedia. Having an understanding of the goal is just as important as understanding how to use the tools to achieve that goal.

The term *interactivity,* or to be interactive, is very confusing today. This is typical for terminology or phrases that get caught up in the buzzword whirlwind. Interactive has become a meaningless marketing term. We have taken products (such as compact discs and televisions) and after outfitting them with a modified remote control have labeled them interactive.

But let's go back to the original definition of interactive: to interact is "to act on one another" (The American Heritage Dictionary of the English Language, Dell Publishing, 1970). That suggests that two or more parties are involved in the creation of a dialog, not a presentation that lacks intellectual and emotional response. By continually diluting the original definition of interactive, we have all become convinced that having control over the pace or sequence of events is interactivity. If that were the case, wouldn't elevators be classified as interactive?

Interactivity is the foundation of a dialog. It consists of two parts: the user talking to the system and the system talking back.

Talking to the System

Talking to the system is the end users' contact with the graphical interface and the means by which they provide information to the system. We're all very familiar with how you talk to an interactive multimedia piece. As a society, we are rapidly growing more comfortable with such communication devices as the mouse, touch screen, or even voice control.

Understanding how users talk to the system is not enough though. Understanding why users talk to the system is also important if you are going to attempt to create truly interactive multimedia. The purpose of users talking to the system is in part so that they can be given information, but users also talk with the system so that the system can learn about them. Every activity should be designed with the goal of the system learning something about the user so that it can in turn provide a specific and relevant response.

 TIP Interaction with the system is more than answering questions. Try to imagine how, if you were face to face with the end user or even watching them trying to apply the content, you would be able to determine which portions were understood and which were confusing. With this in mind, you can begin to build a relevant interaction.

The System Talking Back

Unfortunately, most multimedia designers define the system talking back as simply the displaying of text, graphics, video, or animation in the Presentation Window. By this definition, a dialog with the end user is nothing more than clicking a button or pressing a key so that the next bit of content can be presented.

Is that the definition of interactivity, or is it the definition of control? Is it really any different than using a television remote control or the control panel found on a microwave oven? The system talking back must evolve into the computer's capability to evaluate a student's progress against a stated learning objective then sequence the learning based on that evaluation.

N O T E If the content being displayed does not directly relate to what the system has learned about the end user, you have not created an interactive program. ▪

To make defining interactivity easier, I've broken it into three levels: low-level, mid-level, and high-level. Each level has certain characteristics, and each one also has a unique role for the designer, the end user, and the computer.

Part
VII
Ch
28

N O T E   Just as a piece has a variety of learning objectives, it is possible that a piece will also
contain a mix of interactivity levels. ■

Multimedia is exciting and valuable when the right level of interactivity is matched with
the content and the objective. On the other hand, multimedia is frustrating when the user
has one need and the level of interactivity does not support it.

Adding Low-Level Interactivity

The basic level of interactivity is most commonly defined as a monologue style presentation in which the user is passively involved in the acquisition of information, and the system is not involved in learning about the end user. Additionally, low-level interactivity can
be generally characterized by its interface attributes as well as the roles of the designer,
the end user, and the computer in the presentation of content. Although these characteristics are broad in their application and should not be used as rules, they should help you
determine whether the level of interactivity that you are designing is appropriate for the
learning objective.

N O T E   Think of the piece that contains low-level interactivity as a lecture to the end user. ■

Identifying Interface Characteristics of Low-Level Interactivity

Low-level interactivity can be characterized by its interface features. These are the elements that the end users see and interact with as they move through your piece.

Common Metaphors   Pieces that contain low-level interactivity typically rely on
metaphors common to everyday life. For example, the text book is a popular metaphor
that has been applied to countless computer applications. You're probably familiar with the
page-turning environment that exists in many multimedia pieces, as shown in Figure 28.1.

The content of a book—the text and the graphics—can be embellished with video or audio, but when you look at the Presentation Window, it is formatted very much like a text
book. The user turns pages to go from one piece of content to another.

N O T E   Pieces that can be classified as low-level do not necessarily have common metaphors, but more often than not, a common metaphor is the starting place for
multimedia developers. ■

Standard Computer Widgets   The mechanisms that the user interacts with or that
control the interactivity are often referred to as *widgets*. In low-level interactive situations,

these widgets look very much like the standard computer widgets, as shown in Figure 28.2, that are found in the Windows and Macintosh environments. Beveled buttons, scrolling windows, pull-down menus, and check boxes are all examples of such interface widgets.

FIG. 28.1
The page-turning metaphor is an example of a common metaphor.

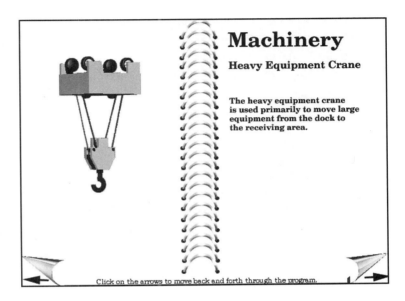

FIG. 28.2
Standard computer widgets are commonly used in the creation of low-level interactive applications.

Pull-down menu located across the top of the screen

Rectangular, beveled buttons

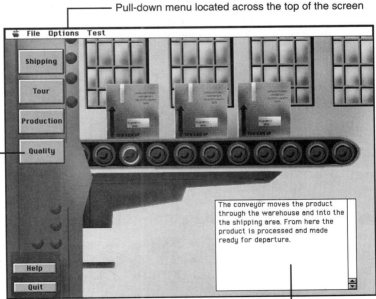

Authorware scrolling text window

N O T E   Applications that can be classified as low-level do not necessarily have standard computer widgets. I have seen many low-level interactive applications with a beautiful interface. More often than not, however, the standard computer widgets do find their way into applications with low-level interactivity. ▧

Linear Presentation and Minimal Branching   Pieces that consist of low-level interactivity typically behave linearly or, at best, contain minimal branching. The paging, or book, metaphor is fairly linear (see Fig. 28.3), and the only branching that might exist enables the user to select a "chapter."

FIG. 28.3
Low-level interactive pieces have a defined starting and stopping point, as well as a defined path to flow between those points.

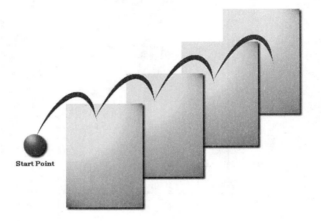

Start Point

Minimal Data Collection   Applications that consist of low-level interactivity can finally be characterized as having minimal data collection. That is, as the user moves through the application, the computer does not keep track of where they've been, what they've done, or information regarding how well they've done. Without this data, the computer cannot create a path through the content. Moreover, without this data, the computer is not able to intelligently converse with the end user.

N O T E   Data collection for the purpose of record keeping is not the same as data collection for the sake of sequencing content. The data collection I am referring to is for sequencing information. ▧

Recognizing the Participants in Low-Level Interactivity

In the development and use of applications that contain low-level interactivity, there are three primary roles that can be explored: the role of the designer, the role of the end user, and the role of the computer.

The Role of the Designer   The designer, or multimedia author, is the person responsible for constructing the program. Whether simply designing the program on paper and then handing it off to a development team or actually doing the development work, the designer is responsible for the overall sequence of events and design of the program.

In the design of pieces with low-level interactivity, the designer typically plays the following two roles:

- Establishing instructional objectives—The length and depth of content is all determined by the designer. For example, the designer decides whether there will be four modules or five; what content will be placed in each module; and at what mastery level the user will be given credit for completing the application.

 TIP Conducting these design efforts is much more efficient and productive if done in collaboration with a subject matter expert.

NOTE Pieces that are for entertainment can be classified with these characteristics as well. ■

- The sequence of events—The designer is responsible for determining the order in which learning objectives are presented. For example, the designer is responsible for determining how many steps will be illustrated in the simulation of a process or how many pages of technical data will be presented in a technical reference guide.

The Role of the End User   In a piece that contains low-level interactivity, the end user is typically responsible for only one thing: controlling the pace at which the content is presented. This has been one of the greatest benefits and selling points of computer-based training and multimedia in general.

Authorware provides a variety of mechanisms that you can incorporate into a program to enable the end user to control the pace, such as the Wait icon, automatic pausing, and a variety of responses for the Interaction icon.

▶ For more information on using the Wait icon to control the pace of a multimedia piece, **see** "Building Pauses," **p. 156**.

▶ For an introduction on using interactions, **see** "Introducing Interactions," **p. 212**.

NOTE No matter what device the users are interacting with, if they are doing nothing more than determining the amount of time between the pieces of content, they are involved in low-level interactivity. ■

Part
VII

Ch
28

The Role of the Computer   The computer plays a unique role in a piece based on low-level interactivity. In most multimedia pieces, the computer is nothing more than a high-priced presentation device. In many cases, the content that is presented by a CD-ROM or over a network could just as well be presented in a slide show, by videotape, or within a workbook. The presentation of the content does not need the computer for anything other than enabling the user to control the pace of the application.

When Is Low-Level Interactivity Appropriate?

Applications that use low-level interactivity are appropriate if you are teaching a process. For example, if you're teaching someone how to use a piece of software; how to repair a piece of equipment; or if you're teaching brain surgery, you more than likely want the user to understand a sequence of events. In each case, the sequence of events is the learning objective.

Low-level interactivity is not appropriate, however, if you are teaching reference material or if you're teaching concepts. Just imagine how frustrating it would be if when looking for a person's phone number you had to search one page at a time from the beginning of the phone book.

Creating Mid-Level Interactivity

Mid-level interactivity is characterized by the user taking greater responsibility and control in the acquisition of content. The computer, however, is still only reacting to the user's control and not entering into a dialog with the end user. Let's again look at some of the common characteristics and roles found at this level of interactivity.

N O T E   As you look at the characteristics of a piece with mid-level interactively, think of such a program as an opportunity for the end user to ask questions of the expert, but the expert does not make assumptions about what the user understands. The expert simply answers the predetermined questions. ▪

Identifying Interface Characteristics of Mid-Level Interactivity

Many of the interface characteristics for mid-level interactivity are similar to those for low-level interactivity.

Forced Metaphors   As common metaphors are used for low-level interactivity, *forced metaphors* are commonly used in pieces that contain or consist of mid-level interactivity. A forced metaphor is a metaphor (or interface) that exists in one environment, which is forced onto the computer (see Fig. 28.4).

For example, I don't know what it is about the game show *Jeopardy* that is so appealing to developers around the world. It seems that every first multimedia application done by a company has got to be made "interactive" and "fun" by making it a game show. In this example, the game show is a forced metaphor.

FIG. 28.4
Forced metaphors apply an interface or theme that has nothing to do with the content of the program.

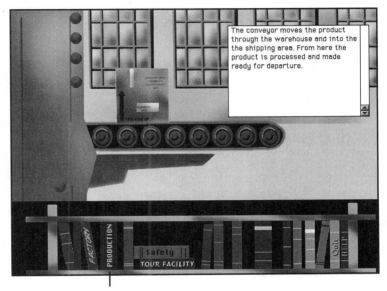

The books are used for navigation instead of traditional buttons.

Other common forced metaphors are the office scene where the end user clicks the items on the desktop to launch portions of the program; the file cabinet where the files represent portions of the program; the book shelf where the various books again are modules of the programs; or a hand-held controller type device with which content is presented on the screen and the controls are used to navigate through the content.

Original Widgets   The widgets in a piece that contains mid-level interactivity begin to vary from those in a low-level interactivity. In low-level interactivity, widgets were very technical or computer looking. (See "Standard Computer Widgets" earlier in this chapter.) Widgets within mid-level interactivity consist of more creative elements. Rather than a button, you now see an icon (see Fig. 28.5). Rather than a scrolling window, you see an actual paper scroll with the words on it.

N O T E   Applications that can be classified as mid-level do not necessarily have original widgets. I have seen many mid-level interactive applications with standard computer widgets. ▪

Part
VII

Ch
28

FIG. 28.5
Widgets begin to appear as icons or objects with which the user interacts.

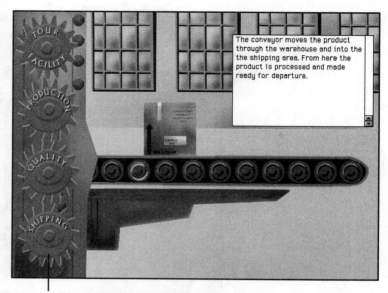

The standard buttons have been substituted with thematic buttons.

Nonlinear Presentation and Minimal Branching   Mid-level interactivity breaks away from the linear presentation by enabling the user to determine to which of the pages they want to go. The content is not necessarily linear in nature, and there is a small amount of branching based on how the user interacts (see Fig. 28.6).

FIG. 28.6
Mid-level interactive pieces have a defined starting point, but do not have a defined stopping point or sequence through the content.

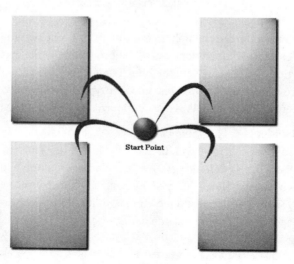

Start Point

The best example for the use of mid-level interactivity that I can think of is the World Wide Web. The information is not linear: the user can move from content area to content area, and every now and then the content seems to organize itself based on characteristics of the user.

Minimal Data Collection   Applications with mid-level interactivity are similar to those with low-level interactivity when it comes to data collection. Although there may be some data collected about the end user in a mid-level interactive application, it is typically only minimal. (See "Minimal Data Collection" earlier in this chapter.)

Recognizing the Participants in Mid-Level Interactivity

Let's explore the same three roles in the development and use of mid-level interactivity as we did for low-level interactivity. (See "Recognizing the Participants in Low-Level Interactivity" earlier in this chapter.)

The Role of the Designer   The role of the designer in mid-level interactive pieces is different than that in a low-level interactive piece. In a mid-level interactive piece, the designer typically has only one main function: establishing instructional objectives. The primary objective of the designer in a piece that contains mid-level interactivity is to determine the outcome objective and to define the content.

Although the designer may suggest a sequence by the design of the interface, that sequence might not be followed because of the interactivity. For example, when somebody is designing a Web page or an interactive catalog, the sequence of content is suggested in the way that it is arranged in menus or on the screen. That does not necessarily mean that the selections will be made by the end user in that order.

The Role of the End User   The role of the end user also changes from that seen in pieces that contain low-level interactivity. (See "Recognizing the Participants in Low-Level Interactivity" earlier in this chapter.) The users now become more involved with the application. Unfortunately, the piece with mid-level interactivity is still not responding to the users based on their interaction. The role of the end user in a piece based on mid-level interactivity is as follows:

- Controlling the pace—As in a low-level interactive piece, the user of a mid-level interactive piece is in control of the pace at which content is presented, either through the use of pause buttons, interactions, or navigation schemes.

- The sequence of events—Although the designer may suggest an order of events in the design of a mid-level interactive piece, the end users are given the freedom to roam the content based on their needs or their interests.

The Role of the Computer   The role of the computer in a mid-level interactive piece is really no different than it is for a low-level interactive piece: it is still that of a high-priced presentation device. The content, whether text, video, sound, or graphics, can still be

Part
VII

Ch
28

presented using another medium. The only benefit of having a computer is that it more efficiently enables the users to randomly access the content in which they are interested.

When Is Mid-Level Interactivity Appropriate?

Pieces that use mid-level interactivity are appropriate for building reference tools. For example, you may provide a picture of a piece of equipment on which the user clicks the various parts to learn more about them; a blueprint of a facility on which the user clicks to find out what operations take place there; or a list of the most commonly asked questions about a product on which the user clicks to learn how to respond to the questions.

Pieces that contain mid-level interactivity are not appropriate for teaching linear sequences and can only occasionally be used to teach the application of concepts.

Implementing High-Level Interactivity

High-level interactivity is best defined as interactivity in which the user becomes involved as an active participant. Not only is the user providing input, but the piece responds to that input. Let's look at some of the common characteristics and roles found at this level of interactivity.

N O T E As we look at the characteristics of a piece with high-level interactivity, think of the interaction with the piece as a casual conversation with the expert. It is not a drill and practice nor a simple exercise of querying, but the expert is actually responding to the end user via dialog. ▓

Identifying Interface Characteristics of High-Level Interactivity

The interface characteristics of a piece that contains high-level interactivity can be much different than other levels of interactivity.

Content-Driven Metaphors   Although the interface metaphors for mid-level interactivity are not common metaphors, they typically do not support the content of the piece. (See "Identifying Interface Characteristics of Mid-Level Interactivity" earlier in this chapter.) The interface of an application that contains high-level interactivity, however, does support the content and interactions much like the backdrop of a play supports the acting and story line.

For example, if you are teaching about a manufacturing process, the interface may look like the manufacturing environment (see Fig. 28.7). Similarly, if you are working for an automotive company, the interface may be that of a dashboard.

FIG. 28.7
Content-driven metaphors apply themes that are derived from the content.

Used by permission from Toyota Motor Manufacturing of America, Inc.

Styled Widgets In pieces with mid-level interactivity, the widgets are not typical computer widgets; however, they are based on metaphors that do not support the content. In an interface that is based on the content, the widgets are objects that are found in the content, such as the buttons at the bottom of Figure 28.8.

FIG. 28.8
Widgets appear as objects found in the content.

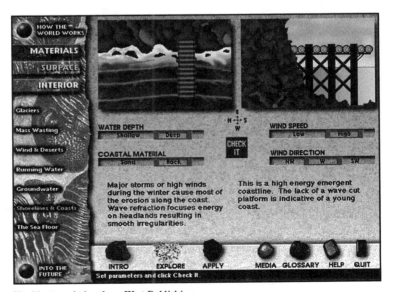

Used by permission from West Publishing.

N O T E Pieces that can be classified as high-level do not necessarily have natural widgets. Sometimes it is necessary to have a slider or mechanism that can only be constructed out of elements derived from the content. ■

Seemingly Infinite Branching   High-level interactivity breaks away from the traditional presentation in which the user has to determine which of the pages to go to—either in a linear or a linked method. In contrast, a piece with high-level interactivity contains a wide variety of branches through which the end user can travel. The paths are not obvious to the user, and the end of a path is determined by a degree of mastery rather than the successful navigation to an ending point (see Fig. 28.9).

FIG. 28.9
High-level interactive pieces have a defined starting point, and a defined stopping point, but the path through the content is unique for each user.

Start Point   End Point

Data-Driven Branching   A piece that contains high-level interactivity is founded on data collection. Every interaction is built with the intention of learning about the end user so that a relevant path of instruction can be taken.

The data that is collected is not used for reporting because the end result is determined by a specific mastery level. Rather, the collected data is used to determine which path through the content is taken.

Recognizing the Participants in High-Level Interactivity

Let's explore the same three roles in the development and use of high-level interactivity as we did for the other levels of interactivity.

The Role of the Designer   The role of the designer in high-level interactive pieces is the same as in a mid-level interactive piece. (See "Recognizing the Participants in Mid-Level

Interactivity" earlier in this chapter.) In a high-level interactive piece, the designer typically has only one main function: establishing instructional objectives. The primary objective of the designer in a piece that contains high-level interactivity is to determine the outcome and to define the content.

Additionally, the designer must determine the standards that are used to judge mastery and to establish the criteria for selecting the various paths. The designer must be able to assume the role of the expert and then determine how the computer will respond to the end user based on the interactions.

The Role of the End User   In a piece that contains high-level interactivity, the role of the end user is the same as that of the user of a piece that contains low-level interactivity: to control the pace at which the content is presented. This has been one of the greatest benefits and selling points for computer-based training and multimedia in general.

> **NOTE** Keep in mind that interactivity is not merely defined by what the user does with the system, but how the system responds. The end user may not perform much action in a piece with high-level interactivity. In such a case, high-level interactivity would be considered low-level interactivity according to the industry's definition.

The Role of the Computer   In a program that contains high-level interactivity, the computer becomes an active participant in the delivery of information—controlling the sequence of events. Using parameters that you define during authoring, the computer will collect information about the end user, then use that information to create a path of instruction. Like the expert sitting at the table, the program begins to assume what the user understands and misunderstands so that an individualized path of instruction can be taken.

When Is High-Level Interactivity Appropriate?

Applications that use high-level interactivity are best employed when the end user must apply what has been learned. Simulations, case examples, or freeform drills can all incorporate high-level interactivity and can be used to ensure that the end user will master the content. Furthermore, there is no need for another form of instruction, nor is there a need for testing. With this model, the instruction and the testing are combined to create the dialog. The result is a piece that is motivating to use and has a predetermined mastery level. ●

CHAPTER 29

A New Look at the Development Process

The professionals that make up the multimedia industry are about as eclectic as the products they create. Although the foundation for multimedia was laid by people with backgrounds in instructional design, video, print, software, and programming. I continue to meet others with seemingly non-related interests who make their way into the industry.

Take yours truly, for example. After completing a four-year degree in technical horticulture, I decided to follow my interest in design and pursue a masters degree in landscape architecture. Sometime during my tour at The Ohio State University, I accidentally discovered computers, and was challenged by my thesis chairman and good friend Professor Brooks Breeden to consider how computers may be used to teach the concepts of landscape architecture. A short time later, I was introduced to a beta version of Course of Action (the predecessor of Authorware), and before I knew it, I was an instructional developer with Authorware, Inc.

Looking at the traditional approach

Before we can search for a new development methodology, it is important to understand the historical phases of current development techniques, including analysis, design, development, implementation, and evaluation.

The pitfalls of traditional development methodologies

There are three pitfalls with the traditional development process that are forcing us to look for a new methodology, including the gap in communication between designers and developers, the fact that the best ideas come during development, and that the end user is involved in the wrong end of the project.

A development approach for today

The development approach that was designed to eliminate the three pitfalls of traditional development still includes the analysis phase, but design and development have been combined into prototyping. Additionally, an emphasis is placed on getting the user involved through implementation and evaluation.

Along with the varied backgrounds of the people who compose the industry came a variety of development methodologies. Although the founding professions had a major influence in forming a standard approach to the creation of multimedia, there are numerous variations on that theme. Regardless, there does not seem to be a methodology created exclusively for multimedia—a methodology that takes advantage of the tools, technologies, and expertise of the profession.

In this chapter, you will begin to learn about a new methodology that has been designed specifically for this industry. ■

Respecting Tradition

Entire books, courses, and journals are dedicated to teaching development methodologies, so I will certainly not be able to give this topic justice in a short chapter. Rather, I hope to contrast development methodologies found in other professions—which have been used to form the basis for creating multimedia—with an approach that takes advantage of today's technologies and multimedia authoring environments. To make this comparison, it is necessary to give a quick tour of the roles and phases involved in the traditional methods of creating interactive programs.

I have selected to highlight only certain tasks so that the contrast between traditional development methodologies and the more contemporary one that my team has successfully implemented can be drawn. The phases that have been described are in no way all inclusive, and the roles and definitions used for these phases are about as varied as the organizations that incorporate them.

With those disclaimers made, I'll try to paint a general picture of the methodology that has been traditionally employed for the development of interactive systems created for training, performance support, kiosk, and entertainment (see Fig. 29.1).

FIG. 29.1
The traditional development process can be generally characterized as a five step approach.

Beginning with Analysis

The first phase in the creation of an interactive program has traditionally been called the *analysis* phase. Once the need for a program is identified, analysis begins in order to determine how the needs of the end user can be met by the program and how behaviors can be changed. Every aspect of the program—from the statement of the problem to the type of hardware needed to run the interactive program—is explored in the analysis phase.

Determining the *Whats* and *Hows* The first step of the analysis phase is to determine what issues need to be addressed by the piece. Whether the piece is an interactive learning tool, a kiosk, or entertainment, having a clear picture of what must be communicated is critical. The collecting of this information is typically referred to as conducting a *needs analysis.*

Once the needs analysis is complete, the team performs further analysis to determine how to test whether the user received and understood the content of the piece. For example, if you were creating an interactive learning tool, you might have determined what questions the user should be able to answer, or if you were developing an in-store kiosk, you might have determined what items would be purchased as a result of the end user using the piece.

Understanding the End User In addition to learning what issues the piece had to address, the analysis phase also attempts to gain an understanding of who will be using the piece. To create a piece that addresses the needs of the end user, it is important to study that user from several perspectives, including psychological condition, informational history, and technical ability, for starters:

- Psychology—The psychological state of the end user is very important if you want to effectively communicate the content of the piece. For example, imagine how difficult it would be to get users to participate with an in-store kiosk designed to provide customer assistance if they had only seen such systems used for sales presentations. Because their perception is that kiosks are used for selling, they might avoid your kiosk even though it was designed to educate.

- Information—To address the needs of the user, it is crucial to deliver relevant information. For example, if you are providing base-level training to employees who have worked on the job for several years, the end user will quickly lose interest in the piece.

■ Technology—Finally, it is important to understand what comfort level the user has with technology. For example, if the user is afraid of, or not familiar with, computers, then the graphical interface—and maybe the physical environment—should not incorporate system standard interface elements such as pull-down menus or scrolling lists.

 It is also helpful to determine the type of on-screen widgets (sliders, dials, check boxes, radio buttons, etc.) and computer input devices (touch screen, trackball, mouse, etc.) that would aid in the end user's comfort level.

Defining the Target Delivery Medium   The final task in conducting an analysis is to determine the delivery medium to use for the interactive program. For example, if you are conducting soft skills training, then a medium that enabled the end user to read body language, such as video, might be appropriate.

Additionally, the mode of delivery is typically determined in the analysis phase. For example, if you are developing a sales support tool that needs regular updating, then you might consider distributing a piece on floppy disk or through the World Wide Web.

The Art of Design

With a clear understanding of the objectives for the piece and a description of the end user's needs, the project moves into the second phase of creation known as *design*. In this phase, every identified need is addressed as the scope of the piece is defined.

Identifying the Piece Content   The first step of the design phase entails the identification of the project content. Based on the issues that were identified during the analysis phase, a list of items that would address those issues is created. (See "Beginning with Analysis" earlier in this chapter.) In many cases, the design team works with subject matter experts, technicians, or trainers to identify content that would directly address each of the issues.

Creating Scripts and Story Boards   The next step in the design phase is to create a detailed blueprint that will be used to actually develop the piece. Every screen is identified, then detailed in terms of content. Scripts for text, video, and audio are written, and thumbnail sketches for graphics, video, and animation are created.

N O T E   In recent years, prototypes have been a partially-functioning, feature incomplete, interactive piece created to demonstrate the direction the final piece will follow or to provide proof that the proposed technology is viable. ▨

The end result is a document that can be used as a set of specifications for a third-party developer.

The Magic of Development

The central phase in the creation of an interactive program is *development*: the blueprint created in the design phase is converted into code that performs according to the specifications.

The client, as well as the end user might be involved in review periods along the way, but for the most part, the development team works according to the direction provided by the design team. When the client or end user is involved, a controlled process for collecting input and changes is enforced by the project team.

Constructing the Code   Beginning with the earliest programming methodologies, the constructing of computer code has always been a specialized science. During this step of the process, the magicians work to transform paper-based ideas into an interactive piece.

Sign-Off and Acceptance   Once development begins, it is not uncommon for everyone—from the development team to the designers to the client—to have new ideas. These new ideas often cause the design to slowly and somewhat unnoticeably drift away from the agreed upon direction. To prevent the design from creeping outside the boundaries of schedule and budget, the project team typically incorporates a procedure for acceptance of completed work. This procedure typically involves the review and sign-off of modules as they are completed.

N O T E   Developers today still use this procedure, and as throughout time, the cost of a change is commonly in direct proportion to the amount of time remaining on the project. ▨

Coping with Revisions   One of the greatest challenges of any development effort is the ability to cope with changes. Changes can impact everything from team morale to budget, time frame, and client/vendor relationship. In any case, a process to manage change is a critical part of the development phase.

Implementing the Final Program

What for many is the last phase of a project is actually the second to last phase. *Implementation* is the point in the project when the piece is delivered to the end user. More than distribution, however, this phase is also designed to ensure that the user is able to use the piece and that the piece functions in the target delivery environment.

The Challenges of Distribution   Once upon a time, distribution was simply the installation of the program on a predefined set of systems. In recent years, however, this phase has been complicated by the need to consider mass distribution. Delivery media such as floppy disks, CD-ROMs, local area networks, and the World Wide Web all brought their own challenges to implementing a piece.

Installation   Along with the complication of distribution is the complication of installation. Drivers for certain media, databases that contain student records, and network devices all require a technical aptitude on the part of the person installing the final piece. A single misplaced file could prevent the entire piece from functioning correctly.

User Guides and Help Files   Because early pieces were so complex and technically challenging, project teams also created detailed user guides and online help files. The level of detail in these documents was based on the technical literacy of the end user as defined in the analysis phase, and the complexity of the piece as defined in the design phase and created in the development phase.

Evaluating the Piece's Effectiveness

The phase that is commonly forgotten, at least in part, is *evaluation*. In this phase, the success of the piece is determined based on the evaluation of four specific criteria.

Reaction   The reaction of the end user has traditionally been collected through questionnaires distributed immediately following the use of the program. These questionnaires became known as *smiley sheets*, however, because they rarely collected much more detail than what the user liked and perhaps did not like about their experience with the interactive piece.

Retention   Retention had only occasionally been measured in a scientific manner. In most cases a pre-test was administered, then following the piece a post-test was administered. The assumption was made that the difference in pre-test and post-test scores reflected retention, and the piece was judged accordingly.

Unfortunately, issues surrounding long-term retention and mastery were not addressed, and only a few project teams returned to the end users after a great amount of time to conduct follow-up testing.

Response   The success of a piece should be measured by the amount of behavioral change in the end user. During the analysis phase, we were able to list objectives, as well as an identified need for which the piece was constructed. By repeating this analysis after a period of time long enough for the piece to have had an impact, we would be able to determine if the objectives were achieved.

Return on Investment   The more common measure of success for an interactive learning piece is the return on investment. The success of the piece is directly proportional to the amount of money that is saved over alternative methods of instruction. Although this was not quite as critical in earlier days, in recent years this factor has become the sole determinant as to whether a project is funded or not.

Evaluation pieces that do not evaluate all four aspects of a project will not be able to truly judge the success of a piece. For example, it is possible to have a phenomenal return on investment while the training actually causes greater problems than it solves.

Pinpointing the Three Pitfalls of Traditional Development Methodologies

Over the last few years, the traditional development approach has been evolving to account for several inefficiencies that have been recognized. Again, I am generalizing, and the inefficiencies that I am pointing out have somewhat been accounted for as organizations begin to make accommodations for the shortfalls of the traditional approach to interactive learning programs. As I will describe in greater detail over the next few sections, the three pitfalls of the traditional development process may be summarized as: the gap in communication between the design and the development teams; the fact that the best ideas arrive after development has begun; and that the end user is involved in the wrong end of the project.

Recognizing the Communication Gap

The first point of confusion caused by the traditional approach to development is the communication gap between the design phase and the development phase, as highlighted in Figure 29.2.

FIG. 29.2
A gap in communication exists between designers and developers that often results in poorly communicated goals and unexpected results.

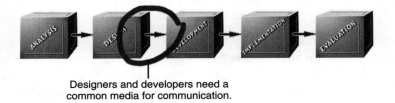

Designers and developers need a
common media for communication.

For years developers have asked designers, "Why didn't you tell me that is how it was to work?" Similarly, the designers have asked, "Why don't those developers build what I ask for?" You see, these two groups of people speak different languages, and despite detailed story boards that attempt to define all dimensions of the interactive experience, there is quite a bit of room left for personal interpretation.

The Point of the Really Good Ideas

The second point of frustration in a project occurs just after development begins, as highlighted in Figure 29.3. This is the point when all of the really good ideas surface.

FIG. 29.3
Once a person begins to experience a design in its final medium, ideas for improvement begin to arise.

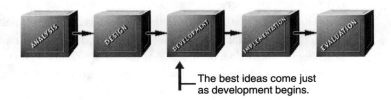

The best ideas come just
as development begins.

I am sure that you have heard the old cliché, "It is easier to critique than create." This is certainly true when it comes to the creation of multimedia. As soon as development has progressed to the point that elements begin to appear in the Presentation Window, everyone—from the designers to the client—begins to critique the design or react with ideas that reach beyond the original concept.

This is certainly understandable when you consider the challenge of designing in two-dimensions for a three- or four-dimensional environment in which the user will experience multiple paths of content. I often equate this experience to the designing of my family's home a few years ago.

As we sat with the architect reviewing the blueprints, we determined that the size of the rooms, the amenities, and the traffic flow made perfect sense. As the construction team dug the foundation and laid the base structure, everything looked great. As soon as they began raising the walls and we could begin to interact with the space by walking through it, however, we quickly discovered windows could be added, a roof line needed to be changed, and only at this point could we determine where light switches and electric outlets could be placed.

Despite the experience of the designers and their ability to describe what this space would look like, there was no way to create the experience in a two-dimensional media. This is true whenever you are building a house, and it is true when you are building an interactive experience.

Moving the Role of the End User

The final concern with the traditional development process is the point at which the end user becomes involved. The end user is involved during analysis—at least in thought—but then not again until the implementation and evaluation phases. More appropriately, however, the end user should be involved in the development process from the very beginning through evaluation, as highlighted in Figure 29.4.

FIG. 29.4
Implementing a portion of the final piece, then evaluating the end user's reaction to and retention of the information is critical throughout the development process, not just at the end.

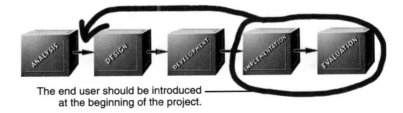

The end user should be introduced at the beginning of the project.

Having the user's reaction throughout the design and development process is critical for two reasons. First, if you are trying to communicate to the end users, their reactions should be assessed so that the results can be used to further guide development.

The second benefit of having the end user involved early in the process is the opportunity to learn what modifications are needed to make the program more usable. When these changes are identified after the program is done, a great deal of effort must be expended to make the corrections.

Carrying Tradition into Today

As Authorware itself was being created, a new approach to multimedia development was being considered. This approach attempted to take what was good from the traditional approach and combine it with the strengths of today's technology to eliminate the three pitfalls.

Goals of the New Approach to Multimedia Development

The new methodology was conceived to accommodate communication and the maintenance of a program as ideas changed throughout the development process.

Eliminating the Communication Gap   At the heart of this new methodology is a process that eliminates the communication gap by incorporating a development tool—Authorware—that can be used in both the design and the development phases. Design specifications, scripts, and story boards are replaced by prototypes that enable all parties to touch and see one another's ideas.

N O T E   Many development teams use the term *prototype* for the final application that is created to convince the client that the team is qualified to do the project; that a specific approach is appropriate; or that computer-based training is the best instructional medium. This piece is commonly discarded once the contract is secured. ■

The prototypes become a common language between the designers and the developers, and a language that can be shared with the end user to obtain valuable information as to the direction the overall project is taking.

Accommodating New Ideas   In addition to being easy to use, Authorware and the Flowline structure are easy to maintain. Therefore, as ideas arise from the client or design team actually seeing segments that have been developed, those ideas can be incorporated with minimal effort.

CAUTION

Be sure not to confuse the notion of accommodation with the ability to constantly make changes. There must come a point when a module is considered done and modifications are only considered if the project is ahead of schedule and budget.

To take advantage of this, development can be approached beginning with a single module. As the end user or client reacts to the development efforts, changes only need to occur in this first module rather than across an entire application. Once the first module is complete, it can be referred to for developing subsequent modules.

Allowing the End User to Participate   Finally, this new methodology was designed with the end user in mind. Because a piece can be built then immediately executed, the end user can actually participate in the development efforts. Bringing the end user to the development team or sending the piece to the end user on a CD-ROM or via the Internet allows the end user to participate in design and development by providing feedback.

The capability to incorporate the end user early in the process is beneficial for several reasons. First, the comments of the end user could be incorporated in real time so that the end user could further react to the direction that the project is heading. This aids in assuring that the user's needs are being met.

Additionally, as the design and development teams discover new requirements, changes only need to take place for the first module because no more than the first module is under construction. The remainder of the modules will simply incorporate the precedent as a part of the design specifications.

The New Phases of Multimedia Development

As the new methodology for creating multimedia was conceived, phases that had the same characteristics as those in the traditional methodology were arranged in a manner that more accurately reflected how development activities needed to occur.

Like the traditional approach to developing multimedia, the new approach begins with an analysis phase. Different from the traditional approach, however, the design and development phases have been combined. This morphing of the phases is made possible by tools such as Authorware that accommodate rapid prototyping, allow non-programmers to participate in development, and result in structures which support the prototypes actually evolving into the final piece. Like the combining of the design and development phases, the implementation and evaluation phases have also been combined to ensure that the end user is incorporated throughout the project.

This new approach to the creation of interactive multimedia programs, as pictured in Figure 29.5, also addresses the three pitfalls of the traditional development approach. Over the next few sections, I will discuss each step of the process in greater detail, as well as give an example of how a project may be approached using this process.

FIG. 29.5
Phases were combined in
the new development
process.

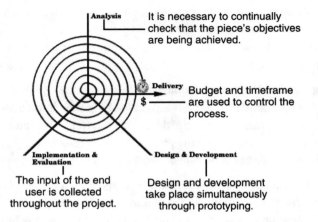

Analysis — It is necessary to continually check that the piece's objectives are being achieved.

Delivery — Budget and timeframe are used to control the process.

Implementation & Evaluation — The input of the end user is collected throughout the project.

Design & Development — Design and development take place simultaneously through prototyping.

It Still Begins with Analysis   The success of a piece is still founded on a solid analysis phase. Learning what the user needs, what behaviors must be changed, and determining what resources are available to meet those needs is critical.

 TIP   When developing an interactive learning piece that employs high-level interactivity, it is important to determine the mastery level that must be obtained.

We must be realistic, however, in understanding that not all of the questions can be answered before development begins. In many cases, more questions will arise after development begins than before. For example, I was recently on a project attempting to determine how the end user would navigate through the content. Despite weeks of developing story boards and concept diagrams, this issue was not resolved until I placed several push buttons on the screen and enabled the client to actually experience moving from one section of the piece to another.

We need to incorporate a methodology that enables us to constantly revisit the analysis phase, if for nothing else than to hold our design accountable for meeting the end user's needs.

Prototyping   Today's development methodology, especially when Authorware is the development tool, combines the traditional design and development phases. Sure, there are portions more dedicated to design (we refer to those as concepting sessions), and there are portions more dedicated to production, but at the heart is a healthy blend.

This blend of designing and developing is referred to as *prototyping*. Because Authorware is so easy to use—and you can rely on models created from previous pieces—the entire team may experience an idea soon after its conception.

Implementation and Evaluation   The third phase of the newer development approach combines implementation with evaluation. It is necessary to get the opinions of the end user early in the process and throughout the process. This phase ideally evaluates not only the end user's reaction to the piece, but also checks to see that the piece is actually teaching as intended.

Walking Through a Project Using the New Development Approach

Over the past six years, my team has taken this concept that was conceived to solve the three pitfalls of the traditional development process—the gap in communication between design and development, the best ideas come during development, and the end user is involved at the wrong end of the project—and we have worked to make it a reality. Today, projects are completed within the allotted time frame and budget; client expectations are met; and the piece are successful at all levels of evaluation. All of this is accomplished without the traditional tools for analysis, design, and development.

N O T E   I will admit and heavily stress that the evolution in development methodologies is not complete. As new technologies find their way into the development arena, I find it necessary to revisit the methodology. For example, as the Internet became a common tool for communication, my team had to figure out how to use it effectively for project communication. We are now looking at new Internet technologies to figure out how they can play a role in multi-location and multinational development efforts. ■

Although it is not possible to write a cookbook for creating multimedia, the following is a set of guidelines for implementing the new approach to multimedia development. Keep in mind that every project has its own set of nuances and that the following outline is merely to serve as a conceptual guide.

1. Define your time frame and budget. Central to this approach of developing multimedia is the need to work backwards from a time frame and budget. These two figures will determine the total possible project resources.

2. Conduct a thorough needs analysis to determine the performance objectives and the outcome objectives (see Fig. 29.6). Further, conduct the task analysis to determine how needs can be addressed, and from that create a content outline for the piece.

FIG. 29.6
Beginning with the seed of an
idea, the first step is to
conduct an analysis.

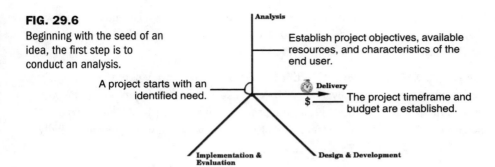

Analysis

Establish project objectives, available
resources, and characteristics of the
end user.

A project starts with an
identified need.

Delivery

The project timeframe and
budget are established.

Implementation &
Evaluation

Design & Development

3. Engineer the outline so that similar tasks are associated into modules and sub-modules. Keep in mind the levels of interactivity, and begin to think of ways to teach multiple tasks together using high-level interactivity.

▶ To refer to the three levels of interactivity, **see** "Defining Interactivity," **p. 536**.

N O T E Although it is important to be as thorough as possible when building the content outline, you will likely find more efficient or appropriate ways to combine the content once development begins. If that happens, it is important to return to this point and re-define the remainder of the project. ▪

4. Determine approximately what percentage (for content, media, time, etc.) of the entire program each module constitutes and then approximately what percentage of the module each sub-module constitutes. Although you have yet to define the content specifically, you should have a pretty good feel about where emphasis must be placed based on information collected in the task analysis.

5. From the budget and time frame, determine what resources should be dedicated to the creation of the user interface and general navigation scheme.

6. Using the remaining resources and the calculated percentages for the content modules and sub-modules, determine what resources should be dedicated to each portion of the program.

7. Using the content outline for reference, create a prototype for the navigation scheme and graphical user interface (see Fig. 29.7). Stay as general as possible, and avoid the temptation to incorporate any graphics or audio. This prototype is only to show functionality.

CAUTION
Avoid developing too much too quickly. Take small steps, and incorporate the feedback of your client or end user along the way.

FIG. 29.7
After the content has been organized, create a prototype for the navigation scheme.

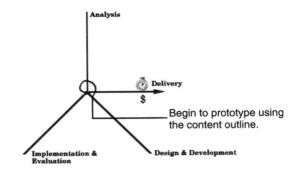

Begin to prototype using the content outline.

8. Conduct user testing with the functioning prototype. Ask colleagues how they feel about the content structure; ask users how they feel about the proposed content; and ask everyone about the functionality (see Fig. 29.8). Keep in mind that this is everyone's first time to critique your work, so be prepared for a lot of opinions and suggestions.

CAUTION

Be sure that you do not simply mail the prototype to an unsuspecting end user for evaluation. Because so many necessary elements for content and navigation will be missing, you need to guide the end user through the piece.

FIG. 29.8
Use the prototype of the navigation scheme to conduct an evaluation.

Check with peers or end users to determine appropriateness of the navigation scheme.

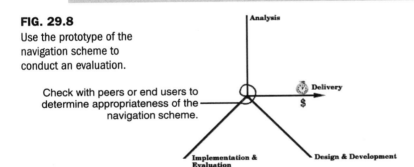

9. Return to the analysis phase with the information you have collected and the experience you have gained. Is the content really organized correctly? Does the navigation scheme support the learning objectives? Is this piece usable by the target population? Ask these questions and more to verify that you are on the right path. Analyze the content to determine the appropriate graphic style and theme for the user interface (see Fig. 29.9). Collect imagery and existing marketing/company material to be used in constructing the actual interface.

FIG. 29.9
Return to the analysis phase to react to what has been learned and to conduct further analysis.

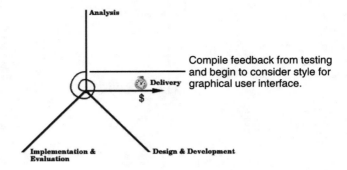

Compile feedback from testing and begin to consider style for graphical user interface.

10. Create illustration mockups that can be used for the graphical interface (see Fig. 29.10). Keep the budget and time frame for the creation of the interface in sight so that too much time is not spent creating detailed mockups.

N O T E Be sure to design an interface that can be easily expanded or collapsed. It is very likely that if the content does not change by the end of this development effort, it will change in future versions. ▪

FIG. 29.10
This prototyping phase cannot incorporate any authoring.

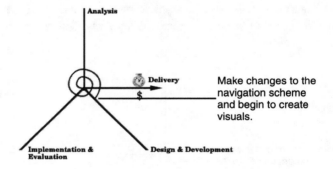

Make changes to the navigation scheme and begin to create visuals.

CAUTION

It is easy to carry the mockups too far. Keep in mind that this work will probably be modified and some part of it will even be thrown away, so only complete as much as you are willing to give up.

11. Ask the end users and your clients to react to the proposed interface concepts; then incorporate all the ideas that have been agreed upon (see Fig. 29.11).

FIG. 29.11
Allow the end users to react
to interface ideas.

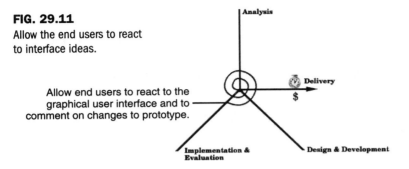

Allow end users to react to the
graphical user interface and to
comment on changes to prototype.

12. Now that the navigation scheme—complete with a graphical user interface—has
been determined, it is time to move to the first bit of content. Select a module (it
does not have to be the first one) that is mid-sized to small in comparison to the
others.

At this point, you must work closely with the subject matter expert to delve deep
into the content (see Fig. 29.12). In a concepting session, ask such questions as,
"How will the users apply this in the real world? If there was something that the
users could hold in their hands to more clearly learn the concept, what would it be?
Why is this so difficult for people to learn? What do you want the end users to walk
away with?"

At the heart of it all, you must get to the instructional goal. Do not worry about the
words or even the pictures yet. Concern yourself with what the user can *do* to learn
and not what they can be told.

FIG. 29.12
Analysis at this point turns
from what should the user
learn to how could they
learn.

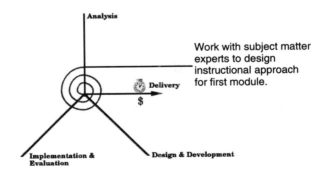

Work with subject matter
experts to design
instructional approach
for first module.

13. With the timeframe and budget for this module in mind, begin to design a way in
which the user can interact with the content. Use the three levels of interactivity—
low, medium, and high—as appropriate to best convey your message.

▶ To refer to the three levels of interactivity, **see** "Defining Interactivity," **p. 536.**

14. As soon as an idea has been touched upon, begin to create a prototype for the idea so that others on the team, including the subject matter expert, can quickly understand the direction that you are heading and can further contribute to the design (see Fig. 29.13).

    Continue to revise the prototype as the idea evolves, but be sure not to spend time incorporating *any media (graphics, digital movies, audio, video, etc.) whatsoever!*

FIG. 29.13
The prototype is to spur the good ideas that arise from development.

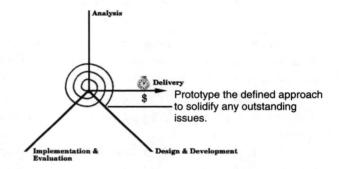

Prototype the defined approach to solidify any outstanding issues.

CAUTION

Avoid the temptation of spending time to make the prototype perfect. This work will surely be modified, and any objects in the Presentation Window will be thrown away.

---

15. Take the prototype—embedded in the navigation scheme using the graphical user interface—and allow end users to work with it (see Fig. 29.14). Observe ways in which they attempt to interact with what you have built, and provide guidance only when they appear confused. Gather as much information from these testers as possible, knowing that they are truly the ones with the need as well as the experience.

 If you create the prototypes using the piece's navigation scheme—inclusive of all buttons, titles, logos, etc.—or at least using a graphic of it so that items do not invade one another's space, it will be much easier to sew the prototype into the master piece once it has been accepted.

FIG. 29.14
The end user should be able
to use the prototype void of
any content.

Once again involve the
end user to ensure the
piece is usable and that it
meets their needs.

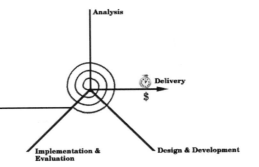

16. Analyze the information received from testing (see Fig. 29.15) to determine which comments were a result of the design and which were a result of the incompleteness of the piece. With the time frame and budget in mind, determine which suggestions are critical to the piece and which can be left as extras.

17. Now that you have a working prototype, conduct the final analysis to determine the media to use as well as the sources for that media.

FIG. 29.15
Use the information from
end-user testing to determine what modifications
need to be made to the
program's functionality.

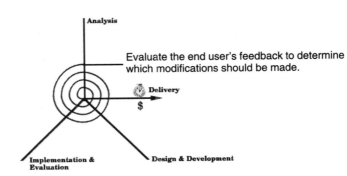

Evaluate the end user's feedback to determine
which modifications should be made.

18. Finish the development of the first module, including all media creation and content implementation. Each element should be constructed with the budget and time frame for the module in mind (see Fig. 29.16). Remember: you may need to return for slight modifications, but for now this module is done.

N O T E Completing the first module will probably take longer than you estimated for a module of its size. This is due to the fact that extra time was used to establish precedents that will be used in future modules. Additionally, team communication needed to be established while working on the first module. ▪

FIG. 29.16
Finish the first module using
the budget, time frame, and
user comments as a guide.

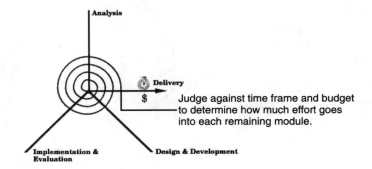

Judge against time frame and budget
to determine how much effort goes
into each remaining module.

19. Distribute the first completed module to a group of end users. Now you should be
     able to gather information on usability and reaction as well as on the effectiveness of
     the piece.

At this point, you have learned enough about communicating as a team, gathering content
from subject matter experts, and the needs of the end user that development can move at
a faster pace and with minimal risk of major modifications. As a next step, take one or two
more modules and begin with the concepting session. Run through all of the steps, being
careful not to make too many assumptions about the end user.

Continue to take small groups of modules and run them through the process—never
biting off more than you can chew. As requests for modifications appear, weigh them
against the time frame and budget to determine whether they should be completed or not.
Because you established many usability factors during the first module, there should be
very few, if any, global issues arising. ●

Delivering the Final Program

CHAPTER 30

Things to Consider for Multi-Platform Development

The battle began in 1984 when the Macintosh made its way onto the playing field. As this exciting new platform took hold, it quickly became the platform of choice for such creative industries as advertising, print design, and multimedia. Shortly thereafter, software providers recognized the need to enable users to move working files from one platform to the other.

Working cross-platform is not much of an issue if you are dealing with text only, so such applications as word processors and spreadsheets quickly made their way to the marketplace. The real challenge was discovered when application developers started moving graphics, sound, animation, and interactivity back and forth.

Dealing with fonts

Unfortunately, fonts in Windows and on the Macintosh are very different. Authorware attempts to accommodate this through the Font Mapping utility, but there are also a few things that you can do to avoid font troubles.

Understanding colors and palettes

When working cross-platform, you can either use a cross-platform palette, use the Macintosh palette in both environments, or create a custom palette.

Working with sound and digital video

While audio is a standard part of the Macintosh, not until recently has it been a standard part of a Windows-based system. Video formats are also considered.

Coping with interface standards

Several interface characteristics are addressed as you move from a Windows platform to a Macintosh.

Understanding external functions

As your piece moves cross platform, you will need to recompile the external function code so that it takes advantage of the target environment.

Today, Authorware is the leading tool for cross-platform interactive learning development between the Macintosh and Windows platforms. Although other authoring tools support cross-platform development, none do it with the accuracy or ease that Authorware provides. Despite the ease of moving a program from one platform to another, there are still a few tricks that can make or break cross-platform development.

In this chapter, you will learn about issues that must be considered for cross-platform development, including the use of fonts, color palettes, performance restraints, sound, digital video, and external functions. ■

Preparing for Multi-Platform Development

As the number of installed personal computers continues to grow along with the need to capture the greatest number of users possible for an interactive multimedia program, the need to accommodate both the Macintosh and the Windows platforms is increasing.

To make delivery in these very different environments cost effective, however, you cannot afford to engineer a program twice—once for each platform. Fortunately, Authorware supports the capability to build an application on one platform, and then edit or distribute that program on the other platform. This also works for a development team where some people like to work on the Macintosh and others like to work in Windows, yet they all are required to work on the same project.

Although Authorware supports cross-platform development, there are certainly a few tricks that must be learned to make this a smooth process. Macromedia estimates that 10 percent to 15 percent of the time it took to originally produce the program will be spent converting it to a second platform. I believe that if you plan carefully and follow the development process outlined in Chapter 29, "A New look at the Development Process," this number can be reduced. Without these considerations, however, you will surely face difficulties when attempting to convert your piece to a second platform.

Dealing with Fonts

Without question, fonts cause the greatest frustration or concern for multimedia developers who work cross-platform. Although Authorware has taken much of the frustration out of development with the font mapping feature, dealing with fonts is still an issue.

As we discussed in Chapter 3, "Presenting Text," fonts on the Macintosh are different than fonts in a Windows environment. Their names are different, their sizes are different, and worst of all, the way each platform applies a font style is different. In an attempt to make it easier to work with fonts on both sides of the aisle, you may want to consider the techniques covered next.

Avoid Strange Fonts

The first rule for cross-platform consistency is to avoid the fonts that are not standard for either the Macintosh or the Windows platform. Although the fonts look great and the style may certainly fit your application, you will find that the aesthetics may not outweigh the problems caused by using nonstandard fonts, unless, of course, these fonts are converted to graphics.

To compound the issue, non-PostScript Type 1 fonts may be packaged and distributed with a Macintosh application but not with a Windows application. This means that nonstandard Windows fonts will have to be distributed and installed for your piece to work.

 To play it absolutely safe, use only system standard fonts or else create a graphic rather than using fonts. Using graphics instead of character fonts, of course, can increase file size and development time.

Beware of Styles

As soon as you get the font type and size issue settled, you will discover another problem with using fonts cross-platform. Although the height of the font in terms of pixels can be closely matched, fonts that have a style applied to them will have different spacing (kerning and leading) dimensions from one platform to another.

For example, if you begin development on the Macintosh and elect to make all text in a content block bold, the number of characters on a line or the number of lines in the block may differ when the piece is moved to the Windows environment. Additionally, the space between the lines will increase. This is due to the fact that the space between the characters is also given bold characteristics in Windows but not on the Macintosh.

 TIP To reduce this issue, try to use text that does not contain hard returns for text wrapping around an object, and leave a little extra space at the bottom of the text block in case the number of lines does increase.

Experiment with Font Mapping

Even if you try to avoid nonstandard fonts and are conscious of using styles, it is a good idea to experiment with the font mapping utility. The Font Mapping dialog box, shown in Figure 30.1, enables you to determine which font will be substituted for the current font after platform conversion.

FIG. 30.1
Use the Font Mapping dialog box to determine equivalent fonts when the piece moves cross-platform.

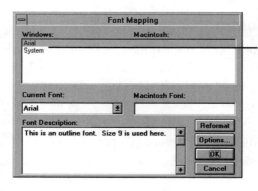

These Windows fonts convert to the corresponding fonts in the Macintosh column.

 TIP When using the font mapping utility, I suggest that you move the piece from platform to platform a few times just to be sure that the selected font for each platform continues to meet your needs. Don't just convert a small block of text and then make the assumption that everything will work. Also, use a grid behind the text so that you can measure the required increase in space.

CAUTION
Authorware does not hyphenate, so words automatically move to the next line if they no longer fit on their current line. This is commonly the case when moving bold text from the Macintosh to Windows. The result is text that is difficult to read and contains an extremely uneven right margin.

Use TrueType Fonts

If possible, use TrueType fonts. Despite platform differences, TrueType fonts are mathematically created so that they look the same on either platform.

> **CAUTION**
>
> TrueType fonts for Windows platforms must be available on the end users' systems if you are using TrueType. Therefore, you must package them separately from your program and either create an installation program or rely on the end users to properly place the fonts on their system. Additionally, most TrueType and PostScript fonts are copyrighted, so you need special permission to use and distribute them.

Use Graphics Instead of Fonts

To avoid the font issue, you can substitute fonts with graphics. As discussed in Chapter 3, "Presenting Text," this also enables you to take advantage of anti-aliasing techniques that result in a much higher quality program.

The drawback, of course, is that anti-aliasing cannot be created in Authorware, so additional steps must be added to the development process. Further, the amount of effort needed to maintain a piece with text that has been converted to a graphic greatly increases.

> **CAUTION**
>
> Although quality may increase, substituting graphics for fonts not only increases development costs but also the overall piece size.

Test, Test, Test

No matter which approach you take in dealing with fonts during cross-platform development, you must continually test the final program. Testing should happen throughout development, and it should include a variety of systems on which the final piece could run.

Understanding Colors and Palettes

As Windows-based systems become more capable of multimedia, the issue of cross-platform color palette compatibility is disappearing. Additionally, Authorware enables you to load a custom palette that can be used for either platform, thereby eliminating the need to rely on a preset system palette.

In the not-so-distant past, however, this was not the case. Until recently, the standard Windows and Macintosh systems shipped with 16 colors that could be upgraded to 256 colors, as shown in Figure 30.2.

FIG. 30.2
An older Macintosh 16-color palette and a current Windows 256-color palette.

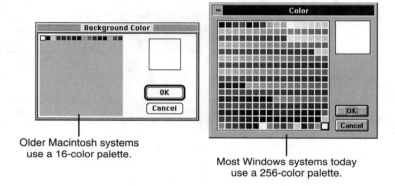

Older Macintosh systems use a 16-color palette.

Most Windows systems today use a 256-color palette.

Unfortunately, the purchasing departments for many companies did not elect to include the upgrade, so delivering desktop training or multimedia solutions was a real trick. Today, however, almost every computer shipped supports at least 256 colors, and most support 32,768 colors. The issue now is that the 256 colors selected for the Windows environment do not align with the 256 colors selected for the Macintosh, as shown in Figure 30.3.

The Macintosh 256-color palette   The Windows 256-color palette

FIG. 30.3
The Macintosh and the Windows 256-color palettes are different.

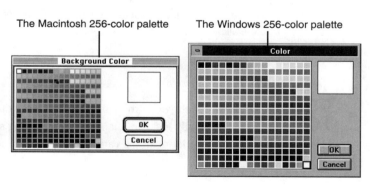

When working across platforms, you may want to consider the techniques discussed next.

Use a Cross-Platform Palette

Authorware, Adobe Photoshop, and Debabelizer all ship with a palette, shown in Figure 30.4, that was designed for cross-platform development. If possible, load one of these palettes into both Authorware for the Macintosh and for Windows prior to beginning development using the techniques discussed in Chapter 2, "Setting Up an Authorware Piece."

▶ For guidance on loading a custom palette, **see** "Palette," **p. 47**.

FIG. 30.4
This palette was designed to take advantage of both platforms.

This universal palette is optimized for both the Macintosh and the Windows platform.

Use the Macintosh Palette

Even if you are developing solely for the Windows environment, you may want to load the Macintosh system palette into Authorware for Windows. This palette seems to be a bit more usable: the hue of the colors is not as high as in the Windows palette, and a greater range of natural tones is available.

N O T E   The active matrix screens on laptops tend to darken all colors, which has caused problems with color choices and has resulted in our team developing a very light custom palette in some applications for Windows laptop delivery. ▮

Create Your Own Palette

If neither the cross-platform palette nor the Macintosh system palette has the colors you need, I suggest creating your own. Palettes can be created using such applications as Adobe Photoshop and then imported into Authorware using the load palette feature (Windows), as shown in Figure 30.5, or using ResEdit or XCMDs (Macintosh). The SetPalette XCMD is included with the Authorware extras, which are distributed on the application disk.

FIG. 30.5
Palettes can be loaded into
Authorware for Windows.

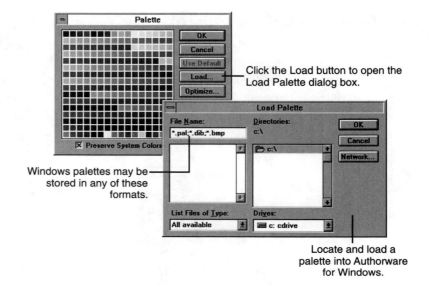

Click the Load button to open the
Load Palette dialog box.

Windows palettes may be
stored in any of these
formats.

Locate and load a
palette into Authorware
for Windows.

> **CAUTION**
> Every monitor is a little different. Do not create a palette that looks good on your monitor without testing it on other systems as well. Additionally, testing should take place throughout the development process to be sure that the final images are acceptable given palette and monitor differences.

Knowing the Performance Issues

Apart from how a piece looks as it moves from one platform to another is how it operates. Each system within an operating environment has unique qualities, and these differences are magnified as you look across platforms. To accommodate these differences, try to follow the techniques described next.

Define the Target Platform

You must first be very specific when determining the target delivery platform. Stipulate performance requirements, minimum configurations for RAM and hard disk space, and transfer rates for CD-ROM drives. This is especially true if you are developing a program that will take advantage of a printer. Because there are hundreds of printers available and each one has a unique driver, printing can vary from system to system.

If the piece will be delivered in a wide variety of systems, I suggest planning and developing for the lowest common denominator and then testing on as many variations as possible.

Access to the Target System

If you are building for an out-of-standard system, I suggest that you purchase or borrow a system that matches the delivery environment. For example, we have been asked to do several projects for trade shows or museums. The systems used in these environments each required a 21-inch monitor. Because not everyone on our development team has such a system, we requested that the client let us use the delivery machines for development to ensure that the final program took full advantage of the targeted system.

If development can't take place on the delivery system, at least one system that matches the final configuration should be nearby so that the program can be transferred to it for performance testing.

TIP When transferring the piece to the delivery system, don't just transfer portions of the piece for testing. Transferring the entire piece will force the delivery system to function just as it will when the final piece is installed.

Catching Performance Problems Early

Whether you are working on the final delivery environment or not, it is critical to the success of the piece to conduct performance testing throughout the development process. This requirement is even more crucial if you are producing a product that will be distributed to a broad market.

This, however, is another one of those lessons that seasoned developers never seem to learn. Last year, for example, we produced a CD-ROM that was to be sold by our client. Even though we conducted in-house testing, we did not spend the time or the money to conduct formal testing. As a result, during the last week of the project, we discovered that the custom video driver used by our client conflicted with the animation played using the Digital Movie icon. The conflict resulted in a serious system crash.

The options were to remove hundreds of animation sequences that were used to create simulations or to work with Macromedia, Microsoft, and our client to secure a new driver. The last week of the project was the wrong time to discover this problem.

Working with Sound and Digital Video

Media elements are always an issue when working across platforms. Performance, support, and quality must be continually checked to ensure that the final piece functions as anticipated. Although there are no hard and fast rules, the rest of this section covers a few issues that you may want to consider.

Missing Sound

Just as most Windows systems shipped with 16 colors, they also shipped without a sound card. Like color, however, the standard for new Windows systems has been raised, and most systems available today provide audio capability.

If you are creating an application that will be distributed to the general market, however, you must be aware that many systems might not have been upgraded. Therefore, you must make the decision to either provide a product that some people cannot use or provide an alternative to using audio when a sound card is not available.

N O T E Keep in mind that most digital video also contains audio, which will not be heard if there is no sound card in the computer. ■

You do not have to worry about audio on the Macintosh because it has been a standard feature since the Macintosh was introduced.

The Problem with Synchronization

Trying to synchronize sound and animation is a real trick. Trying to keep this synchronization consistent from one system to another or from one platform to another is a nightmare.

To ensure that audio and animation remain synchronized, I suggest incorporating the two media elements into a digital movie using such a program as Macromedia Director. In fact, whenever you have a variety of graphics that are being layered together to create a special effect, or a simulation of a process, it is usually easier to create this effect as a digital movie. (See Chapter 20, "Working with Digital Movies," for more information.)

Selecting a Video Format

Although working with digital video across platforms is becoming easier, there are still a number of decisions that must be made. For example, how do you select a digital video file type to use?

If I am developing for the Macintosh only, I would select QuickTime, and if I am developing for the Windows environment only, I would select Video for Windows or MPEG. However, cross-platform developing makes the selection process a bit more complicated.

QuickTime is probably the best alternative because it is available for the Macintosh and for Windows, and using QuickTime does not require you to re-digitize the video. Using QuickTime does require that extensions be installed for both platforms, although it is now a standard part of the Macintosh operating system.

An additional benefit gained from using QuickTime is that a single digital video file can be referenced by either the Macintosh executable or the Windows executable program. This means that you only need one video file for both platforms.

Coping with System Interface Standards

In addition to working with media elements that you create, you should be aware of the graphical interface standards for each platform and the areas in which they differ, as shown in Figure 30.6. For example, buttons in a Windows environment are three-dimensional and actually "depress" when clicked. Not all Macintosh buttons, on the other hand, are three-dimensional.

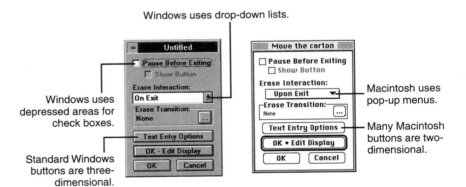

FIG. 30.6
Windows and Macintosh systems vary in the way their interfaces look and function.

As another example, the Macintosh pull-down menu cannot be paused by clicking the menu bar item. In the Windows environment, the user clicks the menu bar title, sees the paused pull-down menu, and then makes a selection from the menu.

Understanding External Functions

The final concern in cross-platform development is the operation of external functions, which—as you may recall—are used by Authorware in the form of XCMDs (Macintosh) and DLLs (Windows). Unfortunately, external functions are ignored when the piece is moved from one platform to another.

▶ To gain insight on using external functions, **see** "Understanding External Code," **p. 416**.

For example, if you are developing a piece on the Macintosh in which external functions have been loaded, then when the piece is moved to the Windows platform, the external functions will not be included or available. To replicate in Windows the functionality of the XCMD, you have to create the external function as a DLL and load it into the Authorware for Windows piece once the conversion process is complete. ●

CHAPTER 31

Preparing for Final Delivery

Before development even begins, you need to start thinking about more than *how* the end user will use the piece. You must also begin to think about *where* the end user will be using the piece and *how* you will get it to them.

In today's academic and corporate environments, the need to deliver interactive multimedia over a variety of platforms and to multiple locations is greater than ever. While traditional interactive learning solutions may have been designed for delivery to a specific platform, or even to a specific classroom-like environment, today's solutions must be able to accommodate the entire range of options.

Authorware has always allowed you to develop on one platform (either Macintosh or Windows) then convert the piece to run on the other. Additionally, successful multimedia pieces have been delivered via CD-ROM, floppy disk, and Local Area Network. With the introduction of Authorware 3.5 and Shockwave for Authorware, you may now create fully interactive pieces to be delivered via the World Wide Web.

The various types of distribution media

You learn about each type of medium and how the scope of the piece determines the file size and therefore the delivery medium.

Distributing your piece to end users

You learn about packaging, which is the ability to create a self-contained executable file from the final piece.

What Shockwave for Authorware is

Shockwave is a tool that simplifies access to and the creation of multimedia programs over the Web.

Preparing for and using Shockwave

You learn the requirements you need to run Shockwave, and the steps necessary to use it.

In this chapter, I will discuss issues regarding preparing a piece for final delivery. Additionally, I will give general guidelines for creating a piece that is to be delivered to a variety of end user systems. ▦

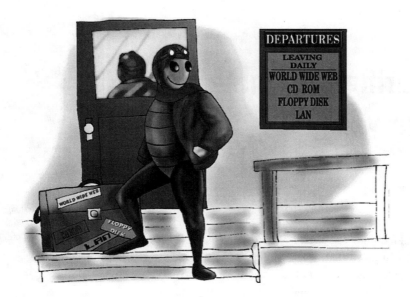

Exploring Various Distribution Media

Once the authoring of a piece has been completed, you will be ready to distribute it to the end users. Unlike a spreadsheet or a word processing document, however, the end user will not need to have a copy of Authorware in order to view your piece. Instead, Authorware provides the ability to create a self-contained executable file from the final piece. This process of creating a self-running file is called *packaging*.

The executable piece can be distributed to the end user in a variety of medium. The type of media and the scope of the piece will determine the file size and, therefore, the delivery medium. In any case, there are a few tricks and benefits for each delivery option.

N O T E The delivery medium and its limitations are typically dictated prior to development. Because the client or end user's system/needs dictates the delivery medium, the limitations of the medium must be taken into consideration during design and development. With this as a beginning point for the project, the content media must be selected to accommodate the limitations of the delivery medium. ▦

Determining the Method of Distribution

Each method of distribution has its own benefits, as well as its limitations. These limitations should be well understood before development begins. Additionally, the piece should be tested using the delivery medium throughout the development process. You should create a copy of the in-progress piece, package it, place it on the desired medium, then install/run it from that medium.

Floppy Disk The most obvious limitation with floppy disks is the amount of information that may be distributed on a reasonable number of diskettes. Despite this limitation, don't assume that multimedia can't be delivered via floppy disk.

In the last couple of years, I have developed a variety of applications that have been delivered via floppy disk. The most recent is an application created for Lutheran Brotherhood Insurance that was mailed to a direct market. While I was not able to use audio or video, I was able to incorporate scanned graphics, animations, and a large number of interactions.

> **N O T E** You may use third-party compression and installation routines to fit a larger piece onto a single or multiple floppy disks. This would require that the user install the final piece to the hard drive or network before executing it. A few of my favorite compression/installation programs include StuffIt for the Macintosh, and DoughBoy or PKZIP for the DOS/Windows environments.

CD-ROM CD-ROM has quickly become the default medium for distribution. Currently capable of holding about 650 MB, a CD-ROM may be created for a single platform or to support both Macintosh and Windows.

I recommend that, when developing a piece that will be distributed via CD-ROM, you create a test CD-ROM as soon as possible in order to monitor performance. Applications on a CD-ROM have a tendency to perform slower than those running from the hard drive. Therefore, if you develop animations, synchronized audio, and other large media elements from the hard drive, their performance may differ when running from the CD-ROM.

> **N O T E** Authorware is extremely efficient in the way in which it reads data from a CD-ROM. Using a process known as "streaming," Authorware will load as much data into RAM as possible, then play that data from RAM rather than directly from the CD-ROM. As memory becomes available, more data is read from the CD-ROM.

Network A network may be used to distribute a final piece to an end user's system, or the piece may actually be accessed directly over the network. In either case, there are advantages and disadvantages that must be considered.

- Local—Using the network solely as a distribution channel is an efficient means of reaching a large group of end users. However, it does require that each end user have enough hard drive space locally to accommodate the piece.

  For example, if you create a performance support tool that people would access only occasionally, users would still require the large amount of disk space locally for the information. Storing this information on the network or even on a CD-ROM would better conserve end user hard drive space.

- Online—If you have a large piece that would be accessed only occasionally or a piece that must be distributed to a large group of people, using a network is a very viable solution.

CAUTION

The greatest disadvantage to using a network is the decrease in performance. For example, the end user may experience the need to wait for large graphics or audio to be displayed, and digital movies or video may appear jerky. Decreased performance is based on the type of network and the amount of activity on the network at the time the multimedia piece is being used. Be sure to do performance testing throughout development.

An Authorware piece that has been made into an executable file can be accessed across a network in a variety of ways. First, the executable file can reside on the network server and be accessed by several people at once. This configuration requires no local hard drive space.

N O T E The file server may be a different platform from the executable file, as long as the client station is able to access it. This includes the support of a UNIX file server, even though Authorware will not run on a UNIX-based client workstation. ■

An alternative to placing the entire file on the network is to place the libraries on the network and allow the end user to download only the executable file, or the RUNA3W (Windows) or RUNA3M (Macintosh) file. Since libraries may be used to store large media elements, the hard drive requirements for the end user would be minimized.

▶ To learn more about working with libraries, **see** "Using Libraries," **p. 518**.

 T I P For best performance, load the RUNA3W (Windows) or RUNA3M (Macintosh) file on the local system even if you keep the remainder of the executable on the server.

A final benefit to the end user accessing the executable file using a network is tracking and data communication. If there is a single executable located on a network, it is much easier to accommodate computer-managed instruction or to access a database which may be used to store product information.

For example, if you are developing a kiosk that will be placed in a retail store, rather than placing the piece on a stand-alone system, you could load it onto a network and tie it to the point-of-sale system. As price and product information change, the kiosk could then be updated automatically.

World Wide Web Like a local area network, the World Wide Web may be used to distribute a final piece to end users. Additionally, Authorware 3.5 now supports the ability to create a piece that can actually be embedded into or on top of a Web page and executed online.

■ Local—The most common use for the World Wide Web at this time is simply to distribute small, downloadable multimedia pieces. These pieces are downloaded to the end user's local system.

The Web can be used during development, as well as for final delivery, to make communication more efficient. For example, we have just finished a series of CD-ROMs for a client located in San Francisco. However, the lead development team was located in Minneapolis, with graphics, animation, and development being completed by our Cincinnati team. To add one more variable to the equation, the subject matter expert was located in London, England.

We used the Internet to pass files from one development team to another; to the subject matter expert for guidance and to add content; and to California for approval. In essence, we used the Internet File Transfer Protocol (FTP) to emulate a Wide Area Network.

■ Online—New with Authorware 3.5 is the ability to create a piece and then, using the Macromedia Afterburner and Shockwave technologies, create a piece which will actually play when embedded into or on top of a web page. This will be discussed in greater detail later in this chapter.

Creating a Packaged Piece

Authorware allows you to create a piece that may be run without having Authorware. This one-time process of making a copy of your piece then compiling it so that it may be executed using the Authorware runtime engine is called "Packaging."

When Authorware packages a piece, it first performs a Save As. Once the Save As is completed, Authorware "compiles" the icons so that editing is no longer possible. Any editing which is required after the piece is packaged must be done in the original source file. After the edits are made, the piece may once again be packaged.

The packaged piece is executed using the Authorware runtime engine A3M (Macintosh) and A3W.EXE (Windows). This engine is simply a player that allows the end user to view your piece without having Authorware. When packaging, you may elect to include the runtime engine as a part of the final piece, or to have it remain separately. Additionally, you must package all library files, either separately or with the final piece.

When preparing the final piece for distribution, you will discover that any media which is linked to the piece (QuickTime, Video for Windows, Director Movies, external audio files, external functions, etc.) are not packaged with Authorware. Therefore, you must be sure that these files are included along with the final piece during distribution.

Packaging a Macintosh Piece

To package a piece on the Macintosh, follow these steps:

1. With the Flowline window active, select the Package option from the File pull-down menu. When this option is selected, the Package Options dialog box, as seen in Figure 31.1, appears.

FIG. 31.1
The Macintosh version of the Package Options dialog box has several unique options for preparing the executable file.

2. Select any of the following packaging options:
   - With RUNA3M—The RUNA3M file is the Macintosh runtime engine required to play an Authorware piece without having the actual Authorware software. When packaging, this file may either be embedded into your piece or it may be distributed separately.

   N O T E If you are distributing more than one final piece via CD-ROM, network, or hard disk, you are required to distribute only one runtime engine, which may be shared among the pieces. Therefore, you would not select to package the file with RUNA3M. ■

- Without RUNA3M—You may elect to package a piece without the runtime engine for a variety of reasons. First, if you are distributing via floppy disk, you may place the runtime file on one disk, then place the piece on another.

  Additionally, a single runtime engine may be used to run several pieces. Therefore, if you have several pieces you may elect to package each without the runtime file, then distribute a single runtime file separately.

N O T E Be sure that you do not forget to distribute the runtime file if you package it separately from your pieces. If the users do not have the runtime engine, they will not be able to play the piece. ■

- Resolve Broken Links at Runtime—Broken links are references from a library to an icon whose address within Authorware has changed. This is typically a result of the icon being cut and then pasted elsewhere in the piece.

  If the icon type and link name have not changed, Authorware will be able to resolve the broken link if this option is selected.

  ▶ To better understand library links, **see** "Working with Library Links," **p. 529**.

T I P Even though this may add a few seconds to the opening process for the piece, I strongly suggest selecting the Resolve Broken Links at Runtime option. The value of ensuring that all content will be displayed far outweighs the impact of a few added seconds at startup.

- Package All Libraries Internally—Selecting this option causes Authorware to package any library icons linked to your piece as a part of the piece. While this may make distribution easier, because you have fewer pieces to keep track of, the size of the file will increase based on the media that have been stored in the library.

T I P If the Package All Libraries Internally option is not selected, but the piece contains icons that are linked to a library, the Package Library Options dialog box will open.

- Include Fonts—This Macintosh-only feature allows you to include any non-PostScript Type 1 font as a part of the packaged piece. This is incredibly beneficial if you want to ensure that the end user will see the piece exactly as it was designed.
- Use Default Names When Packaging—Selecting this option will cause the packaged piece to be named according to the current piece name, with the addition of the .APP (Windows) or .PKG (Macintosh) extension. Libraries will be packaged with the .APR (Windows) or .PKG (Macintosh) extension.

Part
VIII

Ch
31

T I P If you do not select to use the default names when packaging, Authorware will present a dialog box in which you may enter a file name.

3. Select the Save File(s) and Package button to begin packaging the piece. When packaging begins, Authorware prompts you to name the packaged piece, and to select a destination for the packaged piece.

Packaging a Windows Piece

To package a piece in the Windows environment, follow these steps:

1. With the Flowline window active, select the Package option from the File pull-down menu. When this option is selected, the Package Options dialog box, as seen in Figure 31.2, appears.

FIG. 31.2
The Windows version of the Package Options dialog box contains most of the same options as the Macintosh version.

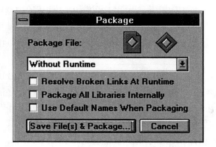

2. The packaging options on the Windows platform are the same as on the Macintosh, with the following exception:

   • Include Fonts—This feature is available only on the Macintosh.

3. Select the Save File(s) and Package button to begin packaging the piece. Authorware will prompt you for a name unless you have selected to use the default name.

Packaging a Library

Just as an Authorware piece must be packaged for distribution, any libraries linked to that piece must also be packaged for distribution. Unless the library has previously been packaged, or you selected to package the library internally, you will be prompted to package the library as soon as the piece has been packaged.

You may also elect to package a library independently of the piece by following the steps given next for each platform.

Packaging a Macintosh Library   To package a library on the Macintosh, follow these steps:

1. With the Library window active, select the Package Library option from the File pull-down menu. When this option is selected, the Package Library Options dialog box, as seen in Figure 31.3, appears.

If you package a piece with linked icons, this dialog box appears.

This dialog box appears if the Package Library option is selected.

FIG. 31.3
The Macintosh version of the Package Library Options dialog box has several unique options for preparing the executable file.

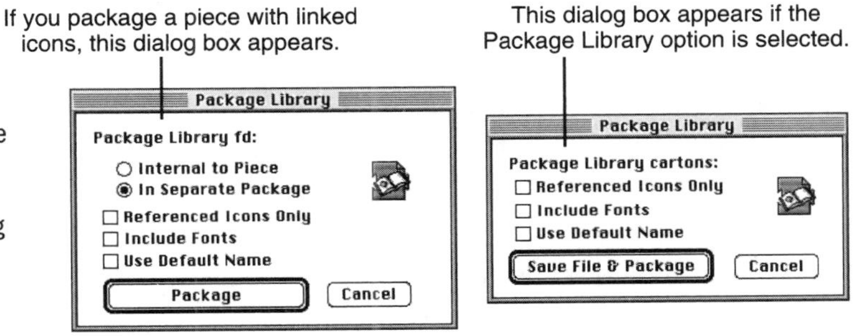

Package Library

Package Library fd:
○ Internal to Piece
◉ In Separate Package
☐ Referenced Icons Only
☐ Include Fonts
☐ Use Default Name
Package   Cancel

Package Library

Package Library cartons:
☐ Referenced Icons Only
☐ Include Fonts
☐ Use Default Name
Save File & Package   Cancel

Part
VIII

Ch
31

2. Select any of the following packaging options:

- Internal to Piece/Separate to Package—These options provide the opportunity to include or exclude the library as a part of the Authorware piece when it is packaged. Therefore, the results are the same as selecting the Package All Libraries option in the Package Options dialog box.

- Referenced Icons Only—Select this option to include only the icons that are directly linked to the Authorware piece. This option is great for eliminating icons which may be increasing file size, but which are not necessary for running the final piece.

- Include Fonts—This Macintosh-only feature has the same results as selecting the Include Fonts option in the Package Options dialog box. When this option is selected, you may include any non-PostScript Type 1 fonts as a part of the packaged piece. This is incredibly beneficial if you want to ensure that the end user will see the piece exactly as it was designed.

- Use Default Name—Selecting this option has the same result as selecting the Use Default Name in the Packaging Options dialog box. When this option is selected, libraries will be packaged with the .APR (Windows) or .PKG (Macintosh) extension.

3. Select the Package button to begin packaging the library.

Packaging a Windows Library   To package a library in Windows, follow these steps:

1. With the Library window active, select the Package Library option from the File pull-down menu. When this option is selected, the Package Library Options dialog box, as seen in Figure 31.4, appears.

FIG. 31.4
The Windows version of the Package Library Options dialog box contains most of the same options as the Macintosh version.

2. The packaging options on the Windows platform are the same as on the Macintosh, with the following exception:

   - Include Fonts—This feature is available only on the Macintosh.

3. Select the Package button to begin packaging the library. Authorware will prompt you for a name unless you have selected to use the default name.

Using Shockwave for Authorware

The Internet and World Wide Web have become the magical technology of the day. Everyone is talking about them, and individuals and mega corporations alike are rushing to build Web sites or gain Internet access.

Unfortunately, on the downside of the excitement is the reality that developing sophisticated Web sites takes a high degree of technical sophistication. TCP/IP, HTTP, ISDN, PPP, HTML, FTP—working with the Web involves a maze of acronyms. But as this technology becomes more prevalent, tools that simplify access to and the creation of multimedia programs over the Web are beginning to surface.

Macromedia, creator of Authorware and Director, is one of the leaders in providing tools that make multimedia development for the Web possible for us all. In June of 1995 Macromedia and Netscape had a release party at Digital World to introduce Shockwave for Director, and in December of 1995, Macromedia unveiled the first interactive multimedia experience over the Internet. With version 3.5 of Authorware and Shockwave for

Authorware, Macromedia is once again putting the power to take advantage of ground breaking technologies in the hands of the end user.

N O T E   Shockwave for Authorware, and the Afterburner compression tool, are available from Macromedia. For more information regarding these products, or to see working examples created with Shockwave, visit Macromedia's web site at **http://www.macromedia.com** or The Human Element, Inc.'s site at **http://www.theinc.com**. ▪

What Is Shockwave?

In its simplest form, Shockwave is a technology that allows real-time of Authorware pieces over the World Wide Web. While past technologies required that multimedia pieces be downloaded, then played on the local drive, Shockwave allows playback over the World Wide Web.

Part VII Ch 31

Additionally, Shockwave brings animation and interactivity to the wealth of content being developed for the Web which, until now, has been a media comprised of text and sprinkled with graphics.

While the Shockwave technology was first developed for Director (Authorware's sister product), it has reached a new plateau by taking advantage of Authorware. The powerful ease of use you will come to appreciate by using Authorware transfers directly to the creation of World Wide Web pieces.

Full Functionality   All of the features that make Authorware such a powerful tool—interactivity, animation, and data collection—are supported by Shockwave.

Compression   Afterburner, the utility that prepares an Authorware file for playback using Shockwave, compresses your Authorware 3.5 file by up to 50 percent.

Unlimited File Size   Interactive multimedia pieces can be huge in terms of file size. Having a requirement to limit that file size for any delivery medium means that either content or media must be sacrificed. But not with Shockwave for Authorware. Authorware pieces that will be delivered via the World Wide Web may be of any size.

In many World Wide Web multimedia delivery tools, the final piece must be downloaded to the local drive. This is not the case with Authorware. With Authorware, data is downloaded to the local system as it is needed. The process of downloading data as needed is known as *streaming*.

Streaming   Streaming is a feature that does not require the entire piece to be downloaded to the local hard drive, but rather allows portions of the piece to be downloaded based on available memory. Streaming results in faster playback and downloads. Authorware 3.5 streams sound, graphics, text, and digital movies (saved as PICS) across the net.

Digital Movies (such as QuickTime, Video for Windows, or Director movies) which have been linked are not streamed, but are downloaded to the user's system.

Full-Screen Playback   Your Authorware 3.5 piece can play as a window within or on top of Netscape Navigator 2.*x* (and other Web browsers which will support Netscape plug-ins in the future), or your end user can minimize the Netscape browser and run the Authorware piece full-screen. Therefore, your end user may see what you see when developing the program, and you may take advantage of pieces developed for delivery via CD-ROM without making major modifications.

Hybrid   Rather than playing all media over the Internet, you may elect to play movies or other large media locally from the hard drive or CD-ROM, while all other parts of the piece remain on the Web.

For example, if you are providing a performance support application which will be used by sales people all across the world, the World Wide Web is an ideal distribution medium. If the application must contain a large number of scanned images of the product, or digital movies which demonstrate how the product is used, the viability of using the World Wide Web may be questioned.

To provide an optimal solution, you could package the large graphic files, and the digital movies, on a CD-ROM. The textual content, and the interactivity, could then be delivered as a Web application. With this solution, the information which will be updated most often will reside on the Web, and the large media files which would not change as often would reside on the more static medium.

Record-Keeping   Just as Authorware allows you to collect information during the running of the piece, and then write that information to an external text file, Authorware using Shockwave has a similar feature. For example, you can write information to the Web using FTP so that it may be placed on the server site.

External Content   External content, such as QuickTime or Dynamic Link Library files, may be played over the Web. These files are downloaded to the local system before they are executed, so be sure that their file size is kept as small as possible for short download times.

Getting Started

To develop truly exciting interactive multimedia pieces for the World Wide Web, there are three technologies which you must have at least a moderate grasp of in order to be successful, described next.

Authorware Despite Authorware's ease of use, and the Afterburner's capability to compress an Authorware piece by up to 50 percent, it is still necessary to be efficient in creating the multimedia file. Graphics should be small and the Flowline should be streamlined.

Additionally, interface design and navigation play a critical role in the usability of your piece. No matter which environment you are developing for, you must always remember how your end users will be using the piece, and what their needs may be. The end user of a Web piece may be different from the user of a CD-ROM, and your piece should reflect that difference in its design.

Be sure that you are confident in your abilities to create an Authorware piece before adding one more bit of confusion—Web technology—to the development process.

Web Development The creation of a Web page may take place using a variety of tools and languages. In any case, an entirely new set of tools, languages, and techniques must be learned in order to create a functional Web site.

One such language is the HyperText Markup Language (HTML). This "programming" language is the core of the World Wide Web. There are numerous tools on the market that enable you to create Web pages with HTML, or use existing content from word processing and page layout documents to create Web documents.

Shockwave and the Afterburner The easiest part of creating a Shockwave for Authorware piece is learning to use the Afterburner utility and the Shockwave player. While there are a few tricks, and even a few steps which may not yet have been implemented, the remainder of this chapter is dedicated to overviewing the process of shocking your Authorware piece.

Preparing for Shockwave

Before developing or viewing a Shockwave piece, make sure you have the appropriate hardware and software.

In terms of the hardware you need, the bigger the better. A Macintosh (preferably a PowerPC) with at least 16MB RAM or a PC (preferably a high-speed pentium) with equivalent RAM, is required for development. Keep in mind that your time is the most valuable asset you have, and anything that reduces development time is worth the investment. In either case, a large hard disk and a connection to an HTTP server are required.

Version 7.5.2 is the recommended system software for the Macintosh, and Windows 95 for Intel-based systems. In addition to the system and Internet connection software, you should be using the latest version of Netscape Navigator, and your server should be equipped with the latest version of the HTTP Server Software.

Using Shockwave

In this section, I discuss, in very general terms, the steps involved with using Shockwave. Because the process is so detailed, and because it may not yet have been finalized, as Shockwave is in the final stages of being developed, I intend only to prepare you for using Shockwave. Please refer to the documentation included with the released version of Shockwave for specific details and steps.

1. Install the Shockwave for Authorware plug-in and the Afterburner for Authorware application. There are several versions of the Shockwave plug-in available, and they are dependent on the type of system you are using, so be careful that you have the right version.

2. Load the plug-in according to Macromedia and Netscape specifications.

3. Install other software, including Netscape Navigator 2.0 or later. Netscape may be downloaded from its Web site: **http://home.netscape.com/**.

4. Configure the HTTP Web server. For Shockwave for Authorware, the only configuration parameter that must be set on the Web server is to specify the MIME types for the Shockwave for Authorware pieces. Specifications for the type of Internet server you are placing the Shockwave piece on and the type of system used to create the piece are available from Macromedia.

5. Create an Authorware 3.5 piece. Pieces that were created with earlier versions of Authorware must be converted to Authorware 3.5 files in order to be used with Shockwave.

6. Package the piece without a runtime player, and package any libraries separately.

7. Use Afterburner for Authorware to segment and compress the piece. The output from Afterburner for Authorware consists of two types of files, one or more "segment" files (extension .AAS) and a single "map" file (extension .AAM). A segment file is a binary file that represents a compressed section of the original Authorware piece. The map file is a text file that contains information the Shockwave for Authorware plug-in will need to retrieve each segment file when playing a piece over the Internet.

8. Create an HTML Web page to access the map file that will launch your piece over the Web. Use an EMBED tag to include your piece on the Web page.

9. Copy your piece and the HTML Web page to the HTTP server. Refer to Macromedia's directions for step-by-step guidance on this process.

10. Start Netscape Navigator 2.0 (or later version).

11. Go to the URL containing your piece.

Index

Licensing Agreement

By opening this package, you are agreeing to be bound by the following: